A SHORT-TITLE CATALOGUE
ARRANGED GEOGRAPHICALLY
OF BOOKS PRINTED AND DISTRIBUTED
BY PRINTERS, PUBLISHERS AND BOOKSELLERS
IN THE ENGLISH PROVINCIAL TOWNS
AND IN SCOTLAND AND IRELAND
UP TO AND INCLUDING THE YEAR 1700

Compiled by E. A. CLOUGH

LONDON

THE LIBRARY ASSOCIATION

1969

SBN 85365 091 8

First published by
The Library Association,
7 Ridgmount Street, London, W.C.1,
1969

HOBBS THE PRINTERS LIMITED
SOUTHAMPTON SO9 2UZ

PREFACE

This is a short-title catalogue of those books which bear an imprint indicating that they were printed, published or distributed in the United Kingdom, other than in London, before 1701. It is based on Pollard and Redgrave's Short-title catalogue 1475-1640 and Wing's Short-title catalogue 1641-1700.

There are three important bibliographies which are concerned with printing and publishing in three different provincial centres:

Harry G. Aldis — List of books printed in Scotland before 1700. Edinburgh. 1904

E.R. McC. Dix — Catalogue of early Dublin-printed books 1601-1700. Dublin. 1898

Falconer Madan — Oxford books. Oxford. 1895-1931

and in order to reduce the size of this catalogue books listed in these bibliographies have not been included. This does not, of course, mean that books with Scottish, Irish or Oxford imprints have been excluded but rather that the entries given in this catalogue should serve as a supplement to these three bibliographies.

No work of this kind is ever complete but this particular catalogue is known to be incomplete because it does not include the large amount of material which Miss Katherine Pantzer of Harvard University Library is cataloguing for a new edition of Pollard and Redgrave. When this is published it is hoped that it may include an index to the place-names appearing in the imprints.

This catalogue is merely a gloss on the monumental work carried out first by Pollard and Redgrave and then later by Donald Wing. The compiler is indebted to Donald Wing for the help and encouragement he gave him.

E.A.C.

A SHORT-TITLE CATALOGUE
ARRANGED GEOGRAPHICALLY
OF BOOKS PRINTED AND DISTRIBUTED
BY PRINTERS, PUBLISHERS AND BOOKSELLERS
IN THE ENGLISH PROVINCIAL TOWNS
AND IN SCOTLAND AND IRELAND
UP TO AND INCLUDING THE YEAR 1700

ABERDEEN

1624　The pack-mans pater noster. Translated out of Dutch, by S[ir] I[ohn] S[empill]. **Aberdeen, E. Raban.** 1624. 4°. STC19087.

1627　TYMME, THOMAS. A silver watch-bell. **Aberdene, E. Raban.** 1627. 8°. STC24430.

1638　FORBES, PATRICK, bp. Eubulus, or a dialogue, etc. **Aberdeen, E. Raban.** 1638. 4°. STC11148.

1638　SCOTLAND. PROCLAMATIONS. Charles etc. [Concerning canons, Service book, etc. 28 June 1638]. [**Aberdeen, E. Raban.** 1638]. Brs. STC21997.

1643　CHURCH OF SCOTLAND. A solemn league and covenant, for reformation. **Aberdene, by Edw. Raban.** 1643. 8pp. 4°. WC4260.

1643　CHURCH OF SCOTLAND. A solemn league and covenant, for reformation. **Aberdene by Edw. Raban.** 1643. 14pp. 4°. WC4261.

1646　ABERDEEN COMMITTEE OF WAR. Proclamation, 13 June. [**Aberdeen, Raban.** 1646]. Brs. WA89.

1646　The committie of warre within the shyrefdom of Aberdene. **At Aberdene.** 13 June 1646. Brs. WC5568.

1651　CHURCH OF SCOTLAND. A short warning and exhortation. **Aberdeen by Iames Brown.** The 22 of August, 1651. Brs. WC4259D.

1651　CHURCH OF SCOTLAND. A solemn warning to all the members of this Kirk. **Aberdene, by James Brown.** 1651. 4°. WC4269.

1651　The coronation of Charles the second. **Aberdeen.** 1651. 4°. WC6341.

1651　[DOUGLAS, ROBERT]. A short information and brotherly exhortation to our brethren. **Aberdene, by James Brown.** [1651] 4°. WD2038.

1663　KENNEDY, Sir JAMES. AEneas Britannicus. [**Aberdeen, John Forbes**]. 1663. WK293.

1665　ALMANACS. CORSS, JAMES. A new prognostication for the year...1665. **Printed in Aberdene by John Forbes.** [1665]. 8°. WA1475.

1665　KEITH, GEORGE. A salutation of dear and tender love. [**Aberdeen**], **printed.** 1665. 4°. WK202.

1666　ALMANACS. An almanack. **Printed in Aberdene by John Forbes.** [1666]. 4°. WA1247.

1666　ALMANACS. CORSS, JAMES. A new prognostication for the year 1666. **Aberdeen.** 1666. 8°. WA1477.

1668　MOORE, ANDREW. Πεγαμα. **Aberdene, by Iohn Forbes younger.** 1668. Brs. WM2533.

1670　TAYLOR, JOHN. Salvator mundi. **Aberdene, by John Forbes.** 1670. WT509.

1671　FULLERTOUNE, JOHN. A short testimony. [**Aberdeen, John Forbes younger**]. 1671. 4°. WF2494.

1671　KEITH, GEORGE. A general epistle to Friends. [**Aberdeen?**], **printed.** 1671. 4°. WK171.

1672　BARCLAY, ROBERT. A seasonable warning. [**Aberdeen.** 1672]. 4°. WB734.

1674　MENZIES, JOHN. Positiones aliquot theologicæ. [**Aberdeen**]. 1674. 4°. WM1726.

1675　SKENE, ALEXANDER. The independencie of the students remonstrance. [**Aberdeen, John Forbes.** 1675]. Brs. WS3934.

1677　KEITH, GEORGE. Way cast up. [**Aberdeen**], **printed.** 1676/77. 8°. WK232.

1678　BARCLAY, ROBERT. An apology for the true Christian divinity. [**Aberdeen, John Forbes**], **printed.** 1678. 4°. WB720.

1678　KEITH, GEORGE. Way cast up. [**Aberdeen.** 1678]. 8°. WK234.

1678　KEITH, GEORGE. The way to the city of God described. [**Aberdeen**], **printed.** 1678. 8°. WK235.

1680　The Lady Bark or, new upstart lady. [**Aberdeen, Forbes.** 1680?]. 4°. WL163.

1681　ALMANACS. A new and exact prognostication for this present year. **Printed in Aberdeen by Iohn Forbes.** 1681. 8°. WA1984.

1683   LORIMER, JAMES. Theoremata. **Abredoniæ, excudebat Joannes Forbesius.** 1683. Brs. WL3072.

1685   JOHNSTON, ARTHUR. Epigrams. **Aberdeen.** 1685. 8°. WJ864.

1686   FORBES, ROBERT. Theses philosophicæ. **Aberdoniæ, excudebat Ioannis Forbes.** 1686. 4°. WF1453.

1688   ALMANACS. Vox uraniæ, or Aberdeen's true astral gazer...1688. **Printed in Aberdeen by John Forbes.** [1688]. 8°. WA2626.

1689   ALMANACS. Vox uraniæ, or Aberdeen's true astral gazer...1689. **Printed in Aberdeen by John Forbes.** [1689]. 8°. WA2627.

1690   ALMANACS. Vox uraniæ, or Aberdeen's true astral gazer...1690. **Printed in Aberdeen by John Forbes.** [1690]. 8°. WA2628.

1690   BLACK, WILLIAM. Illustrissimo ac per honorifico domino D. Alexandro Seton. **Aberdeis: excudebat Joannes Forbesius.** 1690. Fol. WB3037.

1691   ALMANACS. Vox uraniæ, or Aberdeen's true astral gazer...1691. **Printed in Aberdeen by John Forbes.** [1691]. 8°. WA2629.

1691   MORE, ALEXANDER. Theses philosophicæ. **Abredeis.** 1691. 4°. WM2628.

1693   ALMANACS. Vox uraniæ, or Aberdeen's true astral gazer...1693. **Printed in Aberdeen by John Forbes.** [1693]. 8°. WA2631.

1694   ALMANACS. Vox uraniæ, or Aberdeen's true astral gazer...1694. **Printed in Aberdeen by John Forbes.** [1694]. 8°. WA2632.

1694   ROBERTSON, JOHN. Rusticus ad clericum, or, the plowman rebuking the priest. [**Aberdeen**], **printed.** 1694. 8°. WR1607.

1694   SCOTLAND. LORDS OF THE TREASURY. Proclamation, anent production of the tacks... 3 Aug. [**Aberdeen, J. Forbes**]. 1694. Fol. WS1374.

1676   SKENE, GEORGE. Clarissimo nobilissimo ac illustrissimo domino Carolo domino Hay. **Abredeis, excudebat Ioannes Forbesius.** 1696. 4°. WS3937.

1698   ABERDEEN. MARISCHAL COLLEGE. To the Right Honourable the Lord Præses. [**Aberdeen, John Forbes.** 1698]. Brs. WA92.

1698   Aberdeen the 24 Ianuary 1698. Orders ... for the constables. [**Aberdeen, Forbes**]. 1698. Brs. WA94.

1700   A history of Robin Hood and the beggar. **Aberdeen, by John Forbes.** 1700. WH2138.

1700   [SANDILANDS, ROBERT]. Some queries. **Aberdeen, by Iohn Forbes.** [1700]. 4°. WS663.

1700   SMITH, WILLIAM. Theses philosophicae. **Abredeis, excudebat Ioannes Forbesius.** 1700. WS4260.

1700   WHITE, GEORGE. An advertisement anent the reading of the books of Antonia Borignion. **Aberdeen, by John Forbes.** 1700. 8°. WW1767.

ABINGDON

1528   LITURGIES. BREVIARIES. Portiforium. ī **monasterio Abēdonensi, per Ioannem Scholarem.** 1528. 4°. STC15792.

ASHBY - DE - LA - ZOUCH

1687   SHAW, SAMUEL. Grammatica Anglo-Romana: or. **London, for Michael Johnson to be sold at his shops in Litchfield and Uttoxeter: and Ashby-de-la-Zouch.** 1687. 12? WS3035.

AYLESBURY

1650   BURTHALL, RAUNCE, pseud? An old bridle for a wilde asse-colt. **For Stephen Dagnall, at Alsbury.** [1650]. 4°. WB6147.

1651   Severall proposals for the general good of the commonwealth. **London for Stephen Dagnall, at Alsbury.** 1651. 4°. WS2800.

1659   JEFFERY, WILLIAM. The whole faith of man. Second edition. **By G. Dawson, for Francis Smith, and Stephen Dagnal, of Alisbury.** 1659. 8°. WJ524.

1660   WRIGHT, JOSEPH. A testimony for the Son of man. **By S. Dover, for Stephen Dagnall, to be sold at his shop in Alisbury, and at Leyton, and by L. Lloyd** [London]. 1660. 8°. WW3705.

1661   WRIGHT, JOSEPH. A testimony for the Son of Man. **London, for Stephen Dagnal, in Alisbury.** 1661. 8°. WW3706.

BANBURY

1628   WHATELEY, WILLIAM. Sinne no more, or a sermon preached in the parish ch. of Banbury, upon occasion of a fire. The second time published. **For E. Langham in Banbury.** 1628. 4°. STC25322A.

1630   WHATELEY, WILLIAM. Sinne no more, or a sermon preached in the parish ch. of Banbury, upon occasion of a fire. The third time published. **For G. Edwards, sold by E. Langham of Banbury.** 1630. 4°. STC25323.

1634   MATTHEW, ROGER. The flight of time. **G. Miller for E. Langham at Banbery.** [1634]. 4°. STC17654A.

1638   SIBBES, RICHARD. The brides longing for her bride-groomes second comming. A sermon. **E. P[urslow] for E. Langham of Bambury.** 1638. STC22478B.

1682   KNIGHT, JOHN. The Samaritan rebels perjured. [**London**], **for William Thorp in Banbury, to be sold by Randal Taylor.** 1682. 4°. WK688.

1686   ABU BAKR IBN A TUFAIL. The history of Hai Eb'n Yockdan. **For Richard Chiswell, and William Thorp, in Banbury.** 1686. 8°. WA151.

1700   KNIGHT, JOHN. A sermon preach'd...Nov. 18. 1699. **London, for George Thorp, in Banbury** 1700. 4°. WK689.

BATH

1669   JORDEN, EDWARD. A discourse of natural bathes. Third edition. **Imprinted at London, and are to be sold by Thomas Salmon, in Bathe.** 1669. 8°. WJ1074.

1673   JORDEN, EDWARD. A discourse of natural bathes. Fourth edition. **Imprinted at London, for George Sawbridge, and Thomas Salmon, in Bathe.** 1673. 8°. WJ1075.

1685   LEYBOURN, WILLIAM. A platform for purchasers. **For Thomas Raw, of Bath: and sold by Obadiah Blagrave.** 1685. 8°. WL1929.

1697   PIERCE, ROBERT. Bath memoirs. **Bristol, for H. Hammond at Bath, and the Dowzes.** 1697. 8°. WP2163.

BEDFORD

1692 DAVIS, RICHARD. Truth and innocency vindicated. **For Nath. and Robert Ponder, to be sold by Randal Taylor, by Mr. Coolidge at Cambridge Mr. Prior at Colchester, Mr. Noble at St. Edmund's Bury, Mr. Haworth at Ipswich, Northampton, Wellingborow, Kettering, Oundle, Harborow, Litterworth, Upingham, Bedford, Kimbolton and Canterbury.** [1692?]. 4°. WD435.

BELFAST

1697 CRAGHEAD, ROBERT. An answer to the Bishop of Derry's Second admonition. [**Belfast.** 1697]. 4°. WC6793A.

1697 [MACBRIDE, JOHN]. Animadversions on the defence of the answer. [**Belfast**]. 1697. 4°. WM114.

1698 [MACBRIDE, JOHN]. A sermon before the provincial synod...June 1. 1698. [**Belfast?**], **printed.** 1698. 4°. WM115.

1699 BIBLE. ENGLISH. PSALMS. The psalmes of David in meeter. **Belfast, by Patrick Neill & Company,** 1699. 12°. WB2620A.

1699 GUTHRIE, WILLIAM. The Christians great interest. **Belfast, Patrick Neill and Company.** 1699. 12°. WG2275.

1700 ALLEINE, JOSEPH. A most familiar explanation. **Belfast, by Patrick Neill & Company.** 1700. 8°. WA975A.

1700 BIBLE. ENGLISH. PSALMS. The psalms of David in meeter. **Belfast, by Patrick Neill and Company.** 1700. 12°. WB2627.

1700 BUNYAN, JOHN. Sighs from hell. Tenth edition. **Belfast, by Patrick Neill and Company.** 1700. 12°. WB5594.

1700 FLAVELL, JOHN. Mr. John Flavell's remains. **Belfast, by Patrick Neill and Company.** 1700. 8°. WF1182.

1700 FOX, JOHN. Time and the end of time. **Belfast, by Patrick Neill and Company.** 1700. 12°. WF2028.

1700 KEACH, BENJAMIN. War with the devil. **Belfast, by Patrick Neill & Company.** 1700. 12°. WK107.

1700 MEAD, MATTHEW. The almost Christian discovered. **Belfast, by Patrick Neill and Company.** 1700. 12°. WM1543.

1700 MONTGOMERIE, ALEXANDER. The cherry and the slae. **Belfast, printe[sic] and sold by Patrick Neill.** 1700. 8°. WM2503.

1700 PEARSE, EDWARD. The great concern. **Belfast, by Patrick Neill & Company.** 1700. 12°. WP986.

BIRCHLEY HALL, LANCS.

1620 BRERELEY, JOHN. The liturgie of the masse. **Colen [Birchley Hall press, Lancs?].** 1620. 4°. STC3607.

1620 BRERELEY, JOHN. Sainct Austines religion, collected from his owne writtings. [**Birchley Hall press, Lancs?**]. 1620. 4°. STC3608.

BIRMINGHAM

1652 HALL, THOMAS. The font guarded with xx arguments. **By R.W. for Thomas Simmons in Birmingham, and to be sold in London by George Calvert.** 1652. 4°. WH432.

1673 FISHER, SAMUEL. Honour the King. A sermon. **For George Calvert, and Hieron Gregory, in Birmingham.** 1673. 4°. WF1052A.

BLANDFORD

1670 STRAIGHT, JOHN. A sermon preached... the fourth day of March...1669. **London, printed, and are to be sold by William Newton, in Blandford.** 1670. 4°. WS5808.

1694 OLLYFFE, JOHN. A brief defence. **London, for Jonathan Robinson: and are to be sold by John Woolfryes, in Blandford.** 1694. 4°. WO287.

BRIDGWATER

1698 M., J. A contract answer to a correct copy of letters. **For John Roberts, to be sold by him in Bridgewater and by Tho. Cockerill.** 1698. 8°. WM34.

BRISTOL

1634 PURSER, WILLIAM. Compound interest and annuities. **For R. M[ilbourne] and R. Royden of Bristol.** 1634. 8°. STC20513.

1643 The association, agreement and protestation of the covnties of Cornvvall, and Devon. Ianuary 5, 1643. **Bristoll, by Robert Barker and John Bill.** 1643. 4°. WA4053.

1643 CHARLES I, king of England. Military orders and articles established by His Maiesty. **Bristoll, by Robert Barker, and John Bill.** 1643. 4°. WC2497.

1643 CHURCH OF ENGLAND. A forme of common-prayer to be used...second Friday in every month **Bristoll, by Robert Barker, and John Bill.** 1643. 4°. WC4110.

1643 TOWGOOD, RICHARD. Disloyalty of language. **Bristoll, for Rich. Harsell.** 1643. 4°. WT1976.

1644 ANDERSON, FRANCIS. The copy of a letter from...to Sir Thomas Glemham the 20. Ianuary 1643. **Bristoll, by R. Barker and J. Bill.** 1643[4]. 4°. WA3089.

1644 Certain observations vpon the New League. **Bristoll, for Richard Harsell.** 1643[4]. 4°. WC1714.

1644 CHARLES I, king of England. His Majesties speech delivered the twenty second of January, 1643. **Bristoll, by Robert Barker, and John Bill.** 1643[4]. WC2785.

1644 CHARLES I, king of England. His Majesties speech made to the gentlemen...of Sommersot. **Bristoll, by Robert Barker & John Bill.** 1644. 4°. WC2791A.

1644 CHARLES I, king of England. His Majesties speech to the members... the seventh of February, 1643. [**Bristol, printed by John Barker and John Bill**]. Feb., 1643/4. 4°. WC2815.

1644 CHARLES I, king of England. A proclamation to prorogue the Assembly. **Bristol, by R. Barker and J. Bill.** 1644. Brs. WC2705.

1644 DOBSON, EDWARD. The declaration, vindication, and protestation of. **Bristoll [London], printed.** 1644. 4°. WD1751.

1644 ENGLAND. PARLIAMENT. The declaration of the Lords and Commons... concerning their endeavours. **Bristoll, R. Barker and J. Bill.** 1644. 4°. WE1403.

1644 ENGLAND. PARLIAMENT. The petition of the Lords and Commons. **Bristoll, by R. Barker and J. Bill.** 1644. 4°. WE2178.

1644 HOWELL, JAMES. Mercurius Hibernicus. **Printed at Bristoll.** 1644. 14pp. 4°. WH3093.

1644 HOWELL, JAMES. Mercurius Hibernicus. **Printed at Bristoll.** 1644. 28pp. 4°. WH3094.

1644 [MAXWELL, JOHN], abp. An answer to a worthy gentleman who desired. **Bristol.** 1644. 4°. WM1378.

1644 STANDFAST, RICHARD. Clero-laicum condimentum. Or, a sermon. **Bristoll for Thomas Thomas.** 1644. 4°. WS5207.

1645 [ESSEX, ROBERT DEVEREUX, 3rd earl]. A letter from the Earl of Essex. **Bristoll, by Robert Barker, and John Bill.** 1645. 4°. WE3319.

1645 A full relation of the passages concerning the late treaty for a peace. **Bristoll.** 1645. 4°. WF2368.

1645 P[RICKET], R[OBERT]. Newes from the Kings bath. **Bristoll, printed at the authors charge.** 1645. 4°. WP3408.

1645 Relation of the passages concerning the late treaty. **Bristoll,** 1645. 4°. WR856.

1649 The souldiers demand. **Printed at Bristoll.** 1649. 4°. WS4421.

1653 [PURNELL, ROBERT]. The way to Heaven discovered. **[London], for William Ballard of Bristol, and are sold by J. Grismond, London.** 1653. 8°. WP4243.

1655 FARMER, RALPH. The great mysteries. **By S.G. for William Ballard, in Bristoll; and Joshua Kirton.** 1655. 4°. WF441.

1660 BISHOP, GEORGE. A tender visitation of love. **Printed for Robert Wilson, and are to be sold at his shop...and also by Richard Moon in Bristol.** 1660. 4°. WB3007.

1660 BISHOP, GEORGE. To thee, Charls Stuart, king. [Bristol?, c1660]. 4°. WB3010.

1660 BISHOP, GEORGE. To thee, Charls Stuart, king. [Another edition]. [Bristol? 1660]. 4°. WB3011.

1660 BISHOP, GEORGE. The warnings of the Lord to the men. **By M. Inman, to be sold at the Three Bibles, and by Richard Moon, in Bristol.** 1660. 4°. WB3016.

1660 BISHOP, GEORGE. The warnings of the Lord to the men. **Printed, and are to be sold by Tho. Brewster, and Richard Moon in Bristol.** 1660. 4°. WB3017.

1660 BURROUGH, EDWARD. A presentation of wholesome informations. **Printed at London; and are to be sold by Richard Moon, in Bristol.** 1660. 4°. WB6017.

1660 FARMER, RALPH. A plain-dealing, and plain-meaning sermon, preach't...April 16, 1660. **By S. Griffin, to be sold by Thomas Wall, Bristol.** 1660. 4°. WF443.

1661 HODDEN, RICHARD. The one way of God. **By J.C. and are to be sold by Richard Moon in Bristol.** 1661. 4°. WH2283.

1670 WILLINGTON, GEORGE. Cor concussum & contritum: or, a present for Jehova. **By Thomas Milbourn, for Thomas Wall in Bristoll.** 1670. 4°. WW2801.

1672 The oath of a burgess. Civitas Bristol. [Bristol 1672]. Fol. WO68.

1674 C[RUTWELL], N. Bristol drollery. **London, for Charles Allen, in Bristol.** 1674. 8°. WC7447.

1676 STANDFAST, RICHARD. A sermon preached ...August 7th, 1675. **London, by A.M. for Charles Allen, in Bristol.** 1676. 4°. WS5213.

1677 [ALLEN, WILLIAM]. The mystery of the temple. **For B. Harris, to be sold at the Stationers Arms, and by T. Wall in Bristol.** 1677. 12°. WA1076.

1677 COLLINS, RICHARD. The country gaugers vade mecum. **By. W. Godbid, to be sold by M. Pitt, and by Anthony Owen of Bristol.** 1677. 8°. WC5383.

1678 STEEL, LAWRENCE. Short writing begun by nature. **Sold in Bristoll by the author, & also by Charles Allen. And in London by Benjamin Clark.** 1678. 8°. WS5380.

1679 [ALLEN, WILLIAM]. The mystery of the temple. **For B. Harris, to be sold at the Stationers Arms; and by T. Wall in Bristol.** 1679. 8°. WA1077.

1680 STANDFAST, RICHARD. Certain queries. **London, for Charles Allen, in Bristol.** 1680. 8°. WS5206.

1681 CROSSMAN, SAMUEL. Two sermons. **For Henry Brome, sold by Charles Allen in Bristol.** 1681. 4°. WC7271.

1681 Reasons for chusing Sir Robert Atkins. [Bristol? 1680/1]. Brs. WR487.

1681 To the right worshipful Sir Richard Hart. [Bristol?]. 1681. Brs. WT1720.

1682 CHETWIND, JOHN. Eben-ezer, a thankful memorial. **Printed, and are to be sold by Tho. Wall, at Bristol.** 1682. 4°. WC3796.

1683 The presentment of the Grand Jury of Bristol... Mar. 13. 1682. **London, by H. Hills, junr, for Charles Allin in Bristol and published by Ran. Taylor.** 1683. Brs. WP3285.

1683 The presentment of the Grand Jury of Bristol... Mar. 13. 1682. **London, by H. Hills, for Charles Allin in Bristol.** 1683. Brs. WP3286.

1695 CARY, JOHN. An essay on the state of England. **Bristoll: by W. Bonny, for the author, and are to be sold in London by Sam Crouch and Tim Goodwin, also by Tho. Wall and Rich. Gravett, in Bristol.** 1695. 12°. WC730.

1696 CARY, JOHN. An essay, on the coyn. **Bristol, by Will. Bonny.** 1696. 12°. WC728.

1696 CARY, JOHN. An essay, on the coyn. **Bristol; by Will. Bonny, and sold London.** 1696. 8°. WC729.

1696 Civitas Bristoll. To the right worshipful the mayor. **Bristol: W. Bonny.** 1696. Brs. WC4367.

1696 LONDON. By the right worshipful the Mayor and aldermen. These are to give notice. **Bristol: by Will. Bonny.** 1696. Brs. WL2886.

1696 MOORE, JOHN, bp. The banner of Corah. **Bristoll: by W. Bonny, for the author.** 1696. 8°. WM2544.

1696 Proposals for the better maintaining and imploying the poor. **Bristoll: Will. Bonny.** 1696. Brs. WP3747.

1696 To the right worshipful Samuel Wallis. Midsummer sessions, 1696. **Bristol: by Will Bonny.** 1696. Brs. WT1719.

1697 ALLEN, WILLIAM. Several discourses on the unsearchable riches. **Bristol, by Will. Bonny, for J. Allein in Bristol.** 1697. 8°. WA1074.

1697 PIERCE, ROBERT. Bath memoirs. **Bristol, for H. Hammond at Bath, and the Dowzes.** 1697. 8°. WP2163.

1698 HIGNELL, JEREMIAH. Loving and friendly advice and counsel. **Bristol, by Will Bonny.** [1698]. Fol. WH1969A.

1699 COOLE, BENJAMIN. Sophistry detected. **Bristol, Printed and sold by W. Bonny.** 1699. 4°. WC6047B.

1699 KEITH, GEORGE. Sophistry detected. **Bristol, printed and sold by W. Bonny.** 1699. 4°. WK216.

1699 Truth of God. **Bristol, printed and sold by Will. Bonny.** 1699. 8°. WT3157.

1699 WATERMAN, HUGH. A sermon preached... April the 13th, 1699. **Bristol, printed and sold by W. Bonny.** 1699. 4°. WW1053.

1700 ENGLAND, JOHN. Man's sinfulness. **By J. Heptinstall, for John Sprint, and sold by John Miller in Sherborne, and Thomas Wall in Bristol.** 1700. 8°. WE739.

BURY ST. EDMUNDS

1686 BUGG, FRANCIS. The Quakers detected. **For the author, and are to be sold by Edward Gyles in Norwich, and Ralph Watson in St. Edmunds-Bury.** 1686. 4°. WB5387.

1692 DAVIS, RICHARD. Truth and innocency vindicated. **For Nath. and Robert Ponder, to be sold by Randal Taylor, by Mr. Coolidge at Cambridge, Mr. Prior at Colchester, Mr. Noble at St. Edmund's Bury, Mr. Haworth at Ipswich, Northampton, Wellingborow, Kettering, Oundle, Harborow, Litterworth, Upingham, Bedford, Kimbolton and Canterbury.** [1692?]. 4°. WD435.

1695 DARBY, CHARLES. An elegy on the death of the Queen. **For John Chamberlain, in St. Edmunds-Bury: to be sold by Peter Parker and John Whitlock.** 1695. Fol. WD245A.

1699 LEEDES, EDWARD. Methodus Græcam linguam docendi. **Cantabrigiæ, ex officina Johan. Hayes. Impensis Joh. Chamberlayne, Buriensis, et prostant venales apud Pet. Parker, Londini.** 1699. 8°. WL910.

CAMBRIDGE

1521 BALDWIN, abp. De uenerabili, ac diuinissimo altaris sacramento sermo. **J. Siberch, ex Cantab. acad.** 1521. 4°. STC1242.

1521 BULLOCK, HENRY. Doctissimi viri H. Bulloci oratio ad Thomā Cardinalem, archiep. Ebor. **Cantabrigiæ, J. Siberch.** 1521. 4°. STC4082.

1521 ERASMUS, DESIDERIUS. Libellus de conscribendis epistolis. **Cantabrigiæ, per J. Siberch.** 1521. 4°. STC10496.

1521 FISHER, JOHN, cardinal. Contio in Joh. xv. 26. versa in latinum per R. Pacæum. **Cambridge, J. Siberch.** 1521. 4°. STC10898.

1521 GALEN, CLAUDIUS. Galeni Pergamensis de temperamentis et de inæquali intemperie libri tres, T. Linacro interprete. **apud Cantabrigiam per J. Siberch.** 1521. 4°. STC11536.

1521 LUCIAN, OF SAMOSATA. Lepidissimum Luciani opusculū περι, διψαδων H. Bulloco interprete. **Cantabrigiæ, per J. Siberch.** 1521. 4°. STC16896.

1522 GEMINUS, PAPYRIUS. P. Gemini Eleatis Hermathena. **ex præclara Cantabrigia.** 1522. 4°. STC11719.

1584 BRIGHT, TIMOTHY. In physicam G.A. Scribonii animaduersiones. **Cantabrigiæ, ex officina T. Thomasii.** 1584. 8°. STC3745.

1584 LA RAMÉE, PIERRE DE. Dialecticæ libri duo. **Cantabrigiæ, ex off. T. Thomasii.** 1584. 8°. STC15243.

1584 LA ROCHE DE CHANDIEU, ANTOINE. A Sadeelis de rebus gravissimis controversis disputationes. **ex off. T. Thomasij Cantabrigiensis typographi.** 1584. 4°. STC15255.

1584 MARTINIUS, JACOBUS. Jacobi Martini de prima corporum generatione diputatio. **Cantabrigiæ, ex off. T. Thomae.** 1584. 8°. STC 17524.

1584 OVIDIUS NASO, PUBLIUS. [Metamorphoses]. Fabularum Ouidii interpretatio ethica physica et prima corporum generatione diputatio. **Canta-Sabino edita industria T. T[homæ].** **Cantabrigiæ, ex off. T. Thomae.** 1584. 8°. STC 18951.

1584 ROUSPEAU, YVES. Two treatises of the lord his holie supper by Y. Rouspeau and J. de l'Espine. **[Cambridge], T. Thomas.** 1584. 8°. STC21354.

1585 LA RAMÉE, PIERRE DE. The latine grammer of P. Ramus. Whereunto is ioyned an epistle of Tullie. **Cambridge, T. Thomas.** 1585. 8°. STC15253.

1585 Minima vis potest mouere maximum pondus, etc. **[Cambridge. 1585?].** Brs. STC24845.

1585 PILKINGTON, JAMES, bp. A godlie exposition vpon certeine chapters of Nehemiah. **Cambridge, T. Thomas.** 1585. 4°. STC19929.

1585 URSINUS, ZACHARIAS. Doctrinæ christianæ compendium. **ex off. T. Thomasii, Ac. Cantab. Typographi.** 1585. 8°. STC24529.

1585 WHITAKER, WILLIAM. An aunswere to a certaine booke, written by M.W. Rainoldes, etc. **[Cambridge]. T. Thomas, sold at the white Horse, [London].** 1585. 8°. STC25364.

1585 WILLET, ANDREW. De animæ natura et viribus quæstiones quaedam. **ex. off. T. Thomasii, Acad. Cantab. Typog.** 1585. 8°. STC25674.

1586 CHARKE, WILLIAM. A treatise against the Defense of the Censure, giuen upon the bookes of W. Charke and M. Hanmer. **Cambridge, T. Thomas.** 1586. 3vols. 8°. STC5009.

1586 Eadem res duobus vendita, cui prius tradita, debetur. [In verse]. **Cantebrigiæ.** 1586. 4°. STC20893.

1586 An harmony of the Confessions and of the faith of the Christian and reformed churches. **Cambridge, T. Thomas.** 1586. 8°. STC5155.

1586 Legatum distribuendum in nuptiis mulierum pauperum distribui debet in nuptiis virginum, non viduarum. [Cambridge Act verses?]. **Cantebrigiæ.** 1586. 8°. STC15386.

1586 SALUS. Salutis cuique suæ certa sunt inditia. **Cantabrigiæ.** 1586. Brs. STC21648.

1587 CARMICHAEL, JAMES. Grammaticae Latinae, de etymologia, liber secundus. **Cantabrigiæ, T. Thomas.** 1587. 4°. STC4660.

1587 URSINUS, ZACHARIAS. Explicationum catecheticarum editio altera. **Cantebrigiæ, ex off. T. Thomasii.** 1587. 8°. STC24531.

1588 THOMAS, THOMAS. Dictionarium linguae Latinae et Anglicanae. **Cantebrigiae, ex. off. T. Thomasii, Londini, ap R. Boyle.** [1588?]. 8°. STC24008.

1588 WHITAKER, WILLIAM. Disputatio de sacra scriptura. **Cantabrigiae, ex. off. T. Thomasii.** 1588. 4°. STC25366.

1589 ACHILLES TATIUS. De Clitophontis & Leucippes amoribus libri viii. Lat. facti a L. A. Cruceio. **Cantabrigae, J. Legate.** [1589?]. STC89.

1589 BASTINGIUS, JEREMIAS. An exposition or commentarie upon the catechism taught in the Lowe Countryes. **Cambridge, J. Legatt.** 1589. 4°. STC1564.

1589 BEZE, THEODORE DE. Iob expounded, etc. **Cambridge, J. Legatt, sold [in London by A. Kitson].** [1589?]. 8°. STC2020.

1589 CICERO, MARCUS TULLIUS. M.T. Ciceronis de Oratore. **Cantabrigiae, J. Legatt.** 1589. 12°. STC5291.

1589 TERENTIUS, PUBLIUS. P. Terentii Afri comœdia sex. **Cantabrigiae, ex. off. J. Legatt.** 1589. 12°. STC23887.

1590 BIBLE. NEW TESTAMENT. ENGLISH. The new test. of our lord Iesus Christ. **Cambridge, J. Legate.** [1590?]. 32°. STC2889.

1590 GREENWOOD, JOHN. Syntaxis et prosodia versiculis compositae. **J. Legate. Acad. Cantab. typographus.** 1590. 8°. STC12338.

1590 HOLLAND, HENRY. A treatise against witchcraft. **Cambridge, J. Legatt.** 1590. 2vols. 4°. STC13590.

1590 PERKINS, WILLIAM. Armilla aurea, id est, Miranda series causarum et salutis et damnationis iuxta verbum Dei. **Cantabrigiae, ex. off. J. Legatt.** 1590. 8°. STC19655.

1590 WHITAKER, WILLIAM. An aunswere to a certaine booke, written by M. W. Rainoldes, etc. **Cambridge, J. Legat.** 1590. 8°. STC25365.

1590 WILLET, ANDREW. De vniuersali et nouissima Judaeorum vocatione. **ex. off. J. Legati Cantab. Typog.** 1590. 4°. STC 25675.

1591 BIBLE. ENGLISH. The bible etc. **[Cambridge], J. Legate.** 1591. 8°. STC 2155.

1591 PERKINS, WILLIAM. Armilla aurea, id est, theologiae descriptio. Editio secunda. **Cantabrigiae, ex. off. J. Legatt.** [1591?]. 8°. STC19655A.

1591 PERKINS, WILLIAM. A golden chaine, or the description of theologie, containing the order of the cases of saluation and damnation according to Gods woord. **[Cambridge, J. Legate.** 1591?]. 8°. STC19658.

1592 BASTINGIUS, JEREMIAS. An exposition or commentarie upon the catechism taught in the Lowe Countryes. **Cambridge, J. Legatt.** [1592?]. 8°. STC1565.

1592 L'ESPINE, JEAN DE. A very excellent discourse, touching the tranquilitie of the minde. Tr. E. Smyth. **J. Legate, printer to the Vniuer. of Cambridge, [sold by A. Kitson, London].** 1592. 4°. STC15516.

1592 LIPSIUS, JUSTUS. Iusti Lipsii tractatus ad historiam Romanam cognoscendam. **Cantabrigiae, ex. off. J. Legati.** 1592. 8°. STC15702.

1592 PERKINS, WILLIAM. Armilla aurea, id est, theologiae descriptio. Editio tertia. **Cantabrigiae. ex. off. J. Legatt, extant ap. A. Kitson.** [1592]. 8°. STC19656.

1592 PERKINS, WILLIAM. A golden chaine, or the description of theologie, containing the order of the causes of saluation and damnation according to Gods woord. Second edition. **Cambridge, J. Legate.** 1592. 8°. STC19659.

1592 PERKINS, WILLIAM. Prophetica, sive de sacra et vnica ratione concionandi. **[Cambridge], ex. off. J. Legate.** 1592. 8°. STC19735.

1592 SOHN, GEORG. A briefe and learned treatise, conteining a true description of the Anti-Christ Tr. [N.G.]. **Cambridge J. Legate.** 1592. 8°. STC22891.

1592 THOMAS, THOMAS. Dictionarium linguae Latinae et Anglicanae. Tertio emendatum. **Cantabrigiae, ex. off. J. Legate, ap. A. Kitson, Londini.** 1592. 4°. STC24009.

1593 BIBLE. ENGLISH. ECCLESIASTES. Ecclesiastes, with a paraphrase by T. Beza, translated out of Latine. **Cambridge, J. Legatt.** [1593?]. 8°. STC2764.

1593 COWELL, JOHN. Anti-Sanderus, duos continens dialogos. **Cantabrigiae.** 1593. 4°. STC5898.

1593 LYSIAS. Eratosthenes, hoc est, breuis et luculenta defensio Lysiae. **J. Legatus, Acad. Cantab. typographus.** 1593. 8°. STC17121.

1593 MORE, JOHN. A table from the beginning of the world to this day. **J. Legate, pr. to the Univ. of Camb. sold in London. [by A. Kitson].** 1593. 8°. STC18074.

1593 PERKINS, WILLIAM. A direction for the gouernment of the tongue. **J. Legate, pr. to the Vniuer. of Cambridge, solde by A. Kitson.** 1593. 8°. STC19688.

1593 PERKINS, WILLIAM. Two treatises. 1. Of repentance 2. Of the combat of the flesh and the spirit. **J. Legate, pr. to the Vniuer. of Cambridge.** 1593. 8°. STC19758.

1594 DANEAU, LAMBERT. A fruitfull commentarie upon the twelue small prophets. Tr. J. Stockwood. **Cambridge, J. Legatt, printer to the Univ.** 1594. 4°. STC6227.

1594 The death of usury. **Cambridge, J. Legatt.** 1594. 4°. STC6443.

1594 GREAVES, PAUL. Grammatica Anglicana. **Cantabrigiae, ex. off. J. Legatt.** 1594. 8°. STC12208.

1594 HAUWENREUTHER, JOHANN LUDWIG. Σνυόψις της, φυδικης, τοῦ Ἀριστοτέλοῦς Compendium etc. **Cantabrigiae, ex. off. J. Legatt.** 1594. 8°. STC12938.

1594 THOMAS, THOMAS. Dictionarium linguae Latinae et Anglicanae. Quarta editio. **Cantabrigiae, ex. off. J. Legatt, ap. A. Kitson, Londini.** 1594. 8°. STC24010.

1594 WHITAKER, WILLIAM. Aduersus T. Stapletoni Defensionem ecclesiasticae authoritatis. **Cantabrigie, J. Legatus.** 1594. Fol. STC25363.

1595 BASTINGIUS, JEREMIAS. An exposition or commentarie upon the catechism taught in the Lowe Countryes. **Cambridge, J. Legat.** 1595. 8°. STC1566.

1595 COVELL, WILLIAM. Polimanteia, or, the meanes to judge of the fall of a common-wealth. [Init. W.C.] **J. Legate, pr. to the Univ. of Cambridge.** 1595. 4°. STC5883.

1595 LYCOPHRON. Λυκοφρουος τον χαλκιδεως Ἀλεξαυδρα. Lycophronis Chalcidensis Alexandra. [**Cambridge**]. **J. Legatus.** 1595. 8°. STC 17003.

1595 PERKINS, WILLIAM. An exposition of the Lords Prayer. **For J. Legat, pr. to the Vniuer. of Cambridge.** 1595. 4°. STC19702.

1595 PERKINS, WILLIAM. An exposition of the symbole or creed of the Apostles, etc. **J. Legatt, pr. to the Vniuer. of Cambridge.** 1595. 8°. STC19703.

1595 PERKINS, WILLIAM. A golden chaine, or the description of theologie, containing the order of the causes of saluation and damnation according to Gods woord. Second edition, much enlarged. **J. Legat, pr. to the Vniuer. of Cambridge.** 1595. 4°. STC19662.

1595 PERKINS, WILLIAM. A salue for a sicke man. **J. Legate, pr. to the Vniuer. of Cambridge.** 1595. 8°. STC19742.

1595 PERKINS, WILLIAM. Two treatises. 1. Of repentance. 2. Of the combat of the flesh and spirit. Second edition corrected. (A direction for the gouernment of tongues). **J. Legate, pr. to the Vniuer. of Cambridge.** 1595. 2vols. pp 55; 37. 8°. STC19759.

1595 PERKINS, WILLIAM. Two treatises. 1. Of repentance 2. Of the combat of the flesh and spirit. Second edn. corrected. **J. Legate, pr. to the Vniuer, of Cambridge.** 1595. pp. 85. 8°. STC19760.

1595 PLUTARCH. [De recta audiendi ratione]. Πλουταρχου περι του 'ακουειν. **J. Legatus, Acad. Cantab. typographus.** 1595. 8°. STC20058.

1595 RACSTER, JOHN. De hypocritis vitandis. **ex. off. J. Legatt, Cantabrigiæ.** 1595. 4°. STC 20599.

1596 BIBLE. ENGLISH. REVELATION. The apocalyps, or reuelation of S. John with a briefe exposition by F. Du Jon. **J. Legate, printers to the university of Cambridge.** 1596. 4°. STC 2990.

1596 DU JON, FRANCOIS, the Elder. The Apocalyps, or Reuelation of S. John with a briefe exposition. Tr. T. B[arbar]. **Cambridge, J. Legat.** 1596. 4°. STC7296.

1596 G., C. A watch-worde for warre. **Cambridge, J. Legat.** 1596. 4°. STC11492.

1596 PERKINS, WILLIAM. A declaration of the true manner of knowing Christ crucified. **Cambridge, J. Legate.** 1596. 16°. STC19685.

1596 PERKINS, WILLIAM. A discourse of conscience. [**Cambridge**]. **J. Legate.** 1596. 8°. STC19696.

1596 PERKINS, WILLIAM. An exposition of the symbole or creed of the Apostles, etc. Corrected. **J. Legat, pr. to the Vniuer. of Cambridge.** 1596. 4°. STC19704.

1596 SOME, ROBERT. Propositiones tres. **Cantabrigiæ, J. Legat.** 1596. 8°. STC22913.

1596 SOME, ROBERT. Three questions. **J. Legat, printer to the Vniuersity of Cambridge.** 1596. 8°. STC22913A.

1596 THOMAS, THOMAS. Dictionarium linguae Latinae et Anglicanae. Quinta editio auctior. **Cantabrigiæ, ex. off. J. Legati.** 1596. 4°. STC24011.

1596 WILLET, ANDREW. Sacrorum emblematum centuria vna. **ex. off. J. Legate, Acad. Cantab. Typog.** [1596?]. 4°. STC25695.

1597 ABRAHAM, ABEN HASSAN. Haec sunt verba dei. Praecepta in monte Sinai data Judaeis. **Cantabrigiae, ex. officina J. Legat.** 1597. 4°. STC80.

1597 PACIUS, JULIUS. Institutiones logicae. **Cantabrigiæ, ex. off. J. Legat.** 1597. 12°. STC 19083.

1597 PERKINS, WILLIAM. A declaration of the true manner of knowing Christ crucified. **Cambridge, J. Legat.** 1597. 4°. STC19686.

1597 PERKINS, WILLIAM. An exposition of the symbole or creed of the Apostles, etc. Corrected. **J. Legatt, pr. to the Vniuer. of Cambridge.** 1597. 8°. STC19705.

1597 PERKINS, WILLIAM. A golden chaine, or the description of theologie, containing the order of the causes of saluation and damnation according to Gods woord. [**Cambridge**], **J. Legate.** 1597. 4°. STC19663.

1597 PERKINS, WILLIAM. A salue for a sicke man. **J. Legat, pr. to the Vniuer. of Cambridge.** 1597. 4°. STC19743.

1597 PERKINS, WILLIAM. Two treatises. 1. Of repentance 2. Of the combat of the flesh and spirit. Second edn. corrected. **J. Legate, pr. to the Vniuer. of Cambridge.** [**sold by J. Field**]. 1597. 4°. STC19761.

1598 BIRD, SAMUEL. Lectures vpon the 8. and 9. chapters of the sec. Ep. to the Corinthians. **Cambridge, J. Legate.** 1598. 8°. STC3087.

1598 BIRD, SAMUEL. Lectures vpon the II. chapter of Hebrewes and vpon the 38. psalme. **Cambridge, J. Legate.** 1598. 8°. STC3088.

1598 CHEMNITIUS, MARTINUS. A substantial and godly exposition of the Lords praier. Newly translated. **Cambridge, J. Legate.** 1598. 8°. STC5117.

1598 ENGLAND, CHURCH OF. VISITATIONS. Lincoln. **Cambridge, J. Legat.** 1598. 4°. STC10235.

1598 F., I or J. The differences, causes and judgements of vrine. **Cambridge, J. Legat.** 1598. 8°. STC10640.

1598 PERKINS, WILLIAM. De praedestinationis modo et ordine. **Cantabrigiæ, ex. off. J. Legat.** 1598. 8°. STC19682.

1598 PERKINS, WILLIAM. A reformed Catholike. **Cambridge, J. Legat.** 1598. 8°. STC19736.

1598 PERKINS, WILLIAM. Speciman digesti, siue harmoniae Bibliorum. **Cambrigiæ, J. Legat.** 1598. Fol. STC19749.

1598 STOUGHTON, THOMAS. A generall treatise against poperie. **J. Legat, printer to the Vniuer. of Cambridge.** 1598. 8°. STC23316.

1598 TERENTIUS, PUBLIUS. Terence in English: fabulae Anglicae factae opera R. B[ernard]. **Cantabrigiae, ex. off. J. Legat.** 1598. 4°. STC23890.

1598 WILCOX, THOMAS. A discourse touching the doctrine of doubting, etc. **J. Legat, printer to the vniuer. of Camb.** 1598. 8°. STC25621.

1599 DILLINGHAM, FRANCIS. A disswasiue from Poperie, containing twelue effectual reasons etc. [**Cambridge**]. **J. Legat.** 1599. 8°. STC6883.

1599 POLANUS, AMANDUS. Treatise concerning Gods eternal predestination. [Tr. R. Gostwyke] **J. Legat, printer to the Vniuer. of Cambridge.** 1599. 8°. STC20086.

1599 WHITAKER, WILLIAM. Praelectiones in quibus tractatur controuersia de Ecclesia. **ex. off. J. Legat, Acad. Cantab. Typographi.** 1599. 1600. 2 vols. 4°. STC25368.

1599 ZANCHIUS, HIERONYMUS. H. Zanchius his confession of Christian religion. **J. Legat, printer to the Vniuer. of Cambridge.** 1599. 8°. STC26120.

1600 PERKINS, WILLIAM. [Works]. A golden chaine: or, the description of theologie. [With twelve other treatises].. **J. Legat, printer to the Vniuersity of Cambridge.** 1600. 4°. STC19646.

1600 SAVAGE, FRANCIS. A conference betwixt a mother, a recusant, and her sonne a protestant. [**Cambridge**], **J. Legat.** 1600. 8°. STC21781.

1600 THOMAS, THOMAS. Dictionarium linguae Latinae et Anglicanae. Sexta editio. **Cantabrigiae, ex. off. J. Legati.** 1600. 8°. STC24012.

1600 WHITAKER, WILLIAM. Praelecti es in quibus tractatur controuersia de concilis. **Cantabrigiae, J. Legat.** 1600. 8°. STC25367.

1600 WHITAKER, WILLIAM. Praelectiones in quibus tractatur controuersia de Ecclesia. **ex. off. J. Legat, Acad. Cantab. Typographi.** 1599, 1600. 2 vols. 4°. STC25368.

1600 WHITAKER, WILLIAM. Tractatus de peccato originali. **ex. off. J. Legat, Acad. Cantab. Typographi.** 1600. 8°. STC25370.

1601 An ease for overseers of the poore abstracted from the Statutes. **Cambridge, J. Legat.** 1601. 4°. STC7446.

1601 HILL, ROBERT. Life everlasting, or the true knowledge of one Jehovah, three Elohim and Jesus Immanuel. **Cambridge, J. Legat, sold by S. Waterson.** 1601. 4°. STC13479.

1601 PERKINS, WILLIAM. How to live and that well. **J. Legat, pr. to the Vniuer. of Cambridge, sold by S. Waterson.** 1601. 12°. STC19728.

1601 PERKINS, WILLIAM. The true gaine. **Cambridge, J. Legat.** 1601. 8°. STC19757.

1601 PERKINS, WILLIAM. A warning against the idolatrie of the last times. (Christ the true and perfect gain). **J. Legat, pr. to the Vniuer. of Cambridge, sold by S. Waterson.** 1601. 2 vols. 8°. STC19764.

1602 CICERO, MARCUS TULLIUS. M. Tulli Ciceronis Epistolae familiares. **Cantabrigia**[sic], **J. Legat.** 1602. 8°. STC5301.

1602 DILLINGHAM, FRANCIS. Disputatio breuis de limbo patrum. **Cantabrigiae, J. Legat.** 1602. 8°. STC6881.

1602 PERKINS, WILLIAM. A treatise of Gods free grace and mans free will. **J. Legat, pr. to the Vniuer. of Cambridge, sold by S. Waterson.** 1602. 8°. STC19750.

1602 WILLET, ANDREW. A catholicon or remedie against the pseudo-catholike religion. **J. Legat, printer to the Univ. of Cambridge, sold by S. Waterson.** 1602. 8°. STC25673.

1603 CAMBRIDGE UNIVERSITY. Threno-thriambeuticon. Academiae cantabrigiensis ob damnum lucrosum luctuosus triumphus. **Cantabrigiae, J. Legat.** 1603. 4°. STC4493.

1603 DILLINGHAM, FRANCIS. A quartron of reasons, composed by Doctor Hill, vnquartered. [**Cambridge**], **J. Legat, sold by S. Waterson,** [**London**] 1603. 4°. STC6889.

1603 DILLINGHAM, FRANCIS. Tractatus breuis, in quo multa protestantium dogmata tutissima esse concluduntur. **Cantabrigiae, J. Legat.** 1603. 8°. STC6892.

1603 HEYDON, Sir CHRISTOPHER. A defence of judiciall astrologie. [**Cambridge**], **J. Legat, sold by S. Waterson.** 1603. 4°. STC13266.

1603 JAMES I, king of England. A princes looking glasse excerpted out of βασιλικον δωρον and tr. into Latin and English verse by W. Willymat. **J. Legat, printer to the Univ. of Cambridge, sold by S. Waterson.** 1603. 4°. STC14357.

1603 PAGIT, EUSEBIUS. The historie of the Bible. [**Cambridge**], **J. Legate, pr. to the Vniuersity, sold by S. Waterson.** [1603?]. 12°. STC 19106.

1603 PERKINS, WILLIAM. A direction for the gouernment of the tongue. **J. Legat, pr. to the Vniuer. of Cambridge, sold by S. Waterson.** 1603. 12°. STC19690.

1603 PERKINS, WILLIAM. The works of that famous and worthie minister of Christ in the vniuersitie of Cambridge, M. W. Perkins: gathered into one volume and newly corrected according to his owne copies. **J. Legate, printer to the Vniuer. of Cambridge.** 1603. Fol. STC19647.

1603 PLAYFERE, THOMAS. Hearts delight. A sermon. **Cambridge, J. Legat.** 1603. 8°. STC 20010.

1603 PLAYFERE, THOMAS. The power of praier. A sermon. **Cambridge, J. Legat.** 1603. 8°. STC20025.

1603 SHARPE, LEONELL. Dialogus inter Angliam & Scotiam. **Cantabrigiae, ex. off. J. Legat.** 1603. STC22371.

1603 SHARPE, LEONELL. A sermon [on 1 Kings 10.9]. **Cambridge, J. Legat, sold by S. Waterson.** 1603. 8°. STC22376.

1603 SMYTH, JOHN. The bright morning starre. **Cambridge, J. Legat.** 1603. 12°. STC22874.

1603 Sorrowes ioy, or, a lamentation for our late deceased souereigne. **Cambridge, J. Legat.** 1603. 4°. STC7598.

1603 WILLET, ANDREW. Ecclesia triumphans: that is, the joy of the English Church for the coronation of Prince James. **J. Legat, printer to the University of Cambridge, sold by S. Waterson.** 1603. 8°. STC25676.

1604 BOWND, NICH. The holy exercise of fasting described. **Cambridge, J. Legat.** 1604. 8°. STC3438.

1604 ENGLAND, CHURCH OF. VISITATIONS. Lincoln. **Cambridge, J. Legate.** 1604. 4°. STC10236.

1604 GIBBON, CHARLES. The order of equalitie. Contrived for common sessements. **Cambridge, J. Legat.** 1604. 4°. STC11817.

1604 MANNING, JAMES. A new booke, intituled, I am for you all, Complexions castle. **J. Legat, printer to the Univ. of Camb., sold by S. Waterson.** 1604. 4°. STC17257.

1604 OLIVER, THOMAS. T. Oliverii de sophismatum praestigiis cavendis admonitio. **Cantabrigia, ex. off. J. Legat.** 1604. 4 vols. 4°. STC18809.

1604 PERKINS, WILLIAM. The first part of the cases of conscience. **J. Legat, pr. to the Vniuer. of Cambridge, sold by S. Waterson.** 1604. 8°. STC19668.

1604 PERKINS, WILLIAM. A commentarie on the five first chapters of the Epistle to the Galatians. **J. Legat, pr. to the Vniuer. of Cambridge.** 1604. 4°. STC19680.

1604 PERKINS, WILLIAM. Ἐπιείκεια, or a treatise of Christian equity and moderation. **Cambridge, Legat,** 1604. STC19699.

1604 PERKINS, WILLIAM. G. Perkinsi problema de Romanae fidei ementito catholicismo. **Cantabrigiae, ex. off. J. Legat, extant ap. S. Waterson.** 1604. 4°. STC19734.

1604 PERKINS, WILLIAM. A reformed Catholike. **Cambridge, J. Legat, sold by S. Waterson, [London].** 1604. 8°. STC19737.

1604 WILLET, ANDREW. Thesaurus ecclesiae. **Cambridge, J. Legat, sold by S. Waterson.** 1604. 8°. STC25704.

1605 BELL, THOMAS. T. Bels motiues concerning Romish faith. Second edition. **Cambridge, J. Legate, sold [in London by S. Waterson].** 1605. 4°. STC1831.

1605 COWELL, JOHN. Institutiones juris anglicani. **Ex. off. J. Legat, Cantabrigiae, ap. S. Waterson, Londini.** 1605. 8°. STC5899.

1605 DILLINGHAM, FRANCIS. A godly and learned sermon concerning the magistrates dutie and death. **[Cambridge], J. Legat.** 1605. 8°. STC6885.

1605 DILLINGHAM, FRANCIS. Spicilegium de Antichristo contra Bellarmini sophismata. **Cantabrigiae, J. Legat.** 1605. 8°. STC6891.

1605 ENGLAND. PARLIAMENT. In homines nefarios, qui parliamenti domum evertere sunt machinati. **Cantabrigiae, ex. off. J. Legat.** 1605. 4°. STC7737.

1605 LEECH, JAMES. A plaine and profitable catechisme, etc. **J. Legat, printer to the Vniv. of Cambridge.** 1605. 8°. STC15365.

1605 PERKINS, WILLIAM. The works of that famous and worthie minister of Christ in the vniuersitie of Cambridge, M. W. Perkins: gathered into one volume and newly corrected according to his own copies. **Pr. by J. Legat, printer to the Vniuer. of Cambridge, and are to be sold at the Signe of the Crowne in Pauls Church-yard [by S. Waterson]** 1605. Fol. STC19648.

1605 PLAYFERE, THOMAS. The sick-mans couch; a sermon. **J. Legat, printer to the Vniuer. of Cambridge, sold by S. Waterson.** 1605. 4°. STC20027.

1605 WILLET, ANDREW. Hexapla in Genesin. **J. Legate, printer to the University of Cambridge,** 1605. Fol. STC25682.

1606 DILLINGHAM, FRANCIS. Disputatio de natura poenitentiae aduersus Bellarminum, etc. **Cantabrigiae, ex. off. J. Legat.** 1606. 8°. STC 6882.

1606 DILLINGHAM, FRANCIS. The progresse in pietie. **[Cambridge], J. Legat.** 1606. 8°. STC6888.

1606 HIERON, SAMUEL. Truths purchase. Two sermons. **Cambridge, J. Legat, sold by S. Waterson.** 1606. 4°. STC13429.

1606 PERKINS, WILLIAM. The whole treatise of the cases of conscience. **J. Legat, pr. to the Vniuer. of Cambridge, sold by S. Waterson.** 1606. 8°. STC19669.

1606 THOMAS, THOMAS. Dictionarium linguae Latinae et Anglicanae. Septima editio. **Cantabrigiae, ex. off. J. Legati, [ap. S. Waterson], Londini.** 1606. 4°. STC24013.

1607 BERNARD, RICHARD. A double catechisme. **Cambridge, J. Legate.** 1607. 8°. STC1936.

1607 COWELL, JOHN. The interpreter: or booke containing the signification of words. **Cambridge, J. Legate.** 1607. 4°. STC5900.

1607 HIERON, SAMUEL. The dignitie of the scriptures. **Cambridge, J. Legat.** 1607. 4°. STC13398.

1607 HIERON, SAMUEL. Three sermons: 1 the good fight, etc. **Cambridge, J. Legate.** 1607. 4°. STC13426.

1607 PERKINS, WILLIAM. A treatise of mans imagination. **J. Legat, pr. to the Vniuer. of Cambridge, sold by S. Waterson.** 1607. 12°. STC 19751.

1607 ROGERS, THOMAS. The faith, doctrine and religion professed in England. Expressed in 39 articles. **J. Legatt, printer to the University of Cambridge.** 1607. 4°. STC21228.

1607 TERENTIUS, PUBLIUS. P. Terentii Afri comoediae sex. Secunda editio multo emendatior. **Cantabrigiae, ex. off. J. Legat.** 1607. 4°. STC23891.

1607 WILLET, ANDREW. An harmonie upon the first booke of Samuel. **for L. Greene of Cambridge, sold by R. Bankeworth.** 1607. 4°. STC25678.

1607 WILLET, ANDREW. An harmonie upon the first booke of Samuel. **C. Legge, printer to the University of Cambridge.** 1607. STC25678A.

1607 WILLET, ANDREW. Loidoromastix, that is, a scourge for a rayler. **C. Legge, printer to the University of Cambridge.** 1607. 4°. STC25693.

1608 BOWND, NICH. A treatise full of consolation. **Cambridge, C. Legge.** 1608. 8°. STC3441.

1608 HIERON, SAMUEL. Sixe sermons. **Cambridge, J. Legate.** 1608. 4°. STC13422.

1608 KILBY, RICHARD. The burthen of a loaden conscience. **Cambridge, C. Legge.** 1608. 8°. STC14950.

1608 PERKINS, WILLIAM. A discourse of the damned art of witchcraft. **C. Legge, pr. to the Vniuer. of Cambridge.** 1608. 8°. STC19697.

1608 PERKINS, WILLIAM. A godly and learned exposition of Christs sermon in the mount. **T. Brooke and C. Legge, printers to the Vniuer. of Cambridge.** 1608. 4°. STC19722.

1608 PERKINS, WILLIAM. The whole treatise óf the cases of conscience. Newly corrected. **J. Legat, pr. to Vniuer of Cambridge, sold by S. Waterson.** 1608. 3 vols. 8°. STC19670.

1608 PERKINS, WILLIAM. The works of that famous and worthie minister of Christ in the vniuersitie of Cambridge, M. W. Perkins. **J. Legate, printer to the Vniuer. of Cambridge, and are to be sold at the Signe of the Crowne by S. Waterson.** 1608. 3 vols. Fol. STC19649.

1608 WALKINGTON, THOMAS. Salomons sweete harpe. **C. Legge, printer to the Vniversity of Cambridge.** 1608. 8°. STC24971.

1609 BERNARD, RICHARD. A double catechisme. **Cambridge, J. Legate.** 1609. 8°. STC1937.

1609 HIERON, SAMUEL. Three sermons; a remedie for securitie, etc. **Cambridge, C. Legge, sold by S. Macham.** 1609. 4°. STC13427.

1609 PLAYFERE, THOMAS. A funerall sermon preached in S. Maries, 10 May 1665. [sic], [1605?] **Cambridge, C. Legge.** 1609. 4°. STC20009.

1609 PLAYFERE, THOMAS. A sermon preached before the Kings Maiestie at Drayton the sixt day of August, 1605. (A sermon preached the 27 Aug., 1605. - A funerall sermon preached 10 May, 1605. A sermon preached 1609). **Cambridge, C. Legge, sold by S. Macham.** 1609. STC20026.

1610 ANTHONIE, FRANCIS. Medicinæ, chymicae, et veri potabilis auri assertio, ex. lucubrationibus F. Anthonii. **Cantabrigiæ, C. Legge.** 1610. 4°. STC668.

1610 ENGLAND, CHURCH OF VISITATIONS. Ely. **Cambridge, C. Legge.** 1610. 4°. STC10195.

1610 FLETCHER, GILES, the younger. Christs victorie, and triumph. **Cambridge, C. Legge.** 1610. 2 vols. 4°. STC11058.

1610 OWEN, DAVID. Herod and Pilate reconciled: on the concord of a papist and puritan. **C. Legge, printer to Univ. of Camb., sold in Pauls Churchyard, etc.** 1610. 4°. STC18983.

1610 PERKINS, WILLIAM. A salue for a sicke man. [Cambridge], **J. Legatt.** [1610?]. 12°. STC19744.

1610 PERKINS, WILLIAM. A discourse of the damned art of witchcraft. **C. Legge, pr. to the Vniv. of Cambridge.** 1610. 8°. STC19698.

1610 PLAYFERE, THOMAS. Ten sermons by that eloquent divine of famous memory, Th. Playfere. **C. Legge, printer to the University of Cambridge.** 1610. 8°. STC20005.

1610 THOMAS, THOMAS. Dictionarium linguæ Latinae et Anlicanae. Octava editio. **Cantabrigiæ, ex. off. J. Legati [ap. S. Waterson], Londini.** 1610. 8°. STC24014.

1610 WILLET, ANDREW. Hexapla in Danielem. **C. Legge, printer to the University of Cambridge, for L. Greene.** 1610. 2 vols. Fol. STC25689.

1611 PERKINS, WILLIAM. A godly and learned exposition of Christs sermon in the mount. **Cambridge, C. Legge.** 1611. 4°. STC19723.

1611 PERKINS, WILLIAM. A salue for a sicke man. [Cambridge?]. **J. Legat.** 1611. 12°. STC 19745.

1611 PLAYFERE, THOMAS. The power of praier. A sermon. **Cambridge, J. Legat.** 1611. 8°. STC20025A.

1611 PLAYFERE, THOMAS. The sick-mans couch; a sermon. **Cambridge, J. Legat.** 1611. 8°. STC20027A.

1612 CAMBRIDGE UNIVERSITY. Epicedium cantabrigiense in obitum Henrici principis Walliae. **Cantabrigiæ, ex. off. C. Legge.** 1612. pp. 110. 4°. STC4481.

1612 CAMBRIDGE UNIVERSITY. Epicedium cantabrigiense in obitum Henrici principis Walliae. **Cantabrigiæ, ex. off. C. Legge.** 1612. pp. 112. 4°. STC4482.

1612 COLLINS, SAMUEL. Increpatio Andreae Eudaemono - Johannis Jesuitae. **C. Legge, Acad. Cantab. Typographus.** 1612. 4°. STC5563.

1612 NETHERSOLE, Sir FRANCIS. Memoriæ sacra Henrici Walliæ principis laudatio funebris. **Cantabrigiæ, ex. off. C. Legge.** 1612. 4°. STC18473.

1612 PERKINS, WILLIAM. A golden chaine, or the description of theologie, containing the order of the causes of saluation and damnation according to Gods woord. **J. Legate, printer to the Vniuer. of Cambridge.** 1612. 8°. STC19664.

1612 PLAYFERE, THOMAS. Nine sermons by that eloquent divine, Th. Playfere. **C. Legge, printer to the University of Cambridge.** 1612. 8°. STC20005A.

1612 POWNOLL, NATHANIEL. The young divines apologie. **Cambridge, C. Legge, sold by M. Lownes.** 1612. 12°. STC20174.

1612 TAYLOR, THOMAS. A commentarie upon the Epistle to Titus. [Cambridge, C. Legge], **for L. Greene.** 1612. 4°. STC23825.

1612 TAYLOR, THOMAS. A commentaire upon the Epistle to Titus. **C. Legge, printer to the University of Cambridge.** 1612. STC23825A.

1612 TAYLOR, THOMAS. Japhets first publique perswasion into Sems tent. **C. Legge, printer to the University of Cambridge.** 1612. 4°. STC23830.

1613 DESPOTINUS, GASPAR. Hirci mulctra de sanguinis missione in quadam febre quotidiana continua, disceptatio medica. **Cantabrigiæ, C. Legg.** 1613. 4°. STC6786.

1613 ENGLAND, CHURCH OF. VISITATIONS. Ely. **Cambridge, C. Legge.** 1613. 4°. STC10196.

1613 PERKINS, WILLIAM. The works of that famous minister of Christ in the vniuersitie of Cambridge, M. W. Perkins, [vols. 1 and 2] **Printed at London by J. Legatt.** 1612; 13. [vol. 3] **C. Legge, pr. to the Vniuer. of Cambridge.** 1613. 3 vols. Fol. STC19650.

1613 ROBARTES, FOULKES. The revenue of the Gospel is tythes. [Cambridge], **C. Legge.** 1613. 4°. STC21069.

1614 BASTINGIUS, JEREMIAS. An exposition or commentarie upon the catechism taught in the Lowe Countryes. Fifth ed. [Cambridge], **J. Leggatt.** 1614. 4°. STC1567.

1614 KILBY, RICHARD. The burthen of a loaden conscience. Fifth impression. **Cambridge, C. Legge.** 1614. 8°. STC14951.

1614 MOSSE, MILES. Justifying and saving faith. **C. Legge, Pr. to the Univ. of Cambridge, sold by M. Law.** 1614. 4°. STC18209.

1614 WILLET, ANDREW. Ecclesia triumphans: that is, the joy of the English Church for the coronation of Prince James. (Thesaurus ecclesiae; catholicon). **J. Legat, Printer to University of Cambridge.** 1614. 3 vols. Fol. STC25677.

1614 WILLET, ANDREW. An harmonie upon the first booke of Samuel. **C. Legge, printer to the University of Cambridge, for L. Greene.** 1614. Fol. STC25679.

1614 WILLET, ANDREW. An harmonie upon the first cond booke of Samuel. **C. Legge, printer to University of Cambridge.** 1614. Fol. STC25680.

1615 JAMES I, king of England. Deus & Rex; sive dialogus quo demonstratur Jacobum regem immediatè sub Deo constitum justissimè sibi vendicare quicquid in juramento fidelitatis requiritur. [By R. Mocket?]. **Cantabrigiæ, [C. Legge].** 1615. 8°. STC14417.

1615 JAMES I, king of England. God and the King; or a dialogue shewing that King James being immediate under God doth rightfully claime whatsoever is required by the oath of allegiance. **Cambridge.** 1615. STC14419A.

1615 MELANTHE. Fabula pastoralis. **[Cambridge], C. Legge.** 1615. 4°. STC17800.

1615 PERKINS, WILLIAM. A salue for a sicke man. [Cambridge?], **J. Legatt.** 1615. 12°. STC 19746.

1615 YATES, JOHN. Gods arraignment of hypocrites. **Cambridge, C. Legge.** 1615. 4°. STC26081.

1616 FARLEY, HENRY. The complaint of Paules, to all Christian soules. **[Cambridge], C. Legge.** 1616. 4°. STC10688.

1616 GOSTWYKE, ROGER. The anatomie of Ananias. **C. Legge, pr. to the Univ. of Cambridge.** 1616. 4°. STC12100.

1616 JAMES I, king of England. A remonstrance for the right of Kings. Tr. out of His Maiesties French copie [by R. B.]. **C. Legge, printer to the Univ. of Cambridge.** 1616. 4°. STC14369.

1616 JEGON, JOHN, bp. [Direction to archdeacons]. **Cambridge, C. Legge.** 1616. Brs. STC14484.

1616 KILBY, RICHARD. The burthen of a loaden conscience. Sixth impression. **Cambridge, C. Legge.** 1616. 12°. STC14952.

1616 The office of Christian parents. **Cambridge, C. Legge.** 1616. 4°. STC5180.

1616 YATES, JOHN. Gods arraignment of hypocrites. **[Cambridge], C. Legge, sold by A. Johnson.** 1616. 4°. STC26082.

1617 COLLINS, SAMUEL. Epphata to F.T. [i.e. T. Fitzherbert]; or, the defence of the Bishop of Elie concerning the answer to cardinal Bellarmines Apologie. **Cambridge, C. Legge.** 1617. 4°. STC5561.

1617 HIERON, SAMUEL. Davids penitentiall psalme opened: in thirtie lectures. [Anon]. **Cambridge. C. Legge.** 1617. 8°. STC13394A.

1617 PLAYFERE, THOMAS. The sick-mans couch; a sermon. **Cambridge, J. Legatt.** 1617. 8°. STC20027B.

1618 KILBY, RICHARD. The burthen of a loaden conscience. Seauenth impression. **Cambridge, C. Legge, London, M. Law.** 1618. 8°. STC14953.

1618 KILBY, RICHARD. Hallelu-iah: praise yee the Lord, for the unburdening of a loaden conscience **Cambridge, C. Legge, London, M. Law.** 1618. 8°. STC14955.

1618 TAYLOR, THOMAS. Christs combate and conquest **C. Legge, printer to the Univ. of Cambridge.** 1618. 4°. STC23822.

1619 ANGELOS, CHRISTOPHER. Ἐγκωμιον τῆς ἐνδοξοτάτης μεγαλης βρεττανιας An encomion of Great Britaine. **Cambridge, C. Legge.** 1619. 4°. STC635.

1619 ANGELOS, CHRISTOPHER. Σγχειριδcον περι της καταδταεως των οημερον ενρισκομένων Σλληνων. [Enchiridion de institutis Graecorum]. **Cambridge, ex. officina C. Legge.** 1619. 2 vols. 4°. STC636.

1619 CAMBRIDGE UNIVERSITY. Lacrymae cantabrigienses in obitum Reginae Annae. **Cantabrigiæ, ex. off. C. Legge.** 1619. 4°. STC4489.

1619 ENGLAND, CHURCH OF. VISITATIONS. Norwich. **Cambridge, C. Legge.** 1619. 4°. STC 10292.

1619 GURNAY, EDMUND. Corpus Christi. [A sermon]. **[Cambridge], C. Legge.** 1619. 12°. STC12527.

1619 JAMES I, king of England. A remonstrance for the right of kings. Tr. out of His Maiesties French copie [by R.B.]. **C. Legge, printer to the Univ. of Cambridge.** 1619. pp.288. 4°. STC14370.

1619 JAMES I, king of England. A remonstrance for the right of Kings. Tr. out of His Maiesties French copie by R. B. **C. Legge, printer to the Univ. of Cambridge.** 1619. pp.290. 4°. STC 14371.

1619 SYMPSON, WILLIAM. A full and profitable interpretation of all the names within the genealogie of Jesus Christ. **[Cambridge], C. Legge.** 1619. 4°. STC23595.

1619 TAYLOR, THOMAS. A commentarie upon the Epistle to Titus. Reviewed and enlarged. **C. Legge, printer to the University of Cambridge.** 1619. 4°. STC23826.

1620 WILLET, ANDREW. Hexapla: that is a six fold commentarie upon the epistle to the Romans. **C. Legge, printer to the University of Cambridge.** 1620. Fol. STC25691.

1621 PLAYFERE, THOMAS. Ten sermons by that eloquent divine, of famous memory, Th. Playfere. **C. Legge, printer to the Vniu. of Cambridge.** 1621. 8°. STC20006.

1622 OWEN, DAVID. Anti Paraeus: sive determinatio de jure regio. **Ex. off. C. Legge Ac. Cantab. typographi.** 1622. 8°. STC18982.

1623 BIBLE. ENGLISH. PSALMS. The whole book of psalmes. **Cambridge, C. Legge.** 1623. 8°. STC2584.

1623 CAMBRIDGE UNIVERSITY. Gratulatio de principus reditu ex Hispanijs. **Cantabrigiæ, ex. off. C. Legge.** 1623. 4°. STC4487.

1623 CRAKANTHORP, RICHARD. De providentia Dei tractatus. **Cantabrigiæ, [C. Legge]. imp. L. Greene.** 1623. 4°. STC5973.

1623 HERBERT, GEORGE. Oratio quâ principis Caroli reditum ex Hispanijs celebravit G. Herbert. **[Cantabrigiæ], ex. off. C. Legge.** 1623. 4°. STC13181.

1624   CHEVALIER, GUILLAUME de. The ghosts of the deceased Sieurs de Villemor and de Fontaines. The third ed. augmented in French and tr. by T. Heigham. **C. Legge, printer to the University of Cambridge.** 1624. 8°. STC 5129.

1625   ALMANACS. Almanack. **Cambridge, C. Legge.** 1625. 8°. STC405.

1625   CAMBRIDGE UNIVERSITY. Cantabrigiensium dolor et solamen: seu decessio regis Jacobi et successio regis Caroli, etc. **Cantabrigiæ, C. Legge.** 1625. pp.60. 4°. STC4477.

1625   CAMBRIDGE UNIVERSITY. Cantabrigensium dolor et solamen: seu decessio regis Jacobi et successio regis Caroli. [Another edn. with additions]. **Cantabrigiæ, C. Legge.** 1625. pp.72. 4°. STC4478.

1625   CAMBRIDGE UNIVERSITY. Epithalamium Caroli regis et H. Mariæ a musis cantabrigiensibus decantatum. **Cantabrigiæ, C. Legge.** 1625. 4°. STC4484.

1626   ALMANACS. STROF, W. A new almanacke and prognostication for Cambridge. **Cambridge, printers to the Universitie.** 1626. 8°. STC516.

1626   BENLOWES, EDWARD. Sphinx theologica. **Cambridge, printers to the University.** 1626. 8°. STC1879.

1626   HOLLAND, ABRAHAM. Hollandi Post-huma; a funerall elegie of King James, etc. **Cantabrigiæ, imp. H. Holland.** 1626. 4°. STC13579.

1626   NOWELL, ALEXANDER. Christianæ pietatis prima institutio ad vsum scholarum. **Cantabrigiæ, ex. typ. Acad. typographorum.** 1626. 8°. STC18722.

1626   SARPI, PAOLO. Interdicti Veneti historia; recèns ex Italico conversus [by W. Bedell]. **Cantabrigiæ, ap. T. Bucke, J. Bucke et L. Greene.** 1626. 4°. STC21767.

1627   ALMANACS, DOVE. A new almanacke and prognostication. **Cambridge, printers to the University.** 1627. 8°. STC436.

1627   ALMANACS, FROST, W. A new almanacke or prognostication for Cambridge. **Cambridge, printers to the Universitie.** 1627. 8°. STC 446.

1627   ALMANACS, LAKES, T. The countreymans kalendar with a prognostication. **Cambridge, printers to the Universitie.** 1627. 8°. STC 478.

1627   ALMANACS, RIVERS, P. A new almanacke and prognostication for Cambridge. **Cambridge, printers to the Universitie.** 1627. 8°. STC 505.

1627   ALMANACS, WATERS, F. A new almanacke and prognostication for 1627 for Bristol. **Cambridge, printers to the Universitie.** 1627. STC524.

1627   DAVENANT, JOHN, bp. Expositio epistolæ ad colossenses. **Cantabrigiæ, ap T. & J. Bucke.** 1627. Fol. STC6296.

1627   ENGLAND, CHURCH OF. VISITATIONS. Lincoln. **Cambridge.** 1627. 4°. STC10242.

1627   ENGLAND, CHURCH OF. VISITATIONS. Sudbury. **Cambridge, printers to the Univ.** 1627. 4°. STC10338.

1627   FLETCHER, PHINEAS. Locustæ, vel pietas Jesuitica. (The Locusts, or Appollyonists). [**Cambridge**], **T. and J. Bucke.** 1627. 2 vols. 4°. STC11081.

1627   GERHARD, JOHANN. The meditations of J. Gerhard. Tr. R. Winterton. **Cambridge, T. Bucke and J. Bucke.** 1627. 12°. STC11772.

1627   PERROT, RICHARD. Jacobs vowe, or the true historie of tithes. **T. Bucke and J. Bucke, printers to the Vnuier. of Cambridge.** 1627. 2 vols. 4°. STC19770.

1627   WARD, WILLIAM. Short grounds of catechisme. **Cambridge, [T. and J. Buck].** 1627. 8°. STC25058.

1627   WREN, MATTHEW, bp. A sermon preached before the Kings Majestie. **Cambridge, T. and J. Buck.** 1627. 4°. STC26015.

1628   BEDEL, WILLIAM. bp. An examination of certaine motives to recusancie. **Cambridge, printers to the Universitie, sold by R. Daniel, London.** 1628. 8°. STC1786.

1628   BIBLE. ENGLISH. NEW TESTAMENT. The new test. of our lord and saviour Jesus Christ. Newly translated and revised. **Cambridge, printers to the Universitie.** 1628. 24°. STC 2932.

1628   BIBLE. ENGLISH. NEW TESTAMENT. The new test. of our lord and saviour Jesus Christ. Revised by his majesties speciall command. **Cambridge, printers to the Universitie.** 1628. 24°. STC2933.

1628   BIBLE. ENGLISH. NEW TESTAMENT. The new test. of our lord and saviour Jesus Christ. **Cambridge, printers to the Universitie.** 1628. 8°. STC2934.

1628   BIBLE. ENGLISH. PSALMS. The whole book of psalmes. **Printers to the University of Cambridge.** 1628. 8°. STC2608.

1628   BIBLE. ENGLISH. PSALMS. The whole book of psalms. **Printers to the University of Cambridge, sold at London by R. Daniel.** 1628. 8°. STC2609.

1628   BIBLE. ENGLISH. PSALMS. The whole book of psalms. **Printers to the University of Cambridge, sold at London by R. Daniel.** 1628. 12°. STC2610.

1628   CARTER, JOHN. Winter-evenings communication with young novices. **Cambridge, printers to the University.** 1628. 8°. STC4696.

1628   DENT, DANIEL. A sermon against drunkennes, etc. **Cambridge, printers to the Univ.** 1628. 4°. STC6673.

1629   ALMANACS, CLARKE, E. A new almanack for 1629. **Cambridge.** [n. d.]. 8°. STC431.

1629   ALMANACS. POND, F. A new almanacke for 1629. **Cambridge, University printers.** 1629. 8°. STC499.

1629   ALMANACS. RIVERS, P. A new almanacke and prognostication for Cambridge. **Cambridge, printers to the Universitie.** 1629. 8°. STC 505.

1629   BIBLE. ENGLISH. The holy bible. [Roy.]. (The book of common prayer). **Cambridge, T. and J. Buck.** 1629. Fol. STC2285.

1629   BIBLE. ENGLISH. PSALMS. The whole booke of psalmes: collected into English meeter. **Cambridge, T. and J. Buck.** 1629. Fol. STC2613.

1629   LITURGIES. BOOK OF COMMON PRAYER. **Cambridge, T. and J. Buck.** 1629. Fol. STC 16375.

1629 PEMBLE, WILLIAM. De formarum origine. Editio posthuma. **Cambridge. R. Daniel.** [1629?] 16°. STC19572.

1630 ALMANACS. RIVERS, P. A new almanacke and prognostication for Cambridge. **Cambridge, printers to the Universitie.** 1630. 8°. STC 505.

1630 BIBLE. ENGLISH. The holy bible. Rom. **Cambridge, T. and J. Buck.** 1630. 4°. STC2293.

1630 BIBLE. ENGLISH. The holy bible. B.L. **Cambridge, T. and J. Buck.** 1630. 4°. STC 2294.

1630 BIBLE. ENGLISH. PSALMS. The whole booke of Psalmes: collected into English meeter. **Cambridge, T. Buck.** 1630. 4°. STC2624.

1630 CICERO, MARCUS TULLIUS. M.T. Cic. De Officiis de Senectute, de Amicitia, Paradoxa, Somniū Scipionis. **Cantabrigiae, ex. typ. Acad. typographorum.** 1630. 8°. STC5271.

1630 DAVENANT, JOHN, bp. Expositio epistolae ad colossenses. Editio secunda. **Cantabrigiae, ap. T. and J. Buck.** 1630. Fol. STC6297.

1630 ENGLAND, CHURCH OF. VISITATIONS. Lincoln 1630 and 1631. **[Cambridge, Printers to the Univ.** 1630]. 4°. STC10243.

1630 LITURGIES. BOOK OF COMMON PRAYER. **Cambridge, T. and J. Buck.** 1630. 4°. STC16380.

1630 PRESTON, JOHN. Sermons preached before his Majestie, and upon other occasions. **for L. Greene of Cambridge, sold by J. Boler.** 1630. 4°. STC20270.

1630 SARPI, PAOLO. Quæstio quod libetica; an liceat stipendia sub principe religione discrepante merere. [Anon]. **Cantabrigiae,** 1630. 4°. STC21768.

1631 APHTHONIUS, sophista. Progymnasmata Latinitate donata. Nousissima editio. **Cantabrigiae, ex. Acad. typographeo.** 1631. 8°. STC705.

1631 CAMBRIDGE UNIVERSITY. Genethliacum Caroli et Mariae, à musis cantabrigiensibus celebratum. **Cantabrigiae, [R. Daniel].** 1631. 4°. STC4486.

1631 CASTALIO, SEBASTIAN. Dialogorum sacrorum libri quatuor. **Cantabrigiae, ex. acad. celeb. typographeo.** 1631. 8°. STC4775.

1631 CICERO, MARCUS TULLIUS. Epistolarum libri quatuor. **Cantabrigiae, ex. typ. acad.** 1631. 8°. STC5303.

1631 DAVENANT, JOHN, bp. Praelectiones de duobus in theologia controversis capitibus. **Cantabrigiae, ex. Acad. typographeo.** 1631. Fol. STC6301.

1631 GERHARD, JOHANN. The meditations of J. Gerhard. Second edition. (Gerards prayers. Third ed.) **Cambridge, T. and J. Bucke.** 1631. 2 vols. 12°. STC11773.

1631 HIPPOCRATES. Aphorismorum Hippocratis liber primus. Heurnio interprete. **Cantabrigiae.** 1631. 4°. STC13519.

1631 MOSES BEN MAIMON. Canones poenitentiae Hebraicè. Tr. G.N. **Cantabrigiae, ex. Acad. typo.** 1631. 4°. STC18206.

1631 OVIDIUS NASO, PUBLIUS. P. Ouidii Nasonis Metamorphoseωn libri xv. Greg. Bersmani notationibus illustrati. **Cantabrigiae, ex Acad. typog.** 1631. 12°. STC18954.

1631 SETON, JOHN. Dialectica. Huic accessit G. Buclaei Arithmetica. **ex. Acad. typog. Cantabrigiae.** 1631. 8°. STC22257.

1631 TALAEUS, AUDOMARUS. A. Talaei rhetorica. **Cantabrigiae, ex. Acad. typog.** 1631. 8°. STC23661.

1632 BIBLE. NEW TESTAMENT. GREEK. 'H καινη διαθηκη. Novum testamentum. **Cantabrigiae, T. Buck.** 1632. 8°. STC2796.

1632 CAMBRIDGE UNIVERSITY. Anthologia in regis exanthemata; seu gratulatio musarum cantabrigiensium. **Ex. Acad. Cantabrigiensis typographeo.** 1632. 4°. STC4475.

1632 CRUSO, JOHN. Military instructions for the cavallrie. [Init.I.C.] **Cambridge, Printers to the Univ.** 1632. Fol. STC6099.

1632 DALECHAMP, CALEB. Christian hospitalitie, handled common-place-wise. (Harrisonus honoratus, etc.) **Cambridge, T. Buck.** 1632. 2 vols. 4°. STC6192.

1632 FLETCHER, GILES, the younger. Christs victorie, and triumph. Second edition. **Cambridge, for F. Greene.** 1632. 2 vols. 4°. STC11060.

1632 GERHARD, JOHANN. A golden chaine of divine aphorismes. Tr. R. Winterton. **printers to the Univ. of Cambridge.** 1632. 12°. STC11769.

1632 GERHARD, JOHANN. The meditations of J. Gerhard. Third edition. (Gerards prayers. Fourth ed.) **Cambridge, T. Buck.** 1632. 2vols. 12°. STC11774.

1632 HEYWOOD, THOMAS. Englands Elizabeth; her life and troubles. **Cambridge, for P. Waterhouse.** 1632. 12°. STC13314.

1632 MEDE, JOSEPH. Clauis apocalyptica. [Anon]. **Cantabrigiae, T. Buck.** 1632. 2 vols. 4°. STC17767.

1632 PERKINS, WILLIAM. A salue for a sicke man. **[Cambridge?], J. Legatt.** 1632. 12°. STC 19747.

1632 RANDOLPH, THOMAS. The jealous lovers. A comedie presented to their majesties at Cambridge. **Printers to the university of Cambridge.** 1632. 4°. STC20692.

1632 RANDOLPH, THOMAS. The jealous lovers. A comedie presented to their majesties at Cambridge. **Printers to the university of Cambridge, sold by R. Ireland.** 1632. STC20692A.

1632 SCHONAEUS, CORNELIUS. Terentius christianus siue comoediae duae Terentiano stylo conscriptae. **Cantabrigiae, ex. Acad. Typog.** 1632. 8°. STC21823.

1632 SPAGNUOLI, BAPTISTA. B. Mantuani adolescentia seu bucolica. **Cantabrigiae, ex. ac. typog.** 1632. 8°. STC22986.

1632 VIRGILIUS MARO, PUBLIUS. P. Virgilii Maronis opera. **Cantabrigiae.** 1632. 8°. STC24793.

1633 Anthropodaimonomachia. 'Ανθρωποδαιμωνομαχια, or the warre between man & the devil. **Cambridge, printers to the Universitie.** 1633. 4°. STC 669.

1633 BIBLE. ENGLISH. The holy bible etc. [Roy.] **Cambridge, T. and J. Buck.** 1633. 4°. STC 2310.

1633 BIBLE. ENGLISH. NEW TESTAMENT. The new test. of our lord and saviour Jesus Christ. **Cambridge, printers to the university.** 1633. 4°. STC2944.

1633 BIBLE. ENGLISH. PSALMS. The whole booke of psalmes. Collected, etc. **Printers to the University of Cambridge.** 1633. 4°. STC2647.

1633 CAMBRIDGE UNIVERSITY. Ducis Eboracensis fasciae, a musis cantabrigiensibus raptim contextae. **Cantabrigiæ, T. Buck & R. Daniel.** 1633. 4°. STC4480.

1633 CAMBRIDGE UNIVERSITY. Epigrammata Regiorum medicinae professorum in R. Wintertoni Metaphrasin, etc., etc. **Cantabrigiæ, T. Buck and R. Daniel.** 1633. STC4483.

1633 CAMBRIDGE UNIVERSITY. Rex redux; sive musa cantabrigiensis voti damnas de felici reditu regis Caroli. **Ex. Acad. Cantab. typog.** 1633. 4°. STC4491.

1633 CASTALIO, SEBASTIAN. Dialogorum sacrorum libri quatuor. Editio novissima. **Cantabrigiæ, ex. acad. celeb. typographeo.** 1633. 8°. STC 4776.

1633 The Christian's race; a sermon. **Cambridge.** [1633.] 4°. STC5151A.

1633 CICERO, MARCUS TULLIUS. M.T. Cic. De Officiis, de Senectute, de Amicitia, Paradoxa, Somniū Scipionis. **Cantabrigiæ, T. Buck and R. Daniel.** [1633?]. 12°. STC5272.

1633 CORDIER, MATHURIN. Colloquiorum scholasticorum libri quatuor. **Cantabrigiæ, e typog. Acad. typographorum.** 1633. 8°. STC5761.

1633 Daimonōpanōlethria. Δαιμωνοπανωλεθρια, or the devils downfall. **Cambridge, printers to the Univ.** 1633. 4°. STC6189.

1633 DIONYSIUS, PERIEGETES. Διονυσιου ο'ικουμενης περιηγησις **Cantabrigiæ, ap. T. Buck & R. Daniel.** 1633. 8°. STC6900.

1633 ENGLAND, CHURCH OF. VISITATIONS. Norwich. [**Cambridge**], **Printers to the Univ.** 1633. 4°. STC10296.

1633 FLETCHER, GILES, the elder. De literis antiquae Britanniæ. **Cantabrigiæ, ex. acad. typog.** 1633. 8°. STC11054.

1633 FLETCHER, PHINEAS. The purple island. **Printers to the univ. of Cambridge.** 1633. 2 vols. 4°. STC11082.

1633 FLETCHER, PHINEAS. Sylva poetica. **Cantabrigiæ, ex. acad. typog.** 1633. 8°. STC11084.

1633 FOSBROKE, JOHN. Six sermons delivered at Kettering and other places. **Printers to the Univ. of Cambridge.** [T. Buck and R. Daniel]. 1633. 4°. STC11199.

1633 HAGIOSYMPOSION. 'Αγιοσυμπόσιον; or a direction for feasting. **Printers to the Univ. Cambridge.** 1633. 4°. STC12601.

1633 HAUSTED, PETER. Senile odium. Comœdia. **Cantabrigiæ, ex. Ac. typographeo.** 1633. 8°. STC12936.

1633 HERBERT, GEORGE. The Temple. **Cambridge, T. Buck and R. Daniel.** 1633. 12°. STC13183.

1633 HERBERT, GEORGE. The Temple. Second edition. **Cambridge, T. Buck and R. Daniel, sold by F. Green.** 1633. 12°. STC13185.

1633 HIPPOCRATES. 'Ιπποκρατους οι 'Αφορισμοι Hippocratis aphorismi. Greek and Latin. (Epigrammata regiorum medicinæ professorum). **Cantabrigiæ, T. Buck & R. Daniel.** 1633. 2 vols. 8°. STC13518.

1633 KELLET, EDWARD. Miscellanies of divinitie, **printers to the Univ. of Cambridge.** 1633. Fol. STC14903.

1633 MORTON, THOMAS, bp. Sacris ordinibus non rite initiati tenentur ad eos retus ineundos. [**Cambridge**]. 1633. Brs. STC18195.

1633 NOWELL, ALEXANDER. Christinæ pietatis prima institutio ad vsum scholarum. **Cantabrigiæ, ex. Acad. typog.** 1633. 8°. STC18724.

1633 SCOT, THOMAS. God and the King, in a sermon. **printers to the University of Cambridge.** 1633. 4°. STC21873.

1633 Solomon's charity. **Cambridge, printers to the University.** 1633. 4°. STC22903.

1633 VIVES, JOANNES LUDOVICUS. Linguae Latinæ exercitatio. **Cantabrigiæ, ex. Ac. typog.** 1633. 8°. STC24854.

1634 ALMANACS. CLARK. A new almanack and prognostication for 1634 for Ipswich. **Cambridge, printers to the Universitie.** [n.d.] 8°. STC430.

1634 ALMANACS. DOVE. A new almanacke and prognostication. **Cambridge, printers to the University.** 1634. 8°. STC436.

1634 ALMANACS. KIDMAN, T. A new almanack for 1634, etc. **Cambridge, printers to the University.** [n.d.] 8°. STC469.

1634 ALMANACS. RIVERS, P. A new almanacke and prognostication for Cambridge. **Cambridge, printers to the Universitie.** 1634. 8°. STC 505.

1634 ALMANACS. SWALLOW. An almanack for Cambridge. **Cambridge, printers to the Universitie.** 1634. 8°. STC517.

1634 ALMANACS. TURNER, T. An almanack for 1634. **Cambridge, printers to the Universitie.** [1634]. 8°. STC518.

1634 ALMANACS. WINTER, F. An almanack for 1634. **Cambridge, printers to the Universitie.** 1634. STC530.

1634 ARISTOTLE. Epitome doctrinae moralis ex decem libris ethicorum Aristotelis ad Nichomachum collecta per T. Golium. Editio auctior. **Cantabrigiæ, T. & J. Buck.** 1634. 8°. STC 755.

1634 BIBLE. ENGLISH. PSALMS. The whole booke of psalmes. **Printers to the University of Cambridge.** 1634. 4°. STC2654.

1634 CRASHAW, RICHARD. Epigrammatum sacrorum liber. **Cantabrigiæ, ex. Acad. typographeo.** 1634. 8°. STC6009.

1634 DAVENANT, JOHN, bp. Determinationes quaestionum quarundam theologicarum. **Cantabrigiæ, ap. T. & J. Buck, ac R. Daniel.** 1634. Fol. STC6294.

1634 DONNE, JOHN. A sermon upon the xv. verse of the 8 chapter of John. **Cambridge.** 1634. 4°. STC7055.

1634 DONNE, JOHN. Six sermons, upon severall occasions. **Printers to the Univ. of Cambridge, sold by N. Fussell and H. Mosley, London.** 1634. 4°. STC7056.

1634 DONNE, JOHN. Two sermons preached before King Charles upon the xxvi. verse of the first chapter of Genesis. **Printers to the Univ. of Cambridge.** 1634. 4°. STC7058.

1634 ERASMUS, DESIDERIUS. Epitome colloquiorum Erasmi. Editio novissima. **Cantabrigiae, R. Daniel.** 1634. 8°. STC10463.

1634 GARTHWAIT, HENRY. Μονοτεσσαρον, the evangelical harmonie. **T. Buck and R. Daniel, printers to the Univ. of Cambridge.** 1634. 4°. STC11633.

1634 GERHARD, JOHANN. J. Gerhardi meditationes sacrae. Editio postrema. **ex. Acad. typog. Cantabrigiae.** 1634. 12°. STC11771.

1634 HAWKINS, WILLIAM. Corolla varia. Eclogae tres virgilianae. **Cantabrigiae, T. Buck' and ven. Londini ap R. Milbourn.** 1634. 8°. STC12964.

1634 LESSIUS, LEONARDUS. Hygiasticon: or, the right course of preserving life and health unto extream old age; done into English. (A treatise of temperance.By L. Cornarus. Tr. G. Herbert). **Cambridge, R. Daniel.** 1634. 2 vols. 12°. STC15520.

1634 LESSIUS, LEONARDUS. Hygiasticon; or, the right course of preserving life and health unto extream old age; done into English. (A treatise temperance. By. L. Cornarus. Tr. G. Herbert). Second edition. **printers to the University of Cambridge.** 1634. 2 vols. 12°. STC15521.

1634 LILY, WILLIAM and COLET, JOHN. A shorte introduction of grammar. **Cambridge, printers to the Univ.** 1634. 8°. STC15630.

1634 RANDOLPH, THOMAS. The jealous lovers. A comedie presented to their majesties at Cambridge. **Printers to the university of Cambridge, sold by R. Ireland.** 1634. 4°. STC20693.

1634 RUSSELL, JOHN. The two famous pitcht battels of Lypsich and Lutzen. **printers to the University of Cambridge, sold by P. Scarlet.** 1634. 4°. STC21460.

1634 SCOT, ROBERT. The foundation of the Universitie of Oxford. **Cambridge, printers to the University, for J. Scot the elder, sold at the house of R. Peak.** 1634. Fol. STC21868.

1634 SPAGNUOLI, BAPTISTA. B. Mantuani adolescentia seu bucolica. **Cantabrigiae, ex. ac. typog.** 1634. 8°. STC22987.

1635 AESOP. Fabulae. **Cantabrigiae, ex Academia typographeo.** 1635. 8°. STC174.

1635 APHTHONIUS, sophista. Progymnasmata Latinitate donata. Nouissima editio. **Cantabrigiae, ex Acad. typographeo.** 1635. 8°. STC706.

1635 BIBLE, ENGLISH. The holy bible. **Cambridge, T. Buck and R. Daniel.** 1635. 4°. STC2320.

1635 CAMBRIDGE UNIVERSITY. Carmen natalitium ad cunas principis Elisabethae decantatum. **Ex Acad. Cantab. Typog.** 1635. 4°. STC4479.

1635 Cuique suum: αυτωδη contra Cathari cantilenam. **Cantabrigiae, ex acad. typographeo.** 1635. 4°. STC6106.

1635 ENGLAND, CHURCH OF. VISITATIONS. Lincoln. **Cambridge, Printers to the Univ.** 1635. 4°. STC10244.

1635 GERHARD, JOHANN. The meditations of J. Gerhard. Fourth edition. (Gerards prayers. Fifth ed.) **Printers to the Univ. of Cambridge.** 1635. 2 vols. 12°. STC11775.

1635 HERBERT, GEORGE. The Temple. Fourth edition. **Cambridge, T. Buck and R. Daniel.** 1635. 12°. STC13187.

1635 KELLET, EDWARD. Miscellanies of divinitie. **printers to the Univ. of Cambridge,** sold by R. Allott 1635. Fol. STC14904.

1635 LITURGIES. BOOK OF COMMON PRAYER. **Printers to the univ. of Cambridge.** 1635. 4°. STC16401.

1635 OVIDIUS NASO, PUBLIUS. Pub. Ovidii Nasonis Heroidum Epistolae, una cum A. Sabini epistolis tribus, ad totidem Ovidianas responsoriis; Amorum libri tres, etc. [Cambridge], **ex Acad. typog.** 1635. 8°. STC18930.

1635 Poetae minores graeci. **Cantabrigiae, ap. T. and J. Buck and R. Daniel.** 1635. 8°. STC 12211.

1635 RAVISIUS, JOANNES. Epistolae nunc recens in lucem editae. **ex Acad. typ. Cantabrigiae.** 1635. 16°. STC20762.

1635 SCHONAEUS, CORNELIUS. Terentius christianus sive comoediae duae Terentiano stylo conscriptae. **Cantabrigiae, ex Acad. Typog.** 1635. 8°. STC21824.

1635 SHELFORD, ROBERT. Five pious and learned discourses. **printers to the University of Cambridge.** 1635. 4°. STC22400.

1635 SPAGNUOLI, BAPTISTA. B. Mantuani adolescentia seu bucolica. **Cantabrigiae, ex. typog. ac.** 1635. 8°. STC22988.

1635 SWAN, JOHN. Speculum mundi, or, a glasse representing the face of the world [**J. Buck and R. Daniel**], **printers to the University of Cambridge.** 1635. 4°. STC23516.

1636 ALMANAC. DOVE. A new almanacke and prognostication. **Cambridge, printers to the University.** 1636. 8°. STC436.

1636 BENLOWES, EDWARD. Sphinx theologica. **Cantabrigiae, ex acad, typ.** [1636]. 8°. STC 1880.

1636 CADE, ANTHONY. An appendix to a sermon of the nature of conscience. **Cambridge, printers to the University.** 1636. 4°. STC4331.

1636 CADE, ANTHONY. A sermon necessary for these times, showing the nature of conscience. **Cambridge, printers to the University.** 1636. 4°. STC4329A.

1636 DALECHAMP, CALEB. Haeresologia tripartita: vel de pernicie, necessitate et utilitate haerisium in ecclesia. **Cantabrigiae, ex Acad. Typ.** 1636. 4°. STC6194.

1636 DREXELIUS, HIEREMIAS. The considerations of Drexelius upon eternitie. Tr. R. Winterton. **Cambridge, printers to the Univ.** 1636. 12°. STC7236.

1636 DUGRES, GABRIEL. Breve et accuratum grammaticae gallicae compendium. **Cantabrigiae, [Univ. printers].** imp. authoris. 1636. 8°. STC7294.

1636 HODSON, WILLIAM. Credo resurrectionem carnis. (Second edition. Exactly revised and enlarged). **Printers to the Univ. of Cambridge, sold by A. Crook.** 1636. 12°. STC13553.

1636 LESSIUS, LEONARDUS. Hygiasticon: or the right course of preserving life and health unto extream old age; done into English. (A treatise of temperance. By. L. Cornarus. Tr. G. Herbert). Third edition. **printers to the Univ. of Cambridge.** 1636. 12°. STC15522.

1636 MANUZIO, ALDO. Phrases linguae latinae. **ex Acadamiae typ. Cantab.** 1636. 8°. STC 17285.

1636 NOWELL, ALEXANDER. Christianae pietatis prima institutio ad vsum scholarum. **Cantabrigiae, ex Acad. typog.** 1636. 8°. STC 18725.

1636 SALTMARSH, JOHN. Poemata sacra. Latinĕ & Anglicĕ scripta. **ex acad. typog. Cantabrigiae.** 1636. 3 vols. 8°. STC21638.

1636 SIMSON, EDWARD. E. Simsoni Mosaica. **Cantabrigiae, ex acad. typog.** 1636. 2 vols. 4°. STC22571.

1637 BIBLE. ENGLISH. The holy bible. [B.L.] **Printers to the University of Cambridge.** 1637. 4°. STC2326.

1637 BIBLE. ENGLISH. The holy bible with Booke of Common Prayer. **Cambridge, T. Buck and R. Daniel.** 1637. 4°. STC2327.

1637 BIBLE. ENGLISH. PSALMS. The whole booke of psalmes. Both in prose and meeter. [Roman]. **T. Buck and R. Daniel, printers to the University of Cambridge.** 1637. 4°. STC2674.

1637 BIBLE. ENGLISH. PSALMS. The whole booke of psalmes. Both in prose and meeter. [B.L.]. **Printers to the University of Cambridge.** 1637. 4°. STC2675.

1637 BURGERSDIJCK, FRANCO. F. Burgesdicii Institutionum logicarum libri duo. **Cantabrigiae, ex academiae typographeo.** 1637. 8°. STC 4108.

1637 CAMBRIDGE UNIVERSITY. Συνωδ'α, sive musarum cantabrigiensium concentus et congratulatio ad Regem Carolum. **Ex Acad. Cantab. typog.** 1637. 4°. STC4492

1637 DUPORT, JAMES. Oρηνοθριαμβος, sive liber Job Graeco carmine redditus. **Cantabrigiae, ap T. Buck & R. Daniel.** 1637. 8°. STC7365.

1637 ENGLAND, CHURCH OF. VISITATIONS. Peterborough., **Cambridge, Printers to the Univ.** 1637. 4°. STC10319.

1637 LITURGIES. BOOK OF COMMON PRAYER. **Cambridge, T. Buck and R. Daniel.** 1637. 4°. STC16406.

1637 MORTON, THOMAS, bp. Antidotum adversus ecclesiae Romanae de merito propriè dicto ex condigno venenum. **Cantabrigiae, ex Acad. typog.** 1637. 4°. STC18172.

1638 ALMANACS. RIVERS, P. A new almanacke and prognostication for Cambridge. **Cambridge, printers to the Universitie.** 1638. 8°. STC 505.

1638 ALMANACS. SWALLOW. An almanack for Cambridge. **Cambridge, printers to the Universitie.** 1638. 8°. STC517.

1638 ALMANACS. WINTER, F. An almanack for 1638. **Cambridge, printers to the Universitie.** 1638. STC530.

1638 BIBLE. ENGLISH. The holy bible. **Cambridge, T. Buck and R. Daniel.** 1638. Fol. STC 2331.

1638 BIBLE. ENGLISH. The holy bible. **Cambridge, T. Buck and R. Daniel.** 1638. 4°. STC 2332.

1638 BIBLE. ENGLISH. PSALMS. The whole booke of psalms. Both in prose and meeter. **T. Buck and R. Daniel, printers to the University of Cambridge.** 1638. 4°. STC2683.

1638 Directions for musters: wherein is showed the order of drilling, etc. **Cambridge, T. Buck and R. Daniel.** 1638. 4°. STC6903.

1638 ENGLAND, CHURCH OF. VISITATIONS. Norwich. **Cambridge,** [1638]. 4°. STC 10300.

1638 GERHARD, JOHANN. The meditations J. Gerhard. Fifth ed. (Gerards prayers Sixth ed.) **Cambridge, T. Bucke and R. Daniel.** 1638. 2 vols. 8°. STC11778.

1638 HERBERT, GEORGE. The Temple. Fifth edition. **Cambridge, T. Buck and R. Daniel.** 1638. 8°. STC13188.

1638 ISOCRATES. Isocratis orationes tres. **Cantabrigiae, ap. T. Buck and R. Daniel.** 1638. 8°. STC14274.

1638 KING, EDWARD. Justa Edouardo King naufrago. (Obsequies - Lycidas, J. M[ilton]). **Cantabrigiae, ap. T. Buck et R. Daniel.** 1638. 2 vols. 4°. STC14964.

1638 LITURGIES. BOOK OF COMMON PRAYER. **Cambridge, T. Buck and R. Daniel.** 1638. Fol. STC16410.

1638 LITURGIES. BOOK OF COMMON PRAYER. **Printers to the Univ. of Cambridge.** 1638. 4°. STC16412.

1638 OVIDIUS NASO, PUBLIUS. [Tristia]. P. Ovidii Nasonis de tristibus libri V. **Cantabrigiae, ap, T. Buck & R. Daniel.** 1638. 8°. STC18977.

1638 SICTOR, JOANNES. Panegyricon inaugurale. **Cantabrigiae.** [1638?]. 4°. STC22533A.

1639 ALMANACS. SWALLOW. An almanack for Cambridge. **Cambridge, printers to the Universitie.** 1639. 8°. STC517.

1639 BIBLE. ENGLISH. The holy bible. **Cambridge, T. Buck and R. Daniel.** 1639. 4°. STC2338.

1639 BIBLE. ENGLISH. PSALMS. The whole booke of psalms. Both in prose and meeter. **T. Buck and R. Daniel, printers to the University of Cambridge.** 1639. 4°. STC2692.

1639 CADE, ANTHONY. A sermon necessary for these times, shewing the nature of conscience. **Cambridge, printers to the University, sold by J. Sweeting,** [London]. 1639. 4°. STC4330.

1639 CICERO, MARCUS TULLIUS. M.T. Cic. De Officiis, de Senectute, de Amicitia, Paradoxa, Somniũ Scipionis. **Cantabrigiae, ex Acad. typog.** 1639. 8°. STC5273.

1639 DAVENANT, JOHN, bp. Determinationes quaestionum quarundam theologicarum. Editio Secunda. **Cantabrigiae. ap. T. Buck.** 1639. Fol. STC6295.

1639 DAVENANT, JOHN, bp. Expositio epistolae ad colossenses. Editio tertia. **Cantabrigiae, ap. T. Buck.** 1639. Fol. STC6298.

1639 DREXELIUS, HIEREMIAS. The considerations of Drexelius upon eternitie. Tr. R. Winterton. **Cambridge, R. Daniel.** 1639. 12°. STC 7237.

1639 DU PRAISSAC, sieur. The art of warre, or militarie discourses. (A short method for the resolving of any militarie question). Tr. I. C[ruso]. **Cambridge, R. Daniel, sold by J. Williams in London.** 1639. 2 vols. 8°. STC 7366.

1639 ENGLAND, CHURCH OF. VISITATIONS. Peterborough. **Cambridge, T. Buck.** 1639. 4°. STC10320.

1639 ENGLAND, CHURCH OF. VISITATIONS. Sudbury. **Cambridge, T. Buck and R. Daniel.** 1639. 4°. STC10339.

1639 FULLER, THOMAS. The historie of the holy warre. **Cambridge, T. Buck, sold by J. Williams.** 1639. Fol. STC11464.

1639 GURNAY, EDMUND. Toward the vindication of the Second Commandment. [**Cambridge**], **T. Buck.** 1639. 12°. STC12531.

1639 HODSON, WILLIAM. The holy sinner. [**Cambridge University printers**] for A. Crooke. 1639. 12°. STC13555.

1639 MORTON, THOMAS, bp. Antidotum adversus ecclesiae Romanae de merito propriè dicto ex condigno venenum. **Cantabrigiæ, ex. acad. typog. Væneunt à J. Sweeting.** 1639. 4°. STC18173.

1640 ALMANACS. RIVERS, P. A new almanacke and prognostication for Cambridge. **Cambridge, printed at the Universitie.** 1640. 8°. STC 505.

1640 ALMANACS. SWALLOW. An almanack for Cambridge. **Cambridge, printers to the Universitie.** 1640. 8°. STC517.

1640 BALL, JOHN. A friendly triall of the grounds tending to separation. **Cambridge, R. Daniel for E. Brewster in London.** 1640. 4°. STC 1313.

1640 BENLOWES, EDWARD. A buckler against the fear of death. **Cambridge, R. Daniel, sold by M. Sparkes, junior.** 1640. 8°. STC1877.

1640 BIBLE. ENGLISH. The holy bible. **Cambridge, T. Buck and R. Daniel.** 1640. 4°. STC 2346.

1640 CAESAR, CAIUS JULIUS. The complete captain, or, an abbridgement of Cesars warres, with observations... by the Duke de Rohan. Englished by T. C[ruso]. **Cambridge, R. Daniel.** 1640. 8°. STC4338.

1640 CAMBRIDGE UNIVERSITY. Voces votivae ab Academicis cantabrigiensibus pro novissimo Caroli et Mariæ Pr. filio emissae. **Cantabrigæ, ap. R. Daniel.** 1640. 4°. STC4495.

1640 DAVENANT, JOHN, bp. Ad fraternam communionem inter evangelicas ecclesias restaurandem adhortatio. **Cantabrigæ, ex off. Danielis.** 1640. 12°. STC6293.

1640 DOWNAME, GEORGE, bp. A godly and learned treatise of prayer, etc. **Cambridge, R. Daniel for N. Bourne.** 1640. 4°. STC7117.

1640 DREXELIUS, HIEREMIAS. The school of patience. [Tr. D. L.]. **Cambridge, R. Daniel.** 1640. 12°. STC7239.

1640 An endeavour of making the principles of Christian religion plain and easie. **Cambridge, R. Daniel.** 1640. 8°. STC5187.

1640 EUSTACHIUS. Summa philosphiae quadripartita. **Cantabrigiæ, R. Daniel.** 1640. 8°. STC 10578.

1640 FENNER, WILLIAM. The souls looking - glasse. **Cambridge, R. Daniel for J. Rothwell.** 1640. 8°. STC10779.

1640 FLETCHER, GILES, the younger. Christs victorie, and triumph. **Cambridge, R. Daniel for R. Royston.** 1640. 4°. STC11061.

1640 FULLER, THOMAS. The historie of the holy warre. Second edition. **Cambridge, R. Daniel, for T. Buck.** 1640. Fol. STC11465.

1640 GERHARD, JOHANN. Meditations and prayers. (Gerards meditations. Sixth ed. Gerards prayers. Seventh ed.) **Cambridge, R. Daniel for T. Buck.** 1640. 12°. STC11779.

1640 GERHARD, JOHANN. The summe of Christian doctrine. Tr. R. Winterton, **Cambridge, R. Daniel.** 1640. 24°. STC11782.

1640 HENSIUS, DANIEL. D. Heinsii sacrarum exercitationum ad novum testamentum libri XX. Editio secunda. **Cantabrigiæ, ex off. R. Danielis.** 1640. 4°. STC13040.

1640 HODSON, WILLIAM. The divine cosmographer. A tractate on the VIII Psalm. **R. Daniel, printer to the Univ. of Cambridge.** 1640. 12°. STC 13554.

1640 LA RAMEE, PIERRE DE. Dialecticae libri duo. **Cantabrigiæ, ex off. R. Danielis, et veneunt per P. Scarlet.** 1640. 12°. STC15245.

1640 LILY, WILLIAM and COLET, JOHN. A shorte introduction of grammar. **R. Daniel, printer to the Univ. of Cambridge.** 1640. 8°. STC 15633.

1640 LITURGIES. BOOK OF COMMON PRAYER. **Cambridge, T. Buck and R. Daniel.** 1640. 4°. STC16420.

1640 MORTON. THOMAS, bp. Totius doctrinalis controuersiae De eucharistia decisio. **Cantabrigiæ, ex off. R. Danielis.** 1640. 4°. STC18197.

1640 OVIDIUS NASO, PUBLIUS. [Fasti]. Ovids festivalls, or Romane calendar. Tr. into English verse equinumerally by J. Gower, master of arts. **R. Daniel, pr. to the Univ. of Cambridge, sold by M. S[parke, London].** 1640. 8°. STC18948.

1640 POSSELIUS, JOHANNES. J. Posselii Συνταξις Graeca. **Cantabrigiæ, ex off. R. Danielis prostant ap. F. Eaglesfield.** 1640. 8°. STC20130.

1640 RANDOLPH, THOMAS. The jealous lovers. A comedie presented to their majesties at Cambridge. **Cambridge, R. Daniel, sold by R. Ireland.** 1640. 8°. STC20693A.

1640 TORRIANO, GIOVANNI. New and easie directions for the Italian tongue. **Cambridge, R. Daniel.** [1640?]. 4°. STC24139.

1641 ALMANACS. DOVE, JONATHAN. Dove. An almanack. **Cambridge, R. Daniel.** [1641]. 8°. WA1591.

1641 ALMANACS. POND, EDWARD. Almanack for ... 1641. **Cambridge, R. Daniel.** 1641. 8°. WA2127.

1641 ANDREWES, LANCELOT, bp. Nineteen sermons. **Cambridge: by R. Daniel.** 1641. 12°. WA3141.

1641 CAMBRIDGE UNIVERSITY. Irenodia Cantabrigiensis. [Cambridge], ex officina Rogeri Daniel. 1641. 4°. WC340.

1641 Continuatio epicediorvm super octo senatores Londinenses. Cantabrigiae, ex officina Rogeri Danielis. 1641. WC5957.

1641 DAVENANT, JOHN, bp. Animadversions. Cambridge: by Roger Daniel. 1641. 8°. WD315.

1641 DREXEL, JEREMY. Considerations of Drexelius upon eternitie. Cambridge, by Roger Daniel. 1641. 24°. WD2169.

1641 [DURY, JOHN]. Discourse concerning the work. Cambridge. 1641. 4°. WD2852.

1641 [DURY, JOHN]. A summary discourse Cambridge: by Roger Daniel. 1641. 4°. WD 2889.

1641 [GLANVILL, JOSEPH]. Nineteen sermons. Cambridge, Roger Daniel. 1641. 12°. WG816.

1641 HERBERT, GEORGE. The temple. Sixth edition. Cambridge, by Roger Daniel. 1641. 12° WH1516.

1641 HEYWOOD, THOMAS. Englands Elisabeth. Cambridge: by Roger Daniel: to be sold by J. Sweeting. 1641. 12°. WH1779.

1641 [LAYER, JOHN]. The office and dutie of constables. Cambridge, by Roger Daniel, and are to be sold by Francis Eaglesfield [London]. 1641. 8°. WL746.

1641 L'ESTRANGE, HAMON. Gods Sabbath before / under } the law. Cambridge, by Roger Daniel. 1641. 4°. WL1188.

1641 MAISTERSON, HENRY. A sermon preached at St. Pauls. [Cambridge], by Roger Daniel. 1641. 4°. WM304.

1641 A manuell, or a justice of peace his vademecum. By Roger Daniel, Cambridge. 1641. 8°. WM545.

1641 MUNNING, HUMPHREY. A. pious sermon preached. Cambridge, by Roger Daniel. 1641. 4°. WM3079.

1641 SALERNITANUS, BONAVENTURA. De fontibus artium. Cantabrigiae: ex officina R. Danielis. 1641. 12°. WS370.

1641 S[HERMAN] J[OHN]. A Greek in the temple. By Roger Daniel of Cambridge. 1641. 4°. WS 3385.

1641 SICTOR, JAN. Continuatio epicediorum. Cantabrigiae. 1641. 4°. WS3753.

1641 THORNDIKE, HERBERT. Of the government of churches. By Roger Daniel of Cambridge. 1641. 8°. WT1055.

1641 W., F. A treatise of warm beer. Cambridge, by R.D. for H. Overton. [1641?]. 12°. WW 26.

1641 W., F. Warme beere, or a treatise, Cambridge, by R.D. for Henry Overton. 1641. 12°. WW27.

1641 WOTTON, ANTHONY. Mr. Anthony Wotton's defence against Mr. George Walker's charge. Cambridge. by Roger Daniel. 1641. 8°. WW3643.

1642 ALMANACS. Dove. Speculum anni. Cambridge. 1642. 8°. WA1592.

1642 ALMANACS. SWALLOW, JOHN. Swallow. An almanack for 1642. Cambridge. 1642. 8°. WA2410.

1642 BÈZE, THÉODORE DE. Bezae et Camerarii annotationes in Novum Testamentum. Cantabrigiae. 1642. Fol. WB2194.

1642 BIBLE. GREEK. Jesu Christi ... Novum Testamentum. Cantabrigiae, ex officina Rogeri Danielis, et apud Ben. Allin, London. 1642. Fol. WB2729.

1642 BIBLE. GREEK. Jesu Christi ... Novum Testamentum. Cantabrigiae, ex officina Rogeri Danielis. 1642. Londini venales prostant. Fol. WB2729[A].

1642 BIBLE. POLYGLOT. [NEW TESTAMENT]. R. Daniel, Cantabrigiae. 1642. Fol. WB2801.

1642 BUTLER, CHARLES. Rhetoricae libri duo Cantabrigiae, ex officina R. Danielis. 1642. 12°. WB6265.

1642 CHARLES I, king of England. His Majestie's answer to a book, entituled, The declaration, or remonstrance. Cambridge, R. Daniel. 1642. 4°. WC2096.

1642 CHARLES I, king of England. His Majesties answer to a printed book, entituled, A remonstrance. Printed at Cambridge, by Roger Daniel. 1642. 4°. WC2107.

1642 CHARLES I, king of England. His Maiesties answer to the declaration of both Houses ... concerning the commission of array. of the first of July, 1642. Cambridge, by Roger Daniel. WC2116.

1642 CHARLES I, king of England. His Maiesties ansvver to the XIX propositions. Cambridge, by Roger Daniel. 1642. 4°. WC2124A.

1642 CHARLES I, king of England. His Majesties declaration in answer to a declaration. Cambridge, by Roger Daniel. 1642. 4°. WC 2208.

1642 CHARLES I, king of England. His Majestie's declaration to all his loving subjects, occasioned by a false and scandalous imputation. Cambridge, by Roger Daniel. 1642. 4°. WC2238A.

1642 CHARLES I, king of England. His Majesties declaration to all his loving subjects, of August 12, 1642. Printed at Cambridge, by Roger Daniel. 1642. 4°. WC2241.

1642 CHARLES I, king of England. His Majesties declaration to all his loving subjects, of August 12, 1642. Cambridge, by N.N. 1642. 4°. WC2242.

1642 CHARLES I, king of England. His Majesties declaration to all his loving subjects, of August 12, 1642. [Cambridge], by N.N. 1642. 4°. WC2243.

1642 CHARLES I, king of England. His Majesties declarations to all his loving sujects [sic] I. upon occasions. Printed at Cambridge, by Roger Daniel. 1642. 4°. WC2290.

1642 DEMOSTHENES. Δημοσθενους λογοι εκλεκτοι. Selectae Demosthenis orationes. Cantabrigiae, ex officina R. Daniel. 1642. 12°. WD980.

1642 ENGLAND, PARLIAMENT. The humble petition of the Lords and Commons, seventeenth of June. 1642. Cambridge, by Roger Daniel. 1642. 4°. WE1573.

1642 ENGLAND. PARLIAMENT. Nineteen propositions. Cambridge. R. Daniel. 1642. 4° WE1673.

1642 ENGLAND. PARLIAMENT. The petition of the Lords and Commons assembled ... presented to His Majestie at Beverley. **Cambridge, by R. Daniel.** 1642. 4°. WE2176A.

1642 F[ERNE], H[ENRY]. The resolving of conscience. **Cambridge, by Roger Daniel.** 1642. 4°. WF800.

1642 [FULLER, THOMAS]. The holy [and profane] state. **Cambridge: by Roger Daniel for John Williams.** 1642. Fol. WF2443.

1642 HOLDSWORTH, RICHARD. The peoples happinesse. **By Roger Daniel, Cambridge.** 1642. 4°. WH2396.

1642 HOLDSWORTH, RICHARD. A sermon preached. .. 27 of March. **By Roger Daniel, of Cambridge.** 1642. 4°. WH2401.

1642 The humble petition of the Commons of Kent. **Cambridge, by Roger Daniel.** 1642. 4°. WH 3495A.

1642 LOVE, RICHARD. The vvatchmans vvatch-vvord. **By Roger Daniel of Cambridge.** 1642. 4°. WL3193.

1642 MAGIRUS, JOHANN. Physiologiae peripateticae libri sex. **Cantabrigiae: ex officina R. Danielis.** 1642. 8°. WM251.

1642 MORE, HENRY. $\Psi\upsilon\chi\omega\delta\iota\alpha$ Platonica: or a Platonicall song of the soul. **Cambridge, by Roger Daniel.** 1642. 8°. WM2674.

1642 PERKINS, WILLIAM. The foundation of Christian religion. **Cambridge, University press.** 1642. 8°. WP1564.

1642 SPELMAN, Sir JOHN. A Protestants account of his orthodox holding. **By Roger Daniel of Cambridge, 1642. And are to be sold by John Milleson, in Cambridge.** 4°. WS4939.

1642 THORNDIKE, HERBERT. Of religious assemblies. **Cambridge, by Roger Daniel to be sold in London.** 1642. 8°. WT1054.

1642 TORRIANO, GIOVANNI. Select Italian proverbs. **Cambridge, by Roger Daniel.** 1642. 12°. WT1931.

1642 WATSON, RICHARD. A sermon touching schisme. **[Cambridge], by Roger Daniel of Cambridge, 1642. And are to be sold by William Graves [London].** 4°. WW1095.

1643 ALMANACS. POND, EDWARD. Pond's almanack for ... 1643. **By R. Daniel, Cambridge.** 1643. 8°. WA2129.

1643 BEDA, venerabilis. Historiae ecclesiasticae. **Cantabrigiae, excudebat Rogerus Daniel.** 1643. Fol. WB1661.

1643 BURROUGHES, JEREMIAH. Jacob's seed. **By Roger Daniel, Cambridge.** 1643. 12°. WB6090.

1643 FENNER, WILLIAM. The souls looking - glasse. **Cambridge, by Roger Daniel; for John Rothwell.** 1643. WF700.

1643 Introductio ad sapientiam: enchiridion. **Cantabrigiae: ex officina Rogeri Danielis.** 1643. 8°. WI282.

1643 JACKSON, ARTHUR. A help for the understanding. **By Roger Daniel, of Cambridge.** 1643. 4°. WJ67.

1643 MINUCIUS FELIX, MARCUS. Octavius. **Cantabrigiae, R. Daniel.** 1643. 16°. WM2198.

1643 QUARLES, FRANCIS. Emblemes. "Second edition" i.e. fourth edition. **Cambridge, by R: D. for Francis Eglesfield.** 1643. 8°. WQ 77.

1643 A revindication of Psalme 105. 15. **By Roger Daniel, of Cambridge.** 1643. 4°. WR1202.

1644 $A\rho\chi\alpha\iota o\nu o\mu\iota\alpha$, sive de priscis. **Cantabrigiae ex officina Rogeri Daniel; prostant Londini apud Cornelium Bee.** 1644. Fol. WA3605.

1644 BEDA, venerabilis. Historiae ecclesiasticae. **Cantabrigiae, ex officina Rogeri Daniel,** prostant Cornelium Bee. 1644. Fol. WB1662

1644 BURGERSDIJCK, FRANCO. Fr. Burgerdicii Institutionum logicarum. **Cantebrigiae [sic] ex officina Rogeri Daniel.** 1644. 12°. WB5630.

1644 A catalogue of remarkable mercies conferred upon the seven associated counties. **By Roger Daniel, Cambridge.** 1643[4]. 4°. WC1365.

1644 [CROFTS, JOHN]. The copy of a letter sent from the Kings army. **[Cambridge. 1644?].** 4°. WC7005.

1644 C[RUSO], J[OHN]. Military instructions **Cambridge, by Roger Daniel.** 1644. Fol. WC 7433.

1644 DERING, Sir EDWARD. $\Pi\epsilon\rho\iota$ $\iota\delta\iota o$-$\tau\rho o\pi o$-$\Theta\upsilon\sigma\iota\alpha s$. A discourse of proper sacrifice. **Cambridge, for Francis Eglesfield.** 1644. 4°. WD1115.

1644 GRIMSTON, Sir HARBOTTLE. A Christian New-Years gift. **By R. Daniel, Cambridge.** 1644. 16°. WG2029.

1644 H., W. A relation of the good success of the Parliaments forces. **[Cambridge], by W. F.** 1644. 4°. WH161.

1645 BIBLE. ENGLISH. **Cambridge, by Roger Daniel.** [1645]. 8°. WB2208.

1645 BIBLE. ENGLISH. **Cambridge, by Roger Daniel.** 1645. 12°. WB2209.

1645 BIBLE. ENGLISH. PSALMS. The whole book of psalmes. **Cambridge, by Roger Daniel.** 1645. 8°. WB2409.

1645 BIBLE. ENGLISH. PSALMS. The whole book of psalmes. **Cambridge, by Roger Daniel.** 1645. 12°. WB2410.

1645 BYTHNER, VICTORINUS. [Hebrew] lingua eruditorum. **Cantabrigiae, impensis authoris.** 1645. 8°. WB6413.

1645 [CROFTS, JOHN]. The copy of a letter sent from the Kings army. **Printed at Cambridge by R.D.** 1645. 4°. WC7006.

1645 HOWELL, JAMES. $\Delta\epsilon\nu\delta\rho o\lambda o\gamma\iota\alpha$ Dodona's grove. Third edition. **Cambridge: by R. D. for Humphrey Moseley.** 1645. 12°. WH3060.

1645 LOCKYER, NICHOLAS. Christs commvnion with his Chvrch militant. **Cambridge, for J. Rothwell.** 1645. 12°. WL2788.

1645 SARSON, LAURANCE. An analysis of the 1st Timoth. Chap. 1. ver. 15. **Cambridge; by Roger Daniel.** 1645. 4°. WS702.

1645 SHELTON, THOMAS. Tachygraphy. **Cambridge, by R. D.** 1645. 8°. WS3076.

1645 SICTOR, JAN. Chronometra aliquot memorabilium **Cantabrigiae: ex officina Rogeri Daniel.** 1645. 4°. WS3751.

1645 STAHL, DANIEL. Axiomata philosophica. Third edition. **Cantabrigiae, ex officina Rogeri Daniel.** 1645. 12°. WS5163.

1645 TORRIANO, GIOVANNI. New and easy directions. **Cambridge, by Roger Daniel.** [1645?]. 4°. WT1926.

1646 AMES, WILLIAM. Demonstratio logicae. **Cantabrigiae, ex officina Rogeri Danielis.** 1646. 12°. WA2997.

1646 AMES, WILLIAM. Disputatio theologica. **Cantabrigiae, ex officina Rogeri Danielis.** 1646. 12°. WA2998.

1646 AMES, WILLIAM. Philosophemata. Technometria. **Cantabrigiae, ex officina Rogeri Danielis.** 1646. 12°. WA3002.

1646 BIBLE. ENGLISH. PSALMS. The whole book of psalmes. **Printed by the printers to the university of Cambridge.** 1646. 12°. WB2420.

1646 Britannicus his blessing. **Cambridge, by Roger Daniel.** 1646. 4°. WB4821.

1646 BUXTORF, JOHANN. Epitome grammaticae Hebraeae. **Cantabrigiae, R. Daniel.** 1646. 8°. WB6343.

1646 DREXEL, JEREMY. Considerations of Drexelius upon eternitie. **Cambridge, by Roger Daniel.** 1646. 24°. WD2170.

1646 DUPORT, JAMES. Σολομων εμμετρος, sive tres libri Solomonis scilicet. **Cantabrigiae, ex officina Rogeri Danielis.** 1646. 8°. WD2654.

1646 [HALL, JOHN]. Poems. **Cambridge, by Roger Daniel.** 1646. **For J. Rothwell.** [London]. WH355.

1646 HEINSIUS, DANIEL. Crepundia Siliana. **Cantabrigiae: ex officina R. Daniel.** 1646. 12°. WH1372.

1646 JACKSON, ARTHUR. Annotations upon the remaining historicall part. **Cambridge, by Roger Daniel.** 1646. 4°. WJ65.

1646 MORE, HENRY. Democritus Platonissans. **Cambridge, by Roger Daniel.** 1646. 8°. WM 2648.

1646 QUARLES, FRANCIS. Judgement & mercy. **Cambridge, by R. Daniel, for V.Q.** 1646. 8°. WQ102.

1646 SICTOR, JAN. Chronologicum epitaphium. [**Cambridge?** 1646]. Brs. WS3750A.

1646 SICTOR, JAN. Chronometra aliquot memorabilium. **Cantabrigiae.** 1646. 4°. WS 3752.

1646 SLEIDAN, JOHN. De quatuor summis. **Cantabrigiae, ex officina Rogeri Danielis.** 1646. 8°. WS3987.

1646 VALDES, JUAN DE. Divine considerations **Cambridge: for E.D. by Roger Daniel.** 1646. 8°. WV22.

1647 Animadversions upon a declaration of the proceedings against the XI members. **Cambridge, for Will. Armestrong.** 1647. 4° WA3201.

1647 BIBLE. ENGLISH. **Cambridge, R. Daniel; London, R. Barker.** 1647. 12°. WB2220.

1647 BOLTON, SAMUEL. Deliverance in the birth. **Cambridge by Roger Daniel, to be sold by Andrew Kembe in** [London]. 1647. 4°. WB 3519.

1647 BURGERSDIJCK, FRANCO. Fr. Burgerdicii Institutionum logicarum. **Cantabrigiae, ex officina Rogeri Daniel.** 1647. 8°. WB5631.

1647 [BUSBY, RICHARD]. Graecae grammatices rudimenta. **Cantabrigiae.** 1647. 8°. WB6220.

1647 [BUSBY, RICHARD]. A short institution of grammar. **Cambridge.** 1647. 8°. WB6229.

1647 CHARLES I, king of England. The Kings Majesties declaration and profession. **Cambridge: for Nathaniel Smith.** 1647. 4°. WC2181.

1647 CUDWORTH, RALPH. A sermon preached... March 31, 1647. **Cambridge, by Roger Daniel.** 1647. 4°. WC7469.

1647 [FAIRFAX, THOMAS]. baron. A declaration from. **Printed at Cambridge.** 1647. 4°. WF 139.

1647 [FAIRFAX, THOMAS]. baron. A manifesto from...June 27, 1647. **Cambridge, for Benjamin Ridley.** 1647. 4°. WF202.

1647 [FAIRFAX, THOMAS]. baron. A proclamation by...concerning the proceedings of some ministers. **Cambridge, for Nathaniel Smith.** 1647. 4°. WF217.

1647 [FAIRFAX, THOMAS]. baron. A representation. **Cambridge, by Roger Daniel.** 1647. 4°. WF 231.

1647 [FULLER, THOMAS]. The historie of the holy warre. Third edition. **Cambridge, by Roger Daniel, and are to be sold by John VVilliams.** 1647. Fol. WF2438.

1647 HAMMOND, HENRY. Five propositions to the Kings Majesty. **Cambridge, for Nathaniel Smith.** 1647. 4°. WH543.

1647 The heads of a charge delivered. **Cambridge, by Roger Daniel.** 1647. 4°. WH1281.

1647 Heads presented by the Army to the Kings most excellent Majestie, on Saturday, June the 19, 1647. **Cambridge.** [1647]. Brs. WH1300.

1647 J., H. A modell of a Christian society. **Cambridge.** 1647. 8°. WJ16.

1647 A letter from the Kings Majesties court at Oatelands. **Cambridge, for Nathaniel Smith.** 1647. WL1527.

1647 MORE, HENRY. Philosophicall poems. Second edition. **Cambridge, by Roger Daniel.** 1647. 8°. WM2670.

1647 SHELTON, THOMAS. Tachygraphy. **Cambridge, by Roger Daniel.** 1647. 24°. WS 3080.

1647 A solemne engagement of the army. **Cambridge, R. Daniel.** 1647. 4°. WS4438.

1647 STIER, JOHANN. Praecepta doctrinae logicae. **Cantabrigiae, ex officina Rogeri Danielis.** 1647. 4°. WS5538.

1647 Two petitions of the counties of Buckingham and Hertford. **Cambridge, by Roger Daniel.** 1647. 4°. WT3502.

1647 VIGER, FRANCOIS. De praecipuis Graecae. **Cantabrigiae: ex officina Rogeri Daniel.** 1647. 8°. WV374.

1648 ALMANACS. Dove. Speculum anni. 1648. **Cambridge.** [1648]. 8°. WA1596.

1648 ALMANACS. POND, EDWARD. Pond's almanack for...1648. **Cambridge, R. Daniel.** 1648. 8°. WA2132.

1648 BIBLE. ENGLISH. **By Roger Dainel** [sic], **Cambridge.** 1648. 12°. WB2226.

1648 BIBLE. ENGLISH. PSALMS. The whole book of psalms. **By Roger Daniel, Cambridge.** 1648. 18°. WB2432.

1648 BYTHNER, VICTORINUS. Clavis linguae sanctae. **Cantabrigiae, ex officina Rogeri Daniel.** 1648. 8°. WB6412.

1648 Καταχησεις της χριστιανικης πιστεως. Cantabrigiae; ex officina Rogeri Daniel. 1648. 12°. WC1463.

1648 CAUSSIN, NICOLAS. The Christian diary. [**Cambridge**]. 1648. 12°. WC1542.

1648 EUSTACHIUS. Summa philosophiae, **Cantabrigiae, ex officina Rogeri Danielis.** 1648. 8°. WE3432.

1648 [FULLER, THOMAS]. The holy [and profane] state. Second edition. **Cambridge: by R. D. for John Williams.** 1648. Fol. WF2444.

1648 HILL, THOMAS. The best and vvorst of Paul. **By Roger Daniel, Cambridge.** 1648. 4°. WH 2021.

1648 HOMER. 'Oμηρου' Ιλιας. Homeri Ilias. **Cantabrigiae, ex officina Rogeri Daniel.** 1648. 8°. WH2539.

1648 Κατηχησεις της πιστεως. **Cantabrigiae, ex officina Rogeri Daniel.** 1648. 12°. WK29.

1648 WENDELIN, MARCUS FREDERICK. Admiranda nili. **Ex officina Rogeri Danielis. Cantabrigiae.** 1648. 4°. WW1348.

1648 WENDELIN, MARCUS FREDERICK. Contemplationum physicarum. **Ex. officina Rogeri Danielis, Cantabrigiae.** 1648. 8°. WW 1349.

1648 WHITE, THOMAS. The smoak of the botomlesse pit. **By Roger Daniel for Anthony Nicholson, Cambridge.** 1648. 12°. WW1854.

1648 WOLLEB, JOHN. Compendium theologiae. **Ex officina R. Danielis, Cantabrigiensis.** 1648. 12°. WW3259.

1649 ALMANACS. POND, EDWARD. Pond's almanack for 1649. **Cambridge, R. Daniel.** 1649. 8°. WA2133.

1649 DICKSON, DAVID. A short explanation, of the epistle.of Paul to the Hebrevves. **Cambridge, by Roger Daniel for Francis Eglesfield.** 1649. 8°. WD1404.

1649 EUSTACHIUS. Summa philosophiae. **Cantabrigiae, ex officina Rogeri Danielis.** 1649. 8°. WE3433.

1649 HARVEY, WILLIAM. Exercitatio anatomica de circulatione sanguinis. **Cantabrigiae, ex officina Rogeri Danielis.** 1649. 12°. WH1087.

1649 HARVEY, WILLIAM. Exercitatio anatomica de circulatione sanguinis. **Cantabrigiae, ex officina Rogeri Danielis.** 1649. 12°. WH1088.

1649 [JACK, GILBERT]. Primae philosophiae: **Cantabrigiae, ex officina Rogeri Danielis.** 1649. 12°. WJ57.

1649 A letter from the University of Cambridge. **Cambridge.** 1649. Brs. WL1544.

1649 MEDE, JOSEPH. Clavis apocraphica. **Cantabrigiae, apud R. Daniel.** 1649. 4°. WM 1594.

1650 AESOP. AEsop's fables, with their moralls. **Cambridge, by R. D. for Francis Eglesfield.** 1650. 12°. WA688.

1650 BURGERSDIJCK, FRANCO. Collegium physicum. **Ex officina Rogeri Danielis, Cantabrigiensis.** 1650. 12°. WB5625.

1650 DAVENANT, JOHN, bp. Dissertationes duae. [**Cambridge**], **ex officina Rogeri Danielis.** 1650. Fol. WD317.

1650 DREXEL, JEREMY. Considerations of Drexelius upon eternitie. **Cambridge, by Roger Daniel.** 1650. 12°. WD2171.

1650 PEMBLE, WILLIAM. De formarum origine. **Cantabrigiae, ex officina Rogeri Daniel, pro I. B.** [1650?]. 12°. WP1114.

1650 THORNDIKE, HERBERT. Discourses of the primitive government. **Cambridge.** 1650. 8°. WT1047.

1650 THORNDIKE, HERBERT. Two discourses **Cambridge, by Roger Daniel.** 1650. 8°. WT 1057.

1650 VIRGIL. Opera. **Cantabrigiae.** [c.1650]. 12°. WV599.

1651 ALMANACS. Dove. Speculum anni 1651. **Cambridge.** 1651. 8°. WA1598.

1651 ALMANACS, SWALLOW, JOHN. Swallow. An almanack for 1651. **Cambridge, by the printers to the universitie.** [1651]. 8°. WA2416.

1651 [BUSBY, RICHARD]. Graecae grammatices rudimenta. **Cantabrigiae.** 1651. 8°. WB6221.

1651 CHATEILLON, SEBASTIEN. Dialogorum sacrorum. **Cantabrigiae: ex academiae celeberrimae typographeo.** 1651. 8°. WC3732.

1651 CULVERWELL, NATHANIEL. Spiritual opticks. [**Cambridge**], **by Thomas Buck.** 1651. **To be sold by Anthony Nicholson.** 4°. WC7573.

1651 [FULLER, THOMAS]. The historie of the holy warre. Fourth edition. [**Cambridge**], **by Thomas Buck: to be sold by Philemon Stephens.** 1651. Fol. WF2439.

1651 MORE, HENRY. The second lash of Alazonomastix. **By the printers to the University of Cambridge.** 1651. 12°. WM2677.

1651 ROBOTHAM, Dr. Omnium futurorum contingentium certissima est. [**Cambridge.** 1651]. Brs. WR1727.

1651 STATIUS. Publii Papinii Statii Sylvarum libri V. **Cantabrigiae, apud Thomam Buck.** 1651. 8°. WS5336.

1651 WILLAN, EDWARD. Six sermons. **For R. Royston, to be sold by Richard Ireland in Cambridge.** 1651. 4°. WW2261.

1652 ALMANACS. Dove. Speculum anni. 1653. **Cambridge, by the printers to the universitie.** 1652. 8°. WA1599.

1652 ALMANACS. POND, EDWARD. Pond's almanack for ... 1652. **Cambridge: by the printers to the universitie.** 1652. 8°. WA2134.

1652 ALMANACS. POND, EDWARD. Pond an almanack ... 1653. **Cambridge, by the printers to the university.** 1652. 8°. WA2135.

1652 ALMANACS, SWALLOW, JOHN. Swallow. An almanack for 1652. **Cambridge, By the printers to the universitie.** 1652. 8°. WA2417.

1652 AURELIUS ANTONINUS, MARCUS. Μαρου Αυτονονου των εις εαυτον...De rubus suis. **Cantabrigiae, excudebat Thomas Buck, veneunt per Antonium Nicolson.** 1652. 4°. WA4225.

1652 BIBLE. GREEK. Ψαλτεριον του Δαβιδ.
[Cantabrigiae], ex officina Rogeri Danielis.
1652. 12°. WB2721.

1652 MEDE, JOSEPH. Josephi Medi ... opvscvla
Latina. Cantabrigiae: per Thomam Buck,
impensis Gulielmi Morden. 1652. 4°. WM1603.

1652 NICOLS, THOMAS. A lapidary. Cambridge:
by Thomas Buck. 1652. 4°. WN1145.

1652 Poetae minores Graeci. Cantabrigiae, apud
Thom. Buck. 1652. 8°. WP2729.

1652 SCHEINER, CHRISTOPH. Oculus hoc est;
fundamentum opticum. Excudebat J. Flesher,
& prostant apud. Williel. Morden, Cantabrigiae.
1652. 4°. WS858.

1653 ALMANACS. POND, EDWARD. Pond an
almanack ... 1654. Cambridge, by the printers
to the university. 1653. 8°. WA2135A.

1653 ALMANACS. SWALLOW, JOHN. Swallow. An
almanack for 1653. Cambridge, By the printers
to the universitie. 1653. 8°. WA2418.

1653 ALMANACS. SWALLOW, JOHN. Swallow. An
almanack for 1654. Cambridge, By the printers
to the universitie. 1653. 8°. WA2419.

1653 BIBLE. POLYGLOT. [JOB]. Cambridge,
Thos. Buck. 1653. 8°. WB2800.

1653 [DAILLE, JEAN]. An apologie for the Reformed
churches. By Th. Buck, Cambridge. 1653. 8°.
WD113.

1653 DUPORT, JAMES. Θρηνοθριαμβος, sive liber
Job graeco carmine redditus. Cantabrigiae,
apud T. Buck. 1653. 8°. WD2656.

1653 DUPORT, JAMES. Θρηνοθριαμβος, sive liber
Job graeco carmine redditus, Second edition.
Cantabrigiae, apud Thomam Buck. 1653.
Veneunt ibidem per Guliemum Graves. 8°.
WD2657.

1653 HOLDSWORTH, RICHARD. Quaestiones duae.
Excudebat G.D. impensis Gulielmi Nealand,
Cantabrigiensis. 1653. 8°. WH2398.

1653 ISOCRATES. Paraenesis. Cantabrigiae. 1653.
12°. WI1078.

1653 MORE, HENRY. Conjectura cabbalistica. Or,
a conjectural essay. London, by James Flesher,
to be sold by William Morden, Cambridge.
1653. 8°. WM2647.

1653 [SCATTERGOOD, ANTHONY]. Annotationes
in Vetus Testamentum, et in Epistolam ad
Ephesios. Cantabrigiae, per Thomam Buck.
1653. 8°. WS839.

1653 SEDGWICK, JOSEPH. A sermon. preached at ...
Cambridge, May 1st 1653. London, by R.D.
for Edward Story in Cambridge. 1653. 4°.
WS2362.

1654 ALMANACS. Dove. Speculum anni. 1654.
Cambridge, by the printers to the universitie.
1654. 8°. WA1600.

1654 CAMBRIDGE UNIVERSITY. Oliva pacis.
Cantabrigiae: ex academiae typographeo. 1654.
4°. WC348.

1654 EUSTACHIUS. Ethica. Cantabrigiae, ex
academiae typographeo, impensis Gulielmi
Morden. 1654. 8°. WE3429.

1654 JACK, THOMAS. Onomasticon poeticum.
Cantabrigiae; ex academiae typographeo. 1654.
8°. WJ58.

1654 SMET, HENRICH. Prosodia. Cantabrigia,
ex celeberrimae Academiae typographeo. 1654.
8°. WS4017.

1654 WOLLEB, JOHN. Compendium theologiae.
Cantabrigiae, ex academiae typographeo. 1654.
8°. WW3259A.

1655 AESOP. AEsopi Phrygis fabulae. Cantabrigiae:
ex academiae typographeo. 1655. 8°. WA713.

1655 ALMANACS. Dove. Speculum anni. 1655.
Cambridge, by the printers to the universitie.
1655. 8°. WA1601.

1655 ALMANACS. POND, EDWARD. Pond an
almanack ... 1655. Cambridge, by the printers
to the university. 1655. 8°. WA2136.

1655 ALMANACS. SWALLOW, JOHN. Swallow. An
almanack for 1655. Cambridge, By the printers
to the universitie. 1655. 8°. WA2420.

1655 B., R. An idea of arithmetick. By J. Flesher,
and are to be sold by W. Morden in Cambridge.
1655. 8°. WB167.

1655 C., J. The magistrates ministery. Cambridge.
1655. 8°. WC61.

1655 CLARK, JOSHUA. Two sermons preached.
Cambridge, by the printers to the universitie.
1655. Sold by William Morden. 8°. WC4481.

1655 EPICTETUS. Enchiridion. Cantabrigiae,
impensis G. Morden. 1655. 8°. WE3144.

1655 EUCLID. Euclidis elementorum libri xv.
Cantabrigiae, ex academiae typographeo. 1655-
57. 2 vols. 12°. WE3392A.

1655 FROIDMONT, LIBERT. Meteorologica. Typis
E. Tyler, impensis Ed. Story, apud quem
vaeneunt Cantabrigiae. 1655-6. 8°. WF2235.

1655 MORE, HENRY. An antidote against atheisme.
Second edition. London; by J: Flesher, to be
sold by William Morden in Cambridge. 1655.
8°. WM2640.

1655 Officium concionatoris. Cantabrigiae, ex
academiae typographeo. Impensis Gulielmi
Morden. 1655. 4°. WO157.

1655 PORPHYRY ... Περυ αποχης ... de abstinentia.
Cantabrigiae, ex Academiae Typographeo
impensis Guil. Morden. 1655. 8°. WP2978.

1656 AESOP. AEsopi Phrygis fabulae. Cantabrigiae
ex officina Joann. Field. 1656. 8°. WA714.

1656 ALMANACS. Dove. Speculum anni. 1656.
Cambridge, by the printers to the universitie.
1656. 8°. WA1602.

1656 ALMANACS. POND, EDWARD. Pond an
almanack ... 1656. Cambridge, by the printers
to the university. 1656. 8°. WA2137.

1656 Confessio fidei in conventu. Cantabrigiae:
excudebat Johannes Field. 1656. 8°. WC5737.

1656 DILLINGHAM, WILLIAM. Prove all things.
Cambridge, by John Field. To be sold by
William Morden. 1656. 4°. WD1486.

1656 HERBERT, GEORGE. The temple. Seventh
edition. [Cambridge? 1656]. 12°. WH1517.

1656 MORE, HENRY. Enthusiasmus triumphatus,
or, a discourse. London, by J. Flesher, and
are to be sold by W. Morden in Cambridge. .
1656. 8°. WM2655.

1654 TERENTIUS AFER, PUBLICUS. Pub. Terentius
A M. Antonio Mureto emandatus. Cantabrigiae:
ex Academiae typographeo. 1654. 4°. WT732.

1656 TERENTIUS AFER, PUBLICUS. Pub. Terentius A M. Antonio Mureto emendatus. **Cantabrigiæ : ex officina Joann. Field.** 1656. 8°. WT734.

1657 ALMANACS. Dove, Speculum anni. 1657. **Cambridge, by the printers to the universitie.** 1657. 8°. WA1603.

1657 ALMANACS. POND, EDWARD. Pond an almanack ... 1657. **Cambridge, by the printers to the university.** 1657. 8°. WA2138.

1657 ALMANACS. SWALLOW, JOHN. Swallow. An almanack for 1657. **Cambridge, By the printers to the universitie.** 1657. 8°. WA2421.

1657 ALMANACS, SWAN, JOHN. An ephemeris, or almanack for ... 1657. **Cambridge, by John Field.** 1657. 8°. WA2465.

1657 ARROWSMITH, JOHN. Tactica sacra. **Cantabrigiae, excudebat Joannes Field, impensis Joannis Rothwell, Londini.** 1657. 4°. WA 3777.

1657 BIBLE. ENGLISH. **Cambridge, by John Field.** 8°. 1657. WB2252.

1657 BIBLE. ENGLISH. PSALMS. The whole book of psalms. **Cambridge, by John Field.** 1657. 8°. WB2467.

1657 CORDIER, MATHURIN. Colloquiorum scholasticorum libri iiii. **Cantabrigiæ: apud Joann. Field.** 1657. 8°. WC6286.

1657 EUCLID. Euclidis data. **Cantabrigiæ, G. Nealand.** 1657. 8°. WE3390.

1657 FROST, JOHN. Select sermons. **Cambridge, by John Field.** 1657. Fol. WF2246.

1657 VERE, Sir FRANCIS. The commentaries of. **Cambridge, by John Field.** 1657. Fol. WV240.

1658 AESOP. Fabulae. **Cantabrigiæ, ex officina Joann. Field.** 1658. 8°. WA716.

1658 ALMANACS. Dove. Speculum anni 1658 **Cambridge: by John Field.** 1658. 8°. WA1604.

1658 ALMANACS. POND, EDWARD. Pond an almanack ... 1658. **Cambreidg [sic]: printed by John Field.** 1658. 8°. WA2139.

1658 ALMANACS. SWALLOW, JOHN. Swallow. An almanack for 1658. **Cambridge, By John Field.** 1658. 8°. WA2422.

1658 ALMANACS. SWAN, JOHN. An ephemeris, or almanack for ... 1658. **Cambridge, by John Field.** 1658. 8°. WA2466.

1658 ATWELL, GEORGE. The faithfull surveyor. **[Cambridge], for the author, at the charges of Nathanael Rowles.** 1658. 4°. WA4163.

1658 CAMBRIDGE UNIVERSITY. Musarum Cantabrigiensium luctus & gratulatio. **Cantabrigiæ: excudebat Joannes Field.** 1658. **Londini prostant.** 4°. WC345.

1658 CAMBRIDGE UNIVERSITY. Musarum Cantabrigiensium luctus & gratulatio. **Cantabrigiæ: apud Joannem Field.** 1658. 4°. WC346.

1658 FROST, JOHN. Select sermons. **Cambridge: by John Field, to be sold by Thomas Pierrepont, London.** 1658. Fol. WF2247.

1658 [HALL, JOHN]. Emblems. **[Cambridge], By Roger Daniel.** 1658. [cancelled title dated 1648]. 8°. WH344.

1658 [HALL, JOHN]. Emblems. **[Cambridge], By Roger Daniel.** [1658]. 8°. WH344A.

1658 LIGHTFOOT, JOHN. Horae Hebraicae et Talmudicae. Impensae I. In chorographiam ... S. Matthaei. **Cantabrigiae, excudebat Joannes Field, impensis Edovardi Story.** 1658. 4°. WL 2061.

1658 LIGHTFOOT, JOHN. Horae ... In Evangelium sancti Mathæi. **Cantabrigiæ, excudebat Joannes Field.** 1658. 4°. WL2066.

1658 ORIGENES. Οριγινηξ κατα Κελσου ... Contra Celsvm. **Cantabrigiæ, excudebat Joan. Field. impensis Gulielmi Morden.** 1658. 4°. WO424.

1659 ALMANACS. Dove. Speculum anni 1659 **Cambridge: by John Field.** 1659. 8°. WA1605.

1659 ALMANACS. POND, EDWARD. Pond an almanack ... 1659. **Cambridge: by John Field.** 1659. 8°. WA2140.

1659 ALMANACS. SWALLOW, JOHN. Swallow. An almanack for 1659. **Cambridge, By John Field.** 1659. 8°. WA2423.

1659 ALMANACS. SWAN, JOHN. An ephemeris, or almanack for ... 1659. **Cambridge, by John Field.** 1659. 8°. WA2467.

1659 ARROWSMITH, JOHN. Armilla catechetica. A chain of principles. **Cambridge: by John Field, and are to be sold in London.** 1659. 4°. WA3772.

1659 AYLESBURY, THOMAS. Diatribae de aeterno Divini Beneplaciti. **Cantabrigiæ, excudebat Joann. Field.** 1659. 4°. WA4282.

1659 BIBLE. ENGLISH. **Cambridge, John Field.** 1659-60. 2 vols. Fol. WB2255.

1659 BIBLE. ENGLISH. NEW TESTAMENT. The New Testament. **Cambridge: by John Field.** 1659. Fol. WB2662.

1659 MORE, HENRY. The immortality of the soul. **London, by J. Flesher, for William Morden in Cambridge.** 1659. 8°. WM2663.

1659 University queries. **Cambridge, printed.** 1659. 4°. WU80.

1660 ALMANACS. Dove. Speculum anni 1660. **Cambridge: by John Field.** 1660. 8°. WA1606.

1660 ALMANACS. POND, EDWARD. Pond an almanack... 1660. **Cambridge: by John Field.** 1660. 8°. WA2141.

1660 ALMANACS, SWALLOW, JOHN. Swallow. An almanack for 1660. **Cambridge, By John Field.** [1660]. 8°. WA2424.

1660 ALMANACS. SWAN, JOHN. An ephemeris; or almanack for ... 1660. **Cambridge, by John Field.** 1660. 8°. WA2468.

1660 AMYRAUT, MOSES. A treatise concerning religions. **By M. Simons, for Will. Nealand. in Cambridge.** 1660. 8°. WA3037.

1660 BIBLE. ENGLISH. **Cambridge, by John Field.** 1660. Fol. WB2258.

1660 BRADSHAW, WILLIAM. Several treatises of worship. **[London], printed for Cambridge and Oxford, to be sold [London].** 1660. 4°. WB 4161.

1660 BRIGGS, THOMAS. Primaeva communitas. **[Cambridge].** 1660. Brs. WB4666.

1660 BURGERSDIJCK, FRANCO. Fr. Burgerdicii Institutionum logicarum. **Cantabrigiæ, apud Joann. Field.** 1660. 8°. WB5633.

1660   CAMBRIDGE UNIVERSITY. Academiae
Cantabrigiensis Σωστρα. **Cantabrigiae,
excudebat Joannes Field.** 1660. 4°. WC333.

1660   DUNCON, ELEAZAR. Eleazaris Dunconi ...
de adoratione. [**Cambridge?**]. 1660. 12°.
WD2601.

1660   DUPORT, JAMES. Evangelical politie.
Cambridge: by John Field. 1660. 4°. WD2650.

1660   DUPORT, JAMES. Homeri ... gnomologia.
Cantabrigiae, excudebat J. Field. 1660. 4°.
WD2651.

1660   EUCLID. Euclide's elements. **By R. Daniel,
for William Nealand in Cambridge.** 1660. 8°.
WE3397.

1660   FALKLAND, LUCIUS CARY, viscount. A
discourse of infallibility. Second edition. **For
W. Nealand, Cambridge.** 1660. 4°. WF318.

1660   FALKLAND, LUCIUS CARY, viscount. Two
discourses. **For W. Nealand, Cambridge.**
1660. 4°. WF327.

1660   [GARDINER, SAMUEL]. De efficacia gratiae,
Cantabrigiae, per Johannem Field. 1660. 4°.
WG245.

1660   H[ACON], J[OSEPH]. A review of Mr. Horn's
catechisme. **Cambridge, by John Field.** 1660.
8°. WH177.

1660   HOLLINGS, JOHN. Colores sunt variae.
[**Cambridge**]. 1660. Brs. WH2484.

1660   HOMER. Homeri ... gnomologia. **Cantabrigiae,
excudebat Johannes Field.** 1660. 4°. WH2538.

1660   LITURGIES. BOOK OF COMMON PRAYER.
The book of common prayer. [**Cambridge**].
1660. Fol. WB3619.

1660   LOVE, RICHARD. Oratio habita in academia
Cantabrigiensi. **Cantabrigiae, excudebat Joannes
Field.** 1660. 4°. WL3192.

1660   MORE, HENRY. An explanation of the grand
mystery of godliness. **London; by J. Flesher,
for W. Morden, in Cambridge.** 1660. Fol.
WM2658.

1660   PEARSON, JOHN, bp. Critici sacri. **Londini,
excudebat Jacobus Flesher,** 1660. **Prostant
apud** [**Cornelium Bee, Richardum Royston,
Gulielmum Wells, Samuelem Thomson**], **Londini.,
Thomam Robinson, Oxonii, Guilielmum Morden,
Cantabrigiae.** Fol. WP994A.

1660   [RAY, JOHN]. Catalogus plantarum circa
Cantabrigiam. **Cantabrigiae: excudebat Joann.
Field, impensis Gulielmi Nealand.** 1660. 8°.
WR383.

1660   SMITH, JOHN. Select discourses. **London by
J. Flesher, for W. Morden in Cambridg** [sic].
1660. 4°. WS4117.

1660   SMITH, THOMAS. The life and death of Mr.
William Moore. **Cambridge, by John Field.**
1660. 8°. WS4231A.

1660   SPENCER, JOHN. The righteous ruler
[**Cambridge**], **by John Field of Cambridge.** 1660.
4°. WS4952.

1660   [WILLAN, SAMUEL]. A short cut to Cambridge.
[**Cambridge**], **by R. Daniel.** 1660. 12°. WW
2266.

1661   ALMANACS. Dove. Speculum anni 1661.
Cambridge: by John Field. 1661. 8°. WA1607.

1661   ALMANACS. POND, EDWARD. Pond an
almanack ... 1661. **Cambridge: by John Field.**
1661. 8°. WA2142.

1661   ALMANACS, SWALLOW, JOHN. Swallow. An
almanack for 1661. **Cambridge, By John Field.**
[1661]. 8°. WA2425.

1661   ALMANACS. SWAN, JOHN. An ephemeris, or
almanack for ... 1661. **Cambridge, by John
Field.** 1661. 8°. WA2469.

1661   BIBLE. ENGLISH. **Cambridge, by John Field.**
1661. 8°. WB2265.

1661   BIBLE. ENGLISH. PSALMS. The whole booke
of psalmes. **Cambridge, by John Field.** 1661.
8°. WB2476.

1661   CAMBRIDGE UNIVERSITY. Threni Cantabrigienses in funere duorum principum. **Cantabrigiae:
excudebat Joannes Field.** 1661. 4°. WC354.

1661   COLET, JOHN. A sermon of conforming.
Cambridge, W. Morden. 1661. 8°. WC5096.

1661   LILY, WILLIAM. A short introduction of
grammar. **Cambridge, by John Field.** 1661.
8°. WL2282.

1661   Poetae minores Graeci. **Cantabrigiae.** 1661. 8°.
WP2730.

1661   SAVONAROLA, GIROLAMO. Truth of the
Christian faith. **Cambridge, J. Field.** 1661.
12°. WS780.

1661   STEPHENS, THOMAS. Ad magistratum, three
sermons. **Cambridge: by John Field.** 1661. 8°.
WS5456.

1662   ALMANACS. Dove. Speculum anni 1662.
Cambridge: by John Field. 1662. 8°. WA1608.

1662   ALMANACS. POND, EDWARD. Pond an
almanack ... 1662. **Cambridge: by John Field.**
1662. 8°. WA2143.

1662   ALMANACS, SWALLOW, JOHN. Swallow. An
almanack for 1662. **Cambridge, By John Field.**
1662. 8°. WA2426.

1662   ALMANACS. SWAN, JOHN. An ephemeris, or
almanack for ... 1662. **Cambridge, by John
Field.** 1662. 8°. WA2470.

1662   ATWELL, GEORGE. The faithfull surveyor.
Cambridge, for William Nealand. 1662. 4°.
WA4164.

1662   BIBLE. ENGLISH. NEW TESTAMENT. The
New Testament. **Cambridge, by John Field.**
1662. 8°. WB2665.

1662   BIBLE. ENGLISH. PSALMS. The whole book
of psalms. **Cambridge, by John Field.** 1662.
8°. WB2480.

1662   CAMBRIDGE UNIVERSITY. Epithalamia
Cantabrigiensia. **Cantabrigiae, ex officina
Joannis Field.** 1662. 4°. WC335.

1662   [GLANVILL, JOSEPH]. Lux orientalis, or an
enquiry. **Printed, and are to be sold at
Cambridge, and Oxford.** 1662. 8°. WG814.

1662   H[ACON], J[OSEPH]. A vindication of the
review, or... Mr. Horn's catechisme.
Cambridge: by John Field. 1662. 8°. WH178.

1662   HERBERT, GEORGE. Musae responsoriae.
Cambridge, J. Field. 1662. 8°. WH1510.

1662   HYDE, EDWARD. Allegiance and conscience.
Cambridge, by John Field. 1662. 8°. WH3861.

1662   HYDE, EDWARD. The true Catholicke tenure.
Cambridge, by John Field. 1662. 8°. WH3868.

1662   LITURGIES. BOOK OF COMMON PRAYER.
The book of Common Prayer. **Cambridge,
John Field.** 1662. 8°. WB3625.

1662 N[EWMAN], S[AMUEL]. A concordance to the Holy Scriptures. **Cambridge, by John Field.** 1662. Fol. WN925.

1662 P[ATRICK], S[YMON], bp. A brief account of the new sect of Latitude-men. **London, to be sold in St. Pauls ... and Oxford and Cambridge.** 1662. 4°. WP754.

1662 Vindication of the proceedings of the gentlemen of the Inner Temple. **Cambridge, printed.** 1662. 8°. WV527.

1662 VIVIANUS, JOANNES. Ecclesiastes Solomonis. **Cantabrigiae.** 1662. 8°. WV669.

1663 ALMANACS. Dove. Speculum anni 1663 **Cambridge: by John Field.** 1663. 8°. WA1609.

1663 ALMANACS. POND, EDWARD. Pond an almanack ... 1663. **Cambridge: by John Field.** 1663. 8°. WA2144.

1663 ALMANACS, SWALLOW, JOHN. Swallow. An almanack for 1663. **Cambridge, By John Field.** 1663. 8°. WA2427.

1663 ALMANACS. SWAN, JOHN. An ephemeris, or almanack for ... 1663. **Cambridge, by John Field.** 1663. 8°. WA2471.

1663 BIBLE. ENGLISH. **Cambridge, by John Field.** 1663. 4°. WB2268.

1663 BIBLE. ENGLISH. **Cambridge, by John Field.** 1663. 8°. WB2269.

1663 BIBLE. ENGLISH. PSALMS. The whole book of psalms. **By John Field, Cambridge.** 1663. 8°. WB2483.

1663 BROWNE, EDWARD. Judicium de somniis est medico utile. **[Cambridge].** 1663. Brs. WB5113A.

1663 [BUSBY, RICHARD] Graecae grammatices rudimenta. **Cantabrigiae.** 1663. 8°. WB6222.

1663 CAMBRIDGE UNIVERSITY. Selectae aliquot legum, atque ordinationum. **[Cambridge].** Novemb. 24. 1663. Brs. WC351.

1663 CHURCH OF ENGLAND. Articles to be enquired of by the ministers ... of Sudbury. **Cambridge.** 1663. 4°. WC4085.

1663 CLARK, JOHN. Repressaliae sunt licitae. **[Cambridge].** 1663. Brs. WC4476.

1663 FORTREY, SAMUEL. Englands interest. **Cambridge, by John Field.** 1663. 8°. WF1616.

1663 HEEREBOORD, ADRIAN. Ερμηνεια logica. **Cantabrigiae, ex officina Joan. Field.** 1663. 8°. WH1358.

1663 LITURGIES. BOOK OF COMMON PRAYER. The book of common prayer. **Cambridge, John Field.** 1663. 4°. WB3627.

1663 [KERR, THOMAS], bp. Ichabod: or, five groans. **Cambridge: for J. Greaves.** 1663. 4°. WK348.

1663 LE FRANC, JAMES. Ο βασανος της αληθειας. or the touchstone of truth. **Cambridge, by John Field.** 1663. 8°. WL942.

1663 METCALFE, FRANCIS. Cortex Peruvianus. **[Cambridge].** 1663. Brs. WM1919.

1663 MORTON, of St. John's, Cambridge. Sacris ordinibus. **[Cambridge].** 1633 [i.e. 1663]. Brs. WM2816.

1663 [PERRENCHIEF, RICHARD]. Potestas ecclesiae. **[Cambridge].** 1663. Brs. WP1600.

1663 [RAY, JOHN]. Appendix ad catalogam. **Cantabrigiae.** 1663. 8°. WR379.

1663 SPENCER, JOHN. A discourse concerning prodigies. **[Cambridge], by John Field for Will. Graves in Cambridge.** 1663. 4°. WS4947.

1663 VOSS, GERARD JOHANN. Elementa rhetorica. **Cantabrigiae.** 1663. 8°. WV689.

1664 ALMANACS. Dove. Speculum anni 1664. **Cambridge: by John Field.** 1664. 8°. WA1610.

1664 ALMANACS. POND, EDWARD. Pond an almanack for ... 1664. **Cambridge; by John Field.** 1664. 8°. WA2145.

1664 ALMANACS. SWALLOW, JOHN. Swallow. An almanack for 1664. **Cambridge, By John Field.** 1664. 8°. WA2428.

1664 ALMANACS. SWAN, JOHN. An ephemeris, or almanack for ... 1664. **Cambridge, by John Field.** 1664. 8°. WA2472.

1664 BIBLE. ENGLISH. **Cambridge, by John Field.** 1664. 12°. WB2272.

1664 BYTHNER, VICTORINUS. Lyra prophetica. **Typis Jacobi Flesher: prostat vero apud Edm. Beechinoe, Cantabrigiae.** 1664. 4°. WB6421.

1664 BYTHNER, VICTORINUS. Lyra prophetica. **Typis Jacobi Flesher: prostat vero venalis apud Gul. Morden, Cantabrigiae.** 1664. 4°. WB6422.

1664 FLORUS, LUCIUS ANNÆUS. L. Julii Flori. Rerum à Romanis gestarvm. **Cantabrigiae, ex officina Ioannis Field.** 1664. 12°. WF1373.

1664 HOMER. 'Ομηρου 'Ιλιας. Homeri Ilias. **Cantabrigiae, excudebat Joannes Field.** 1664. 4°. WH2540.

1664 HOMER. Homeri Odyssea. **Cantabrigiae, excudebat J. Field.** 1664. 8°. WH2553.

1664 LIGHTFOOT, JOHN. Horae ... I Corinthians. **Cantabrigiae, excudebat Joannes Field.** 1664. 4°. WH2067.

1664 MORE, HENRY. Epistola H. Mori ad V. C. **Londini, typis J. Flesher & venales prostat apud G. Morden, Cantabrigiensem.** 1664. 8°. WM2656.

1664 MORE, HENRY. A modest enquiry. **London, by J. Flesher, for W. Morden, in Cambridge.** 1664. Fol. WM2666.

1665 ALMANACS. Dove. Speculum anni 1665. **Cambridge: by John Field.** 1665. 8°. WA1611.

1665 ALMANACS. POND, EDWARD. Pond an almanack for ... 1665. **Cambridge; by John Field.** 1665. 8°. WA2146.

1665 ALMANACS. SWALLOW, JOHN. Swallow. An almanack for 1665. **Cambridge, By John Field.** 1665. 8°. WA2429.

1665 ALMANACS. SWAN, JOHN. An ephemeris, or almanack for ... 1665. **Cambridge, by John Field.** 1665. 8°. WA2473.

1665 BEAUMONT, JOSEPH. Some observations upon the apologie of H. More. **Cambridge, by John Field.** 1665. 4°. WB1628.

1665 Bellum Belgicum secundum, or a poem attempting something. **Cambridge, by J. Field and are to be sold by Robert Nicholson.** 1665. 4°. WB1860.

1665   BIBLE. GREEK. 'Η παλια Διαθηκη κατα τους εβδομηκοντα. **Cantabrigiae, excusum per Joannem Field.** 1665. 12°. WB2719.

1665   DU HAMEL, JEAN BAPTISTE. Elementa astronomica. **Cantabrigiae,** 1665. 12°. WD 2498.

1665   EDWARDS, JOHN. The plague of the heart. **Cambridge: by John Field, for Edmund Beechinoe.** 1665. 4°. WE209.

1665   EUCLID. Euclidis sex primi elementorum. **Cantabrigiae, excudebat J. Field, impensis Edwardi Story.** 1665. 12°. WE3406.

1665   Liber precvm pvblicarvm. **Cantabrigiae.** 1665. 8°. WL1953.

1665   SALLUST ... Cum historiarū fragmentis. **Cantabrigiae, ex officina Ioannis Field.** 1665. 12°. WS405.

1665   SOPHOCLES. ΣοΦοκλης Τραγωδιαυ Z' ... tragoediae VII. **Cantabrigiae, excudebat Joannes Field.** 1665. 8°. WS4691.

1666   ALMANACS. Dove. Speculum anni 1666. **Cambridge: by John Field.** 1666. 8°. WA1612.

1666   ALMANACS. POND, EDWARD. Pond an almanack for ... 1666. **Cambridge; by John Field.** 1666. 8°. WA2147.

1666   ALMANACS. SWALLOW, JOHN. Swallow. An almanack for 1666. **Cambridge, By John Field.** 1666. 8°. WA2430.

1666   ALMANACS. SWAN, JOHN. An ephemeris, or almanack for ... 1664. [sic] **By John Field, Cambridge.** 1666. 8°. WA2474.

1666   BIBLE. ENGLISH. **Cambridge, by John Field.** 1666-8. 4°. WB2275.

1666   BIBLE. ENGLISH. NEW TESTAMENT. The New Testament. **Cambridge, by John Field.** 1666. 4°. WB2667.

1666   BIBLE. ENGLISH. PSALMS. The whole book of psalms. **By John Field, Cambridge.** 1666. 4°. WB2490.

1666   BIBLE. GREEK. Δαβιδης 'εμμετρος. **Cantabrigiae, excudit Ioannes Field.** 1666. 4°. WB2723.

1666   BURGERSDIJCK, FRANCO. Fr. Burgersdicii Institutionum logicarum. **Cantabrigiae, apud Joann. Field.** 1666. 8°. WB5634.

1666   BURGERSDIJCK, FRANCO. Institutionum logicarum synopsis. **Cantabrigiae, apud Joann. Field.** 1666. 8°. WB5637.

1666   DREXEL, JEREMY. Considerations of Drexelius upon eternitie. **Cambridge, by Roger Daniel. To be sould by Tho. Rooks** [London]. 1666. 12°. WD2175.

1666   DUPORT, JAMES. Δαβιδης 'εμμετρος, sive metaphrasis. **Cantabrigiae, excudebat J. Field.** 1666. 4°. WD2648.

1666   LILY, WILLIAM. A short introduction of grammar. **Cambridge, by John Field.** 1666. 8°. WL2284.

1666   LITURGIES. BOOK OF COMMON PRAYER. The book of common prayer. **By John Field, Cambridge.** 1666. 4°. WB3633.

1667   ALMANACS. Dove. Speculum anni 1667. **Cambridge: by John Field.** 1667. 8°. WA1613.

1667   ALMANACS. POND, EDWARD. Pond. An almanack for ... 1667. **Cambridge; by John Field.** 1667. 8°. WA2147A.

1667   ALMANACS. SWALLOW, JOHN. Swallow. An almanack for 1667. **Cambridge, By John Field.** 1667. 8°. WA2431.

1667   ALMANACS. SWAN, JOHN. An ephemeris, or almanack for ... 1667. **By John Field, Cambridge.** 1667. 8°. WA2475.

1667   ALMANACS. SWAN, JOHN. An ephemeris, or almanack for ... 1668. **By John Field, Cambridge.** 1667. 8°. WA2476.

1667   B[ULLOKAR], J[OHN]. An English expositor. "Fourth" edition. **Cambridge, by John Field.** 1667. 12°. WB5431.

1667   CHURCH OF ENGLAND. Articles to be enquired of, and answered. **Cambridge: by John Field.** 1667. 4°. WC4010.

1667   CHURCH OF ENGLAND. Articles to be enquired of ... Bedford. **Cambridge, printed.** 1667. 4°. WC4017.

1667   CICERO. De officiis. Libri III. **Cantabrigiae, apud Joannem Field.** 1667. 8°. WC4292.

1667   FLORUS, LUCIUS ANNAEUS. L. Julii Flori. Rerum à Romanis gestarvm. **Cantabrigiae, ex officina Ioannis Field.** 1667. 12°. WF1374.

1667   Poetae minores Graeci. **Cantabrigiae, apud Joann. Field.** 1667. 8°. WP2731.

1668   AESOP. Fabulae. **Cantabrigiae, ex officina Joann. Field.** 1668. 8°. WA720.

1668   ALMANACS. CLARKE, WILLIAM. Synopsis anni: or, An almanack for ... 1668. **Cambridge, for John Field.** 1668. 8°. WA1415.

1668   ALMANACS. Dove. Speculum anni 1668. [Cambridge], **by John Field.** 1668. 8°. WA 1614.

1668   ALMANACS. HOOKER, RICHARD. Coelestis legatus: or, an astrological diarie for ... 1668. **Cambridge, by John Field.** 1668. 8°. WA1829.

1668   ALMANACS. POND, EDWARD. Pond. An almanack for ... 1668. **Cambridge, by John Field.** 1668. 8°. WA2148.

1668   ALMANACS. SWALLOW, JOHN. Swallow. An almanack for 1668. **Cambridge, By John Field.** 1668. 8°. WA2432.

1668   BIBLE. ENGLISH. **Cambridge, by John Field.** 1668. 4°. WB2277.

1668   [COLLIER, JEREMY]. The office of a chaplain enquir'd into. **Cambridge, by John Hayes; for Henry Dickinson. And are to be sold by Sam Smith, London.** 1668. 4°. WC5258.

1668   ELLIS, JOHN. Clavis fidei. **Cambridge, by John Field.** 1668. 8°. WE585.

1668   GAUTRACHE, PIERRE. Mathematicae totius. **Cantabrigiae, excudebat Joan. Field. Impensis Edwardi Story.** 1668. 8°. WG382.

1668   H[OAR], L[EONARD]. Index Biblicus. **Cambridge, J. Field.** 1668. 4°. WH2196.

1668   JACKSON, JOHN. Index Biblicus; or an exact concordance. **Cambridge, by John Field.** 1668. 4°. WJ79.

1668   KEMP, EDWARD. Reasons for the sole use of the church prayers. **Cambridge, by John Field, 1668, to be sold by Edward Story in Cambridge.** 4°. WK258.

1668   KEMP, EDWARD. A sermon preached ... September the 6. 1668. **Cambridge, by John Field, 1668. To be sold by Edward Story.** 4°. WK259.

1668 LILY, WILLIAM. A short introduction of grammar. **Cambridge, by John Field.** 1668. 8°. WL2287.

1668 SCHREVELIUS, CORNELIUS. Lexicon manuale. **Cantabrigiæ, ex officina Joannes Field.** 1668. 8°. WS894.

1668 SOPHOCLES. Σοφοκληος τραγωδιαυ Ζ' ... tragoediae VII. Κανταβριγα. [1668]. WS4692.

1668 STARKEY, WILLIAM. The divine obligation. **Cambridge: by John Field, to be sold by Henry Dickinson.** 1668. 4°. WS5294.

1669 ALMANACS. Dove. Speculum anni 1669. **[Cambridge], by John Field.** 1669. 8°. WA 1615.

1669 ALMANACS. POND, EDWARD. Pond. An almanack for ... 1669. **Cambridge; by John Field.** 1669. 8°. WA2149.

1669 ALMANACS. The Protestant almanack for ... 1669. **Cambridge; printed.** 1669. 8°. WA2223.

1669 ALMANACS. SWALLOW, JOHN. Swallow. An almanack for 1669. **Cambridge, By John Field.** 1669. 8°. WA2433.

1669 ALMANACS. SWAN, JOHN. An ephemeris, or almanack for 1669. **By John Field, Cambridge.** 1669. 8°. WA2477.

1669 ALMANACS. WHITING, JAMES. An ephemeris for ... 1669. **By John Field, Cambridge.** 1669. 8°. WA2762.

1669 CAMBRIDGE UNIVERSITY. Threni Cantabrigiensis in exequiis. **Cantabrigiæ, ex officina typographica academiae.** 1669. 4°. WC355.

1669 CASAUBON, MERIC. A letter of. **Cambridge, for William Morden.** 1669. 4°. WC805.

1669 [CHARLETON, WALTER]. Oeconomia animalis, novis. Fourth edition. **Ex officina Johannis Redmayne, prostant venales apud Johannem Creed, Cantab.** 1669. 12°. WC3687.

1669 CICERO. De officiis. Libri III. **Cantabrigiæ, apud Joannem Field.** 1669. 8°. WC4293.

1669 ELLIS, JOHN. Clavis fidei. **Cambridge, J. Creed.** 1669. 8°. WE586.

1669 GOULDMAN, FRANCIS. A copious dictionary. Second edition. **Cambridge, by John Field, to be sold by George Sawbridge.** 1669. 4°. WG1444.

1669 GOULDMAN, FRANCIS. Dictionarium etymologicum. **Cantabrigiæ.** 1669. 4°. WG 1447.

1669 LA RAMEE, PIERRE DE. P. Rami dialecticae libro duo. **Ex officina Johannis Redmayne, & veneunt per Robertum Nicholson & Henricum Dickinson. Cantabrigiæ.** 1669. 8°. WL434.

1669 MORE, HENRY. Enchiridion ethicum. Second edition. **Londini, excudebat J. Flesher, venale autem habetur apud Gulielmum Morden, Cantabrigiensem.** 1669. 8°. WM2653.

1669 SCARGILL, DANIEL. The recantation of. **Cambridge, by the printers to the university.** 1669. 4°. WS823.

1669 SOPHOCLES. Σοφοκληος τραγωδιαυ Ζ'... tragoediae VII. **Cantabrigiæ, excudebat Johannes Field.** 1669. **Prostant venales apud Edmundum Beechinoe.** 8°. WS4693.

1669 SOPHOCLES. Σοφοκληος τραγωδιαυ Ζ' ... tragoediae VII. **Cantabrigiæ, excudebat Joannes Field.** 1669. **Prostant venales apud Joham Hart.** 8°. WS4694.

1669 Speculum Papismi: or, a looking-glasse for Papists. **Cambridge.** 1669. 8°. WS4851.

1669 SPENCER, JOHN. Dissertatio de Urim & Thummin. **Cantabrigiæ, impensis T. Garthwait.** 1669. 8°. WS4950.

1670 AESOP. AEsopi Phrygis fabulae. **Cantabrigiæ, ex officina Joann. Hayes.** 1670. 8°. WA721.

1670 ALMANACS. Dove. Speculum anni 1670. **[Cambridge], by John Field.** 1670. 8°. WA1616.

1670 ALMANACS. POND, EDWARD. Pond. An almanack for ... 1670. **Cambridge, by John Field.** 1670. 8°. WA2150.

1670 ALMANACS. SWALLOW, JOHN. Swallow. An almanack for 1670. **Cambridge, by the printers to the university.** 1670. 8°. WA2434.

1670 ALMANACS. SWAN, JOHN. An ephemeris, or almanack for 1670. **By John Field, Cambridge.** 1670. 8°. WA2478.

1670 BARNE, MILES. A sermon preached before the king at Newmarket April 24, 1670. **Cambridge, by John Hayes and to be sold by Edm. Story in Cambridge.** 1670. 4°. WB860.

1670 BARROW, ISAAC, Spiritus sanctus est persona distincta. **[Cambridge].** July 4, 1670. Brs. WB960.

1670 BIBLE. ENGLISH. **Cambridge, by John Hayes.** 1670. 4°. WB2281.

1670 BIBLE. ENGLISH. PSALMS. The vvhole book of psalms. **By John Hayes, of Cambridge.** 1670. 8°. WB2503.

1670 CAMBRIDGE UNIVERSITY. Lacrymae Cantabrigienses in obitum... Henriettae. **Cantabrigiæ, ex officina Joann. Hayes.** 1670. 4°. WC341.

1670 CAMBRIDGE UNIVERSITY. Musarum Cantabrigiensium threnodia. **Cantabrigiæ, ex officina Joann. Hayes.** 1670. 4°. WC347.

1670 CAMBRIDGE UNIVERSITY. Threnodia in obitum. **Cantabrigiæ J. Hayes.** 1670. 4°. WC356.

1670 CHURCH OF ENGLAND. Articles of enquiry ... Bedford. **Cambridge, printed.** 1670. 4°. WC4016.

1670 CICERO. M. Tullii Ciceronis epistolarum libri IV. **Cantabrigiæ: ex officina Joann. Hayes.** 1670. 8°. WC4302.

1670 C[RASHAW], R[ICHARD]. Richardi Crashawi poemata et epigrammata. Second edition. **Cantabrigiæ, ex officina Joan. Hayes.** 1670. 8°. WC6834.

1670 [DU MOULIN, PETER, younger], Petri Molinaei P.F. Παρεργα. Poematvm libri tres. **Cantabrigiæ, excudebat Joann. Hayes. Impensis Joannis Creed.** 8°. WD2561.

1670 GERHARD, JOHANN. Gerards meditations. **Cambridge, by John Hayes.** 1670. 12°. WG610.

1670 HEEREBOORD, ADRIAN. Ερμηνεια logica. **Cantabrigiæ, ex officina Joan. Hayes.** 1670. 8°. WH1359.

1670 HELIODORUS OF LARISSA. Ηλιοδωρον.. capita opticorum. **Cantabrigiæ, ex officina J. Hayes, impensis Joann. Creed.** 1670. 8°. WH1375.

1670 HUME JOHN. βios επουρανιοξ, or the character of an heavenly conversation. **Cambridge, J. Hayes.** 1670. 4°. WH3661.

1670 JOHNSON, JAMES. The judge's authority. **Cambridge, by John Hayes, for Samuel Simpson in Cambridge.** 1670. 4°. WJ777.

1670 JOHNSON, JAMES. Nature inverted. **Cambridge by John Hayes, for Samuel Simpson.** 1670. 4°. WJ778.

1670 LANE, ERASMUS. Divinitas Christi. [Cambridge]. 1670. Brs. WL336.

1670 LITURGIES. BOOK OF COMMON PRAYER. The book of common prayer. **Cambridge, by John Hayes.** 1670. 4°. WB3637.

1670 OCELLUS, LUCANUS. Οκελλος δ Λευκανος Φιλοσφος... De universi naturâ. **Cantabrigiæ, ex officina J. Hayes, impensis Joann. Creed.** 1670. 8°. WO125

1670 A poem on that execrable treason plotted... 1605. **Cambridge, by John Hayes, for Robert Nicholson.** 1670. 4°. WP2685.

1670 [RAY, JOHN]. A collection of English proverbs. **Cambridge by John Hayes, for W. Morden.** 1670. 8°. WR386.

1670 SALLUST. Σαλλουστιου... de diis & mundo. **Cantabrigiæ ex officina J. Hayes, impensis Joann. Creed.** 1670. WS407.

1670 SEIGNIOR, GEORGE. Moses and Aaron. **Cambridge, by John Hayes.** 1670. 4°. WS2418.

1670 SHERINGHAM, ROBERT. De anglorum gentis origine. **Cantabrigiæ, excudebat Jo. Hayes, impensis Edvardi Story.** 1670. 8°. WS3236.

1670 SPENCER, JOHN. Dissertatio de Urim & Thummin. Second edition. **Cantabrigiæ, impensis Gualteri Kettilby.** 1670. 8°. WS4951.

1671 ALMANACS. Dove. Speculum anni 1671. **Cambridge, by John Hayes.** 1671. 8°. WA1617.

1671 ALMANACS. POND, EDWARD. Pond. An almanack for...1671. **Cambridge, by John Hayes.** 1671. 8°. WA2151.

1671 ALMANACS. SWALLOW, JOHN. Swallow. An almanack for 1671. **Cambridge, by the printers to the university.** 1671. 8°. WA2435.

1671 ALMANACS. SWAN, JOHN. An ephemeris, or almanack for 1671. **By John Field, Cambridge.** 1671. 8°. WA2479.

1671 CAMBRIDGE UNIVERSITY. Epicedia Cantabrigiensia in obitum...Annae. **Cantabrigiæ, ex officina Joann. Hayes.** 1671. 4°. WC334.

1671 CHURCH OF ENGLAND. Articles for visitation ...Ely. **Cambridge, by John Hayes.** 1671. 4°. WC4036.

1671 [DU MOULIN, PETER, Younger]. Petri Molinaei P. F. Παρεργα Poematvm libri tres. **Cantabrigiæ excudebat Joann. Hayes,** 1671. **Impensis Joannis Creed.** 8°. WD2562.

1671 [DU MOULIN, PETER, Younger]... Παρεργων incrementum. **Cantabrigiæ, excudebat Joann. Hayes.** 1671. **Impensis Joannis Creed.** 8°. WD2563.

1671 GALE, THOMAS. Opuscula mythologica. **Cantabrigiæ, ex officina J. Hayes, impensis Joann. Creed.** 1671. 8°. WG156.

1671 MORE, HENRY. Enchiridion metaphysicum: ...pars prima. **Londini, typis E. Flesher. Prostat apud Gulielmum Morden, Cantabrigiensem.** 1671. 4°. WM2654.

1671 NORTH, JOHN. A sermon preached...October 8, 1671. **Cambridge, by John Hayes, and are to be sold by Edw. Story in Cambridge.** 1671. 4°. WN1289.

1671 NORTH, JOHN. A sermon preached...October 8, 1671. Second edition. **Cambridge, by John Hayes, and are to be sold by Edw. Story in Cambridge.** 1671. 4°. WN1290.

1671 Poetae minores Graeci. **Cantabrigiæ, ex officina Joan Hayes.** 1671. 8°. WP2732.

1672 ALMANACS. Dove. Speculum anni 1672. **Cambridge, by John Field.** 1672. 8°. WA1618.

1672 ALMANACS. POND, EDWARD. Pond. An almanack for...1672. **Cambridge, by John Hayes.** 1672. 8°. WA2152.

1672 ALMANACS. SWALLOW, JOHN. Swallow. An almanack for 1672. **Cambridge, by the printers to the university.** 1672. 8°. WA2436.

1672 ALMANACS. SWAN, JOHN. An ephemeris, or almanack for 1672. **By John Field, Cambridge.** 1672. 8°. WA2480.

1672 The foundation of the University of Cambridge, vvith a catalogue. **By John Hayes, Cambridge for John Ivory.** 1672. 4°. Brs. WF1646.

1672 HESIOD. Ἡσιοδου ασκραιου τα ευρισκομενα. Hesiodi...quae extant. **Cantabrigiæ, J. Hayes.** 1672. 8°. WH1606.

1672 HOMER. Ὁμηρου Ιλιας. Homeri Ilias. **Cantabrigiæ, excudebat Joannes Hayes.** 1672. 8°. WH2541.

1672 LANGBAINE, GERARD. The foundation of the Universitie of Cambridge. **Cambridge, by John Hayes, for John Ivory.** 1672. Brs. WL369.

1672 LA RAMEE, PIERRE DE. P. Rami dialeticae libro duo. **Cantabrigiæ ex officina Joann. Hayes, impensis G. Morden.** 1672. 8°. WL435.

1672 N[EWMAN], S[AMUEL]. An exact concordance. Second edition. **Cambridge, by John Hayes: for George Sawbridge. And also to be sold by John Martin, Robert Horne, Henry Brome, Richard Chiswell, Robert Boulter, John Wright, and William Jacob, in London.** 1672. Fol. WN926.

1672 OVID. Metamorphosewn. **Cantabrigiæ, ex officina Joann. Hayes.** 1672. 8°. WO680A.

1672 PEARSON, JOHN, bp. Vindiciae Epistolarum S. Ignatii. **Cantabrigiae, typis Joann. Hayes; prostant Londini, apud Guil. Wells & Rob. Scott.** 1672. 4°. WP1010.

1672 PUFENDORF, SAMUEL. Elementorum jurisprudentiae. **Cantabrigiæ, ex officina Joann. Hayes.** 1672. Impensis Joann. Creed. 8°. WP4175.

1672 TIXIER, JEAN. Epistolae. **Cantabrigiæ, ex officina Joannis Hayes.** 1672. 8°. WT1317B.

1672 VAREN, BERNHARD. Geographia generalis. **Cantabrigiæ, ex officina J. Hayes, sumptibus Henrici Dickinson.** 1672. 8°. WV106.

1673 ALMANACS. POND, EDWARD. Pond. An almanack for...1673. **Cambridge, by John Hayes.** 1673. 8°. WA2153.

1673 ALMANACS. SWALLOW, JOHN. Swallow. An almanack for 1673. **Cambridge, by the printers to the university.** 1673. 8°. WA2437.

1673 ALMANACS. SWAN, JOHN. An ephemeris, or almanack for 1673. **By John Field, Cambridge.** 1673. 8°. WA2481.

1673 BARCLAY, JOHN. Jo. Barclaii Argenis. **Cantabrigiæ, ex officina Joann. Hayes.** 1673. **Impensis Joann. Creed.** 8°. WB714.

1673 BIBLE, ENGLISH. **Cambridge, by John Hayes.** 1673. 4°. WB2289.

1673 BIBLE. ENGLISH. NEW TESTAMENT. The New Testament. **Cambridge, by John Hayes.** 1673. 4°. WB2671.

1673 BIBLE. ENGLISH. PSALMS. Psalms in metre. ⌊**Cambridge**⌋. 1673. 4°. WB2512.

1673 BIBLE. ENGLISH. PSALMS. The whole book of psalms. **By John Hayes, Cambridge.** 1673. 8°. WB2513.

1673 COMBERLADGE, JOHN. Putredo. ⌊**Cantabrigiae**⌋. 1673. Brs. WC5497.

1673 The friendly vindication of Mr. Dryden. **Cambridge, printed.** 1673. 4°. WF2229

1673 GROOT, WILLIAM. De principiis juris naturalis enchiridion. **Cantabrigiæ for John Creed.** 1673. 8°. WG2067.

1673 HIEROCLES. ῾Ιεροκλεους. Commentarivs in aurea Pythagoreorum. **By J.R. for J. Williams, and are to be sold by Henry Dickenson in Cambridge.** 1673. 2 vols. 8°. WH1935.

1673 HIEROCLES. De providentia & fato. **By J.R. for J. Williams, and are to be sold by Henry Dickinson of Cambridge.** 1673. 8°. WH1937.

1673 LILY, WILLIAM. A short introduction of grammar. **Cambridge, John Hayes.** 1673. 8°. WL2290.

1673 LILY, WILLIAM. A short introduction of grammar. **Cambridge, by John Hayes.** 1673. 8°. WL2292.

1673 LITURGIES. BOOK OF COMMON PRAYER. The book of Common Prayer. **Cambridge, by John Hayes.** 1673. 4°. WB3640.

1673 PLATO...De rebus divinis dialogi select. **Cantabrigiæ, ex officina Joann Hayes. Impensis Joann. Creed.** 1673. 8°. WP2406.

1673 A poem attempting something upon the rarities of...Cambridge. **For Robert Nicolson in Cambridge.** 1673. 4°. WP2669.

1673 SMITH, JOHN. Select discourses. Second edition. **Cambridge, by John Hayes, for W. Morden.** 1673. 4°. WS4118.

1673 SMITH, SAMUEL. Select discourses. Second edition. **Cambridge, J. Hayes.** 1673. 4°. WS4192.

1673 SOPHOCLES Σοφοκλης ΤραγωδιαυΖ'... tragoediae VII. **Cantabrigiæ, excudebat J.F. prostant Londini apud Rob. Scott.** 1673. 8°. WS4695.

1673 TEMPLER, JOHN. Idea theologiae Leviathanis. **Londini, typis E. Flesher, impensis G. Morden, Cantabrigiæ.** 1673. 8°. WT664.

1673 TERENTUIS AFER, PUBLICUS. Pub. Terentius AM. Antonio Mureto emendatus. **Cantabrigiæ, ex officina Johannis Hayes.** 1673. 8°. WT739.

1673 VAREN, BERNHARD. Descriptio regni Iaponiæ. **Cantabrigiæ, ex officina Joan. Hayes.** 1673. **Impensis Samuelis Simpson.** 8°. WV105.

1674 ALMANACS. Dove. A new almanack for... 1674. **Cambridge, by John Hayes.** 1674. 8°. WA1619.

1674 ALMANACS. POND, EDWARD. Pond. An almanack for...1674. **Cambridge by John Hayes.** 1674. 8°. WA2154.

1674 ALMANACS. SWALLOW, JOHN. Swallow. An almanack for 1674. **Cambridge, by the printers to the university.** 1674. 8°. WA2438.

1674 ALMANACS. SWAN, JOHN. Swan. A new almanack for...1674. **By John Hayes, Cambridge.** 1674. 8°. WA2482.

1674 BIBLE, ENGLISH. **Cambridge, by John Hayes.** 1674. Fol. WB2291.

1674 CICERO. De officiis. Libri III. **Cantabrigiæ, apud J. Hayes.** 1674. 8°. WC4294.

1674 C⌊RASHAW⌋, R⌊ICHARD⌋. Richardi Crashawi poemata et epigrammata. Second edition. **Cantabrigiae, ex officina Joan. Hayes.** 1674. 8°. WC6835.

1674 GOULDMAN, FRANCIS. A copious dictionary. Third edition. **Cambridge, by John Hayes, to be sold by George Sawbridge, John Place, William Place, Thomas Bassett, Thomas Dring, and John Leigh, London.** 1674. 4°. WG1445.

1674 LIGHTFOOT, JOHN. Horae Hebraicae et Talmudicae in Evangelium S. Lucae. **Cantabrigiæ, impensis Ed. Story.** 1674. 4°. WL2063.

1674 OLIVIER, PIERRE. Dissertationes academiæ. **Cantabrigiæ, ex officina Johan. Hayes.** 1674. **Impensis Jon. Hart, Cantab.** 8°. WO285.

1675 ALMANACS. Dove. Speculum anni or an almanack for...1675. **Cambridge, by John Hayes.** 1675. 8°. WA1620.

1675 ALMANACS. POND, EDWARD. Pond. An almanack for...1675. **Cambridge, by John Hayes.** 1671. WA2155.

1675 ALMANACS. SWALLOW, JOHN. Swallow. An almanack for 1675. **Cambridge, by the printers to the university.** 1675. 8°. WA2439.

1675 ALMANACS. SWAN, JOHN. Swan. A new almanack for...1675. **By John Hayes, Cambridge.** 1675. 8°. WA2483.

1675 BIBLE. ENGLISH. **Cambridge, by John Hayes.** 1675. 4°. WB2294.

1675 BIBLE. ENGLISH. NEW TESTAMENT. The New Testament. **Cambridge, by John Hayes.** 1675. 4°. WB2672.

1675 BIBLE. ENGLISH. PSALMS. The whole book of psalms. **By John Hayes, Cambridge.** 1675. 4°. WB2517.

1675 GASSENDI, PIERRE. ...Institutio astronomica. Fifth edition, **Typis Eliz. Flesher. Prostant apud Gulielmum Morden, Cantab.** 1675. 8°. WG292.

1675 JACKSON, WILLIAM. Of the rule of faith. **Cambridge, by John Hayes for Henry Dickinson, and to be sold by R. Chiswel, in London.** 1675. 4°. WJ95.

1675 LITURGIES. BOOK OF COMMON PRAYER. The book of common prayer. **Cambridge, by John Hayes.** 1675. 4°. WB3643.

1675 LUCRETIUS. De rerum natura. **Cantabrigiæ ex officina Joann. Hayes.** 1675. **Impensis W. Morden.** 12°. WL3442.

1675 Magna et antiqua charta Quinque Portuum. **Cantabrigiæ.** 1675. 8°. WM254.

1675 ⌊MARVELL, ANDREW⌋. Plain-dealing: or, a full. **London, by Andr. Clark, for Henry Dickinson in Cambridge.** 1675. 12°. WM876.

1675 [MARVELL, ANDREW]. Plain-dealing: or, a full. **Cambridge, by J. Hayes, for Henry Dickinson.** 1675. 12°. WM877.

1675 [ROGERS, THOMAS]. The faith, doctrine, and religion. **Cambridge, by John Hayes, to be sold by George Sawbridge, London.** 1675. 4°. WR1835.

1676 ALMANACS. Dove. Speculum anni or an almanack for...1676. **Cambridge, by John Hayes.** 1676. 8°. WA1621.

1676 ALMANACKS. POND, EDWARD. Pond. A new almanack for...1676. **Cambridge, by John Hayes.** 1676. 8°. WA2156.

1676 ALMANACS. SWALLOW, JOHN. Swallow. An almanack for 1676. **Cambridge, by the printers to the university.** 1676. 8°. WA2440.

1676 ALMANACS. SWAN, JOHN. Swan. A new almanack for...1676. **By John Hayes, Cambridge.** 1676. 8°. WA2484.

1676 APPLEFORD, ROBERT. Mechanica-rerum explicatio. [Cantabrigiae]. 1676. Brs. WA3581.

1676 BIBLE. ENGLISH. PSALMS. The whole book of psalms. **[Cambridge], by John Hayes.** 1676. 4°. WB2523.

1676 BIBLE. LATIN. NEW TESTAMENT. Novum testamentum. **Cantabrigiae, ex officina Ioannis Field.** 1676. 12°. WB2788.

1676 BRIGGS, WILLIAM. Opthalmo-graphia. **Cantabrigiae, excudebat J. Hayes, impensis J. Hart.** 1676. 12°. WB4668.

1676 B[ULLOKAR], J[OHN]. An English expositor. Fifth edition. **Cambridge, by John Hayes to be sold by G. Sawbridge, London.** 1676. 12°. WB5432.

1676 CULMAN, LEONARD. Sententiae pueriles. **Cantabrigiae, ex officina Joann. Hayes.** 1676. 8°. WC7477.

1676 DUPORT, JAMES. Musae subsecivae, seu poetica stromota. **Cantabrigiae, ex officina Joann Hayes.** 1676. 8°. WD2652.

1676 LITURGIES. BOOK OF COMMON PRAYER. The book of common prayer. **Cambridge, John Hayes.** 1676. 4°. WB3648.

1676 MACE, THOMAS. Musick's monument. **By T. Ratcliffe and N. Thompson, for the author, and are to be sold by himself in Cambridge and by John Carr [London].** 1676. Fol. WM120.

1676 Officium concionatoris. **Cantabrigiae, ex officina Joan. Hayes.** 1676. **Impensis Gulielmi Morden, Cantabr.** 8°. WO158.

1676 RHODOCANAKIS, KONSTANTINES. Tractatus de resolutione. **Cantabrigiae.** 1676. 8°. WR1337.

1676 ROBERTSON, WILLIAM. Thesaurus Graecae linguae. **Cantabrigiae, excudebat Johannes Hayes, impensis Georgii Sawbridge, Londini.** 1676. 4°. WR1619.

1676 ROCHE, T. Ad musas. **Cantabrigiae, J. Hayes.** 1676. 4°. WR1738.

1676 SCATTERGOOD, SAMUEL. A sermon preached ...April 2, 1676. **Cambridge, by John Hayes.** 1676. 4°. WS843.

1676 TEMPLER, JOHN. The reason of Episcopall inspection. **Cambridge, by John Hayes, for William Morden.** 1676. 4°. WT665.

1676 TERENTIUS AFER, PUBLICUS. Comoediae sex. **Cantabrigiae ex officina Joannis Hayes 1676. Prostant venales apud Edvar. Story, Joan. Creed, Henric. Dicksonson.** 12°. WT742.

1677 AESOP. Fabulae AEsopi. **Cantabrigiae, ex officina Jonna. Hayes.** 1677. 8°. WA725

1677 ALMANACS. Dove. Speculum anni or an almanack for...1677. **Cambridge, by John Hayes.** 1677. 8°. WA1622.

1677 ALMANACS. POND, EDWARD. Pond. An almanack for...1677. **Cambridge, by John Hayes.** 1677. 8°. WA2157.

1677 ALMANACS. SWALLOW, JOHN. Swallow. An almanack for 1677. **Cambridge, by the printers to the university.** 1677. 8°. WA2441.

1677 ALMANACS. SWAN, JOHN. Swan. A new almanack for...1677. **By John Hayes, Cambridge.** 1677. 8°. WA2485.

1677 BIBLE. ENGLISH. **Cambridge, by John Hayes.** 1677. 4°. WB2303.

1677 BIBLE. ENGLISH. NEW TESTAMENT. The New Testament. **Cambridge, by John Hayes.** 1677. 4°. WB2677.

1677 BIBLE. LATIN. NEW TESTAMENT. Novum testamentum. **Cantabrigiae,** 1677. 24°. WB2789.

1677 CAMBRIDGE UNIVERSITY. Epithalamium in desideratissimis nuptiis. **Cantabrigiae, ex officina Joann. Hayes.** 1677. 4°. WC336.

1677 ORIGENES. Ωριγινηξ κατα Κελσου...Contra Celsvm. **Cantabrigiae, excudebat Joan. Hayes, impensis Guli. Morden.** 1677. 4°. WO425.

1677 Poetae minores Graeci. **Cantabrigiae, ex officina Joan. Hayes.** 1677. 8°. WP2733.

1677 WALKER, WILLIAM. A modest plea for infants baptism. **Cambridge, by John Hayes: to be sold by Henry Dickinson.** 1677. 12°. WW430.

1677 WITTY, ROBERT. Gout raptures. Αστρωμαχια. **Cambridge, by John Hayes, to be sold by John Creed.** 1677. 8°. WW3228.

1678 ALMANACS. Dove. Speculum anni or an almanack for...1678. **Cambridge, by John Hayes.** 1678. 8°. WA1623.

1678 ALMANACS. POND, EDWARD. Pond. An almanack for...1678. **Cambridge, by John Hayes.** 1678. 8°. WA2158.

1678 ALMANACS. SWALLOW, JOHN. Swallow. An almanack for 1678. **Cambridge, by the printers to the university.** 1678. 8°. WA2442.

1678 ALMANACS. SWAN, JOHN. Swan. A new almanack for...1678. **By John Hayes, Cambridge.** 1678. 8°. WA2486.

1678 BABINGTON, HUMFREY. Mercy & judgment. **Cambridge, by John Hayes, for Henry Dickinson.** 1678. 4°. WB247.

1678 GOULDMAN, FRANCIS. A copious dictionary. Fourth edition. **Cambridge, by John Hayes.** 1678. 4°. WG1446.

1678 [RAY, JOHN]. A collection of English proverbs. Second edition. **Cambridge, by John Hayes, for W. Morden.** 1678. 8°. WR387.

1678 ROBERTSON, WILLIAM. Thesaurus Graecae linguae. **Cantabrigiae, excudebat Johannes Hayes, impensis Georgii Sawbridge, Londini.** 1678. 4°. WR1620.

1679 ALMANACS. Dove. Speculum anni or an almanack for...1679. **Cambridge, by John Hayes.** 1679. 8°. WA1624.

1679 ALMANACS. POND, EDWARD. Pond. An almanack for...1679. **Cambridge, by John Hayes.** 1679. 8°. WA2159.

1679 ALMANACS. SWALLOW, JOHN. Swallow. An almanack for 1679. **Cambridge, by the printers to the university.** 1679. 8°. WA2443.

1679 ALMANACS. SWAN, JOHN. Swan. A new almanack for...1679. **By John Hayes, Cambridge.** 1679. 8°. WA2487.

1679 ARISTOTLE. - Aνξρονικου ροδιου παραφρασις ..... Ethicorum Nichomacheorum. **Cantabrigiae, excudebat Johannes Hayes, impensis Johannis creed.** 1679. 8°. WA3688.

1679 BIBLE. ENGLISH. PSALMS. The whole book of psalms. |**Cambridge**|, **by John Hayes.** 1679. 4°. WB2534.

1679 BYTHNER, VICTORINUS. Lyra prophetica. **Typis E. Flesher, apud G. Morden, Cantabrigiae** 1679. 4°. WB6423.

1679 CATO, DIONYSIUS. Catona disticha de moribvs. **Cantabrigiae, ex officina Joan. Hayes.** 1679. 8°. WC1507.

1679 GERHARD, JOHANN. Gerard's meditations. **Cambridge, by John Hayes.** 1679. 12°. WG611.

1679 HOMER. ˊOμηρου Iλιαs. Homeri Ilias. **Cantabrigiae, excudebat J. Hayes.** 1679. 8°. WH2543.

1679 LITURGIES. BOOK OF COMMON PRAYER. The book of common prayer. **Cambridge, by John Hayes.** 1679. 4°. WB3656.

1679 LIVIUS, TITUS. Qui extant historiarum libri. **Cantabrigiae, ex officina Joan. Hayes. Impensis Joan. Creed & Henr. Dickinson.** 1679. 8°. WL2612.

1679 SALLUST...Cum historiarū fragmentis. **Cantabrigiae, ex officina Ioannis Hayes.** 1679. 12°. WS406.

1679 SPAGNUOLI, BAPTISTA, Mantuanus... Adolescentia. **Cantabrigiae, ex officina Joan. Hayes.** 1679. 8°. WS4790.

1680 ALMANACS. CULPEPER, NATHANIEL. Culpeper revived. **Cambridge, by John Hayes.** 1680. 8°. WA1501.

1680 ALMANACS. Dove. Speculum anni or an almanack for...1680. **Cambridge, by John Hayes.** 1680. 8°. WA1625.

1680 ALMANACS. POND, EDWARD. Pond. An almanack for...1680. **Cambridge, by John Hayes.** 1680. 8°. WA2160.

1680 ALMANACS. SWALLOW, JOHN. Swallow. An almanack for 1680. **Cambridge, by the printers to the university.** 1680. 8°. WA2444.

1680 ALMANACS. SWAN, JOHN. Swan. A new almanack for...1680. **By John Hayes, Cambridge.** 1680. 8°. WA2488.

1680 ALMANACS. WING, JOHN. Ολυμπια δωματα, or an almanack for...1680. **Cambridge, by John Hayes.** 1680. 8°. WA2771.

1680 BIBLE. ENGLISH. NEW TESTAMENT. The New Testament. **Cambridge, by John Hayes.** 1680. 4°. WB2684.

1680 B|ULLOKAR| J|OHN|. An English expositor. Sixth edition. **Cambridge, for J. Hays.** 1680. 12°. WB5433.

1680 BURGERSDIJCK, FRANCO. Fr. Burgerdicii Institutionvm logicarum. **Cantabrigiae, apud Joann. Hayes,** 1680. **Prostant venales apud Guil. Graves jun.** 8°. WB5636.

1680 FLORUS, LUCIUS ANNAEUS. L. Julii Flori. Rerum à Romanis gestarvm. **Cantabrigiae, ex officina Ioannis Hayes.** 1680. 12°. WF1376.

1680 HEEREBOORD, ADRIAN. Eρμηνεια logica. **Cantabrigiae, ex officina Joan. Hayes.** 1680. 8°. WH1361.

1681 ALMANACS. CULPEPER, NATHANIEL. Culpeper revived. **Cambridge, by John Hayes.** 1681. 8°. WA1502.

1681 ALMANACS. Dove. Speculum anni or an almanack for...1681. **Cambridge, by John Hayes.** 1681. 8°. WA1626.

1681 ALMANACS. POND, EDWARD. Pond. An almanack for...1681. **Ca̅mbridge, by John Hayes.** 1681. 8°. WA2161.

1681 ALMANACS. SWALLOW, JOHN. Swallow. An almanack for 1681. **Cambridge, by the printers to the university.** 1681. 8°. WA2445.

1681 ALMANACS. SWAN, JOHN. Swan. A new almanack for...1681. **By John Hayes, Cambridge.** 1681. 8°. WA2489.

1681 ALMANACS. WING, JOHN. Ολυμπια δωματα, or an almanack for...1681. **Cambridge, by John Hayes.** 1681. 8°. WA2772.

1681 CORDIER, MATHURIN. Colloquiorum scholasticorum libri iiii. **Cantabrigiae, ex officina Joann. Hayes.** 1681. 8°. WC6290.

1681 |HILL, WILLIAM|. Omnium febrium causa latet in sanguine. [**Cambridge, 1681**]. Brs. WH2035A.

1681 LILY, WILLIAM. Brevissima institvtio. **Cantabrigiae, apud Johannem Hayes.** 1681. 8°. WL2258A.

1681 LILY, WILLIAM. A short introduction of grammar. **Cambridge, by John Hayes.** 1681. 8°. WL2297.

1681 ROBERTSON, WILLIAM. Phraseologia generalis. **Cambridge, by J. Hayes.** 1681. **And are to be sold by George Sawbridge, London.** 8°. WR1616.

1681 |ROGERS, THOMAS|. The faith, doctrine, and religion. **Cambridge, by John Hayes, to be sold by George Sawbridge, London.** 1681. 4°. WR1836.

1681 SHOULDAM, ROBERT. Affectus Cvulgo dicto hypocondrracus. |**Cambridge**|. 1681. Brs. WS3647A.

1681 VAREN, BERNHARD. Geographia generalis. Second edition. **Cantabrigiae, ex officina Joann. Hayes.** 1681. 8°. WV107.

1682 ALMANACS. CULPEPER, NATHANIEL. Culpeper revived. **Cambridge, by John Hayes.** 1682. 8°. WA1503.

1682 ALMANACS. Dove. Speculum anni or an almanack for...1682. **Cambridge, by John Hayes.** 1682. 8°. WA1627.

1682   ALMANACS. POND, EDWARD. Pond. An almanack for...1682. **Cambridge, by John Hayes.** 1682. 8°. WA2162.

1682   ALMANACS. SWALLOW, JOHN. Swallow. An almanack for 1682. **Cambridge, by the printers to the university.** 1682. 8°. WA2446.

1682   ALMANACS. SWAN, JOHN. Swan. A new almanack for...1682. **By John Hayes, Cambridge,** 1682. 8°. WA2490.

1682   ALMANACS. WING, JOHN. Ολυμπια δωματα, or an almanack for...1682. **Cambridge, by John Hayes.** 1682. 8°. WA2773.

1682   ⌊ARNAULD, ANTOINE⌋. Logica, sive ars cogitandi. Second edition. **Impensis R. Littlebury, R. Scot, G. Scot, G. Wells, Londinensium, & J. Green, Cantaboigiensis.** ⌊sic⌋. 1682. 8°. WA3726.

1682   BARNE, MILES. A discourse concerning the nature of Christ's Kingdom. **Cambridge, by J. Hayes, for R. Green.** 1682. 4°. WB857.

1682   BARNE, MILES. A discourse concerning the nature of Christ's Kingdom. Second edition. **Cambridge, by J. Hayes, for R. Green.** 1682. 4°. WB858.

1682   BIBLE. ENGLISH. **Cambridge, J. Hayes.** 1682. 4°. WB2323.

1682   ⌊JENNER, DAVID⌋. Beavfrons; or a new-discovery. **London, for Charles Morden in Cambridge.** 1682. 4°. WJ656.

1682   N⌊EWMAN⌋, S⌊AMUEL⌋. An exact concordance. Third edition. **Cambridge, by John Hayes for Hannah Sawbridge i London.** 1682. Fol. WN927.

1682   PUFENDORF, SAMUEL. De officio hominis. **Cantabrigiae, ex officina Joan.Hayes.** 1682. **Impensis Joan. Creed.** 8°. WP4174.

1682   SCHULER, JOANNES. Exercitationes. **Cantabrigiae, excudebat Joannis Hayes, impensis Joan. Creed.** 1682. 8°. WS900.

1682   SHERINGHAM, ROBERT. The Kings supremacy asserted. Third edition. **London, for Jonas Hart and Charles Morden in Cambridge.** 1682. 4°. WS3238.

1682   To his grace Christopher Duke of Albermarle. **Cambridge, by John Hayes: for Francis Hicks.** 1682. Fol. WT1361.

1683   ALMANACS. CULPEPER, NATHANIEL. Culpeper revived. **Cambridge, by John Hayes.** 1683. 8°. WA1504.

1683   ALMANACS. Dove. Speculum anni or an almanack for...1683. **Cambridge, by John Hayes.** 1683. 8°. WA1628.

1683   ALMANACS. POND, EDWARD. Pond. An almanack for...1683. **Cambridge, by John Hayes.** 1683. 8°. WA2163.

1683   ALMANACS. SWALLOW, JOHN. Swallow. An almanack for 1683. **Cambridge, by the printers to the university.** 1683. 8°. WA2447.

1683   ALMANACS. WING, JOHN. Ολυμπια δωματα, or an almanack for...1683. **Cambridge, by John Hayes.** 1683. 8°. WA2774.

1683   BIBLE. ENGLISH. **Cambridge by John Hayes.** 1683. 4°. WB2333.

1683   BIBLE. ENGLISH. NEW TESTAMENT. The New Testament. **Cambridge, by John Hayes.** 1683. 4°. WB2690.

1683   BIBLE. ENGLISH. PSALMS. The whole book of psalms. ⌊Cambridge⌋, **by John Hayes.** 1683. 4°. WB2552A.

1683   BIBLE. LATIN. NEW TESTAMENT. Novum testamentum. **Cantabrigiae.** 1683. 12°. WB2791.

1683   BURRELL, JOHN. The divine right of kings. **Cambridge, by John Hayes, for Sam. Simpson.** 1683. 4°. WB5974.

1683   CAMBRIDGE UNIVERSITY. Hymenaeus Cantabrigiensis. **Cantabrigiae, ex officina Johannis Hayes.** 1683. 4°. WC338.

1683   CICERO. De officiis. Libri III. **Cantabrigiae, apud J. Hayes.** 1683. 8°. WC4295.

1683   DAVENANT, JOHN. bp. Dissertatio de morte Christi. **Ex officina Rogeri Danielis, Cantabrigiensis.** 1683. 12°. WD316.

1683   EUSEBIUS PAMPHILI, bp. The history of the church. **Cambridge, by John Hayes, for Han. Sawbridge.** 1683. Fol. WE3423.

1683   GAUTRACHE, PIERRE. Mathematicae totius. **Typis M. Clarke, impensis Richardi Green, Cantabrigiensis.** 1683. 8°. WG383.

1683   ⌊JENNER, DAVID⌋. Beavfrons; or, a new-discovery. **London, for Charles Morden. in Cambridge.** 1683. 4°. WJ657.

1683   JEWEL, JOHN. bp. Apologia ecclesiae Anglicanae. **Cantabrigiae, excudebat Joannes Hayes; impensis Joannis Creed.** 1683. 12°. WJ733.

1683   LITURGIES. BOOK OF COMMON PRAYER. The book of common prayer. **Cambridge, John Hayes.** 1683. 4°. WB3670.

1683   PLATO. De rebus divinis dialogi select. Second edition. **Cantabrigiae, ex officina Joann. Hayes. Impensis Joann. Creed.** 1683. 8°. WP2407.

1683   ROBERTSON, WILLIAM. ⌊Hebrew⌋. Manipulus linguae sanctae. **Cantabrigiae; ⌊pro authore⌋ typis Johannis Hayes. Prostant venales Londini.** 1683. 4°. WR1614.

1683   TURNER, JOHN. The middle way. **For Samuel Sympson in Cambridge, to be sold by him, and Fincham Gardiner.** 1683. 8°. WT3312.

1684   ALBERMARLE, CHRISTOPER, duke of. I, Christopher Duke of Albemarle, &c. Chancellour ... Orders and rules. ⌊Cambridge⌋. June 27, 1684. Brs. WA839.

1684   ALMANACS. CULPEPER, NATHANIEL. Culpeper revived. **Cambridge, by John Hayes.** 1684. 8°. WA1505.

1684   ALMANACS. Dove. Speculum anni or an almanack for...1684. **Cambridge by John Hayes** 1684. 8°. WA1629.

1684   ALMANACS. Fly: an almacack for...**Cambridge by John Hayes.** 1684. 8°. WA1686.

1684   ALMANACS. POND, EDWARD. Pond. An almanack for...1684. **Cambridge, by John Hayes.** 1684. 8°. WA2164.

1684   ALMANACS. SWALLOW, JOHN. Swallow. A new almanack for 1684. **Cambridge, by the printers to the university.** 1684. 8°. WA2448.

1684   ALMANACS. SWAN, JOHN. Swan. A new almanack for...1684. **By John Hayes, Cambridge.** 1684. 8°. WA2491.

1684   ALMANACS. WING, JOHN. Ολυμπια δωματα, or an almanack for...1684. **Cambridge, by John Hayes.** 1684. 8°. WA2775.

1684 ANACREON. Ανακρεοντος πηιου μελη. **Cantabrigiæ, ex officina Joan. Hayes, impensis Rich. Green, Cantabr.** 1684. 12°. WA3044

1684 Ανθολογια seu selecta quaèdam poemata Italorum. **Impensis R. Green & F. Hicks, Cantab.** 1684. 12°. WA3476.

1684 BARNE, MILES. A sermon preached... July 10th. 1684. **Cambridge, by J. Hayes: for R. Green,** 1684. **To be sold by Walt. Davis in London.** 4°. WB864.

1684 Bibliotheca Sturbitchiana. **Cambridge.** 8 Sept. 1684. 4°. WB2857.

1684 B[ULLOKAR], J[OHN]. An English expositor. Seventh edition. **Cambridge, for John Hayes, to be sold by H. Sawbridge.** 1684. 8°. WB5434

1684 CAMBRIDGE UNIVERSITY. Statuta quaedam. **Cantabrigiæ, ex officina Joan. Hayes.** 1684. 8°. WC353.

1684 CASIMIR, MATHIAS. Lyricorum libri IV. **Cantabrigiæ; apud Ricardum Green.** 1684. 12°. WC1213.

1684 COURCELLES, ETIENNE DE. Stephani Curcellæi synopsis ethices. Second edition. **Excudebat M.C. sumptibus H. Dickinson, Cantabrigiæ.** 1684. 8°. WC6583A.

1684 P., H. A satyr against common-wealths. **For Joseph Hindmarsh, and Francis Hicks, in Cambridge.** 1684. Fol. WP34.

1684 Poetae minores Graeci. **Cantabrigiæ,** 1684. 8°. WP2734.

1684 SAUMAISE, CLAUDE DE. Defensio regia, pro Carolo I. **Cantabrigia: apud Franciscum Hicks.** 1684. 12°. WS738.

1684 TURNER, JOHN. The middle way. The second part. **For Samuel Sympson in Cambridge to be sold by him, and Fincham Gardiner.** 1684. 8°. WT3312A.

1684 WHEAR, DEGORY. Relectiones Hyemales. Fifth edition. **Cantabrigiæ, ex officinâ Joan. Hayes, impensis H. Dickenson, & B. Green.** 1684. 8°. WW1596.

1685 ALMANACS. CULPEPER, NATHANIEL. Culpeper revived. **Cambridge, by John Hayes.** 1685. 8°. WA1506.

1685 ALMANACS. Dove. Speculum anni or an almanack for...1685. **Cambridge, by John Hayes.** 1685. 8°. WA1630.

1685 ALMANACS. Fly: an almacack for...**Cambridge by John Hayes.** 1685. 8°. WA1687.

1685 ALMANACS. POND, EDWARD. Pond. An almanack for...1685. **Cambridge, by John Hayes.** 1685. 8°. WA2165.

1685 ALMANACS. SWALLOW, JOHN. Swallow. A new almanack for 1685. **Cambridge, by the printers to the university.** 1685. 8°. WA2449.

1685 ALMANACS. WING, JOHN. Ολυμπια δωματα, or an almanack for...1685. **Cambridge, by John Hayes.** 1685. 8°. WA2776.

1685 BARON, ROBERT. Rob. Baronii... Metaphysica generalis. **Cantabrigiæ, ex officina Johan. Hayes. Impensis H. Sawbridge.** 1685. 12°. WB885.

1685 BIBLE. HEBREW. [Hebrew]. Sepher Tehellim. **Cantabrigiæ, typis Johen, Hayes, prostant, vero, venales London.** 1685. 12°. WB2743.

1685 BRIGGS, WILLIAM. Opthalmo-graphia. **Typis J.P., impensis Sam. Simpson, Cantabrig. & prostant venales apud Sam. Smith, London.** 1685. 8°. WB4668A.

1685 CAMBRIDGE UNIVERSITY. Mœstissimae ac laetissimae academiæ. **Cantabrigiæ, ex officina Joan. Hayes.** 1684/5. 4°. WC343.

1685 ERASMUS, DESIDERIUS. Enchiridion militis Christiani. **Cantabrigiæ, ex officina Joh. Hayes, impensis Guil. Graves, jun.** 1685. 8°. WE3200

1685 GOSTWYKE, WILLIAM. A sermon preached... 26th of July 1685. **Cambridge, by John Hayes, To be sold by H. Dickinson and by Walter Davis, London.** 1685. 4°. WG1323.

1685 GOWER, HUMFREY. A discourse, deliver'd... September 1684. **Cambridge, by John Hayes. For John Creed.** 1685. 4°. WG1458.

1685 In homines nefarios qui scelere ausuq; immani. **Cantabrigiæ, Ioannis Legat.** 1685. 4°. WI110.

1685 JENNER, DAVID. Beavfrons; or, a new-discovery. **For Charles Morden in Cambridge, and are to be sold by Joseph Hindmarsh.** 1685. 4°. WJ658.

1685 LACTANTIUS. Lucii Cœlii Lactantii Firmiani opera quae extant. **Cantabrigiæ, ex officina Johan. Hayes, impensis Hen. Dickinson, & Rich. Green.** 1685. 8°. WL140.

1685 LILY, WILLIAM. A short introduction of grammar. **Cambridge, by John Hayes.** 1685. 8°. WL2298A.

1685 [RAY, JOHN]. Appendix ad catalogam. Second edition. **Cantabrigiæ.** 1685. 8°. WR380.

1685 [RYVES, BRUNO]. Mercurius Rusticus: or, the countries complaint of the barbarous. **For Richard Green, Cambridge.** 1685. 8°. WR2450.

1685 SCHREVELIUS, CORNELIUS. Lexicon manuale. Sixth edition. **Cantabrigiæ, ex officina Joan. Hayes, impensis H. Sawbridge, Londini.** 1685. 8°. WS895.

1685 SCRIVENER, MATTHEW. A treatise against drunkennesse. **London, for Charles Broun, in Cambridge,** 1685. 12°. WS2119.

1685 SPENCER, JOHN. De legibus hebraeorum ritualibus. **Cantabrigiæ, ex officina Joan. Hayes, impensis Richardi Chiswel, Londini.** 1685. Fol. WS4946.

1685 Tabula chronologica regum. **Cantabrigiæ, ex officina Joan. Hayes, impensis Guilielmi Graves.** 1685. Brs. WT94.

1685 THOMAS À KEMPIS. De Christo imitando. **Cantabrigiæ, ex officinâ Joh. Hayes.** 1685. **Impensis G. Graves, jun.** 12°. WT949.

1686 ALMANACS. CULPEPER, NATHANIEL. Culpeper revived. **Cambridge, by John Hayes.** 1686. 8°. WA1507.

1686 ALMANACS. Dove. Speculum anni or an almanack for...1686. **Cambridge, by John Hayes.** 1686. 8°. WA1631.

1686 ALMANACS. Fly: an almacack for... **Cambridge, by John Hayes.** 1686. 8°. WA1688.

1686 ALMANACS. POND, EDWARD. Pond. An almanack for...1686. **Cambridge, by John Hayes.** 1686. 8°. WA2166.

1686 ALMANACS. SWALLOW, JOHN. Swallow. A new almanack for 1686. **Cambridge, by the printers to the university.** 1686. 8°. WA2450.

1686 ALMANACS. WING, JOHN. Ολυμπια δωματα, or an almanack for...1686. **Cambridge, by John Hayes.** 1686. 8°. WA2777.

1686 BIBLE. LATIN. NEW TESTAMENT. Novum testamentum. **Cantabrigiæ.** 1686. 8°. WB2792

1686 HOMER. 'Ομηρου 'Ιλιος'. Homeri Ilias. **Cantabrigiæ, ex officina Joan. Hayes.** 1686. 8°. WH2544.

1686 ISOCRATES. Orationes et epistolæ. **Cantabrigiæ, ex officina Johan. Hayes.** 1686. 12°. WI1077.

1686 LUCRETIUS. De rerum natura. **Cantabrigiæ, officina Joann. Hayes.** 1686. Impensis H. Dickenson. 12°. WL3444.

1686 NEWTON, Sir ISAAC. Tables for renewing. **Cambridge, by John Hayes.** 1686. 8°. WN1050.

1686 SCHULER, JOANNES. Exercitationes. **Cantabrigiæ,** 1686. 8°. WS901.

1686 SEDGWICK, OBADIAH. Catalogus variorum librorum theologicorum, philologicor, &c. **Cambridge,** 29 March 1686. Fol. WS2367.

1686 SLEIDAN, JOHN....De quatuor monarchiis. **Cantabrigiæ, ex officina Johan. Hayes. Impensis H. Sawbridge, Londini.** 1686. 12°. WS3986.

1686 TERTULLIAN. ... Apologeticus. **Cantabrigiæ, ex officina Joan. Hayes.** 1686. Impensis Henr. Dickinson & Rich. Green. 12°. WT784.

1686 THURLIN, THOMAS. The necessity of obedience. **Cambridge, by John Hayes, to be sold by H. Dickinson.** 1686. 4°. WT1138.

1686 TURNER, FRANCIS, bp. A letter to the clergy. **Cambridge, by J. Hayes.** 1686. 4°. WT3277.

1687 ALMANACS. CULPEPER, NATHANIEL. Culpeper revived. **Cambridge, by John Hayes.** 1687. 8°. WA1508.

1687 ALMANACS. Dove. Speculum anni or an almanack for...1687. **Cambridge, by John Hayes.** 1687. 8°. WA1632.

1687 ALMANACS. Fly: an almacack for... **Cambridge, by John Hayes.** 1687. 8°. WA1689.

1687 ALMANACS. POND, EDWARD. Pond. An almanack for...1687. **Cambridge, by John Hayes.** 1687. 8°. WA2167.

1687 ALMANACS. SWALLOW, JOHN. Swallow. A new almanack for 1687. **Cambridge, by the printers to the university.** 1687. 8°. WA2451.

1687 ALMANACS. WING, JOHN. Ολυμπια δωματα, or an almanack for...1687. **Cambridge, by John Hayes.** 1687. 8°. WA2778.

1687 CALAMY, BENJAMIN. Sermons preached upon several occasions. First edition. **By M. Flesher, for Henry Dickenson and Richard Green in Cambridge, to be sold by Walter Davis.** 1687. 8°. WC221.

1687 OVID. Metamorphoseos. **Cantabrigiæ. J. Hayes.** 1687. 8°. WO681.

1687 VINCENTIUS, Saint, of Lérins. Adversus profanas. **Cantabrigiæ.** 1687. 12°. WV453.

1687 VINCENTIUS, Saint, of Lérins. Perigrini, commonitorium. **Cantabrigiæ.** 1687. 12°. WV457.

1688 ALMANACS. CULPEPER, NATHANIEL. Culpeper revived. **Cambridge, by John Hayes.** 1688. 8°. WA1509.

1688 ALMANACS. Dove. Speculum anni or an almanack for 1688. [**Cambridge**], by John Hayes. 1688. 8°. WA1633.

1688 ALMANACS. POND, EDWARD. Pond. An almanack for...1688. **Cambridge, by John Hayes.** 1688. 8°. WA2168.

1688 ALMANACS. SWALLOW, JOHN. Swallow. A new almanack for 1688. **Cambridge, by the printers to the university.** 1688. 8°. WA2452.

1688 ALMANACS. WING, JOHN. Ολυμπια δωματα, or an almanack for...1688. **Cambridge, by John Hayes.** 1688. 8°. WA2779.

1688 BARNES, JOSHUA. The history of... Edward IIIᵈ. **Cambridge, by John Hayes for the author.** 1688. Fol. WB871.

1688 BROWNE, THOMAS. Concio ad clerum. **Cantabrigiæ, ex officina Joan. Hayes, impensis H. Dickinson, Cantab. & Sam. Smith, Lond.** 1688. 4°. WB5184.

1688 BROWNE, THOMAS. Concio habita coram. **Cantabrigiæ, ex officina Joan. Hayes, impensis H. Dickinson, Cantab. & Sam. Smith, Lond.** 1688. 4°. WB5184A.

1688 B[ULLOKAR], J[OHN]. An English expositor. Eighth edition. **Cambridge, by John Hayes.** 1688.12°. WB5435.

1688 CAMBRIDGE UNIVERSITY. Illustrissimi principis Ducis Cornubiae. **Cantabrigiæ, ex officina Joan. Hayes.** 1688. 4°. WC339.

1688 LOGGAN, DAVID. Cantabrigia illustrata. **Cantabrigiæ.** 1688. Fol. WL2836.

1688 [SANDERSON, ROBERT], bp. Casus conscientiae. **Cantabrigiæ, ex officina Jo. Hayes. Impensis Hen. Dickinson, & Rich. Green.** 1688. 8°. WS581.

1688 SAYWELL, WILLIAM. The reformation of the Church of England justified. **Cambridge, by John Hayes; for Edward Hall. To be sold by Luke Meredith, London.** 1688. 29pp. 4°. WS804.

1688 THOMAS À KEMPIS. De Christo imitando. **Cantabrigiæ, ex officina Joh. Hayes.** 1688. 12°. WT950.

1688 VALLA, LORENZO. De linguae latinae elegantia. **Cantabrigiæ, apud Edvardum Hall.** 1688. 8°. WV46.

1689 ALMANACS. CULPEPER, NATHANIEL. Culpeper revived. **Cambridge, by John Hayes.** 1689. 8°. WA1510.

1689 ALMANACS. Dove. Speculum anni or an almanack for 1689. **Cambridge, by John Hayes.** 1689. 8°. WA1634.

1689 ALMANACS. POND, EDWARD. Pond. An almanack for...1689. **Cambridge, by John Hayes.** 1689. 8°. WA2169.

1689 ALMANACS. SWALLOW, JOHN. Swallow. A new almanack for 1689. **Cambridge, by the printers to the university.** 1689. 8°. WA2453.

1689 ALMANACS. WING, JOHN. Ολυμπια δωματα, or an almanack for...1689. **Cambridge, by John Hayes.** 8°. WA2780.

1689 CAMBRIDGE UNIVERSITY. Musae Cantabrigiensis. **Cantabrigiæ, ex officina Joann. Hayes.** 1689. 4°. WC344.

1689 |FLEETWOOD, WILLIAM|, bp. A sermon preached before the university...25th of March, 1689. **Cambridge, by John Hayes; for William Graves there.** 1689. 4°. WF1251.

1689 HOMER. 'Ομηρου 'Ιλιας. Homeri Ilias. **Cantabrigiæ, ex officina Joann. Hayes; vendit Ed. Brewster, Londini.** 1689. 4°. WH2545.

1689 LAUNOY, JEAN DE. Joannis Launoii epistolae omnes. **Cantabrigiæ, ex Officina J. Hayes, impensis E. Hall.** 1689. Fol. WL621.

1689 VINCENTIUS, Saint, of Lérins. Adversus profanas. **Cantabrigiæ, J. Hayes.** 1689. 12°. WV454.

1690 ALMANACS. CULPEPER, NATHANIEL. Culpeper revived. **Cambridge, by John Hayes.** 1690. 8°. WA1511.

1690 ALMANACS. Dove. Speculum anni or an almanack for 1690. **Cambridge, by John Hayes** 1690. 8°. WA1635.

1690 ALMANACS. POND, EDWARD. Pond. An almanack for...1690. **Cambridge, by John Hayes.** 1690. 8°. WA2170.

1690 ALMANACS. SWALLOW, JOHN. Swallow. A new almanack for 1690. **Cambridge, by the printers to the university.** 1690. 8°. WA2454.

1690 ALMANACS. WING, JOHN. Ολυμπια δωματα, or an almanack for...1690. **Cambridge, by John Hayes.** 1690. 8°. WA2781.

1690 CALAMY, BENJAMIN. Sermons preached upon several occasions. Second edition. **By M. Clark, for Henry Dickenson and Richard Green, in Cambridge, to be sold by Walter Davis.** 1690. 8°. WC222.

1690 FULLER, SAMUEL. Canonica svccessio. **Cantabrigiæ, ex officina J. Hayes, 1690. Impensis H. Dickinson, Cantab. Et prostant venales apud S. Smith.** 4°. WF2396.

1690 LOGGAN, DAVID. Cantabrigia illustrata. **Cantabrigiæ.** [1690?]. Fol. WL2837.

1690 MILNER, JOHN. De Nethinim sive Nethinaeis. **Cantabrigiæ, impensis C. Brown.** 1690. 4°. WM2079.

1691 ALMANACS. Dove. Speculum anni or an almanack for 1691. **Cambridge, by John Hayes.** 1691. 8°. WA1636.

1691 ALMANACS. POND, EDWARD. Pond. An almanack for...1691. **Cambridge, by John Hayes.** 1691. 8°. WA2171.

1691 ALMANACS. SWALLOW, JOHN. Swallow. A new almanack for 1691. **Cambridge, by the printers to the university.** 1691. 8°. WA2455.

1691 ALMANACS. WING, JOHN. Ολυμπια δωματα, or an almanack for...1691. **Cambridge, by John Hayes.** 1691. 8°. WA2782.

1691 FLEETWOOD, WILLIAM, bp. Inscriptionum antiquarum sylloge. **Impensis Guil. Graves, Cantabrigiansis, & prostant apud Tim. Childe.** 1691. 8°. WF1247.

1691 HAMMOND, HENRY. A practicall catechisme. Thirteenth edition. **By M. Clark, for Henry Dickenson, and Richard Green, in Cambridge.** 1691. 8°. WH595.

1691 HANBURY, NATHANIEL. Supplementum analyticum. **Cantabrigiæ, ex officina Johann. Hayes. Impensis authoris, 1691. Prostant venales per Edvardum Hall.** 4°. WH638.

1691 HEYRICK, THOMAS. Miscellany poems. **Cambridge, by John Hayes, for the author and are to be sold by Francis Hicks and Thomas Basset and Samuel Heyrick in London.** 1691. 4°. WH1753.

1691 MILTON, JOHN. Johannis Miltoni paradisi amissi. **Cantabrigiæ, ex officina Jo. Hayes, impensis Sam. Simpson.** 1691. 4°. WM2156.

1691 |ROGERS, THOMAS|. The faith, doctrine, and religion. **Cambridge, by John Hayes, to be sold by Edw. Brewster, London.** 1691. 4°. WR1837.

1691 WALKER, THOMAS. Divine hymns. **Cambridge, by J. Hayes; for W. Graves.** 1691. 4°. WW415.

1692 ALMANACS. CULPEPER, NATHANIEL. Culpeper revived. **Cambridge, by John Hayes.** 1692. 8°. WA1512.

1692 ALMANACS. Dove. Speculum anni or a almanack for 1692. **Cambridge, by John Hayes.** 1692. 8°. WA1637.

1692 ALMANACS. POND, EDWARD. Pond. An almanack for...1692. **Cambridge, by John Hayes.** 1692. 8°. WA2172.

1692 ALMANACS. SWALLOW, JOHN. Swallow. A new almanack for 1692. **Cambridge, by the printers to the university.** 1692. 8°. WA2456.

1692 ALMANACS. WING, JOHN. Ολυμπια δωματα, or an almanack for...1692. **Cambridge, by John Hayes.** 1692. 8°. WA2783.

1692 The anatomy of a Jacobite, or the Jacobites heart laid open. **Cambridge, printed.** 1692. 8°. WA3052.

1692 DAVIS, RICHARD. Truth and innocency vindicated. **For Nath. and Robert Ponder, to be sold by Randal Taylor, by Mr. Coolidge at Cambridge, Mr. Prior at Colchester, Mr. Noble at St. Edmund's Bury, Mr. Haworth at Ipswich, Northampton, Wellingborow, Kettering, Oundle, Harborow, Litterworth, Upingham, Bedford, Kimbolton and Canterbury.** [1692?]. 4°. WD435.

1692 EDWARDS, JOHN. An enquiry into four remarkable texts. **Cambridge, by J. Hayes; for W. Graves.** 1692. 4°. WE208.

1692 EUSEBIUS PAMPHILI, bp. The history of the church. **Cambridge, by John Hayes, for N. Rolls.** 1692. Fol. WE3424.

1692 SAYWELL, WILLIAM. The necessity of adhering. **Cambridge, by J. Hayes; for Edw. Hall.** 1692. 4°. WS801.

1692 TERENTIUS AFER, PUBLICUS. Comoediae sex. **Cantabrigiæ, ex officina Johannis Hayes.** 1692. 12°. WT745.

1693 ALMANACS. CULPEPER, NATHANIEL. Culpeper revived. **Cambridge, by John Hayes.** 1693. 8°. WA1513.

1693 ALMANACS. Dove. Speculum anni or an almanack for 1693. **Cambridge, by John Hayes.** 1693. 8°. WA1638.

1693 ALMANACS. POND, EDWARD. Pond. An almanack for...1693. **Cambridge, by John Hayes.** 1693. 8°. WA2173.

1693 ALMANACS. SWALLOW, JOHN. Swallow. A new almanack for 1693. **Cambridge, by the printers to the university.** 1693. 8°. WA2457.

1693 ALMANACS. WING, JOHN. Ολυμπια δωματα, or an almanack for...1693. **Cambridge, by John Hayes.** 1693. 8°. WA2784.

1693 EUSTACHIUS. Ethica. **Ex officina Elizabethæ Redmayne.** 1693. **Prostant venales apud H. Dickinson, E. Hall, Cantab.** 8°. WE3431.

1693 JEFFERY, JOHN. The duty & encouragement of religious artificers. **Cambridge, by John Hayes. for Samuel Oliver in Norwich.** 1693. 4°. WJ515.

1693 KNATCHBULL, Sir NORTON. Annotations upon some difficult texts. **Cambridge, by J. Hayes, for W. Graves.** 1693. 8°. WK672.

1693 Linguae Romanæ dictionarium...a new dictionary. **Cambridge, for W. Rawlins, T. Dring, R. Chiswell, C. Harper, W. Crook, J. place** [sic], **and the executors of S. Leigh.** 1693. 4°. WL2354.

1693 LITTLETON, ADAM. Linguae Romanæ dictionarium...A new dictionary. **Cambridge, for W. Rawlins, T. Dring, R. Chiswell, C. Harper, W. Crook, J. Place, and the executors of S. Leigh** [London]. 1693. Fol. WL2565.

1693 ROBERTSON, WILLIAM. Phraseologia generalis. **Cambridge, by J. Hayes.** 1693. **And are to be sold by George Sawbridge, London.** 8°. WR1617.

1693 ROBERTSON, WILLIAM. Phraseologia generalis. **Cambridge, by John Hayes. To be sold by Daniel Browne, John Laurence, Henry Bonwick, and John Taylor, London.** 1693. 8°. WR1617A.

1693 WALKER, THOMAS. A sermon preached... August 1. 1693. **Cambridge, by John Hayes, for William Graves.** 1693. 4°. WW416.

1694 ALMANACS. CULPEPER, NATHANIEL. Culpeper revived. **Cambridge, by John Hayes.** 1694. 8°. WA1514.

1694 ALMANACS. Dove. Speculum anni or an almanack for 1694. **Cambridge, by John Hayes.** 1694. 8°. WA1639.

1694 ALMANACS. POND, EDWARD. Pond. An almanack for...1694. **Cambridge, by John Hayes,** 1694. 8°. WA2174.

1694 ALMANACS. SWALLOW, JOHN. Swallow. A new almanack for 1694. **Cambridge, by the printers to the university.** 1694. 8°. WA2458.

1694 ALMANACS. WING, JOHN. Ολυμπια δωματα, or an almanack for...1694. **Cambridge, by John Hayes.** 1694. 8°. WA2785.

1694 Articuli Lambethanii. **Cantabrigiae.** 1694. 8°. WA3891.

1694 Articulorum xxxix. Second edition. **Cantabrigiae.** 1694. 12°. WA3893.

1694 COGA, NATHANIEL. Catalogue of library. **Cambridge,** 27 Nov., 1694. 4°. WC4890.

1694 ELLIS, JOHN. Articulorum xxxix...Defensio. Second edition. **Cantabrigiae, ex officina Johann Hayes.** 1694. **Impensis Hen. Dickinson, et prostant venales apud S. Smith, Lond.** 12°. WE581.

1694 EURIPIDES. Ευριπιδου σωξομδυα απαυτα... Euripidis quae extant omnia. **Cantabrigiae ex officina Johan. Hayes. Impensis Richardi Green Cantab.** 1694. Brs. WE3415.

1694 EURIPIDES. Ευριπιδου σωξομδυα απαντα... Euripidis quae extant omnia. **Cantabrigiae, ex officina J. Hayes, impensis R. Green.** 1694. Fol. WE3416.

1694 MILNER, JOHN. A defence of Arch-Bishop Usher. **Cambridge, by J. Hayes for Benj. Tooke, to be sold by W. Graves in Cambridge.** 1694. 8°. WM2080.

1695 ALMANACS. CULPEPER, NATHANIEL. Culpeper revived. **Cambridge, by John Hayes.** 1695. 8°. WA1515.

1695 ALMANACS. Dove. Speculum anni or an almanack for 1695. **Cambridge by John Hayes.** 1695. 8°. WA1640.

1695 ALMANACS. POND, EDWARD. Pond. An almanack for...1695. **Cambridge, by John Hayes.** 1695. 8°. WA2175.

1695 ALMANACS. SWALLOW, JOHN. Swallow. A new almanack for 1695. **Cambridge, by the printers to the university.** 1695. 8°. WA2459.

1695 ALMANACS. WING. JOHN. Ολυμπια δωματα, or an almanack for...1695. **Cambridge, by John Hayes.** 1695. 8°. WA2786.

1695 CAMBRIDGE UNIVERSITY. Lacrymae Cantabrigienes in obitum...Mariae. **Cantabrigiae, ex officina Johan. Hayes.** 1694/5. 4°. WC342.

1695 CAMBRIDGE UNIVERSITY. Statuta legenda. [**Cantabrigiae.** 1695]. Brs. WC352.

1695 CENSORINUS. De die natali. **Cantabrigiae, ex officina Joh. Hayes, impensis Tho. Dawson, jun.** 1695. 8°. WC1664.

1695 LILY, WILLIAM. A short introduction of grammar. **Cambridge, by John Hayes.** 1695. 8°. WL2301.

1695 PHILLIPS, JOHN. A reflection on our modern poesy. **London: for W. Rogers in London; and F. Hicks in Cambridge.** 1695. Fol. WP2096.

1695 WHITEFOOT, JOHN. A discourse upon I Peter IV. VII...the power...of charity. **Cambridge, by John Hayes.** 1695. **For William Graves, to be sold by Samuel Oliver in Norwich,** 8°. WW1862.

1696 ALMANACS. CULPEPER, NATHANIEL. Culpeper revived. **Cambridge, by John Hayes.** 1696. 8°. WA1516.

1696 ALMANACS. Dove. Speculum anni or an almanack for 1696. **Cambridge by John Hayes.** 1696. 8°. WA1641.

1696 ALMANACS. POND, EDWARD. Pond. An almanack for...1696. **Cambridge, by John Hayes.** 1696. 8°. WA2176.

1696 ALMANACS. SWALLOW, JOHN. Swallow. A new almanack for 1696. **Cambridge, by the printers to the university.** 1696. 8°. WA2460.

1696 ALMANACS. WING, JOHN. Ολυμπια δωματα, or an almanack for...1696. **Cambridge, by John Hayes.** 1696. 8°. WA2787.

1696 BIBLE. ENGLISH. PSALMS. The whole book of psalms. **Cambridge, by John Hayes.** 1696. Fol. WB2600.

1696 BRIGGS, JOSEPH. Catechetical exercises. **Cambridge, by Joh. Hayes, for Edw. Hall. To be sold by Luke Meredith, London.** 1696. 8°. WB4662.

1696 BUSTEED, MICHAEL. Orationes duae funebres. [**Cantabrigiae**], **ex officina Joh. Hayes.** 1696. **Impensis Edm. Jeffery Cantab.** 12°. WB6260.

1696 GURDON, BRAMPTON. Probabile est animam. [**Cambridge**]. 1696. Brs. WG2250.

1696 LITURGIES. BOOK OF COMMON PRAYER. The book of common prayer. **Cambridge.** 1696. Fol. WB3693.

1697 AEsop naturaliz'd. **Cambridge, by John Hayes, for Edward Hall.** 1697. 8°. WA744.

1697 ALMANACS. CULPEPER, NATHANIEL. Culpeper revived. **Cambridge, by John Hayes.** 1697. 8°. WA1517.

1697 ALMANACS. Dove. Speculum anni or an almanack for 1697. **Cambridge, by John Hayes.** 1697. 8°. WA1642.

1697 ALMANACS. POND, EDWARD. Pond. An almanack for...1697. **Cambridge, by John Hayes.** 1697. 8°. WA2177.

1697 ALMANACS. SWALLOW, JOHN. Swallow. A new almanack for 1697. **Cambridge, by the printers to the university.** 1697. 8°. WA2461.

1697 ALMANACS. WING, JOHN. Oλυμπια δωματα, or an almanack for...1697. **Cambridge, by John Hayes.** 1697. 8°. WA2788.

1697 AYLOFFE, WILLIAM. Gulielmus pacifus: sive oratio de pace. **Cantabrigiæ, typis academias.** [1697]. 4°. WA4291.

1697 CAMBRIDGE UNIVERSITY. Gratulatio academiæ Cantabrigiensis de reditu. **Cantabrigiæ, typis academicis.** [1697]. Fol. WC337.

1697 Miscellany poems; with the cure of love. **For Will Rogers: and Fr. Hicks in Cambridge.** 1697. 8°. WM2232A.

1697 Request of the tutors to the vice-chancellor. [**Cambridge**]. 1697. Brs. WR1118.

1698 ALMANACS. CULPEPER, NATHANIEL. Culpeper revived. **Cambridge, by John Hayes.** 1698. 8°. WA1518.

1698 ALMANACS. Dove. Speculum anni or an almanack for 1698. **Cambridge, by John Hayes.** 1698. 8°. WA1643.

1698 ALMANACS. POND, EDWARD. Pond. An almanack for...1698. **Cambridge, by John Hayes.** 1698. 8°. WA2178.

1698 ALMANACS. SWALLOW, JOHN. Swallow. A new almanack for 1698. **Cambridge, by the printers to the university.** 1698. 8°. WA2462.

1698 ALMANACS. WING, JOHN. Oλυμπια δωματα, or an almanack for...1698. **Cambridge, by John Hayes.** 1698. 8°. WA2789.

1698 BARKER, THOMAS. Nassau: a poem. **For Will Rogers, and F. Hicks, in Cambridge.** 1698. Fol. WB787.

1698 BIBLE. ENGLISH. PSALMS. The whole book of psalms. **Cambridge, by Roger Daniel.** 1698. 8°. WB2611.

1698 HUTCHINSON, FRANCIS, bp. A sermon preached ...July iij. 1698. **Cambridge, for Edmund Jeffery.** 1698. 4°. WH3831.

1698 N[EWMAN], S[AMUEL]. An exact concordance. Fourth edition. **Cambridge, by John Hayes: for Awnsham and John Churchill, London.** 1698. Fol. WN928.

1698 NOURSE, PETER. A sermon preached... July iij. 1698. **Cambridge, at the University's printing-house, for Edward Hall, in Cambridge, to be sold by Luke Meredith, in London.** 1698. 4°. WN1415.

1698 OVID. Metamorphoseos. **Cantabrigiæ, ex officina Joann. Hayes.** 1698. 8°. WO683.

1699 ALMANACS. CULPEPER, NATHANIEL. Culpeper revived. **Cambridge, by John Hayes.** 1699. 8°. WA1519.

1699 ALMANACS. Dove. Speculum anni or a almanack for 1699. **Cambridge, by John Hayes.** 1699. 8°. WA1644.

1699 ALMANACS. POND. EDWARD. Pond. An almanack for ...1699. **Cambridge, for John Hayes.** 1699. 8°. WA2179.

1699 ALMANACS. SWALLOW, JOHN. Swallow. A new almanack for 1699. **Cambridge, by the printers to the university.** 1699. 8°. WA2463.

1699 ALMANACS. WING, JOHN. Oλυμπια δωματα, or an almanack for...1699. **Cambridge, by John Hayes.** 1699. 8°. WA2790.

1699 BIBLE. ENGLISH. PSALMS. Some of the psalms of David. **Cambridge.** 1699. 8°. WB2619.

1699 CEBES. The tablet of. **Cambridge, for John Pindar.** 1699. 12°. WC1653A.

1699 CICERO. M.T. Ciceronis orationes quaedam selectae. **Cantabrigiæ, ex officina Johan. Hayes impensis R. Clavell, S. and J. Spring, S. Smith. and B. Walford.** 1699. 8°. WC4316.

1699 EDWARDS, JOHN. The eternal and intrinsick reasons. **Cambridge, at the university press, for Edmund Jeffery,** 1699. 4°. WE204.

1699 HORACE. Opera. **Cantabrigiæ, typis academicis impensis Jacobi Tonson.** 1699. 4°. WH2764.

1699 LEEDES, EDWARD. Methodus Græcam linguam docendi. **Cantabrigiæ, ex officina Johan. Hayes. Impensis Joh. Chamberlayne, Buriensis, et prostant venales apud Pet. Parker, Londini.** 1699. 8°. WL910.

1699 LENG, JOHN. bp. A sermon preach'd...16th day of April 1699. **Cambridge, at the University Press, for R. Clavel, London, and Edmund Jeffery in Cambridge.** 1699. 4°. WL1050.

1699 MARSH, RICHARD. The vanity and danger of modern theories. **Cambridge, at the University press, for Edmund Jeffery, in Cambridge.** 1699. 4°. WM738.

1699 The sceptical muse; or, a paradox. **For R. Basset; sold by Fr. Hicks, in Cambridge.** 1699. Fol. WS847.

1699 WALKER, OBADIAH. Of education especially of young gentlemen. "Sixth" edition. **By H. Gellibrand, for Richard Wellington and are to be sold by Francis Hicks, in Cambridge.** 1699. 12°. WW404A.

1700 ALMANACS. CULPEPER, NATHANIEL. Culpeper revived. **Cambridge, by John Hayes.** 1700. 8°. WA1520.

1700 ALMANACS. Dove. Speculum anni or an almanack for 1700. **Cambridge, by John Hayes.** 1700. 8°. WA1645.

1700 ALMANACS. POND. EDWARD. Pond. An almanack for...1700. **Cambridge, for John Hayes.** 1700. 8°. WA2180.

1700 ALMANACS. SWALLOW, JOHN. A new almanack for 1700. **Cambridge, by the printers to the university.** 1700. 8°. WA2464.

1700 BARKER, THOMAS. A poem, dedicated to the memory of Dr. Joseph Beaumont. **Cambridge, by John Hayes, for Edward Hall.** 1700. 4°. WB788.

1700 [BENNET, THOMAS]. An answer to the dissenters pleas. **Cambridge, at the university press for A. Bosvile.** 1700. 8°. WB1888.

1700 [BENNET, THOMAS]. An answer to the dissenters pleas. **Cambridge, at the university press for Alexander Bosvile.** 1700. 8°. WB1889.

1700 BIBLE. GREEK. Tης χαινης Διαθηχης Απαντα. Novi Testamenti. **Cantabrigiæ. 1700.** 8°. WB2739.

1700 BLACKALL, OFFSPRING. bp. St. Paul and St. James reconcil'd. **Cambridge, at the University Press, for Edmund Jeffery, in Cambridge.** 1700. 4°. WB3050.

1700 CAMBRIDGE UNIVERSITY. Threnodia academiae Cantabrigiensis. **Cantabrigiæ, typis academicis.** 1700. 12°. WC357.

1700 COBB, SAMUEL. Poetæ Britannici. A poem. **For A. Roper and R. Basset, sold by Mr. Jeffries in Cambridge.** 1700. Fol. WC4773.

1700 DILLINGHAM, WILLIAM. Vita Laurentii Chaderton. **Cantabrigiæ, typis academicis.** 1700. 8°. WD1488.

1700 EDWARDS, JOHN. Concio et determinatio. **Cantabrigiæ, typis academicis, impensis Edmundi Jeffery.** 1700. 8°. WE200.

1700 EDWARDS, JOHN. The eternal and intrinsick reasons. **Cambridge, for E. Jeffery.** 1700. 8°. WE205.

1700 GASKARTH, JOHN. A description of the unregenerate. **Cambridge, at the University Press, for Edmund Jeffery.** 1700. 4°. WG286.

1700 GASKARTH, JOHN. Insanientis sapientiae. **Cantabrigiæ, typis academicis, impensis Edmundi Jeffery.** 1700. 4°. WG287.

1700 HARE, FRANCIS. A sermon preach'd... January the 6th. **Cambridge, at the University Press, for Edmund Jeffery.** 1700. 4°. WH757.

1700 LE CLERC, JEAN. Joan. Clerici Physica. **Cantabrigiæ, typis academicis, sumtibus Timothei Child, & Roberti Knaplock, Londoni.** 1700. 12°. WL824.

1700 NEWTON, Sir ISAAC. Tables for renewing. Second edition. **Cambridge, by John Hayes, to be sold by Ed. Hall.** 1700. 8°. WN1051.

1700 PHILIPS, AMBROSE. The life of John Williams. **Cambridge, at the University Press, for A. Bosvile.** 1700. 8°. WP2025.

1700 Poetae minores Graeci. **Cantabrigiæ, ex officina Joan. Hayes.** 1700. Impensis A. & J. Churchill, Lond. 12°. WP2735.

CAMPBELTOWN

1685 ARGYLE, ARCHIBALD CAMPBELL, 9th earl. The declaration and apology of the Protestant people. **Reprinted at Campbell-toun, in Kintyre, in the Shire of Argyle.** [1685]. 4°. WA3677.

CANTERBURY

1549 BIBLE. ENGLISH. PSALMS. PROSE VERSIONS. The psalter poynted. **Cantorbury, J. Mychell,** 1549. 4°. STC2380.

1549 GREGORY I, Saint. Here after foloweth the lyfe of Saynt Gregoryes mother. [**Canterbury.**] **J. Mychell.** [1549?]. STC12353.

1550 BIBLE. ENGLISH. PSALMS. PROSE VERSIONS. The psalter poynted. **Cantorbury, J. Mychell.** 1550. 4°. STC2380A.

1550 HURLESTONE, RANDALL. Newes from Rome concerning the papisticall Masse. **Cantorbury, J. Mychell for E. Campion.** [1550?]. 8°. STC14006.

1550 LAMBERT, JOHN. Minister of Elham. Of predestinacion & election. **Cātorbury, J. Mychell.** [1550?]. 8°. STC15181.

1550 LITURGIES. HOURS AND PRIMERS. Salisbury and General. [The primer in English and Latin.] **Canterbury, J. Mychell** [1550?]. STC16052.

1550 LYDGATE, JOHN. The churle and the byrde. **Canterbury, J. Mychel.** [1550?]. 4°. STC 17013.

1550 RIDLEY, LANCELOT. An exposytion in Englyshe vpon the epistyll to the Phillipiās. **Cantorbury, J. Mychell.** [1550?]. 8°. STC21040.

1550 RIDLEY, LANCELOT. An exposytion in Englyshe vpon the epistyll to the Philippiās. **Cantorbury, J. Mychyll for E. whitchurche.** [1550?]. STC21041.

?1550 SALTWOOD, ROBERT. A comparyson bytwene iiij. byrdes, the larke, the nyghtyngale, ỹ thrusshe & the cucko. [**Canterbury**], **J. Mychel.** [n. d.]. 4°. STC21647.

1551 A breuiat cronicle contaynynge all the kinges from brute to this daye. **Cantorbury, J. Mychell.** [1551]. 8°. STC9968.

1552 A breuiat cronicle contaynynge all the kinges from brute to this daye. **Canterbury, J. Mychell.** [1552]. 8°. STC9969.

1553 A breuiat cronicle contaynynge all the kinges from brute to this daye. **Cāterbury, J. Mychel.** 1553. 8°. STC9970.

1556 ENGLAND, CHURCH OF. Visitation Articles. Canterbury. M. V. C. LVI. [**Canterbury, J. Michel?**]. 1556. 4°. STC10149.

1556 ENGLAND, CHURCH OF. Visitation Articles. Canterbury. MDCLVI. [**Canterbury, J. Michel?** 1556]. 4°. STC10150.

1687 Cynthia: with the tragicall account. **By R. Holt for T. Passinger, and R. Fenner, in Canterbury.** 1687. 8°. WC7710A.

1690 A short account of the mineral waters lately found out in the city of Canterbury. [**Canterbury 1690?**] 4°. WS3541.

1692 DAVIS, RICHARD. Truth and innocency vindicated. **For Nath. and Robert Ponder, to be sold by Randal Taylor, by Mr. Coolidge at Cambridge, Mr. Prior at Colchester, Mr. Noble at St. Edmund's Bury. Mr. Haworth at Ipswich, Northampton, Wellingborow, Kettering, Oundle, Harborow, Litterworth, Upingham, Bedford, Kimbolton and Canterbury.** [1692?] 4°. WD435.

CARLISLE

1656 [GILPIN, RICHARD]. The agreement of the associated ministers...Cumberland. **By T. L. for Simon VVaterson, & are sold by Richard Scott in Carlisle.** 1656. 4°. WG774.

1658 GILPIN, RICHARD. The temple re-built. **By E. T. for Luke Fawne, to be sold by Richard Scott, in Carlisle.** 1658. 4°. WG778.

1658 POLWHEILE, THEOPHILUS. Αυθεντης; or a treatise. **London, for Thomas Johnson and are to be sold by Richard Scott in Carlisle.** 1658. 8°. WO2782.

CHELMSFORD

1680 A full and true relation of all the proceedings at the Assizes holden at Chelmsford. [**Chelmsford? 1680**]. Fol. WF2316.

CHESTER

1681 DELAMERE, HENRY BOOTH, earl of. The speech of... March 2, 1680/1. **For John Minshall in Chester, and are to be sold by Langley Curtis.** 1681. Fol. WD881.

1682 ALLEN, JOHN, of Trinity College, Cambridge. Of perjury. A sermon. **For Benj. Tooke, and George Atkinson, in Chester.** 1682. 4°. WA1034.

1682 OLIVER, JOHN. The last judgment. **London, for John Minshull, to be sold at his shop in Chester, and Ric. Chiswell.** 1682. 4°. WO275.

1688 HOLME, RANDLE. The academy of armory. **Chester, for the author.** 1688. Fol. WH2513.

CIRENCESTER

1681 CHARLES II, king of England. Aurea dicta. The king's gracious words. **By J. Grantham, for Walter Davis, and are to be sold by John Barksdale, in Cirencester.** 1681. 4°. WC2929.

1682 Epigrammata sacra selecta. **For John Barksdale — in Cirencester.** 1682. 8°. WE3157.

1700 HILTON, THOMAS. A funeral sermon occasion'd by the death of John Barksdale. **For J. Nutt and J. Barksdale, in Cirencester.** 1700. 4°. WH2041.

COGGESHALL

1697 FENN, MATTHEW. A few lines touching baptism. **For Matthew Fenn at Coggshall.** 1697. 8°. WF677.

COLCHESTER

1648 A choak-peare for the Parliament. **Printed at Colechester.** 1648. 4°. WC3921.

1692 DAVIS, RICHARD. Truth and innocency vindicated. **For Nath. and Robert Ponder, to be sold by Randal Taylor, by Mr. Coolidge at Cambridge, Mr. Prior at Colchester, Mr. Noble at St. Edmund's Bury, Mr. Haworth at Ipswich, Northampton, Wellingborow, Kettering, Oundle, Harborow, Litterworth, Upingham, Bedford, Kimbolton and Canterbury.** [1692?]. 4°. WD435.

CORK

1648 A continuation of the narrative; being. **By P. Cole, Corck, reprinted.** 1648. 4°. WC5968.

1648 ORMONDE, JAMES BUTLER, duke of. The declaration of. **Printed at Corke, and now reprinted.** 1648. 4°. WO442.

1649 Εμκων βασιλικη. The pourtraicture of His Sacred Maiesty. **Corck, by Peter de Pienne.** 1649. 12°. WE291.

1649 IRELAND. Whereas I am informed... 8, Decemember 1649. **Cork.** 1649. Brs. WI812.

1649 O'NEILL, OWEN. The propositions of. **Printed at Corck.** 1649. 4°. WO340.

1649 You are forthwith, on receipt hereof, to prepare an accompt. **Printed at Corcke.** 1649. Brs. WY52.

1650 CROMWELL, OLIVER. A letter from the Lord Generall Cromvvell to the Parliament of England. **Printed at Corcke.** 1650. 4°. WC7104.

1657 The agreement and resolution of severall associated ministers in... Corke. **Corke,** 1657. 4°. WA768.

1660 DAUNCEY, JOHN. The history of His sacred Majesty Charles the II. **Cork, reprinted by William Smith.** 1660. 12°. WD292.

1675 MERCER, WILLIAM. The moderate cavalier. **[Cork?] printed.** 1675. 4°. WM1739.

1691 WETENHALL, EDWARD, bp. Pastoral admonitions. **Cork, by John Brent, for David Jones.** 1691. 4°. WW1508.

COVENTRY

1589 PENRY, JOHN. A viewe of some part of such publike wants as are in the seruice of God within Wales. **[Coventry? 1589].** 8°. STC19613.

1589 MARPRELATE, MARTIN, pseud. Certaine minerall and metaphisicall school points to be defended by the reuerende bishops, etc. **[Coventry, 20 fb. 1589].** Brs. STC17455.

1589 MARPRELATE, MARTIN, pseud. Hay any worke for Cooper or a brief epistle directed to the reuerende Byshopps. **[Coventry, R. Waldegrave. march 1589].** 4°. STC17456.

1669 GREW, OBADIAH. The Lord Jesus Christ. **For John Brooke in Coventry.** 1669. 12°. WG1963.

DAVENTRY

1693 P[ALMER], C[HARLES]. The danger of a total and wilful neglect. **By J. A. for Tho. Parkhurst, to be sold by Obed. Smith at Daventry.** 1693. 8°. WP221.

DEVIZES

1697 PIERCE, ROBERT. Bath memoirs. **Bristol, for H. Hammond at Bath, and the Dowzes.** 1697. 8°. WP2163.

DORCHESTER

1660 USSHER, JAMES, abp. Eighteen sermons preached in Oxford 1640. **By S. Griffin, for Will. Churchill in Dorchester.** 1660. 4°. WU173.

1663 GLOVER, HENRY. An exhortation to prayer for Jerusalems peace. **By E. Cotes for William Church-hill, in Dorchester.** 1663. 4°. WG890.

1680 REYNER, SAMUEL. A sermon preached at the funeral of the Right Honourable Denzell Lord Holles. **London, for William Churchill, in Dorchester.** 1680. 4°. WR1233.

1687 H., S. A second guide to heaven. **For A. Churchill, and sold by W. Churchill, in Dorset.** 1687. 8°. WH124.

1688 H., S. The godly man's enquiry. **For W. Churchill, in Dorset.** 1688. 8°. WH118.

DUBLIN

1551 LITURGIES. BOOK OF COMMON PRAYER. The Boke of the common praier, after the vse of the Churche of England. **Dubliniae, in off. H. Poweli.** 1551. Fol. STC16277.

1561 IRELAND. A proclamacyon set fourth by the Erle of Sussex, etc. [Against Shan Onell. 8 June 1561]. **Dublyn, H. Powell.** [1561]. Fol. STC14138.

1564 IRELAND. A proclamacyon, sett furthe by the Lorde Iustice and Counsell. [Outlawry of rebels, 16 Aug. 1564]. **Dublin, H. Powell.** 1564. Fol. STC14139.

1566 IRELAND, CHURCH OF. A brefe declaration of certein articles of religion. **Dublin, H. Powel.** 1566. 4°. STC14259.

1571 O'KEARNEY, JOHN. Aibidil Gaoidheilge & Caiticiosma. **Dublin, J. Usher.** 1571. 8°. STC18793.

1595 IRELAND. The Queenes Maiesties proclamation against the Earle of Tirone, etc. [12 June 1595]. **Dublin, W. Kearney.** 1595. Fol. STC14145.

1595 IRELAND. The Queenes Maiesties proclamation against the Earle of Tirone, etc. [In Irish]. **Dublin, W. Kearney.** 1595. Fol. STC14145A.

1600 IRELAND. By the L. Deputie. [Offering a reward for Hugh O'Neale. 22 Nov. 1600] **Dublin, J. Francke.** 1600. Brs. STC14147.

1602 BIBLE. NEW TESTAMENT. IRISH. Tiomna nuadh ar d Tighearna agus ar slanaightheora Iosa Criosd. [Tr.] Huilliam O Domhnuill. [**Dublin**], **Seón Francke.** [**J. Franckton**]. 1602. Fol. STC2958.

1603 IRELAND. By the Lord Deputie. [Against traffic with Spain. 10 Mar. 1603]. **Dublin, J. Franckton.** 1602. [1603]. Brs. STC14150.

1603 IRELAND. By the Lord Deputie. [Fixing a new standard of silver coin. 11 Oct.1603]. **Dublin, J. Franckton.** 1603. Brs. STC14151.

1605 IRELAND. By the Lord Deputie. [Revoking commissions of martial law. 20 Feb.1605]. **Dublin, J. Franckton.** 1604. [1605]. Brs. STC14152.

1605 IRELAND. By the Lord Deputie. [Concerning the carrying of arms. 20 Feb.1605]. **Dublin, J. Franckton.** 1604. [1605]. Brs. STC14153.

1605 IRELAND. By the Lord Deputie. [Pardon for offences before the King's accession. 11 Mar. 1605]. **Dublin, J. Franckton.** 1604. [1605]. Fol. STC14154.

1605 IRELAND. By the King. [For uniformity in religion. 4 July 1605]. **Dublin, J. Franckton.** 1605. Fol. STC14155.

1606 IRELAND. By the Lord Deputie. [Against importation of arms, etc. 10 Mar.1606]. **Dublin, J. Franckton.** 1605. [1606]. Fol. STC14156.

1606 IRELAND. By the Lord Deputie. [Abolishing the term 'sterling'. 11 Nov.1606]. **Dublin, J. Franckton.** 1606. Brs. STC14158.

1607 IRELAND. By the Lord Deputie. [Concerning the lands of Tyrone and Tyrconnell. 9 Nov. 1607]. **Dublin, J. Franckton.** 1607. Brs. STC14159.

1607 IRELAND. By the Lord Deputie. [Against Lord Delvin. 23 Nov.1607]. **Dublin, J. Franckton.** 1607. Brs. STC14160.

1608 O'DOGHERTY, Sir CAHIR. The overthrow of an Irish rebell. On the death of Sir C. Odoughertie. **Dublin, J. Franckton, London for J. Wright.** 1608. 4°. STC18786.

1609 IRELAND. By the Lord Deputie. [Continuing the commission for surrendering lands in Tanistry, etc. 19 June, 1609]. **Dublin, J. Frankton.** [1609]. Brs. STC14162.

1611 IRELAND. By the Lord Deputy. [Republishing the proclamation of 4 July 1605. 13 July 1611]. **Dublin, J. Franckton.** [1611]. Fol. STC14163.

1612 IRELAND. A proclamation set forth by Sir J. Carroll. [Enforcing certain laws. 31 Oct.1612]. **Dublin, J. Franckton.** 1612. Fol. STC14164.

1614 IRELAND. A proclamation set forth by Sir J. Carroll. [Fixing wages. 3 Feb. 1614]. **Dublin, J. Franckton.** 1613. [1614]. Fol. STC14165.

1618 IRELAND. By the Lord Deputie. [Against usury. 3 Oct.1618]. **Dublin, F. Kingston.** 1618. Brs. STC14170.

1618 IRELAND. By the Lord Deputie. [Expelling Irish from Ulster plantations. 1 Oct.1618]. **Dublin, F. Kingston.** 1618. Brs. STC14169.

1618 IRELAND. By the Lord Deputie. [For registering births, deaths, and marriages. 25 Apr. 1618]. **Dublin, J. Franckton.** 1618. Fol. STC14168.

1619 IRELAND. By the Lord Deputie. [Against importation of arms, etc. 20 Mar.1619]. **Dublin, F. Kyngston.** 1619. Fol. STC14172.

1620 HAMPTON, CHRISTOPHER. A sermon preached before the Kings Maiestie, in the church of Beauly. (An addition etc.) **Dublin, Society of Stationers.** 1620. 2 vols. 4°. STC12738.

1620 IRELAND. By the Lord Deputie. [Patent to F. Kingston, and T. Downes. 15 July 1620]. **Dublin, Company of Stationers.** 1620. Brs. STC14173.

1621 IRELAND. By the Lord Deputie; concerning alehouses, [3 Mar.1621]. **Dublin, Company of Stationers.** 1620. [1621]. Fol. STC14174.

1622 IRELAND. By the Lord Deputie; against transportation of corne. [23 Nov.1622]. **Dublin, Company of Stationers.** 1622. Brs. STC14181.

1622 IRELAND. By the Lord Deputie; for farthing tokens. [28 Sept.1622]. **Dublin, Company of Stationers.** 1622. Fol. STC14180.

1622 IRELAND. By the Lord Deputie; for the banishment of Scottish-men. [21 Sept.1622]. **Dublin, Company of Stationers.** 1622. Brs. STC14179.

1622 IRELAND. By the Lords Justices; concerning the commissioners proceedings. [27 July 1622]. **Dublin, Company of Stationers.** 1622. Brs. STC14176.

1622 IRELAND. By the Lords Justices; concerning the late plantations. [24 Aug.1622]. **Dublin, Company of Stationers.** 1622. Brs. STC14177.

1622 IRELAND. By the Lords Justices; concerning the payment of his Majest. revennue. [5 Sept. 1622]. **Dublin, Company of Stationers.** 1622. Brs. STC14178.

1622 IRELAND. His Maiesties directions for the courts of justice within Ireland. **Dublin, Society of Stationers.** 1622. 4°. STC14134.

1623 IRELAND. By the Lord Deputy; for prevention of dearth of corne. [18 Apr.1623]. **Dublin, Company of Stationers.** 1623. Brs. STC14182.

1623 IRELAND. By the Lord Deputie; concerning iron ordinance. [19 July 1623]. **Dublin, Company of Stationers.** 1623. Brs. STC14183.

1624 IRELAND. By the Lord Deputie. [Against unlicensed importation of arms. 5 Apr.1624]. **Dublin, Society of Stationers.** 1624. Brs. STC14190.

1624 IRELAND. By the Lord Deputie; concerning the officers of the Custome-house. [27 Feb. 1624]. **Dublin, Company of Stationers.** 1623. [1624]. Brs. STC14188.

1624 IRELAND. By the Lord Deputie; concerning the planters in Ulster. [21 Jan.1624]. **Dublin, Company of Stationers.** 1623. [1624]. Brs. STC14186.

1624 IRELAND. By the Lord Deputie; for the banishment of Jesuites and priests. [21 Jan. 1624]. **Dublin, Society of Stationers.** 1623. [1624]. Brs. STC14185.

1624 IRELAND. By the Lord Deputie; prohibiting sale of cattell out of faires or markets. [26 Feb. 1624]. **Dublin, Company of Stationers.** 1623. [1624]. Brs. STC14187.

1624 IRELAND. By the Lord Deputie; prohibiting the use of logwood. [13 Jan.1624]. **Dublin, Company of Stationers.** 1623. [1624]. Brs. STC14184.

1624 IRELAND. By the Lord Deputie; touching weights and measures. [1 Mar.1624]. **Dublin, Company of Stationers.** 1623. [1624]. Brs. STC14189.

1624 IRELAND. By the Lord Deputie; tythes, offrings, etc. to be taken in Ulster. [6 July 1624]. **Dublin, Society of Stationers.** 1624. Brs. STC14191.

1624 USHER, JAMES, abp. An answer to a challenge made by a Jesuite in Ireland. **Dublin, Society of Stationers.** 1624. 4°. STC24542.

1625 IRELAND. By the King; for the due administration of justice. [7 Nov.1625]. **Dublin, Society of Stationers.** 1625. Brs. STC.14203.

1625 IRELAND. By the Lord Deputy. [Accession of Charles I, 10 Apr.1625]. **Dublin, Society of Stationers.** 1625. Brs. STC14191A.

1625 IRELAND. By the Lord Deputie; an act of State touching beggers, etc. [24 Aug.1625]. **Dublin, Society of Stationers.** 1625. Fol. STC14201.

1625 IRELAND. By the Lord Deputie. [Against keeping markets on the sabbath. 23 July 1625]. **Dublin, Society of Stationers.** 1625. Brs. STC14197.

1625 IRELAND. By the Lord Deputie. [Against unlicensed importation of arms. 25 June 1625]. **Dublin, Company of Stationers.** 1625. Brs. STC.14195.

1625 IRELAND. By the Lord Deputy; all men being in office shall continue etc. [10 Apr.1625]. **Dublin, Society of Stationers.** 1625. Brs. STC14193.

1625 IRELAND. By the Lord Deputie. [For issue of warrants for gunpowder. 9 July 1625]. **Dublin, Company of Stationers.** 1625. Brs. STC14196.

1625 IRELAND. By the Lord Deputy. [The King's proclamation to his people. 10 Apr.1625]. **Dublin, Society of Stationers.** 1625. Brs. STC14192.

1625 IRELAND. By the Lord Deputie. [Quarantine orders, 4 Aug.1625]. **Dublin, Company of Stationers.** 1625. Fol. STC14198.

1625 IRELAND. By the Lord Deputie; for the banishing of idle persons. [22 Aug.1625]. **Dublin, Company of Stationers.** 1625. Brs. STC14199.

1625 IRELAND. By the Lord Deputie; for publike fasting, etc. [13 Oct.1625]. **Dublin, Society of Stationers.** 1625. Brs. STC14202.

1625 IRELAND. By the Lord Deputie; forbidding drovers to drive cattle by night. [22 Aug.1625]. **Dublin, Company of Stationers.** 1625. Brs. STC14200.

1625 IRELAND. Lawes and orders of warre. [11 June 1625]. **Dublin, Society of Stationers.** 1625. Fol. STC14194.

1625 JEROME, STEPHEN. Englands iubilee, or Irelands ioyes io-pæan, for King Charles his welcome. **Dublin, Society of Stationers.** 1625. 4°. STC14509.

1626 ENGLAND. By the King. that ships carying corne for Spain be lawfull prize. [31 Dec.1625]. **Dublin, Society of Stationers.** 1625 [1626]. Fol. STC8814.

1626 IRELAND. By the Lord Deputie; against the transportation of cattle. [23 Sept.1626]. **Dublin, Society of Stationers.** 1626. Brs. STC14206.

1626 IRELAND. By the Lord Deputie; concerning the obstinate returning of the transplanted Irish Septs. [30 Sept.1626]. **Dublin, Society of Stationers.** 1626. Brs. STC14207.

1626 IRELAND. By the Lord Deputie; concerning the payment of his Maiesties revenues, etc. [20 July 1626]. **Dublin, Society of Stationers.** 1626. Brs. STC14205.

1626 IRELAND. By the Lord Deputie; to forbid trade within the dominions of the King of Spaine. [9 Jan.1626]. **Dublin, Society of Stationers.** 1625. [1626]. Brs. STC14204.

1627 IRELAND. By the Lord Deputie; a stay of the transportation of cattle. [1 Sept.1627]. **Dublin, Society of Stationers.** 1627. Brs. STC14209.

1627 IRELAND. By the Lord Deputie. [Renewing grants of Ulster Undertakers. 13 Dec.1627]. **Dublin, Society of Stationers.** 1627. Brs. STC14210.

1628 IRELAND. By the Lord Deputie; for reformation of abuses in weights and measures. [5 Feb. 1628]. **Dublin, Society of Stationers.** 1627. [1628]. Fol. STC14211.

1629 IRELAND. By the Lord Deputy. [Against Roman jurisdiction. 1 Apr.1629]. **Dublin, Society of Stationers.** 1629. Brs. STC14215.

1629 IRELAND. By the Lord Deputy. [Concerning heralds' fees at funerals. 4 Aug.1627]. **Dublin Society of Stationers.** 1629. Brs. STC14208.

1629 IRELAND. By the Lords Justices. [Soldiers not to collect assignments. 23 Nov.1629]. **Dublin, Society of Stationers.** 1629. Brs. STC14216.

1629 IRELAND, CHURCH OF. Articles of religion agreed upon in the convocation. **For the Company of Stationers of the Irish Stocke.** 1629. 4°. STC14263.

1630 C., T. A short discourse of the New-Foundland. **Dublin, Society of Stationers.** 1630. 4°. STC4311.

1630 IRELAND. By the Lords Justices; concerning dying woods. [20 May 1630]. **Dublin, Society of Stationers.** 1630. Brs. STC14218.

1630 IRELAND. By the Lords Justices; instructions to be observed by the sheriffes. [13 Jan.1630]. **Dublin, Society of Stationers.** 1629. [1630]. Brs. STC14217.

1630 IRELAND. By the Lords Justices. [Revenues to be paid at fixed places. 30 June 1630]. **Dublin, Society of Stationers.** 1630. Brs. STC14219.

1631 IRELAND. By the Lords Justices. [Against unauthorized fasts and festivals. 21 July 1631]. **Dublin, Society of Stationers.** 1631. Brs. STC14223.

1631 IRELAND. By the Lords Justices. [Concerning the monopoly of starch. 21 May 1631]. **Dublin, Society of Stationers.** 1631. Fol. STC14222.

1631 USSHER, JAMES, abp. Gotteschalci, et praedestinatianae controversiae ab eo motae historia. **Dublinii, ex typ.Soc. Bibliopolarum.** 1631. 4°. STC24550.

1632 IRELAND. By the Lords Justices. [Concerning licenses of alehouses, etc. 4 Feb.1632]. **Dublin, Society of Stationers.** 1631. [1632]. Fol. STC14224.

1632 IRELAND. By the Lords Justices. [Continuing impost on wine. 24 Feb.1632]. **Dublin, Society of Stationers.** 1631. [1632]. Brs. STC14225.

1632 IRELAND. By the Lords Justices; to confirm defective titles. [21 July 1632]. **Dublin, Society of Stationers.** 1632. Brs. STC14227.

1632 IRELAND. By the Lords Justices; upon the new Booke of Rates. [20 Apr. 1632]. **Dublin, Society of Stationers.** 1632. Fol. STC14226.

1633 HARRIS, PAUL. The excommunication published by the Archbp. of Dublin against the inhabitants of Dublin, proved of no validity. Second edition. [**Dublin?**] 1633. 4°. STC12810.

1633 IRELAND. By the Lord Deputy; concerning the payments of 12 pence in the pound of all merchandizes, etc. [17 Dec.1633]. **Dublin, Society of Stationers.** 1633. Brs. STC14231.

1633 SYMS, CHRISTOPHER. An apology for C. Syms and his way and method of teaching. **Dublin, [Society of Stationers].** 1633. 4°. STC23596.

1633 WARE, Sir JAMES. Two histories of Ireland, etc. [A view of the state of Ireland]. **Dublin, Society of Stationers.** 1633. 2 vols. Fol. STC25067.

1634 IRELAND. By the Lord Deputy; concerning coales. [16 Jan.1634]. **Dublin, Society of Stationers.** 1633. [1634]. Brs. STC14233.

1634 IRELAND. By the Lord Deputy. [Concerning heralds' fees at funerals. 4 Aug.1627]. **Dublin, Society of Stationers.** 1634. Brs. STC14208A.

1634 IRELAND. By the Lord Generall; instructions to be observed by officers of musters. [13 Mar. 1634]. **Dublin, Society of Stationers.** 1633. [1634]. Fol. STC14234.

1635 IRELAND, CHURCH OF. Constitutions and canons ecclesiastical. 1634. **Dublin, A. Crook and S. Helsham, sold by S. Helsham.** [1635?] 4°. STC14264.

1636 IRELAND. By the Lord Deputy. [Concerning heralds' fees at funerals. 4 Aug.1627]. **Dublin, Society of Stationers.** 1636. Brs. STC14208B.

1637 IRELAND. By the Lord Deputy; concerning licences for selling wine, etc. [31 Dec.1637]. **Dublin, Society of Stationers.** 1637. Brs. STC14244.

1637 IRELAND. By the Lord Deputy. [For proving titles to lands. 31 Oct.1637]. **Dublin, Society of Stationers.** 1637. Brs. STC14243.

1638 IRELAND. By the Lord Deputy; concerning linnen yarne. [22 Feb.1638]. **Dublin, Society of Stationers.** 1637. [1638]. Brs. STC14246.

1638 IRELAND. By the Lord Deputy; prohibiting the importation of allome. [20 Dec.1638]. **Dublin, Society of Stationers.** 1638. Fol. STC14249.

1638 IRELAND. By the Lord Deputy; concerning the importation of tobaccoe. [9 Jan.1638]. **Dublin, Society of Stationers.** 1637. [1638]. Brs. STC14245.

1638 IRELAND. By the Lord Deputy; concerning the sealing of tobaccoe. [23 Feb.1638]. **Dublin, Society of Stationers.** 1637. [1638]. Brs. STC14247.

1638 IRELAND. By the Lord Deputy; to preventing the defrauding of his Majesties customes. [16 Oct.1638]. **Dublin, Society of Stationers.** 1638. Fol. STC14248.

1638 IRELAND. By the Lord Deputy; touching times for passing of patents for defective titles. [20 Dec.1638]. **Dublin, Society of Stationers.** 1638. Brs. STC14250.

1638 SHIRLEY, JAMES. The royall master. **T. Cotes, sold by T. Allott and E. Crooke in Dublin.** 1638. 4°. STC22454A.

1639 USHER, JAMES, abp. Britannicarum ecclesiarum antiquitates. **Dublinii, ex off. typ. Soc. Bibliopolarum.** 1639. 4°. STC24548A.

1640 INCE, WILLIAM. Lot's little one: or meditations on Gen. 19. vers. 20. **J. R[aworth], London, for J. Crook and R. Sergier in Dublin.** 1640. 12°. STC14073.

1640 IRELAND, CHURCH OF. [Visitation articles]. Dublin — Province. **Dublin, Society of Stationers.** 1640. 4°. STC14266.

1640 SHIRLEY, JAMES. The opportunitie. A comedy. **Dublin, for A. Crooke.** 1640. 4°. STC22452.

1641 IRELAND. These are to make knowne ... 23 October 1641. **Dublin, Society of Stationers.** 1641. Brs. WI653.

1641 IRELAND. Whereas a petition hath ... 29 October 1641. **Dublin, Society of Stationers.** 1641. Brs. WI703.

1641 IRELAND. Whereas by the frequent concourse... 28 December 1641. **Dublin.** 1641. Brs. WI 759.

1641 CHARLES I, king of England. A proclamation containing and declaring. **Dublin, Society of Stationers.** 1641. Fol. WC2570.

1641 ENGLAND. PARLIAMENT. An order of the Lords and Commons ... concerning Ireland. **Dublin.** 12 November, 1641. Brs. WE1703.

1641 IRELAND. By the Lords, Justices, and Councell. Will. Parsons. Jo. Borlase. Whereas. **Imprinted at Dublin by the Society of Stationers.** [1641]. Brs. W1345.

1641 IRELAND. A proclamation for a publique fast ... 27 November 1641. [**Dublin.** 1641]. Brs. WI613.

1641 IRELAND. A proclamation for assembling of both Houses. **Dublin.** 1641. Brs. WI621.

1641 IRELAND. A proclamation for sewring mens estates. **Dublin, Society of Stationers.** 1641. WI626.

1641 IRELAND. A proclamation for the disbanding of the New Irish Army. **Dublin, Society of Stationers.** 1641. Brs. WI627.

1641 IRELAND. A proclamation for the further adjournment. **Dublin, Society of Stationers.** 1641. Fol. WI630.

1641 IRELAND. A proclamation for the immediate fortifying. **Dublin.** 1641. Brs. WI631.

1641 IRELAND. A proclamation for the prorogation of the Parliament. **Dublin, Society of Stationers.** 1641. Brs. WI633.

1641 IRELAND. A proclamation for the prorogation of the Parliament. 27 December 1641. **Dublin.** 1641. Brs. WI634.

1641 IRELAND. The protestation and declaration of the Lords. **Dublin.** 1641. Brs. WI642.

1641 IRELAND. These are to make knowne ... 23 October 1641. **Dublin, Society of Stationers.** 1641. Brs. WI653.

1641 IRELAND. Whereas a petition hath ... 29 October 1641. **Dublin, Society of Stationers.** 1641. Brs. WI703.

1641 IRELAND. Whereas by the frequent concourse ... 28 December 1641. **Dublin.** 1641. Brs. WI759.

1641 IRELAND. Whereas sundrie persons have ... 16 November 1641. **[Dublin.** 1641]. Brs. WI887.

1641 IRELAND. Whereas the present condition ... 16 November 1641. **Dublin.** 1641. Brs. WI930.

1641 IRELAND. Whereas we ... have issued ... 1 November 1641. **Dublin, Society of Stationers.** 1641. Brs. WI989.

1641 IRELAND. Whereas we ... have lately found ... 30 October 1641. **Dublin, Society of Stationers.** 1641. Brs. WI990.

1641 ORMONDE, JAMES BUTLER, duke of. Lawes and orders of warre. **Dublin, by the Society of Stationers.** 1641. 4°. WO447.

1642 IRELAND. Although by proclamation ... 15 January 1641 [2]. **Dublin** 1641 [2]. Brs. WI333.

1642 IRELAND. Forasmuch as Almighty God ... 30 April 1642. **Dublin, 1642.** Brs. WI395.

1642 IRELAND. It is well known to all men ... 8 February 1641 [2]. **Dublin** 1641 [2]. Fol. WI422.

1642 IRELAND. We doe hereby in His ... 18 January 1641 [2]. **Dublin.** 1641 [2]. Brs. WI677.

1642 IRELAND. Whereas by severall warrants ... 31 December 1642. **Dublin, by W. Bladen.** 1642. Brs. WI751.

1642 IRELAND. Whereas for speciall reasons of state ... 10 June 1642. **Dublin, by William Bladen.** 1642. Fol. WI777.

1642 IRELAND. Whereas His Maistie is at ... 18 November 1642. **[Dublin.** 1642]. Brs. WI804.

1642 IRELAND. Whereas in the beginning of ... 19 August 1642. **Dublin, by W. Bladen.** 1642. Brs. WI828.

1642 IRELAND. Whereas it is observed ... 14 January 1641 [2]. **[Dublin.** 1642]. Brs. WI844.

1642 IRELAND. Whereas it is observed that ... 21 June 1642. **Dublin, by W. Bladen.** 1642. Brs. WI845.

1642 IRELAND. Whereas many malignant ... 14 October 1642. **[Dublin.** 1642]. Brs. WI849.

1642 The propositions made by the citie of London. **Dublin** [1642]. 4°. WP3791.

1643 CHARLES I, king of England. A proclamation concerning a cessation of armes. **Dublin.** 1643. WC2559.

1643 IRELAND. By the Lords, Iustices and Councell. **Imprinted at Dublin by William Bladen.** 1643. Fol. WI347.

1643 IRELAND. A proclamation concerning a cessation of armes. **Printed at Dublin by William Bladen.** 1643. 4°. WI604.

1643 IRELAND. We doe by this proclamation ... 29 May 1643. **Dublin, by W. Bladen.** 1643. Brs. WI672.

1643 IRELAND. We doe by this proclamation ... 2 August 1643. **Dublin, by W. Bladen.** 1643. Brs. WI673.

1643 IRELAND. We ... having received His Majesties ... 8 July 1643. **Dublin, by W. Bladen.** 1643. Fol. WI681.

1643 IRELAND. We ... having taken into consideration ... 1 April 1643. **Dublin, by W. Bladen.** 1643. Brs. WI682.

1643 IRELAND. We having taken into our ... 24 June 1643. **Dublin, by W. Bladen.** 1643. Fol. WI683.

1643 IRELAND. We having taken into our serious ... 19 August 1643. **Dublin, by W. Bladen.** 1643. Fol. WI684.

1643 IRELAND. We having taken into our serious ... 19 August 1643. **Dublin, by W. Bladen.** 1643. Fol. WI685.

1643 IRELAND. We having taken into our serious ... 19 August 1643. **Dublin, by W. Bladen.** 1643. Brs. WI686.

1643 IRELAND. We the Lords Iustices and Councell ... 9 February 1642 [3]. **Dublin, by W. Bladen.** 1642/3. Brs. WI696.

1643 IRELAND. Whereas by proclamation ... 6 March 1642 [3]. **Dublin, by W. Bladen.** 1642 [3]. Brs. WI741.

1643 IRELAND. Whereas the persons to ... 10 February 1642 [3]. **Dublin, by W. Bladen.** 1642 [3]. Brs. WI929.

1643 IRELAND. Whereas we the Lords Justices ... 14 January 1642 [3]. **Dublin, by W. Bladen.** 1642/3. Brs. WI1009.

1644 IRELAND. The copy of a letter written by direction of the Lords ... 18 April 1644. **[Dublin.** 1644.] Brs. WI359.

1644 IRELAND. For speciall reasons of state ... 3 December 1644. **Dublin, by W. Bladen.** 1644. Brs. WI402.

1644 IRELAND. A proclamation for an imposition. **Dublin, by William Bladen.** 1644. 4°. WI619A.

1644 IRELAND. Vpon consideration of the ... 5 September 1644. **Dublin, by W. Bladen.** 1644. Fol. WI657.

1644 IRELAND. Vpon consideration of the ... 18 November 1644. **Dublin, by W. Bladen.** 1644. Brs. WI658.

1644 IRELAND. Wee ... doe by this proclamation ... 20 September 1644. **Dublin, by W. Bladen.** 1644. Brs. WI674.

1644 IRELAND. Wee doe hereby declare and ... 4 December 1644. **Dublin, by W. Bladen.** 1644. Brs. WI676.

1644 IRELAND. We having taken into our serious ... 20 May 1644. **Dublin, by W. Bladen.** 1644. Fol. WI687.

1644 IRELAND. We have taken into our serious ... 12 October 1644. **Dublin, by W. Bladen.** 1644. Fol. WI688.

1644 IRELAND. Whereas by former orders made ... 14 December 1644. **Dublin, by W. Bladen.** 1644. Brs. WI727.

1644 IRELAND. Whereas sundry lands, tenements ... 11 November 1644. **Dublin, by W. Bladen.** 1644. Brs. WI886.

1644 IRELAND. Whereas sundry persons who ... 28 August 1644. **Dublin, by W. Bladen.** 1644. Brs. WI888.

1644 IRELAND. Whereas the late Lord Justices ... 20 May 1644. **Dublin, by W. Bladen.** 1644. Fol. WI910.

1644 IRELAND. Whereas we have lately seen ... 18 December 1644. **Dublin, by W. Bladen.** 1644. Brs. WI991.

1644 IRELAND. Whereas wee are informed ... 29 March 1644. **Dublin, by W. Bladen.** 1644. Brs. WI958.

1644 IRELAND. Whereas wee are informed ... 12 April 1644. **Dublin, by W. Bladen.** 1644. WI959.

1644 IRELAND. Whereas we observe that ... 20 May 1644. **Dublin, by W. Bladen.** 1644. Brs. WI1000.

1645 IRELAND. An addition to the late proclamation ... 7 February 1644 [5]. **Dublin, W. Bladen.** 1644 [5]. Brs. WI331.

1645 IRELAND. Vpon consideration of the annexed ... 13 January 1644 [5]. **Dublin, by W. Bladen.** 1644 [5]. Brs. WI659.

1645 IRELAND. Vpon consideration of the annexed ... 2 April 1645. **Dublin, by W. Bladen.** 1645. Brs. WI660.

1645 IRELAND. Vpon consideration of the annexed ... 22 April 1645. **Dublin, by W. Bladen.** 1645. Brs. WI661.

1645 IRELAND. Vpon consideration of the annexed ... 22 May 1645. **Dublin, by W. Bladen.** 1645. Brs. WI662.

1645 IRELAND. Vpon consideration of the annexed ... 4 June 1645. **Dublin, by W. Bladen.** 1645. Brs. WI663.

1645 IRELAND. Vpon consideration of the annexed ... 21 June 1645. **Dublin, by W. Bladen.** 1645. Brs. WI664.

1645 IRELAND. Vpon consideration of the annexed ... 30 June 1645. **Dublin, by W. Bladen.** 1645. Brs. WI665.

1645 IRELAND. Vpon consideration of the annexed ... 24 July 1645. **Dublin, by W. Bladen.** 1645. Brs. WI666.

1645 IRELAND. Vpon consideration of the annexed ... 29 July 1645. **Dublin, by W. Bladen.** 1645. Brs. WI667.

1645 IRELAND. We finding great abuse in the ... 7 February 1644 [5]. **Dublin, by W. Bladen.** 1644 [5]. Brs. WI679.

1645 IRELAND. Whereas in the present treaty ... 8 January 1644 [5]. **Dublin.** 1644 [5]. Brs. WI829.

1645 IRELAND. Whereas we observe that these ... 16 April 1645. **Dublin, by W. Bladen.** 1645. Brs. WI1001.

1645 IRELAND. Whereas wee issued a proclamation ... 17 July 1645. **Dublin, by W. Bladen.** 1645. Brs. WI998.

1646 Articles of peace, made, concluded. **Dublin, W. Bladen.** 1646. 4°. WA3864.

1646 CHARLES I, king of England. The kings letter to the Marquesse of Ormond. **Dublin, Wm. Bladen.** 1646. Brs. WC2416.

1646 CHARLES I, king of England. Right trusty and entirely beloved cousin ... third day of April, 1646. **Imprinted at Dublin by VVilliam Bladen.** 1646. Brs. WC2761.

1646 IRELAND. It is ordered that any commander ... 3 March 1645 [6]. **Dublin.** 1645/6. Brs. WI421.

1646 IRELAND. Right trusty and entirely ... 21 May 1646. **Dublin, by W. Bladen.** 1646. Brs. WI643.

1646 IRELAND. Whereas wee issued a proclamation ... 13 January 1645 [6]. **Dublin, by W. Bladen.** 1645 [6]. Brs. WI999.

1647 ENGLAND. PARLIAMENT. A remonstrance from the Lords and Commons ... concerning the estate of Ireland. **Dublin: by William Bladen.** 1646 [7]. 4°. WE2218.

1647 IRELAND. Whereas wee ... 23 June 1647. **Dublin, by W. Bladen.** 1647. Brs. WI953.

1647 Lawes and ordinances of warre. **Dublin, by William Bladen.** 1647. 4°. WL696A.

1648 The humble petition of us the Parliaments poore souldiers. **Dublin: by W. B.** 1648. Brs. WH3588.

1648 IRELAND. Whereas Colonell Owen ONeill, coming into this kingdome ... 30 September 1648. [**Dublin.** 1648]. Brs. WI763.

1649 ORMONDE, JAMES BUTLER, duke of. A true copy of two letters. **Dublin, by William Bladen, 1649, and now re-printed.** [1649]. 4°. WO462.

1650 Death's universal summons. **Dublin.** [1650?] 8°. WD505A.

1651 FITZGERALD, GERALD. A letter, or paper, signed by ... **Printed at Dublin, by W. Bladen.** 1651. 4°. WF1073.

1652 A declaration and instructions, for bringing. **Dublin, by W. Bladen.** 1652. 4°. WD530A.

1653 IRELAND. By the commissioners for the settling and securing ... Ulster. **Dublin, by William Bladen.** 1653. Brs. WI341.

1654 CROMWELL, OLIVER. An ordinance for indempnity to the English Protestants of ... Minster. **Dublin reprinted, W. Bladen.** 1654. Fol. WC7131.

1654 IRELAND. For the better destroying of wolves ... 23 December 1654. **Dublin, by W. Bladen.** 1654. Brs. WI405.

1654 IRELAND. Whereas great complaint is made ... 25 November 1654. **Dublin, by W. Bladen.** 1654. Brs. WI783.

1655 CROMWELL, OLIVER. A declaration of ... shewing the reasons. **Dublin.** 1655. 4°. WC7084.

1655 IRELAND. A declaration and commission for three months assessment ... 27 June 1655. **Dublin, by W. Bladen.** 1655. Brs. WI368.

1655 IRELAND. A declaration and commission for three months assessment ... 6 September 1655. **Dublin, by W. Bladen.** 1655. Fol. WI369.

1655 IRELAND. A declaration concerning the fines to be imposed. **Dublin, by W. Bladen.** 1655. Brs. WI372.

1655 IRELAND. A declaration directing the officers. **Dublin, by W. Bladen.** 1654 [5]. Brs. WI375.

1655 IRELAND. A declaration for making sale of the corn. **Dublin, by W. Bladen.** 1654 [5]. Brs. WI376.

1655 IRELAND. A declaration that all Irish Papists. **Dublin, by W. Bladen.** 1655. Brs. WI390.

1655 IRELAND. A declaration, that all persons holding custodiums. **Dublin, by W. Bladen.** 1655. Brs. WI391.

1655 IRELAND. A declaration, that no transplanted person. **Dublin, by W. Bladen.** 1655. Brs. WI392.

1655 IRELAND. The Lord ... in their late march ... 9 July 1655. **Dublin, by W. Bladen.** 1655. Fol. WI424.

1655 IRELAND. Ordered that all persons ... 2 April 1655. **Dublin, by W. Bladen.** 1655. Fol. WI425.

1655 IRELAND. Ordered that Thursday ... 15 June 1655. **Dublin, by W. Bladen.** 1655. Fol. WI426.

1655 IRELAND. Vpon consideration had ... 12 February 1654 [5]. **Dublin, by W. Bladen.** 1654 [5]. Brs. WI655.

1655 IRELAND. Whereas by an order ... 27 February 1654 [5]. **Dublin, by W. Bladen.** 1654 [5]. Brs. WI725.

1655 IRELAND. Whereas his highness ... 1 January 1654 [5]. **Dublin, by W. Bladen.** 1654 [5]. Brs. WI785.

1655 IRELAND. Whereas his highness ... 7 August 1655. **Dublin, by W. Bladen.** 1655. Brs. WI786.

1655 IRELAND. Whereas in pursuance of ... 14 July 1655. **Dublin, by W. Bladen.** 1655. Brs. WI821.

1655 IRELAND. Whereas several murthers ... 24 January 1654 [5]. **Dublin, by W. Bladen.** 1654[5]. Brs. WI870.

1655 IRELAND. Whereas several murthers ... 28 May 1655. **Dublin, by W. Bladen.** 1655. Brs. WI871.

1655 IRELAND. Whereas several officers and ... 27 July 1655. **Dublin, by W. Bladen.** 1655. Brs. WI873.

1655 IRELAND. Whereas the late commissioners ... 21 May 1655. **Dublin, by W. Bladen.** 1655. Brs. WI905.

1656 IRELAND. For the better destroying of wolves ... 23 December 1654. **Dublin, by W. Bladen.** 1656. Brs. WI406.

1656 IRELAND. His Highness Council having taken ... 7 April 1656. **Dublin, by W. Bladen.** 1656. Brs. WI411.

1656 IRELAND. Whereas by a declaration. **Dublin, by W. Bladen.** 1656. Fol. WI717.

1656 IRELAND. Whereas Dermott Riane ... 15 April 1656. **Dublin, by W. Bladen.** 1656. Brs. WI764.

1656 IRELAND. Whereas it hath been by many ... 14 April 1656. **Dublin, by W. Bladen.** 1656. Fol. WI838.

1657 LOFTUS, DUDLEY. Logica seu introductio. **Dublin, William Bladen.** 1657. 12°. WL2823.

1658 IRELAND. Whereas in and by an act ... 29 January 1657 [8]. **Dublin, by W. Bladen.** 1657 [8]. Brs. WI819.

1658 IRELAND. Whereas in pursuance of ... 20 January 1657 [8]. **Dublin, by W. Bladen.** 1657 [8]. Brs. WI822.

1658 MAXWELL, ROBERT, bp. In obitum Richardi Pepys. **Dublinii.** 1658. Brs. WM1387.

1658 ROBERT, Kilmorensis. In obitum clarissimi ... Richardi Pepys. **Dublinii, apud Gul. Bladen.** 1658. Brs. WR1572.

1659 HARRISON, THOMAS, of St. Dunstan. Threni Hybernici; or, Ireland sympathising. **By E. Cotes, and are to be sold by John North at Dublin.** 1659. 4°. WH916.

1660 CHARLES II, king of England. A proclamation against the rebels in Ireland. **Dublin, W. Bladen.** 1660. Brs. WC3223.

1660 CHARLES II, king of England. A proclamation against vicious, debauch'd and prophane persons ... thirtieth day of May. **Dublin, W. Bladen.** 1660. Brs. WC3229.

1660 CHARLES II, king of England. A proclamation. Whereas by the death ... May the 14, 1660. **Dublin, by William Bladen.** 1660. Brs. WC3596.

1660 CHARLES II, king of England. To our trusty and well-beloved General Monck. **Dublin, by William Bladen.** 1660. Brs. WC3612.

1660 The declaration and engagement of the army ... in Ireland. [**Dublin, W. Bladen.** 1660]. Brs. WD525.

1660 IRELAND. A declaration of the General Convention of Ireland ... 1 May 1660. **Dublin, by W. Bladen.** 1660. Brs. WI379.

1660 IRELAND. A declaration of the General Convention of Ireland ... 28 May 1660. **Dublin, by W. Bladen.** 1660. Brs. WI382.

1660 IRELAND. Forasmuch as we the Lords ... 12 March 1660. **Dublin, by W. Bladen.** 1660. Brs. WI401.

1660 IRELAND. A proclamation ... [14 May 1660]. **Dublin, by W. Bladen.** 1660. Brs. WI427.

1660 MOUNTRATH, CHARLES COOTE, earl of. The declaration of. **Dublin, by William Bladen.** 1659 [60]. Brs. WM2979.

1660 PRESSICK, GEORGE. A briefe relation, of some of the most remarkable passages. [**Dublin?**]. 1660. 4°. WP3295.

1660 WALLER, Sir HARDRESSE. A letter from. **Dublin, by William Bladen.** 1659 [60]. Brs. WW536A.

1661 CHARLES II, king of England. A proclamation for the entring and putting in of claims in Ireland. **Dublin, W. Bladen.** 1661. Brs. WC3481.

1661   IRELAND. An act for the continuance of the customs. **Dublin, J. Crook.** 1661. Brs. WI316.

1661   IRELAND. By the Lords Iustices and Council. **Dublin, by William Bladen.** 1661. Brs. WI348.

1661   IRELAND. The declaration concerning the continuance of the customs. **Dublin, John Crook, sold by John North.** 1661. Brs. WI385.

1661   IRELAND. The declaration concerning the continuance ... 7 December 1661. **Dublin, J. Crook.** [1661.] Brs. WI386.

1661   IRELAND. The declaration for the speedy raising of moneys. **Dublin, John Crook.** 1661. Brs. WI389.

1661   IRELAND. A declaration of the Lords and Commons concerning ecclesiastical government. **Dublin, by W. Bladen.** 1661. Brs. WI383.

1661   IRELAND. The declaration of the Lords ... and Commons ... concerning His Majesties intended match. **Dublin, by W. Bladen.** 1661. Brs. WI384.

1661   IRELAND. His Majesty taken into His ... 5 January 1660 [1]. **Dublin, by W. Bladen.** 1660 [1]. Brs. WI413.

1661   IRELAND. In pursuance of a proclamation ... 16 February 1660 [1]. **Dublin, by W. Bladen.** 1660 [1]. Fol. WI415.

1661   IRELAND. In pursuance of a proclamation ... 16 February 1660 [1]. **Dublin, by W. Bladen.** 1660 [1]. Brs. WI416.

1661   IRELAND. A proclamation 27 March 1661. **Dublin, by W. Bladen.** 1661. Brs. WI429.

1661   IRELAND. A proclamation ... 1 April 1661. **Dublin, by W. Bladen.** 1661. Brs. WI431.

1661   IRELAND. A proclamation concerning a Parliament ... 26 March 1661. **Dublin, by W. Bladen.** 1661. Brs. WI602.

1661   IRELAND. A proclamation concerning gunpowder ... 10 October 1661. **Dublin, J. Crook.** 1661. Fol. WI606.

1661   IRELAND. A proclamation concerning gunpowder ... 14 October 1661. **Dublin, J. Crook.** 1661. Fol. WI607.

1661   IRELAND. A proclamation for a day of humiliation ... 21 January 1660 [1]. **Dublin, by W. Bladen.** 1660 [1]. Brs. WI610.

1661   IRELAND. A proclamation for the due and speedy execution. **Dublin, by W. Bladen.** 1660 [1]. Brs. WI628.

1661   IRELAND. We ... taking into our consideration ... 1 April 1661. **Dublin, W. Bladen.** 1661. Brs. WI692.

1661   IRELAND. We the Lords Iustices and Councell ... 15 January 1660 [1]. **Dublin, by W. Bladen.** 1660 [1]. Brs. WI697.

1661   IRELAND. Whereas a committee of the General ... 23 February 1660 [1]. **Dublin, by W. Bladen.** 1660 [1]. Brs. WI699.

1661   IRELAND. Whereas a committee of the ... 21 June 1661. **Dublin, by W. Bladen.** 1661. Brs. WI700.

1661   IRELAND. Whereas amongst many other ... 17 August 1661. **Dublin, J. Crook.** 1661. Brs. WI707.

1661   IRELAND. Whereas amongst many other ... 13 September 1661. **Dublin, J. Crook.** 1661. Brs. WI708.

1661   IRELAND. Whereas by reason that diverse ... 15 August 1661. **Dublin, J. Crook, sold by John North.** 1661. Fol. WI749.

1661   IRELAND. Whereas divers persons in seveal [sic] ... 19 January 1660 [1]. **Dublin, by W. Bladen.** 1660 [1]. Brs. WI769.

1661   IRELAND. Whereas for sundry good causes and ... 10 December 1661. **Dublin, J. Crook.** 1661. Brs. WI778.

1661   IRELAND. Whereas for the better enabling ... 7 February 1660 [1]. **Dublin, by W. Bladen.** 1660 [1]. Brs. WI781.

1661   IRELAND. Whereas ... Halsey and Walter Butler ... 10 September 1661. **Dublin, J. Crook.** 1661. Brs. WI784.

1661   IRELAND. Whereas His Majesty by his ... 9 January 1660 [1]. **Dublin, by W. Bladen.** 1660 [1]. Brs. WI795.

1661   IRELAND. Whereas his Majestie (out of ...) ... 30 March 1661. **Dublin, by W. Bladen.** 1661. Brs. WI805.

1661   IRELAND. Whereas in pursuance to a ... 29 June 1661. **Dublin, by W. Bladen.** 1661. Brs. WI825.

1661   IRELAND. Whereas it is a certain truth ... 15 April 1661. **Dublin, by W. Bladen.** 1661. Brs. WI843.

1661   IRELAND. Whereas on the nineteenth of ... 7 November 1661. **Dublin, J. Crook.** 1661. Fol. WI853.

1661   IRELAND. Whereas the Duke of Albemarle ... 17 April 1661. **Dublin, by W. Bladen.** 1661. Brs. WI898.

1661   IRELAND. Whereas the kings most excellent Maiesty ... 29 January 1660 [1]. **Dublin, by W. Bladen.** 1660 [1]. Brs. WI900.

1661   IRELAND. Whereas the kings most excellent Maiesty ... 20 August. **Dublin, J. Crook.** 1661. Fol. WI901.

1661   IRELAND. Whereas the late General Convention ... 2 January 1660 [1]. **Dublin, by W. Bladen.** 1660 [1]. Brs. WI907.

1661   IRELAND. Whereas the lords spiritual ... 20 November 1661. **Dublin, J. Crook, sold by S. Dancer.** 1661. Fol. WI914.

1661   IRELAND. Whereas there was a letter ... 24 December 1661. **Dublin, J. Crook.** 1661. Brs. WI945.

1661   IRELAND. Whereas upon the humble application ... 7 January 1660 [1]. **Dublin, by W. Bladen.** 1660 [1]. Brs. WI952.

1661   IRELAND. Whereas we are given to understand by ... 22 January 1660 [1]. **Dublin, by W. Bladen.** 1660 [1]. Brs. WI955.

1661   IRELAND. Whereas wee are informed ... 10 September 1661. **Dublin, J. Crook.** 1661. Brs. WI960.

1661   IRELAND. Whereas we are informed and ... 16 September 1661. **Dublin, T. Crook.** 1661. Brs. WI961.

1661   IRELAND. Whereas we are informed that ... 7 November 1661. **Dublin, J. Crook.** Brs. WI962.

1661   IRELAND. Whereas we formerly issued a ... 22 November 1661. **Dublin, J. Crook.** 1661. Fol. WI985.

1661   IRELAND. Whereas we the Lords Justices ... 10 December 1661. **Dublin, J. Crook.** 1661. Fol. WI1010.

1662   IRELAND. An act for incouraging Protestant strangers. **Dublin.** 1662. Brs. WI303

1662   IRELAND. All persons that shall have occasion ... 29 August 1662. **Dublin, J. Crook.** 1662. Brs. WI332.

1662   IRELAND. By His Majesties commissioners, appointed for putting in execution. **Dublin, J. Crook.** 1662. Fol. WI339.

1662   IRELAND. A declaration concerning the continuance. **Dublin, J. Crook.** 1661 [2]. Brs. WI387.

1662   IRELAND. An expectation concerning the continuance. **Dublin, J. Crook.** 1662. Brs. WI388.

1662   IRELAND. For the more due and ... 14 November 1662. **Dublin, J. Crook.** 1662. Brs. WI407.

1662   IRELAND. A proclamation appointing the time ... 23 September 1662. **Dublin, J. Crook.** 1662. Brs. WI601.

1662   IRELAND. A proclamation for the suppressing of unlawful assemblies. **Dublin, J. Crook.** 1662. Fol. WI637.

1662   IRELAND. We ... considering the duty incumbent ... 13 December 1662. **Dublin, J. Crook.** 1662. Fol. WI671.

1662   IRELAND. Whereas at the Parliament ... 24 March 1661 [2]. **Dublin, T. Crook.** 1661 [2]. Brs. WI714.

1662   IRELAND. Whereas by act of Parliament ... 23 June 1662. **Dublin, J. Crook.** 1662. Fol. WI722.

1662   IRELAND. Whereas by an act intituled ... 19 September 1662. **Dublin, J. Crook.** 1662. Fol. WI753.

1662   IRELAND. Whereas by occasion of the ... 23 July 1662. **Dublin, J. Crook.** 1662. Brs. WI729.

1662   IRELAND. Whereas by one act of Parliament ... 17 October 1662. **Dublin, J. Crook.** 1662. Fol. WI731.

1662   IRELAND. Whereas by proclamation ... 19 September 1662. **Dublin, J. Crook.** 1662. Fol. WI742.

1662   IRELAND. Whereas for sundry good causes and ... 20 January 1661 [2]. **Dublin, J. Crook.** 1661 [2]. Brs. WI779.

1662   IRELAND. Whereas for sundry good causes and ... 19 February 1661 [2]. **Dublin, J. Crook.** 1661 [2]. Brs. WI780.

1662   IRELAND. Whereas in expectation of ... 30 April 1662. **Dublin, J. Crook.** 1662. Brs. WI820.

1662   IRELAND. Whereas on the seventh day ... 27 February 1661 [2]. **Dublin, J. Crook.** 1661 [2]. Fol. WI855.

1662   IRELAND. Whereas Popish priests, friers ... 17 March 1661 [2]. **Dublin, J. Crook.** 1661 [2]. Brs. WI857.

1662   IRELAND. Whereas Robert Brown vicar of ... 16 July 1662. **Dublin, John Crook.** 1662. Brs. WI862.

1662   IRELAND. Whereas the late Lord Justices ... 15 August 1662. **Dublin, J. Crook.** 1662. Fol. WI911.

1662   IRELAND. Whereas there was an ordinance ... 13 February 1661 [2]. **Dublin, J. Crook.** 1661 [2]. Brs. WI946.

1662   IRELAND. Whereas we are informed ... 4 August 1662. **Dublin, J. Crook.** 1662. Fol. WI963.

1662   IRELAND. Whereas we are informed ... 22 September 1662. **Dublin, J. Crook.** 1662. Brs. WI964.

1662   IRELAND. Whereas we are informed that ... 18 December 1662. **Dublin, J. Crook.** 1662. Brs. WI965.

1662   IRELAND. Whereas we understand ... 18 August 1662. **Dublin, J. Crook.** 1662. Brs. WI1014.

1662   ORMONDE, JAMES BUTLER, duke of. The speech of ... 27 September, 1662. **Dublin: by John Crook, to be sold by Sam. Dancer.** 1662. Fol. WO459.

1662   WALSH, PETER. A letter desiring a just and merciful regard of the Roman Catholicks of Ireland. [**Dublin**? 1662]. 4°. WW636.

1662   [WILLIAMSON, CAESAR]. Oratio in suscepti diadematis. **Dublinii, typis & impensis J. C.** 1662. WW2793A.

1663   Account of the daily proceedings of the Commissioners of Oyer and Terminer at York. **Dublin.** 1663. 4°. WA268.

1663   IRELAND. For the more ready dispatch of such petitions ... 30 April 1663. **Dublin, J. Crooke.** 1663. Brs. WI408.

1663   IRELAND. Forasmuch as His Majesties service ... 22 May 1663. **Dublin, J. Crooke.** 1663. Brs. WI396.

1663   IRELAND. A proclamation concerning licences. **Dublin, J. Crooke.** 1663. Brs. WI608.

1663   IRELAND. We cannot but call to mind ... 29 June 1663. **Dublin, J. Crooke.** 1663. Fol. WI669.

1663   IRELAND. Whereas by an act made ... 27 May 1663. **Dublin, J. Crook.** 1663. Fol. WI720.

1663   IRELAND. Whereas by an act made ... 3 June 1663. **Dublin, J. Crooke.** 1663. Fol. WI721.

1663   IRELAND. Whereas by one act of Parliament ... 18 March 1662 [3]. **Dublin, J. Crook, sold by S. Dancer.** 1663. Fol. WI732.

1663   IRELAND. Whereas by our proclamation ... 10 April 1663. **Dublin, J. Crook.** 1663. Fol. WI736.

1663   IRELAND. Whereas, by the direction ... 5 August 1663. **Dublin, J. Crooke.** 1663. Fol. WI758.

1663   IRELAND. Whereas certain wicked persons ... 21 May 1663. **Dublin, J. Crooke.** 1663. Fol. WI762.

1663   IRELAND. Whereas in an act intituled ... 11 November 1663. **Dublin, J. Crooke.** 1663. Fol. WI814.

1663   IRELAND. Whereas in an act lately ... 28 January 1662 [3]. **Dublin, J. Crook, sold by S. Dancer.** 1662 [3]. Fol. WI815.

1663   IRELAND. Whereas in the act intituled ... 9 September 1663. **Dublin, J. Crooke.** 1663. Fol. WI826.

1663   IRELAND. Whereas since His Majesties ... 28 August 1663. **Dublin, J. Crook.** 1663. Fol. WI884.

1663   IRELAND. Whereas the present Parliament ... 21 May 1663. **Dublin, J. Crook.** 1663. Brs. WI931.

1663   IRELAND. Whereas the present Parliament ... 1 July 1663. **Dublin, J. Crook.** 1663. Brs. WI932.

1663   IRELAND. Whereas the present Parliament ... 3 August 1663. **Dublin, J. Crook.** 1663. Brs. WI933.

1663   IRELAND. Whereas the present Parliament ... 4 September 1663. **Dublin, J. Crook.** 1663. Brs. WI934.

1663   IRELAND. Whereas the present Parliament ... 31 October 1663. **Dublin, J. Crook.** 1663. Brs. WI935.

1663   IRELAND. Whereas the present Parliament ... 19 December 1663. **Dublin, J. Crook.** 1663. Brs. WI936.

1663   IRELAND. Whereas we are informed ... 8 September 1663. **Dublin, J. Crooke.** 1663. Brs. WI966.

1663   IRELAND. Whereas we have by the blessing ... 23 May 1663. **Dublin, J. Crooke.** 1663. Fol. WI988.

1663   IRELAND. Whereas we have seen a ... 26 June 1663. **Dublin, J. Crook.** 1663. Brs. WI995.

1664   IRELAND. Whereas in an act ... 27 February 1663 [4]. **Dublin, J. Crooke.** 1663 [4]. Fol. WI813.

1664   IRELAND. Whereas the Parliament is prorogued ... 2 February 1663 [4]. **Dublin, J. Crook.** 1663[4]. Brs. WI916.

1664   IRELAND. Whereas the Parliament stands ... 12 September 1664. **Dublin, J. Crooke.** 1664. Brs. WI917.

1664   IRELAND. Whereas the Parliament stands ... 13 October 1664. **Dublin, J. Crooke.** 1664. Brs. WI918.

1664   IRELAND. Whereas the Parliament stands ... 17 November 1664. **Dublin, J. Crooke.** 1664. Brs. WI919.

1644   IRELAND. Whereas the Parliament stands ... 19 December 1664. **Dublin, J. Crooke.** 1664. Brs. WI920.

1664   IRELAND. Whereas the present Parliament ... 22 January 1663 [4]. **Dublin, J. Crook.** 1663 [4]. WI937.

1664   IRELAND. Whereas the present Parliament ... 6 February 1663 [4]. **Dublin, J. Crook.** 1663 [4]. WI938.

1664   IRELAND. Whereas we are informed ... 27 May 1664. **Dublin, J. Crooke.** 1664. Brs. WI967.

1664   IRELAND. Whereas we are informed ... 1 October 1664. **Dublin, J. Crooke.** 1664. Brs. WI968.

1664   ORMONDE, JAMES BUTLER, duke of. L'oratione ... fatta. **Stampata in Dublino, per Giov. Crooke e sivendono appresso Sam. Dancer.** 1664. 4°. WO454.

1664   STEARNE, JOHN. Le electione & reprobatione dissertatio. **Dublinii.** 1664. 4°. WS5370.

1664   VAN GOGH, MICHIEL. A memorial delivered to His Majesty. **Dublin, for Samuel Dancer.** 1664. 4°. WV92.

1665   Articles of presentments, to be inquired of. **Dublin, by John Crook.** 1665. 4°. WA3865.

1665   IRELAND. As by proclamation bearing ... 19 August 1665. **Dublin, J. Crook.** 1665. WI335.

1665   IRELAND. Forasmuch as the infection ... 28 July 1665. **Dublin, J. Crook.** 1665. Fol. WI397.

1665   IRELAND. A proclamation for a thanksgiving. ... 22 June 1665. **Dublin, J. Crook.** 1665. Fol. WI616.

1665   IRELAND. A proclamation for publique prayer. **Dublin, J. Crook.** 1665. Fol. WI624.

1665   IRELAND. We ... considering that at this ... 26 July 1665. **Dublin, J. Crook.** 1665. Fol. WI670.

1665   IRELAND. Whereas an act lately ... 16 August 1665. **Dublin, J. Crook.** 1665. Fol. WI709.

1665   IRELAND. Whereas notwithstanding ... 15 April 1665. **Dublin, J. Crook.** 1665. Fol. WI851.

1665   IRELAND. Whereas notwithstanding ... 16 September 1665. **Dublin, J. Crook.** 1665. Fol. WI852.

1665   IRELAND. Whereas the kings most excellent Maiesty ... 7 January 1664 [5]. **Dublin, J. Crook.** 1664 [5]. Fol. WI902.

1665   IRELAND. Whereas the late Lord Deputy ... 19 October 1665. **Dublin, J. Crook.** 1665. Fol. WI909.

1665   IRELAND. Whereas the Parliament stands ... 10 February 1664 [5]. **Dublin, J. Crooke.** 1664 [5]. Brs. WI921.

1665   IRELAND. Whereas the Parliament stands ... 30 March 1665. **Dublin, J. Crooke.** 1665. Brs. WI922.

1665   IRELAND. Whereas the Parliament stands ... 18 April 1665. **Dublin, J. Crooke.** 1665. Brs. WI923.

1665   IRELAND. Whereas the Parliament stands ... 18 May 1665. **Dublin, J. Crooke.** 1665. Brs. WI924.

1665   IRELAND. Whereas the Parliament stands ... 22 June 1665. **Dublin, J. Crooke.** 1665. Brs. WI925.

1665   IRELAND. Whereas the Parliament stands ... 24 July 1665. **Dublin, J. Crooke.** 1665. Brs. WI926.

1665   IRELAND. Whereas the Parliament stands ... 21 August 1665. **Dublin, J. Crooke.** 1665. Brs. WI927.

1665   IRELAND. Whereas the Parliament stands ... 18 September 1665. **Dublin, J. Crooke.** 1665. Brs. WI928.

1666   ENGLAND. PARLIAMENT. By the knights citizens and burgesses in Parliament assembled. It is this day ordered ... 14 April 1666. **Dublin, J. Crook.** 1666. Brs. WE1266.

1666   ENGLAND. PARLIAMENT. By the knights citizens and burgesses in Parliament assembled. It is this day ordered ... 3 August 1666. **Dublin, J. Crook.** 1666. Brs. WE1267.

1666   A form of consecration or dedication of churches. **Dublin.** 1666. 4°. WF1566.

1666   IRELAND. By His Majesties commissioners appointed for executing the act of settlement ... 25 June. **Dublin, J. Crook.** 1666. Brs. WI338.

1666   IRELAND. A proclamation for a thanksgiving ... 15 August 1666. **Dublin, J. Crook.** 1666. Fol. WI617.

1666   IRELAND. Rules, orders and directions. **Dublin,** 1666. Fol. WI646.

1666   IRELAND. We ... do order, command, ... 8 June 1666. **Dublin, J. Crooke.** 1666. Brs. WI678.

1666   IRELAND. Whereas a writing under ... 16 May 1666. **Dublin, J. Crooke.** 1666. Fol. WI706.

1666   IRELAND. Whereas by an act of ... 15 August 1666. **Dublin, J. Crook.** 1666. Fol. WI723.

1666   IRELAND. Whereas by an act ... 17 September 1666. **Dublin, J. Crook.** 1666. Fol. WI724.

1666   IRELAND. Whereas by an act ... 3 January 1665 [6]. **Dublin, J. Crook.** 1665 [6]. Brs. WI754.

1666   IRELAND. Whereas by direction ... 15 August 1666. **Dublin, J. Crook.** 1666. Brs. WI726.

1666   IRELAND. Whereas Dualtagh ... 25 June 1666. **Dublin, J. Crook.** 1666. Fol. WI775.

1666   IRELAND. Whereas for the better ... 12 July 1666. **Dublin, J. Crook.** 1666. Fol. WI782.

1666   IRELAND. Whereas His Majestie ... 4 September 1666. **Dublin, J. Crook.** 1666. Fol. WI787.

1666   IRELAND. Whereas in the tenth ... 15 August 1666. **Dublin, J. Crook.** 1666. Fol. WI830.

1666   IRELAND. Whereas on the second day ... 22 September 1666. **Dublin, J. Crook.** 1666. Fol. WI854.

1666   IRELAND. Whereas several felonies...24 March 1665 [6]. **Dublin, J. Crooke.** 1665 [6]. Fol. WI868.

1666   IRELAND. Whereas the commissioners ... 22 January 1665 [6]. **Dublin, J. Crooke.** 1665 [6]. Fol. WI892.

1666   IRELAND. Whereas the commissioners ... 26 March 1666. **Dublin, J. Crooke.** 1666. Fol. WI893.

1666   IRELAND. Whereas the commissioners ... 27 April 1666. **Dublin, J. Crooke.** Fol. WI894.

1666   IRELAND. Whereas the sins of ... 8 February 1665 [6]. **Dublin, J. Crooke.** 1665 [6]. Brs. WI941.

1666   IRELAND. Whereas this house have taken notice ... 12 April 1666. **Dublin, J. Crooke.** 1666. Brs. WI947.

1666   IRELAND. Whereas upon the French ... 28 February 1665 [6]. **Dublin, J. Crooke.** 1665 [6]. Fol. WI951.

1666   IRELAND. Whereas we the Lord Lieutenant ... 26 September 1666. **Dublin, J. Crook.** 1666. Fol. WI1003.

1667   CHARLES II, king of England. A proclamation for publishing the peace ... Denmark. **Dublin, J. Crook.** 1667. Brs. WC3387.

1667   CHARLES II, king of England. A proclamation for publishing the peace ... French king. **Dublin, J. Crooke.** 1667. Brs. WC3389.

1667   CHARLES II, king of England. A proclamation for publishing the peace ... Netherlands. **Dublin, J. Crook.** 1667. Brs. WC3391A.

1667   IRELAND. As by proclamation dated ... 7 June 1667. **Dublin, J. Crooke.** 1667. Brs. WI336.

1667   IRELAND. For speciall reasons of state ... 5 January 1666. **Dublin, J. Crook.** 1666 [7]. Brs. WI403.

1667   IRELAND. A proclamation for bringing in a proportion of corn. **Dublin, J. Crooke.** 1666 [7]. Fol. WI622.

1667   IRELAND. A proclamation for publishing an act. **Dublin, J. Crooke.** 1666 [7]. Fol. WI625.

1667   IRELAND. Wee the Lord Lieutenant ... 7 January 1666 [7]. **Dublin, J. Crook.** 1666 [7]. Brs. WI693.

1667   IRELAND. Whereas by a clause in the ... 15 October 1667. **Dublin, J. Crooke.** 1667. Fol. WI715.

1667   IRELAND. Whereas by a proclamation ... 29 April 1667. **Dublin, J. Crooke.** 1667. Fol. WI718.

1667   IRELAND. Whereas by act of Council ... 29 April 1667. **Dublin, J. Crooke.** 1667. Brs. WI719.

1667   IRELAND. Whereas by occasion of the backwardness ... 11 September 1667. **Dublin, J. Crook.** 1667. Fol. WI730.

1667   IRELAND. Whereas divers complaints ... 15 October 1667. **Dublin, J. Crook.** 1667. Brs. WI765.

1667   IRELAND. Whereas His Majesties ... 31 July 1667. **Dublin, J. Crooke.** 1667. Fol. WI788.

1667   IRELAND. Whereas in an act ... 23 January 1666 [7]. **Dublin, J. Crooke.** 1666 [7]. Brs. WI816.

1667   IRELAND. Whereas several complaints ... 14 September 1667. **Dublin, J. Crook.** 1667. Brs. WI866.

1667   IRELAND. Whereas we have been necessarily ... 21 March 1666 [7]. **Dublin, J. Crooke.** 1666 [7]. Fol. WI987.

1667   LOWER, RICHARD. Willisius male vindicatvs. **Dublini.** 1667. 8°. WL3313.

1668   IRELAND. Whereas by proclamation ... 14 September 1668. **Dublin, J. Crook.** 1668. Brs. WI743.

1668   IRELAND. Whereas in the act, entituled ... 10 July 1668. **Dublin, J. Crook.** 1668. Fol. WI827.

1668   IRELAND. Whereas Rory macRandal ... 3 June 1668. **Dublin, J. Crook.** 1668. Fol. WI864.

1669   IRELAND. Whereas divers persons ... 26 November 1669. **Dublin, B. Tooke.** [1669]. Brs. WI770.

1669   IRELAND. Whereas in an act of ... 26 August 1669. **Dublin, B. Tooke.** 1669. Brs. WI817.

1669   IRELAND. Whereas several proclamations ... 3 August 1669. **Dublin, Benjamin Tooke.** 1669. Brs. WI881.

1669   IRELAND. Whereas several rolls ... 1 October 1669. **Dublin, B. Tooke.** [1669]. Brs. WI882.

1669   IRELAND. Whereas the commissioners ... 29 October 1669. **Dublin, B. Tooke.** [1669]. Fol. WI895.

1669   IRELAND. Whereas the Lords of his ... 9 August 1669. **Dublin, B. Tooke.** 1669. Fol. WI912.

1669   IRELAND. Whereas we are informed ... 29 January 1668 [9]. **Dublin, J. Crooke.** 1669. Brs. WI969.

1669   WINCHELSEA, HINEAGE FINCH, earl. True relation of the late prodigious earthquake. **Dublin, by Benj. Tooke.** 1669. 4°. WW2970.

1670   IRELAND. We ... for prevention of ... 2 September 1670. **Dublin, B. Tooke.** 1670. Brs. WI680.

1670   IRELAND. Whereas by one clause ... 6 July 1670. **Dublin, B. Tooke.** 1670. Fol. WI733.

1670   IRELAND. Whereas divers persons ... 28 March 1670. **Dublin, B. Tooke.** 1670. Brs. WI771.

1670   IRELAND. Whereas Edmund mac Gilaspy ... 1 June 1670. **Dublin, B. Tooke.** 1670. Fol. WI776.

1670   IRELAND. Whereas His Most Excellent ... 21 March 1669 [70]. **Dublin, B. Tooke.** 1669 [70]. Brs. WI810.

1670   IRELAND. Whereas in pursuance of ... 21 March 1669 [70]. **Dublin, B. Tooke.** 1669 [70]. Brs. WI823.

1670   IRELAND. Whereas Rory macRandall ... 29 April 1670. **Dublin, B. Tooke, sold by Mary Crooke.** 1670. Fol. WI865.

1670   IRELAND. Whereas Thurloe Boyle, Thurloe ... 17 August 1670. **Dublin, B. Tooke.** 1670. Fol. WI948.

1670   IRELAND. Whereas we are highly sensible ... 22 June 1670. **Dublin, B. Tooke, sold by Joseph Wilde.** 1670. Fol. WI956.

1670   IRELAND. Whereas we are highly sensible ... 22 June 1670. **Dublin, B. Tooke, sold by Mary Crooke.** [1670]. Brs. WI957.

1671   IRELAND. Whereas His Majesty ... 9 October 1671. **Dublin, B. Tooke.** 1671. Fol. WI789.

1671   IRELAND. Whereas His Majesty by His ... 20 October 1671. **Dublin, B. Tooke.** 1671. Fol. WI792.

1671   IRELAND. Whereas information hath been made ... 15 April 1671. **Dublin, B. Tooke.** 1671. Brs. WI833.

1671   IRELAND. Whereas the commissioned ... 24 November 1671. **Dublin, B. Tooke.** 1671. Fol. WI891.

1672   CHARLES II, king of England. His Majesties declaration against the States Generall. **Dublin, B. Tooke.** 1672. Brs. WC2955.

1672   IRELAND. Forasmuch as we judge it fit ... 24 March 1672. **Dublin, B. Tooke.** 1672. Brs. WI399.

1672   IRELAND. Rules, orders and directions, made and establish'd. [**Dublin.** 1672]. Fol. WI647.

1672   IRELAND. We ... do command and ... 27 March 1672. **Dublin, B. Tooke.** 1672. Brs. WI675.

1672   IRELAND. We judging it requisite ... 22 November 1672. **Dublin, B. Tooke.** 1672. Brs. WI690.

1672   IRELAND. Whereas by the antient ... 9 July 1672. **Dublin, B. Tooke.** 1672. Fol. WI755.

1672   IRELAND. Whereas His Majestie by his letters ... 29 July 1672. **Dublin, B. Tooke.** 1672. Fol. WI793.

1672   IRELAND. Whereas we are informed ... 25 October 1672. **Dublin, B. Took.** 1672. Fol. WI970.

1672   IRELAND. Whereas we the Lord Lieutenant ... 8 March 1671 [2]. **Dublin, B. Tooke, sold by Joseph Wilde.** 1671 [2]. Fol. WI1004.

1672   IRELAND. Whereas we the Lord Lieutenant ... 21 October 1672. **Dublin, B. Took.** 1672. Fol. WI1005.

1672   LOUIS XIV, king of France. The most Christian Kings declaration of war against the States-Generall. **And reprinted at Dublin by Benjamin Tooke, and are to be sold by Joseph Wilde.** 1672. Fol. WL3115.

1672   Orders and instructions to be observed. **Dublin,** 1672. 4°. WO395.

1672   WETENHALL, EDWARD, bp. Collyrium. A sermon. **Dublin, by Thomas Rooks, and are to be sold by Joseph Wilde.** 1672. 4°. WW1493.

1673   CHARLES II, king of England. A proclamation for the suppression of Popery. **Dublin, B. Tooke.** 1673. Brs. WC3430.

1673   EGAN, ANTHONY. The Franciscan convert; ... preached at St. Maudlins. **Dublin.** 1673. 4°. WE249.

1673   IRELAND. Forasmuch as we judge it fit ... 27 October 1673. **Dublin, B. Tooke.** 1673. Brs. WI400.

1673   IRELAND. Whereas divers persons ... 17 October 1673. **Dublin, B. Tooke.** 1673. Brs. WI772.

1673   IRELAND. Whereas His Majesty by his ... 24 January 1672 [3]. **Dublin, B. Tooke.** 1672[3]. Fol. WI796.

1673   IRELAND. Whereas His Majesty by ... 7 February 1672 [3]. **Dublin, B. Tooke.** 1672 [3]. Fol. WI797.

1673   IRELAND. Whereas in pursuance of ... 29 November 1673. **Dublin, B. Tooke.** 1673. Fol. WI824.

1673   IRELAND. Whereas information hath been given ... 8 November 1673. **Dublin, B. Tooke.** 1673. Fol. WI832.

1673   IRELAND. Whereas information is given ... 28 July 1673. **Dublin, B. Tooke.** 1673. Fol. WI834.

1673   IRELAND. Whereas our very good Lord ... 18 February 1672 [3]. **Dublin, B. Tooke.** 1672 [3]. Fol. WI856.

1673   IRELAND. Whereas the Lords of his ... 27 October 1673. **Dublin, B. Tooke.** 1673. Fol. WI913.

1673   IRELAND. Whereas we are informed ... 4 February 1672 [3]. [**Dublin.** 1673]. Brs. WI971.

1674   CHARLES II, king of England. A proclamation for publishing the peace ... Netherlands. **Dublin, B. Tooke.** 1673 [4]. Brs. WC3394.

1674   IRELAND. Whereas by proclamation ... 14 December 1674. **Dublin, B. Tooke.** 1674. Fol. WI744.

1674 IRELAND. Whereas Donnell ODowd ... 2 March 1673 [4]. **Dublin, B. Tooke.** 1673 [4]. Fol. WI774.

1674 IRELAND. Whereas Redmond OHanlon ... 14 December 1674. **Dublin, B. Tooke.** 1674. Fol. WI858.

1674 IRELAND. Whereas we are informed ... 18 May 1674. **Dublin, B. Tooke.** 1674. Fol. WI972.

1674 IRELAND. Whereas we held it necessary ... 5 October 1674. **Dublin, B. Tooke.** 1674. Fol. WI997.

1674 IRELAND. Whereas we the Lord Lieutenant ... 27 April 1674. **Dublin, B. Took.** 1674. Fol. WI1006.

1675 CHARLES II, king of England. His Majesties gracious speech to both Houses ... 9th of June 1675. **Dublin, reprinted by Benjamin Tooke.** 1675. Fol. WC3059A.

1675 CHARLES II, king of England. At the Court at Whitehall ... His Majesty was this day pleased ... 3 February 1674/5. **Dublin, B. Tooke.** 1674 [5]. Brs. WE810.

1675 CHARLES II, king of England. A proclamation commanding the immediate return. **Dublin, B. Tooke.** 1675. Brs. WC3248.

1675 IRELAND. Whereas divers disloyal ... 10 June 1675. **Dublin, B. Tooke.** 1675. Fol. WI766.

1675 IRELAND. Whereas His Majesty by ... 1 March 1674 [5]. **Dublin, B. Tooke.** 1674 [5]. Fol. WI798.

1675 IRELAND. Whereas His Majesty by ... 20 December 1675. **Dublin, B. Tooke.** 1675. Brs. WI799.

1675 IRELAND. Whereas in an act ... 25 February 1674 [5]. **Dublin, B. Tooke.** 1674 [5]. Fol. WI818.

1675 IRELAND. Whereas in the twenty ... 7 July 1675. **Dublin, B. Tooke.** 1675. Fol. WI831.

1675 IRELAND. Whereas information is ... 26 July 1675. **Dublin, B. Tooke.** 1675. Fol. WI835.

1675 IRELAND. Whereas the kings most excellent Maiesty ... 15 December 1675. **Dublin, B. Tooke.** 1675. Brs. WI903.

1676 An indenture, containing a grant. **Dublin.** 1676. Fol. WI144.

1676 IRELAND. By the commissinors [sic] apointed for hearing and determining ... 30 June. **Dublin, B. Tooke.** 1676. Brs. WI340.

1676 IRELAND. Wee the Lord Lieutenant ... 23 August 1676. **Dublin, B. Tooke.** 1676. Fol. WI694.

1676 IRELAND. Whereas by a clause ... 30 June 1676. **Dublin, B. Tooke.** 16[76]. Fol. WI716.

1676 IRELAND. Whereas His Majestie by his letters ... 29 July 1672. **Dublin, B. Tooke.** 1676. Fol. WI794.

1676 IRELAND. Whereas His Majesty by ... 26 May 1676. **Dublin, B. Tooke.** 1676. Fol. WI800.

1676 IRELAND. Whereas His Majesty by ... 26 June 1676. **Dublin, B. Tooke.** 1676. Fol. WI801.

1676 IRELAND. Whereas His Majesty by ... 26 June 1676. **Dublin, B. Tooke.** 1676. Fol. WI802.

1676 IRELAND. Whereas his Majestie upon ... 30 June 1676. **Dublin, B. Tooke.** 1676. Fol. WI806.

1676 IRELAND. Whereas Redmond O Hanlon ... 16 October 1676. **Dublin, B. Tooke.** 1676. Fol. WI859.

1676 LA BASTIDE, MARC ANTOINE DE. An answer to the Bishop of Condom's book. **Dublin, Benjamin Tooke.** 1676. 12°. WL100.

1676 WALKER, JOSEPH. An answer to the bishop of Condom's book. **Dublin.** 1676. 8°. WW394.

1677 DAVIES, JOHN. Les reports des cases. **Dublin.** 1677. Fol. WD408A.

1677 IRELAND. Complaint having been ... 26 April 1677. **Dublin, B. Tooke.** 1677. Fol. WI358.

1677 IRELAND. A proclamation concerning passes for ships. **Dublin, B. Tooke.** 1676 [7]. Fol. WI609.

1677 IRELAND. Whereas a most barbarous ... 19 October 1677. [**Dublin.** 1677]. Fol. WI702.

1677 IRELAND. Whereas application hath ... 21 May 1677. **Dublin, B. Tooke.** 1677. Fol. WI711.

1677 IRELAND. Whereas by our proclamation ... 19 February 1676 [7]. **Dublin, B. Tooke.** 1676 [7]. Fol. WI737.

1677 IRELAND. Whereas by the good and ... 19 December 1677. **Dublin, B. Took.** 1677. Fol. WI760.

1677 IRELAND. Whereas the farmers of his ... 5 February 1676 [7]. **Dublin, B. Tooke.** 1676 [7]. Fol. WI899.

1677 IRELAND. Whereas we are authorized ... 16 August 1677. **Dublin, B. Tooke.** 1677. Fol. WI954.

1677 IRELAND. Whereas we are informed ... 9 April 1677. **Dublin, B. Tooke.** 1677. Fol. WI973.

1678 CHARLES II, king of England. At the court at Whitehall ... whereas His Majesty by His ... 19 November 1678. **Dublin, B. Took.** 1678. Brs. WE843.

1678 CHARLES II, king of England. A proclamation commanding all persons being Popish recusants. **Dublin, B. Took.** 1678. Brs. WC3244.

1678 CHARLES II, king of England. A proclamation for the discovery and apprehending all Popish priests. **Dublin, B. Took.** 1678. Brs. WC3464.

1678 IRELAND. A collection of all the statutes now in use in ... Ireland. **Dvblin, by Benjamin Tooke.** 1678. Fol. WI356.

1678 IRELAND. For the prevention of all evil ... 20 November 1678. **Dublin, B. Took.** 1678. Fol. WI409.

1678 IRELAND. A proclamation having ... 6 November 1678. **Dublin, B. Tooke.** 1678. Fol. WI638.

1678 IRELAND. We judging it requisite ... 14 October 1678. **Dublin, B. Tooke, sold by Mary Crook.** 1678. Brs. WI691.

1678 IRELAND. We the Lord Lieutenant and ... 20 November 1678. **Dublin, B. Took.** 1687 [i.e. 1678]. Brs. WI695.

1678 IRELAND. Whereas by order ... 28 March 1678. **Dublin, B. Tooke.** 1678. Fol. WI734.

1678 IRELAND. Whereas by proclamation ... bearing ... 12 December 1678. **Dublin, B. Took.** 1678. Fol. WI745.

1678 IRELAND. Whereas by some letters ... 13 December 1678. **Dublin, B. Took.** 1678. Brs. W I752.

1678 IRELAND. Whereas by two several ... 16 October 1678. **Dublin, B. Took**e. 1678. Fol. W I761.

1678 IRELAND. Whereas His Majesty by ... 12 April 1678. **Dublin, B. Tooke.** 1678. Brs. WI803.

1678 IRELAND. Whereas the process of His ... 27 April 1678. **Dublin, B. Tooke, sold by Joseph Wilde.** 1678. Brs. WI939.

1678 IRELAND. Whereas we are informed ... 9 January 1677 [8]. **Dublin, B. Tooke.** 1677 [8]. Fol. WI974.

1678 IRELAND. Whereas we are informed ... 22 March 1677 [8]. **Dublin, B. Tooke.** 1677 [8]. Brs. WI975.

1678 IRELAND. Whereas we have received ... 2 November 1678. **Dublin, B. Tooke.** 1678. Fol. WI992.

1679 An account of the public affairs in Ireland. **Dublin,** 1679. 4°. WA375.

1679 CHARLES II, king of England. There having been lately presented ... 17 January 1678/9. **Dublin, B. Took.** 1678 [9]. Brs. WE821.

1679 CHURCH OF ENGLAND. A form of prayer, to be used May 29. **Dublin.** 1679. 4°. WC4147.

1679 IRELAND. Vpon consideration had ... 10 December 1679. **Dublin, Took & Crook.** 1679. Brs. WI656.

1679 IRELAND. We ... being deeply sensible ... 14 May 1679. **Dublin, Took & Crook.** 1679. Fol. WI668.

1679 IRELAND. Whereas by our proclamation ... 26 March 1679. **Dublin, B. Took.** 1679. Fol. WI738.

1679 IRELAND. Whereas it appears by the examination ... 14 April 1679. **Dublin, B. Tooke & J. Crook.** 1679. Fol. WI836.

1679 IRELAND. Whereas the late horrid plot ... 10 December 1679. **Dublin, Took & Crook.** 1679. Fol. WI908.

1679 IRELAND. Whereas there hath been a ... 30 June 1679. **Dublin, Tooke & Crook.** [1679]. Fol. WI943.

1679 IRELAND. Whereas, tobacco is one of... 21 July 1679. **Dublin, Tooke & Crook.** 1679. Fol. WI949.

1679 IRELAND. Whereas we are informed ... 26 March 1679. **Dublin, B. Tooke.** 1679. Fol. WI976.

1679 IRELAND. Whereas we have received ... 23 December 1679. **Dublin, Took & Crook.** 1679. Fol. WI993.

1679 Narrative of the late design. **Dublin, reprinted.** 1679. 4°. WN191.

1679 SCOTLAND. PRIVY COUNCIL. By the Privy Council of Scotland. 23 January 1678/9. **Dublin.** 1679. Brs. WS1481.

1680 CARGILL, DONALD. A true and exact copy of a treasonable and bloody paper ... taken from. **Dublin.** 1680. 4°. WC570.

1680 CHARLES II, king of England. His Majesties gracious speech to both Houses ... 26th of January 1679/80. **Dublin, reprinted by Benjamin Took and John Brook.** 1679/80. Fol. WC3065A.

1680 DANGERFIELD, THOMAS. The information of. **[Dublin], reprinted.** 1680. 4°. WD188.

1680 DUGDALE, STEPHEN. The information of. **Reprinted at Dublin.** 1680. 4°. WD2476.

1680 [FLATMAN, THOMAS]. On the death of the Rt. honourable Thos. Earl of Ossory. **Printed at Dublin by Benjamin Tooke and John Crooke. Sold by Mary Crooke.** 1680. Fol. WF1146.

1680 IRELAND. Whereas by proclamation ... 26 April 1680. **Dublin, Took & Crook.** 1680. Brs. WI746.

1680 IRELAND. Whereas by several proclamations ... 29 November 1680. **Dublin, Took & Crook.** 1680. Fol. WI750.

1680 IRELAND. Whereas divers officers of His Majesties ... 29 November 1680. **Dublin, Took & Crook.** 1680. Fol. WI768.

1680 IRELAND. Whereas His Majesty ... 19 July 1680. **Dublin, Tooke & Crook.** 1680. Fol. WI807.

1680 IRELAND. Whereas His Majesty ... 15 November 1680. **Dublin, Took & Crook.** 1680. Fol. WI808.

1680 IRELAND. Whereas Redmond OHanlon ... 21 January 1679[80]. **Dublin, Took & Crook.** 1679[80]. Fol. WI860

1680 IRELAND. Whereas we are informed ... 24 March 1679[80]. **Dublin, Took & Crook.** 1679[80]. Brs. WI977.

1680 [LOWTHER, LUKE]. By the Lord Mayor of ... Dublin. [**Dublin.** 1680]. Brs. WL3333.

1680 NOTTINGHAM, HINEAGE FINCH, earl of. The speech of ... in Westminster Hall, ... Seventh of December, 1680. **Reprinted at Dublin, by Benjamin Took and John Crook: to be sold by Mary Crook.** 1680. Fol. WN1410.

1680 STILLINGFLEET, EDWARD, bp. The mischief of separation. Second edition. **Dublin, Ben. Took & J. Crook.** 1680. 4°. WS5606.

1680 STILLINGFLEET, EDWARD, bp. The mischief of separation. Third edition. **Dublin, Ben. Took & J. Crook.** 1680. 4°. WS5607.

1680 STILLINGFLEET, EDWARD, bp. The mischief of separation. Fourth edition. **Dublin, Ben. Took & J. Crook** 1680. 4°. WS5608.

1681 CHARLES II, king of England. A proclamation for dissolving this present Parliament. **Dublin, by Benjamin Tooke and John Crook.** [1680/1]. Brs. WC3335.

1681 DRYDEN, JOHN. Absalom and Achitophel. A poem with all the additions. [**Dublin.** 1681]. 4°. WD2213.

1681 DRYDEN, JOHN. Absalom and Achitophel. A poem. The second edition. [**Dublin.** 1681]. 4°. WD2214.

1681 IRELAND. Whereas by former orders ... 7 November 1681. **Dublin, Took & Crook.** 1681. Brs. WI728.

1681 IRELAND. Whereas we are informed ... 1 July 1681. **Dublin, Took & Crook.** 1681. Brs. WI978.

1682 COALES, JOHN. The coat of arms of N.T. J.F. & R.L. An answer to Thomson's ballad call'd The loyal feast. **Dublin, for A. Banks.** [1682?] Brs. WC4763.

1682 DRYDEN, JOHN. An elegy on the usurper O.C. [**Dublin?**] reprinted. 1682. 4°. WD2269.

1682 DRYDEN, JOHN. The second part of Absalom. **Dublin, for Robert Thornton**. 1682. 4°. WD2352.

1682 IRELAND. Whereas we the Lord Lieutenant ... 10 April 1682. **Dublin, Took & Crook**. 1682. Fol. WI1007.

1682 LAWRENCE, RICHARD. The interest of Ireland. **Dublin, by Jos. Ray, for Jos. Howes, and are to be sold by Awnsham Churchill, London**. 1682. 8°. WL680A.

1682 [WARE, ROBERT]. The second part of Foxes and firebrands. **Dublin, by Jos. Ray, for Jos. Howes, to be sold by Awnsham Churchill, in London**. 1682. 8°. WW853.

1683 IRELAND. It having pleased Almighty God ... 13 August 1683. [**Dublin, Took & Crook**. 1683]. Brs. WI420.

1683 IRELAND. Whereas many and ... 6 June 1683. **Dublin, Tooke & Crooke**. 1683. Fol. WI848.

1683 IRELAND. Whereas Robert Robinson late of ... 2 July 1683. **Dublin, Took & Crook**. 1683. Fol. WI863.

1683 IRELAND. Whereas the commissioners ... 15 January 1682[3]. **Dublin, Tooke & Crooke**. 1682[3]. Fol. WI896.

1683 IRELAND. Whereas the late farmers of his ... 12 January 1682[3]. **Dublin, Tooke & Crooke**. 1682[3]. Brs. WI906.

1683 IRELAND. Whereas we have received ... 12 October 1683. **Dublin, Took & Crook**. [1683]. Fol. WI994.

1683 MATHER, SAMUEL. The figures or types. [**Dublin**], **printed**. 1683. 4°. WM1279.

1683 OXFORD, UNIVERSITY OF. The judgment and decree of the ... July 21, 1683. **Dublin, reprinted**. 1683. Fol. WO892.

1683 SLEIGH, JOSEPH. Good advice and counsel. [**Dublin?**]. 1683. 8°. WS3991.

1683 WARBURTON, GEORGE. These are to give notice. [**Dublin**. 1683]. Brs. WW728.

1684 Carolina described more fully. **Dublin, printed**. 1684. 4°. WC606.

1684 IRELAND. A collection of all the statutes now in use in ... Ireland. **Dublin**. 1684. 12°. WI357.

1684 IRELAND. His Majesties chief commissioner ... 22 August 1684. **Dublin, B. Took**. 1684. Fol. WI412.

1684 IRELAND. Whereas by proclamation ... 21 June 1684. **Dublin, B. Took**. [1684]. Brs. W1747.

1684 IRELAND. Whereas His Majestie being ... 4 June 1684. **Dublin, B. Took**. [1684]. Fol. WI790.

1684 IRELAND. Whereas we are informed ... 5 May 1684. **Dublin, B. Took** [**sold by Mary Crook**]. [1684]. Brs. WI979.

1684 IRELAND. Whereas we are informed ... 9 June 1684. **Dublin, B. Took**. [1684]. Fol. WI980.

1684 Some reflections on the paper delivered unto the sheriffs ... by James Holloway. **Dublin**. 1684. 4°. WS4588.

1685 An account of the manner of taking the late Duke of Monmouth. **Dublin, by Benjamin Tooke; to be sold by Andrew Crook, and by Samuel Helsham**. [1685]. Fol. WA323.

1685 An account of what passed at the execution of the late Duke of Monmouth. **Dublin, reprinted by Andrew Crook and Samuel Helsham: to be sold by Andrew Crook, and Samuel Helsham**. 1685. Fol. WA435.

1685 CHURCH OF ENGLAND. A form of prayer with thanksgiving ... sixth day of February. **Dublin, by Benjamin Tooke; to be sold by Andrew Crook, and by Samuel Helsham**. 1685. 4°. WC4174.

1685 A consolatory epistle to D. T[itus] O[ates]. **Dublin**. 1685. 4°. WC5929.

1685 An elegy on the death of ... Richard, Earl of Arran. **Dublin**. 1685. Brs. WE378.

1685 An elegy on the death of the right honble. Richard Butler. **Dublin**. 1685. Brs. WE405.

1685 An elegy on the death of the right honourabe [sic] Richard Earl of Arran. **Dublin, printed**. 1685. Brs. WE406.

1685 ENGLAND. PARLIAMENT. The votes and farther proceedings. **Dublin, by Benjamin Took, to be sold by Samuel Helsham**. 1685. Fol. WE2440.

1685 IRELAND. We hereby think fit ... 10 February 1684/5. **Dublin, B. Took**. [1684/5]. Brs. WI689.

1685 IRELAND. Whereas by proclamation ... 16 October 1685. **Dublin, B. Tooke**. [1685]. Fol. WI748.

1685 IRELAND. Whereas by the ancient laws ... 10 July 1685. **Dublin, B. Tooke**. 1685. Fol. WI756.

1685 IRELAND. Whereas His Majesty being informed ... 11 August 1685. **Dublin, B. Tooke**. 1685. Brs. WI791.

1685 IRELAND. Whereas it appears by ... 23 December 1685. **Dublin, B. Tooke**. 1685. Fol. WI837.

1685 IRELAND. Whereas it hath pleased ... 11 February 1684[5]. **Dublin, B. Tooke, sold by Andrew Crook and Samuel Helsham**. 1684[5]. Fol. WI839.

1685 IRELAND. Whereas Richard Power, late. **Dublin, B. Tooke**. 1685. Brs. WI861.

1685 IRELAND. Whereas several of the ... 12 June 1685. **Dublin, B. Took, sold by Samuel Helsham**. [1685]. Fol. WI872.

1685 IRELAND. Whereas the kings most excellent Maiesty ... 6 February 1684[5]. **Dublin, Andrew Crook**. 1684[5]. Brs. WI904.

1685 IRELAND. Whereas upon information ... 20 June 1685. **Dublin, B. Tooke**. [1685]. Fol. WI950

1685 IRELAND. Whereas we are informed ... 24 July 1685. **Dublin, B. Took**. [1685]. Fol. WI981.

1685 IRELAND. Whereas we the Lord Lieutenant ... 11 February 1684[5]. **Dublin, B. Tooke**. 1684[5]. Brs. WI1008.

1685 IRELAND. Whereas we the Lords Justices ... 22 June 1685. **Dublin, B. Tooke**. [1685]. Fol. WI1011.

1685 IRELAND. Whereas we the Lords Justices ... 22 June 1685. **Dublin, B. Tooke**. [1685]. Fol. WI1012.

1685 IRELAND. Whereas we the Lords Justices ... 22 June 1685. **Dublin, B. Tooke**. [1685]. Brs. WI1013.

1685 JAMES II, king of England. An account of what His Majesty said. **Dublin, B. Took**. 1684[5]. Brs. WJ151.

1685   JAMES II, king of England. His Majesties most gracious speech to both Houses ... 9th of November 1685. **Dublin, reprinted by Benjamin Took, to be sold by Andrew Crook, and Samuel Helsham.** 1685. Fol. WJ230.

1685   JAMES II, king of England. A proclamation ... 13 June 1685. **Dublin, B. Tooke.** 1685. Fol. WJ241.

1685   JAMES II, king of England. A proclamation ... 16 June 1685. **Dublin, B. Tooke.** 1685. 4°. WJ244.

1685   JAMES II, king of England. A proclamation against spreading. **Dublin, B. Tooke.** 1685. Fol. WJ311.

1685   MATHER, SAMUEL. The figures or types. **Dublin, printed.** 1685. sold at London by H. Sawbridge, and A. Churchill. 4°. WM1280.

1685   On His Majesties sending the right honourable Henry Earl of Clarendon. **Dublin, by Andrew Crook and Samuel Helsham, to be sold by Andrew Crook, and by Samuel Helsham.** [1685?]. Brs. WO297.

1685   PENN, WILLIAM. The Quakers elegy on the death of Charles. **Dublin, by Andrew Crook and Samuel Helsham, to be sold by Samuel Helsham.** 1685. Brs. WP1350.

1685   SCOTLAND. ESTATES. The proceedings of the Parliament of Scotland. **Dublin, reprinted for William Mendey, Eliphal Dobson, and Robert Thornton.** 1685. 4°. WS1305.

1685   Upon the arrival of ... Henry, Earl of Clarendon. **Dublin.** 1685. Fol. WU107.

1686   CHARLES II, king of England. Copies of two papers written by. **Dublin, reprinted for Robert Thornton.** 1686. 4°. WC2945.

1686   CHARLES II, king of England. Copies of two papers written by. **Dublin, reprinted by Jos. Ray, for Rob. Thornton.** 1686. 4°. WC2946.

1686   IRELAND. For the quieting of the minds ... 28 July 1686. **Dublin, Crook & Helsham.** 1686. Brs. WI410.

1686   IRELAND. Whereas not only the pious ... 27 January 1685[6]. **Dublin, B. Tooke.** 1685[6]. Fol. WI850.

1686   IRELAND. Whereas there have been ... 8 December 1686. **Dublin, Crook & Helsham.** 1686. Fol. WI944.

1686   JAMES II, king of England. A proclamation of the kings Majesties ... pardon. **Dublin, by Andrew Crook & Samuel Helsham, sold by Samuel Helsham, Joseph Howes, and Eliphal Dopson.** 1686. Brs. WJ364.

1686   JAMES II, king of England. To the most reverend fathers in God, William. **Dublin, re-printed by Andrew Crook, and Samuel Helsham, assigns of Benjamin Tooke, to be sold by Andrew Crook and Samuel Helsham.** 1686. 8°. WJ391.

1686   KING, WILLIAM, abp. Catholick religion asserted. **Dublin.** 1686. 4°. WK525.

1686   STILLINGFLEET, EDWARD, bp. An answer to some papers. **Dublin, by Jos. Ray for Rob. Thornton.** 1686. 4°. WS5563.

1686   WARREN, ALBERTUS. A panegyrick to his excellency Richard, Earl of Tirconnell. **Dublin, for Joseph Ray.** 1686. Brs. WW953A.

1686   WETENHALL, EDWARD, bp. Hexapla Jacobæa: a specimen. **Dublin, by A. Crook and S. Helsham, for W. Norman, S. Helsham, E. Dobson.** 1686. 8°. WW1501.

1687   IRELAND. A declaration ... 18 July 1687. **Dublin, Crook & Helsham.** 1687. Brs. WI360.

1687   IRELAND. A declaration concerning the pay ... 29 April 1687. **Dublin, Crook & Helsham.** 1687. Fol. WI373.

1687   IRELAND. Whereas a late proclamation ... 21 February 1686[7]. **Dublin, Crook & Helsham.** 1686[7]. Fol. WI701.

1687   IRELAND. Whereas a petition was ... 2 May 1687. **Dublin, Crook & Helsham.** 1687. Fol. WI704.

1687   IRELAND. Whereas an act of Council ... 18 July 1687. **Dublin, Crook & Helsham.** 1687. Fol. WI710.

1687   IRELAND. Whereas several merchants ... 7 March 1686[7]. **Dublin, Crook & Helsham.** 1686[7]. Brs. WI869.

1687   IRELAND. Whereas the commissioners ... 11 April 1687. **Dublin, Crook & Helsham.** 1687. Fol. WI897.

1687   IRELAND. Whereas we are informed ... 21 February 1686[7]. **Dublin, Crook & Helsham.** 1686[7]. Fol. WI982.

1687   IRELAND. Whereas we are informed ... 4 April 1687. **Dublin, Crook & Helsham.** 1687. Brs. WI984.

1687   [PRIOR, MATTHEW]. The hind and the panther transvers'd. [**Dublin**]. 1687. 4°. WP3512.

1688   IRELAND. A declaration ... 1 June 1688. **Dublin, Crook & Helsham.** 1688. Brs. WI361.

1688   IRELAND. A declaration ... 25 September 1688. **Dublin, Crook & Helsham.** 1688. Brs. WI362.

1688   IRELAND. A declaration ... 29 December 1688. **Dublin, Crook & Helsham.** 1688. Fol. WI363.

1688   IRELAND. A declaration concerning the incamping of the horse. **Dublin, Crook & Helsham.** 1688. Brs. WI371.

1688   IRELAND. A declaration for the good government ... 20 July 1688. **Dublin, Crook & Helsham.** Fol. WI377.

1688   IRELAND. A declaration for the good government ... 24 August 1688. **Dublin, Crook & Helsham.** 1688. Fol. WI378.

1688   IRELAND. Whereas a proclamation ... 16 January 1687[8]. **Dublin, Crook and Helsham.** 1687[8]. Fol. WI705.

1688   IRELAND. Whereas by the ancient laws ... 15 October 1688. **Dublin, Crook & Helsham.** 1688. Fol. WI757.

1688   IRELAND. Whereas His Sacred Majesty ... 4 April 1688. **Dublin, Crook & Helsham.** 1688. Fol. WI811.

1688   IRELAND. Whereas it hath pleased ... 8 February 1687[8]. **Dublin, Crook & Helsham.** 1687[8]. Fol. WI841.

1688   IRELAND. Whereas several persons ... 20 September 1688. **Dublin, Crook & Helsham.** 1688. Fol. WI874.

1688 IRELAND. Whereas several persons ... 20 September 1688. **Dublin, Crook & Helsham.** [1688]. Brs. WI875.

1688 IRELAND. Whereas several persons ... 7 December 1688. **Dublin, Crook & Helsham.** 1688. Fol. WI876.

1688 IRELAND. Whereas the master-porters ... 31 May 1688. [**Dublin.** 1688]. Brs. WI915.

1688 IRELAND. Whereas we have ... 28 December 1688. **Dublin, Crook & Helsham.** 1688. Fol. WI986.

1688 JAMES II, king of England. A declaration ... 21 September 1688. **Dublin, Crook & Helsham.** 1688. Brs. WJ159.

1688 JAMES II, king of England. A declaration ... 6 November 1688. **Dublin, Crook & Helsham.** 1688. Brs. WJ162.

1688 JAMES II, king of England. A proclamation ... 28th day of September 1688. **Dublin, by Andrew Crook & Samuel Helsham.** 1688. Brs. WJ261.

1688 JAMES II, king of England. A proclamation for the speedy calling of a Parliament. **Dublin, by Andrew Crook & Samuel Helsham.** 1688. Brs. WJ359.

1688 LOUIS XIV, king of France. The French King's declaration of war by sea and land against the Spaniards. **Dublin, reprinted.** 1688. Brs. WL3113.

1688 SEATON, ALEXANDER. A testimony of tender advice. [**Dublin.** 1688]. 4°. WS2252.

1689 An account of a late, horrid and bloody massacre in Ireland. [**Dublin?**], **printed.** 1689. 4°. WA186.

1689 IRELAND. At a General Court Martial held at the Inns in Dublin. Whereas information ... 14 August 1689. **Dublin, Crook and Helsham.** [1689]. Brs. WI337.

1689 IRELAND. A declaration of ... 2 February 1688/9. **Dublin, Crook & Helsham.** 1688[9]. Brs. WI364.

1689 IRELAND. A declaration of ... 25 February 1688[9]. **Dublin, Crook & Helsham.** 1688[9]. Brs. WI365.

1689 IRELAND. A declaration of ... 1 March 1688[9]. **Dublin, Crook & Helsham.** 1688[9]. Brs. WI366.

1689 IRELAND. Whereas several persons ... 25 January 1688[9]. **Dublin, Crook & Helsham.** 1688[9]. Fol. WI878.

1689 IRELAND. Whereas several persons ... 7 March 1688[9]. **Dublin, Crook & Helsham.** 1689. Brs. WI879.

1689 JAMES II, king of England. A declaration ... 1 April 1689. **Dublin, Crook & Helsham.** 1689. WJ164.

1689 JAMES II, king of England. A declaration ... 28 June 1689. **Dublin, Crook & Helsham.** 1689. Fol. WJ166.

1689 JAMES II, king of England. A declaration ... 2 September 1689. **Dublin, by Andrew Crook and Samuel Helsham, assigns of Benjamin Tooke.** 1689. Brs. WJ169.

1689 JAMES II, king of England. A declaration... 3 September 1689. **Dublin, Crook & Helsham.** 1689. Brs. WJ170.

1689 JAMES II, king of England. A declaration... 12 November 1689. **Dublin, by Andrew Crook the assign of Benjamin Tooke.** 1689. Brs. WJ172.

1689 JAMES II, king of England. A declaration... 24 November 1689. **Dublin, by Andrew Crook the assign of Benjamin Tooke.** 1689. Brs. WJ173.

1689 JAMES II, king of England. A declaration for the better government. **Dublin, by Andrew Crook the assignee of Benjamin Tooke.** 1689. Brs. WJ181.

1689 JAMES II, king of England. His Majesties most gracious speech to both Houses ... seventh of May. 1689. **Dublin, Dublin [sic] by Andrew Crook and Samuel Helsham.** 1689. Fol. WJ232.

1689 JAMES II, king of England. An order...23 August 1689. **Dublin, by Andrew Crook and Samuel Helsham, assigns of Benjamin Tooke.** 1689. Brs. WJ234.

1689 JAMES II, king of England. Our will and pleasure is that you ... 25 August 1689. **Dublin, by Andrew Crook and Samuel Helsham, assigns of Benjamin Tooke.** 1689. Brs. WJ237.

1689 JAMES II, king of England. A proclamation... 25 March 1689. **Dublin, by Andrew Crook and Samuel Helsham.** 1689. Brs. WJ265.

1689 JAMES II, king of England. A proclamation... 25 March 1689. **Dublin; by Andrew Crook and Samuel Helsham.** 1689. Brs. WJ267.

1689 JAMES II, king of England. A proclamation... 25 March 1689. **Dublin, by Andrew Crook & Samuel Helsham.** 1689. Brs. WJ269.

1689 JAMES II, king of England. A proclamation... 25 March 1689. **Dublin, by Andrew Crook and Samuel Helsham.** 1689. Fol. WJ271.

1689 JAMES II, king of England. A proclamation... 1 April 1689. **Dublin, by Andrew Crook and Samuel Helsham, assigns of Tooke.** 1689. Fol. WJ272.

1689 JAMES II, king of England. A proclamation... 4 May 1689. **Dublin, by Andrew Crook and Samuel Helsham, assigns of Tooke.** 1689. Brs. WJ273.

1689 JAMES II, king of England. A proclamation... 4 May 1689. **Dublin, by Andrew Crook and Samuel Helsham.** 1689. Brs. WJ274.

1689 JAMES II, king of England. A proclamation... 14 June 1689. **Dublin, by Andrew Crook and Samuel Helsham, assigns of Benjamin Tooke.** 1689. Brs. WJ275.

1689 JAMES II, king of England. A proclamation... 18 June 1689. **Dublin, by Andrew Crook and Samuel Helsham, assigns of Benjamin Tooke.** 1689. Fol. WJ276.

1689 JAMES II, king of England. A proclamation... 24 June 1689. **Dublin, by Andrew Crook and Samuel Helsham, assigns of Benjamin Tooke.** 1689. Brs. WJ277.

1689 JAMES II, king of England. A proclamation... 27 June 1689. **Dublin, by Andrew Crook and Samuel Helsham, assigns of Benjamin Tooke.** 1689. Fol. WJ278.

1689 JAMES II, king of England. A proclamation... 20 July 1689. **Dublin, by Andrew Crook and Samuel Helsham, assigns of Benjamin Tooke.** 1689. Brs. WJ279.

1689   JAMES II, king of England. A proclamation...
20 July 1689. **Dublin, by Andrew Crook and
Samuel Helsham, assigns of Benjamin Tooke.**
1689. Brs. WJ280.

1689   JAMES II, king of England. A proclamation...
26 July 1689. **Dublin, by Andrew Crook and
Samuel Helsham, assigns of Benjamin Tooke.**
1689. Brs. WJ281.

1689   JAMES II, king of England. A proclamation...
26 July 1689. **Dublin, by Andrew Crook and
Samuel Helsham, assigns of Benjamin Tooke.**
1689. Brs. WJ282.

1689   JAMES II, king of England. A proclamation...
27th day of July 1689. **Dublin, by Andrew Crook
and Samuel Helsham, assigns of Benjamin Tooke.**
1689. Brs. WJ283.

1689   JAMES II, king of England. A proclamation...
30 July 1689. **Dublin, by Andrew Crook and
Samuel Helsham, assigns of Benjamin Tooke.**
1689. Brs. WJ284.

1689   JAMES II, king of England. A proclamation...
5 August 1689. **Dublin, by Andrew Crook and
Samuel Helsham, assigns of Benjamin Tooke.**
1689. Brs. WJ285.

1689   JAMES II, king of England. A proclamation...
20 August 1689. **Dublin, by Andrew Crook and
Samuel Helsham, assigns of Benjamin Tooke.**
1689. Brs. WJ286.

1689   JAMES II, king of England. A proclamation...
31 October 1689. **Dublin, by Andrew Crook
the assign of Benjamin Tooke.** 1689. Brs.
WJ287.

1689   JAMES II, king of England. A proclamation...
[31 October 1689.] **Dublin, by Andrew Crook the
assign of Benjamin Tooke.** 1689. Brs. WJ288.

1689   JAMES II, king of England. A proclamation...
18 November 1689. **Dublin, by Andrew Crook the
assign of Benjamin Tooke.** 1689. WJ289.

1689   JAMES II, king of England. A proclamation...
29 November 1689. **Dublin, by Andrew Crook the
assign of Benjamin Tooke.** 1689. Brs. WJ290.

1689   JAMES II, king of England. A proclamation...
30 November 1689. **Dublin, by Andrew Crook the
assign of Benjamin Tooke.** 1689. Brs. WJ291.

1689   JAMES II, king of England. A proclamation...
13 December 1689. **Dublin, by Andrew Crook the
assign of Benjamin Tooke.** 1689. Brs. WJ292.

1689   JAMES II, king of England. A proclamation for
27 December 1689. **Dublin, by Andrew Crook the
assignee of Benjamin Tooke, to be sold by Andrew
Crook.** 1689. Brs. WJ293.

1689   JAMES II, king of England. A proclamation for
the better government. **Dublin, by Andrew Crook
the assignee of Benjamin Tooke.** 1689. Fol.
WJ350.

1689   JAMES II, king of England. We are graciously
pleased to declare ... 2 September. [**Dublin.**
1689]. Brs. WJ398.

1689   JAMES II, king of England. Whereas all reason-
able means are ... 14 September 1689. **Dublin,
by Andrew Crook and Samuel Helsham, assigns of
Benj. Tooke.** 1689. Brs. WJ400.

1689   JAMES II, king of England. Whereas an address
hath been ... 5 August 1689. **Dublin, by Andrew
Crook and Samuel Helsham, assigns of Benjamin
Tooke.** 1689. Brs. WJ401.

1689   JAMES, II, king of England. Whereas great disorders have been ... 24 September 1689.
**Dublin, by Andrew Crook and Samuel Helsham,
assigns of Benjamin Tooke.** 1689. Brs. WJ403.

1689   JAMES II, king of England. Whereas several of
our troops of horse ... 2 November 1689.
Dublin, by Andrew Crook. 1689. Brs. WJ408.

1689   JAMES II, king of England. Whereas we are
informed that ... 24 September 1689. **Dublin,
by Andrew Crook and Samuel Helsham, assigns of
Benjamin Tooke.** 1689. Brs. WJ409.

1689   JAMES II, king of England. Whereas we have
issued a proclamation ... 8 October 1689.
**Dublin, by Andrew Crook and Samuel Helsham,
assigns of Benj. Tooke.** 1689. Brs. WJ410.

1689   JAMES II, king of England. Whereas we have
prorogued the ... 17 October 1689. **Dublin, by
Andrew Crook and Samuel Helsham the assign of
Benjamin Tooke.** 1689. Brs. WJ411.

1689   REILY, EDMOND. Whereas several of the
inhabitants ... 27 September 1689. **Dublin,
Crook & Helsham.** 1689. Brs. WR766.

1690   ATHLONE, GODERT GINKELL, earl of. Their
majesties forces. **Dublin, by Andrew Crook,
assignee of Benjamin Tooke.** 1690. Fol. WA4118.

1690   [DOPPING, ANTHONY, bp]. A speech spoken by
the Bishop of Meath ... July the 7th, 1690.
**Dublin, by Andrew Crook assignee of Benjamin
Tooke.** [1690]. Brs. WD1916.

1690   IRELAND. By the right honorable the Commissioners ... 16 July 1690. **Dublin, A. Crook.**
[1690]. Brs. WI352.

1690   IRELAND. By the right honorable the Commissioners ... 19 July 1690. **Dublin, A. Crook.**
[1690]. Brs. WI353.

1690   IRELAND. A proclamation ... 18 September
1690. **Dublin, A. Crook.** 1690. Brs. WI432.

1690   IRELAND. A proclamation ... 19 September
1690. **Dublin, A. Crook.** 1690. Brs. WI434.

1690   IRELAND. A proclamation ... 26 September
1690. **Dublin, A. Crook.** [1690]. Brs. WI436.

1690   IRELAND. A proclamation ... 26 September
1690. **Dublin, A. Crook.** 1690. Brs. WI437.

1690   IRELAND. A proclamation ... 26 September
1690. **Dublin, E. Jones.** 1690. Brs. WI438.

1690   IRELAND. A proclamation ... 30 September
1690. **Dublin, A. Crook.** 1690. Brs. WI439.

1690   IRELAND. A proclamation ... 7 October 1690.
Dublin, A. Crook. [1690]. Brs. WI440.

1690   IRELAND. A proclamation ... 22 October 1690.
Dublin, A. Crook. 1690. Brs. WI441.

1690   IRELAND. A proclamation ... 14 November
1690. **Dublin, A. Crooke.** [1690]. Brs. WI442.

1690   IRELAND. A proclamation ... 19 November
1690. **Dublin, A. Crook.** [1690.] Brs. WI443.

1690   IRELAND. A proclamation ... 20 November
1690. **Dublin, A. Crook.** [1690.] Brs. WI444.

1690   IRELAND. A proclamation ... 2 December
1690. **Dublin, A. Crook.** [1690.] Brs. WI445.

1690   IRELAND. A proclamation ... 8 December
1690. **Dublin, A. Crook.** 1690. Brs. WI446.

1690   IRELAND. A proclamation ... 8 December
1690. **Dublin, A. Crook.** [1690]. Brs. WI447.

1690   IRELAND. A proclamation ... 8 December
1690. **Dublin, A. Crook.** [1690.] Brs. WI448.

1690 IRELAND. A proclamation ... 12 December 1690. **Dublin, A. Crook.** [1690]. Brs. WI449.

1690 IRELAND. A proclamation ... 29 December 1690. **Dublin, A. Crook.** [1690]. Brs. WI450.

1690 IRELAND. A proclamation ... 31 December 1690. **Dublin, A: Crook.** [1690]. Brs. WI451.

1690 IRELAND. Rules to be observed ... 9 October 1690. **Dublin, Joseph Ray.** 1690. Brs. WI650.

1690 IRELAND. Whereas His Majesty in ... 14 April 1690. [**Dublin**. 1690]. Brs. WI809.

1690 IRELAND. Whereas it is of great importance ... 16 September 1690. **Dublin, A. Crook.** [1690]. Brs. WI846.

1690 IRELAND. Whereas it is of great importance ... 16 September 1690. [**Dublin**]. **For A. Crook.** 1690. Brs. WI847.

1690 IRELAND. Whereas the city of Dublin ... 16 September 1690. **Dublin, A. Crook.** 1690. Brs. WI889.

1690 IRELAND. Whereas the city of Dublin ... 16 September 1690. [**Dublin**]. **For A. Crook.** 1690. Brs. WI890.

1690 IRELAND. Whereas the several ... 24 July 1690. **Dublin, E. Jones.** 1690. Brs. W1940.

1690 IRELAND. Whereas the wives children and family ... 26 September 1690. **Dublin, A. Crook.** 1690. Brs. WI942.

1690 JAMES II, king of England. A declaration... 24 January 1689[90]. **Dublin, A. Crook.** 1689[90]. Brs. WJ174.

1690 JAMES II, king of England. A declaration... 14 February 1689[90]. **Dublin, for James Malone.** 1689[90]. Fol. WJ175.

1690 JAMES II, king of England. A declaration... 18 February 1689[90]. **Dublin, for James Malone.** 1689[90]. Fol. WJ176.

1690 JAMES II, king of England. A declaration... 28 February 1689[90]. **Dublin, for James Malone, to** [**be**] **sold at his shop. And by Andrew Crook.** 1689[90]. Brs. WJ177.

1690 JAMES II, king of England. A declaration... 19 March 1689[90]. **Dublin, for James Malone, to** [**be**] **sold at his shop. And by Andrew Crook.** 1689[90]. Brs. WJ178.

1690 JAMES II, king of England. A declaration... 26 April 1690. **Dublin, for James Malone.** [1690]. Brs. WJ179.

1690 JAMES II, king of England. A declaration... 9 June 1690. **Dublin, for James Malone.** [1690]. Brs. WJ180.

1690 JAMES II, king of England. A proclamation... 3 January 1689[90]. **Dublin, by Andrew Crook the assignee of Benjamin Tooke, to be sold by Andrew Crook.** 1689[90]. Brs. WJ294.

1690 JAMES II, king of England. A proclamation... 10 January 1689[90]. **Dublin by Andrew Crook the assignee of Benjamin Tooke, to be sold by Andrew Crook.** 1689[90]. Brs. WJ295.

1690 JAMES II, king of England. A proclamation... 21 January 1689[90]. **Dublin, by Andrew Crook, the assignee of Benjamin Tooke.** 1689[90]. Brs. WJ296.

1690 JAMES II, king of England. A proclamation... [21 January 1689[90]]. [**Dublin**] **By Andrew Crook, the assignee of Benjamin Tooke.** 1689[90]. Brs. WJ297.

1690 JAMES II, king of England. A proclamation... 4 February 1689[90]. **Dublin, for James Malone.** 1689[90]. Brs. WJ298.

1690 JAMES II, king of England. A proclamation... 4 February 1689[90]. **Dublin, for James Malone.** 1689[90]. Brs. WJ299.

1690 JAMES II, king of England. A proclamation... 28 February 1689[90]. **Dublin, for James Malone.** 1689[90]. Fol. WJ300.

1690 JAMES, II, king of England. A proclamation... 25th day of March 1690. **Dublin, for James Malone; to** [**be**] **sold at his shop, and by Andrew Crook.** 1690. Fol. WJ301.

1690 JAMES II, king of England. A proclamation... 28 March 1690. **Dublin, for James Malone; to** [**be**] **sold at his shop, and by Andrew Crook.** 1689[90]. Brs. WJ302.

1690 JAMES II, king of England. A proclamation... 4 April 1690. **Dublin, for James Malone; to** [**be**] **sold at his shop, and by Andrew Crook.** 1690. Brs. WJ303.

1690 JAMES II, king of England. A proclamation... 15 April 1690. **Dublin, for James Malone; to** [**be**] **sold at his shop, and by Andrew Crook.** 1690. Brs. WJ304.

1690 JAMES II, king of England. A proclamation... 21 April 1690. **Dublin, for James Malone.** 1690. Fol. WJ305.

1690 JAMES II, king of England. A proclamation... 13 June 1690. **Dublin, for James Malone.** 1690. Brs. WJ306.

1690 JAMES II, king of England. A proclamation... 15 June 1690. **Dublin, for James Malone.** 1690. Brs. WJ307.

1690 JAMES II, king of England. A proclamation... [15 June 1690.] [**Dublin**], **for James Malone.** 1690. Brs. WJ308.

1690 JAMES II, king of England. A proclamation... 15 June 1690. **Dublin, for James Malone.** [1690.] Brs. WJ309.

1690 JAMES II, king of England. We having thought fit ... 10 June 1690. **Dublin, by Andrew Crook.** [1690]. Brs. WJ359.

1690 WILLIAM III, king of England. Most gracious speech to both Houses – second of October, 1690. **Dublin, reprinted by Andrew Crook, assignee of Benjamin Tooke.** 1690. Fol. WW2385.

1690 WILLIAM AND MARY, king and queen of England. The declaration of ... seventh day of July, 1690. **By Edw. Jones, Dublin.** 1690. Brs. WW2512.

1690 WILLIAM AND MARY, king and queen of England. The declaration of ... 22 February, 1688[9]. **Dublin, reprinted by A. Crook.** [1690]. Brs. WW2508.

1690 WILLIAM AND MARY, king and queen of England. An order ... 20 June, 1690. **Dublin, by Andrew Crook.** 1690. Brs. WW2520.

1690 WILLIAM AND MARY, king and queen of England. A proclamation ... 19 June 1690. **By Edward Jones, Dublin.** 1690. Brs. WW2532.

1690 WILLIAM AND MARY, king and queen of England. A proclamation 24 June 1690. **Dublin, by A. Crook.** 1690. Brs. WW2534.

1690 WILLIAM AND MARY, king and queen of England. A proclamation 10 July, 1690. **By Edward Jones, Dublin.** 1690. Brs. WW2535.

1690   WILLIAM AND MARY, king and queen of England.
        A proclamation 31 July, 1690. **Dublin, by E. Jones.**
        1690. Brs. WW2542.

1690   WILLIAM AND MARY, king and queen of England.
        A proclamation 15 August 1690. **Dublin, by**
        Edward Jones. 1690. Brs. WW2544.

1690   WILLIAM AND MARY, king and queen of England.
        A proclamation for a fast. **By Edw. Jones, Dublin.**
        1690. Brs. WW2567.

1690   WILLIAM AND MARY, king and queen of England.
        The second declaration of. **By Edw. Jones in**
        Dublin. 1690. Brs. WW2633.

1690   WILLIAM AND MARY, king and queen of England.
        The second declaration of. **Dublin, by A. Crook.**
        1690. Brs. WW2634.

1691   ATHLONE, GODERT GINKELL, earl of. His
        Majesty by ... 27 April 1691. **Dublin, A. Crooke.**
        [1691]. Brs. WA4115.

1691   ATHLONE, GODERT GINKELL, earl of. The
        stealing of horses ... 12 May 1691. **Dublin,**
        A. Crook. [1691]. Brs. WA4116.

1691   ATHLONE, GODERT GINKELL, earl of. By ...
        4 February 1690[1]. **Dublin, A. Crook.** [1691].
        Brs. WA4117.

1691   ATHLONE, GODERT GINKELL, earl of. Whereas
        directions ... 25 November 1691. **Dublin,**
        A. Crook. [1691]. WA4119.

1691   ATHLONE, GODERT GINKELL, earl of. Whereas
        several considerable ... 4 December 1691.
        Dublin, A. Crook. [1691]. Brs. WA4120.

1691   ATHLONE, GODERT GINKELL, earl of. Whereas
        the right honourable ... [23 May 1691]. **Dublin,**
        A. Crook. [1691]. Brs. WA4121.

1691   IRELAND. By the Lords-Justices of Ireland,
        a proclamation ... 21st day of February, 1691.
        Dublin, by Andrew Crook, assignees of Benjamin
        Took. [1691]. Brs. WI351.

1691   IRELAND. For stating the accounts of the army
        ... 17 February 1690[1]. **Dublin, A. Crook.**
        [1691]. Brs. WI404.

1691   IRELAND. A proclamation ... 17 January
        1690[1]. **Dublin, A. Crook.** [1691]. Brs. WI452.

1691   IRELAND. A proclamation ... 27 January
        1690[1]. **Dublin, A. Crook.** 1691. Fol. WI453.

1691   IRELAND. A proclamation ... 6 February
        1690[1]. **Dublin, A. Crook.** 1691. Fol. WI454.

1691   IRELAND. A proclamation ... 21 February
        1690[1]. **Dublin, A. Crook.** [1691]. Brs. WI455.

1691   IRELAND. A proclamation ... 23 February
        1690[1]. **Dublin, A. Crook.** [1691]. Brs. WI456.

1691   IRELAND. A proclamation ... 24 February
        1690[1]. **Dublin, A. Crook.** [1691]. Brs. WI457.

1691   IRELAND. A proclamation ... 27 February
        1690[1]. **Dublin, A. Crook.** [1691]. Brs. WI458.

1691   IRELAND. A proclamation ... 28 February
        1690[1]. **Dublin, A. Crook.** 1691. Fol. WI459.

1691   IRELAND. A proclamation ... 26 March 1691.
        Dublin, A. Crook. [1691]. Brs. WI460.

1691   IRELAND. A proclamation ... 15 April 1691.
        Dublin, A. Crook. [1691]. Brs. WI461.

1691   IRELAND. A proclamation ... 30 April 1691.
        Dublin, A. Crook. [1691]. Brs. WI462.

1691   IRELAND. A proclamation 14 May 1691. **Dublin,**
        A. Crook. [1691]. Brs. WI463.

1691   IRELAND. A proclamation ... 23 May 1691.
        Dublin, A. Crook. [1691]. Brs. WI464.

1691   IRELAND. A proclamation ... 15 June 1691.
        Dublin, A. Crook. [1691]. Fol. WI465.

1691   IRELAND. A proclamation ... 17 June 1691.
        Dublin, A. Crook. [1691]. Fol. WI466.

1691   IRELAND. A proclamation ... 17 June 1691.
        Dublin, A. Crook. [1691]. Brs. WI467.

1691   IRELAND. A proclamation ... 22 June 1691.
        Dublin, A. Crook. [1691]. Brs. WI468.

1691   IRELAND A proclamation ... 22 June 1691.
        Dublin, A. Crook. 1691. Brs. WI469.

1691   IRELAND. A proclamation ... 1 July 1691.
        Dublin, A. Crook. 1691. Fol. WI470.

1691   IRELAND. A proclamation ... 7 July 1691.
        [**Dublin.** 1691]. Brs. WI471.

1691   IRELAND. A proclamation ... 15 July 1691.
        Dublin, A. Crook. [1691]. Fol. WI472.

1691   IRELAND. A proclamation ... 16 July 1691.
        Dublin, A. Crook. [1691]. Brs. WI473.

1691   IRELAND. A proclamation ... 24 July 1691.
        Dublin, A. Crook. [1691]. Brs. WI474.

1691   IRELAND. A proclamation ... 4 August 1691.
        Dublin, A. Crook. [1691]. Brs. WI475.

1691   IRELAND. A proclamation ... 16 September
        1691. **Dublin, A. Crook.** [1691]. Brs. WI476.

1691   IRELAND. A proclamation ... 18 September
        1691. **Dublin, A. Crook.** [1691]. Fol. WI477.

1691   IRELAND. A proclamation ... 25 September
        1691. **Dublin, A. Crook.** [1691]. Fol. WI478.

1691   IRELAND. A proclamation ... 14 October 1691.
        Dublin, A. Crook. [1691]. Brs. WI479.

1691   IRELAND. A proclamation ... 14 October 1691.
        Dublin, A. Crook. [1691]. Brs. WI480.

1691   IRELAND. A proclamation ... 7 November
        1691. **Dublin, A. Crook.** [1691]. Fol. WI481.

1691   IRELAND. A proclamation ... 9 November
        1691. **Dublin, A. Crook.** [1691]. Brs. WI482.

1691   IRELAND. A proclamation ... 9 November
        1691. **Dublin, A. Crook.** 1691. Brs. WI483.

1691   IRELAND. A proclamation ... 14 December
        1691. **Dublin, A. Crook.** [1691]. Brs. WI484.

1691   IRELAND. A proclamation ... 16 December
        1691. **Dublin, A. Crook.** [1691]. Brs. WI485.

1691   IRELAND. A proclamation against duelling.
        Dublin, A. Crook. [1691]. Brs. WI600.

1691   IRELAND. A proclamation for the encouragement
        of sutlers. **Dublin, A. Crook.** [1691.] Brs. WI629.

1691   IRELAND. Whereas by our proclamation ...
        25 June 1691. **Dublin, A. Crook.** 1691. Brs.
        WI739.

1691   IRELAND. Whereas divers persons ...
        9 December 1691. **Dublin, A. Crook.** [1691]. Brs.
        WI773.

1691   IRELAND. Whereas we have sent our ... 9 May
        1691. **Dublin, A. Crook.** [1691]. Brs. WI996.

1692   CHURCH OF ENGLAND. The form of prayer to
        be used ... twentieth of ... July. **Dublin, by**
        Andrew Crook, assignee of Benjamin Tooke.
        1692. 4°. WC4155.

1692   [DOPPING, ANTHONY, bp]. Modus tenendi Parlia-
        menta in Hibernia. **Dublin.** 1692. 4°. WD1912.

1692 IRELAND. Acts and statutes made in a Parliament. **Dublin, by Andrew Crook.** 1692. Fol. WI329.

1692 IRELAND. A declaration ... 20 January 1691[2]. **Dublin, A. Crook.** 1691[2]. Brs. WI367.

1692 IRELAND. A declaration concerning the pay ... 29 April 1687. **Dublin, A. Crook.** 1692. Fol. WI374.

1692 IRELAND. Information haveing been ... 4 January 1691. **Dublin, A. Crook.** [1691/2]. Brs. WI417.

1692 IRELAND. Information having been given ... March 1691/2. **Dublin, A. Crook.** 1691[2]. Brs. WI418.

1692 IRELAND. A proclamation ... 11 January 1691[2]. **Dublin, A. Crook.** 1691[2]. Brs. WI486.

1692 IRELAND. A proclamation ... 4 February 1691/2. **Dublin, A. Crook.** 1691/2. Brs. WI487.

1692 IRELAND. A proclamation ... 4 February 1691/2. **Dublin, A. Crook.** 1691[2]. Brs. WI488.

1692 IRELAND. A proclamation ... 23 March 1691[2]. **Dublin, A. Crook.** 1691[2]. Fol. WI489.

1692 IRELAND. A proclamation ... 20 May 1692. **Dublin, A. Crook.** 1691[2]. Brs. WI490.

1692 IRELAND. A proclamation ... 20 May 1691[2]. **Dublin, A. Crook.** 1691[2]. Brs. WI491.

1692 IRELAND. A proclamation ... 1 July 1692. **Dublin, A. Crook.** 1692. Brs. WI492.

1692 IRELAND. A proclamation ... 7 July 1692. **Dublin, A. Crook.** 1692. Brs. WI493.

1692 IRELAND. A proclamation ... 21 October 1692. **Dublin, A. Crook.** 1692. Fol. WI494.

1692 IRELAND. A proclamation ... 7 November 1692. **Dublin, A. Crook.** 1692. Fol. WI495.

1692 IRELAND. A proclamation ... 18 November 1692. **Dublin, A. Crook.** 1692. Brs. WI496.

1692 IRELAND. A proclamation ... 19 December 1692. **Dublin, A. Crook.** 1692. Fol. WI497.

1692 IRELAND. A proclamation ... 19 December 1692. **Dublin, A. Crook.** 1692. Brs. WI498.

1692 IRELAND. A proclamation requireing all officers. **Dublin, A. Crook.** 1692. Fol. WI640.

1692 IRELAND. Whereas several soldiers ... 5 March 1691[2]. **Dublin, A. Crook.** 1691[2]. Brs. WI883.

1692 A list of the persons to whom lycences ... 22 February 1691/2. [**Dublin.** 1691/2]. Fol. WL2484.

1692 LLOYD, WILLIAM, bp. The pretences of the French invasion examined. **Dublin, reprinted for William Norman, Eliphalet Dobson, and Patrick Campbell.** 1692. 4°. WL2691.

1692 The military articles of Lymerick. **Dublin.** 1692. 4°. WM2050.

1692 SCOBELL, HENRY. Modus tenendi Parliamenta & consilia in Hibernia. **Dublin, by Andrew Crook, assignee of Ben. Tooke.** [1692]. 8°. WS926.

1692 SCOBELL, HENRY. Rules and customs. **Dublin, re-printed by Andrew Crook, assignee of Benjamin Tooke.** 1692. 8°. WS932.

1692 WILLIAM AND MARY, king and queen of England. A proclamation declaring the war in Ireland ... ended. **Dublin, by A. Crook.** 1691[2]. Brs. WW2564.

1693 CHURCH OF ENGLAND. A form of prayer and thanksgiving. **Dublin, by Andrew Crook.** 1693. 4°. WC4130.

1693 IRELAND. A proclamation ... 2 January 1692[3]. **Dublin, A. Crook.** 1692[3]. Fol. WI499.

1693 IRELAND. A proclamation ... 17 February 1692[3]. **Dublin, A. Crook.** 1692[3]. Brs. WI500.

1693 IRELAND. A proclamation ... 17 February 1692[3]. **Dublin, A. Crook.** 1692[3]. Brs. WI501.

1693 IRELAND. A proclamation ... 27 March 1693. **Dublin, A. Crook.** 1693. Brs. WI502.

1693 IRELAND. A proclamation ... 8 April 1693. **Dublin, A. Crook.** 1693. Brs. WI503.

1693 IRELAND. A proclamation ... 28 April 1693. **Dublin, A. Crook.** 1693. Brs. WI504.

1693 IRELAND. A proclamation ... 3 May 1693. **Dublin, A. Crook.** 1693. Fol. WI505.

1693 IRELAND. A proclamation ... 17 May 1693. **Dublin, A. Crook.** 1693. Brs. WI506.

1693 IRELAND. A proclamation ... 26 June 1693. **Dublin, A. Crook.** 1693. Brs. WI507.

1693 IRELAND. A proclamation ... 18 August 1693. **Dublin, A. Crook.** 1693. Fol. WI508.

1693 IRELAND. A proclamation ... 18 October 1693. **Dublin, A. Crook.** 1693. Fol. WI509.

1693 IRELAND. A proclamation ... 19 October 1693. **Dublin, A. Crook.** 1693. Brs. WI510.

1693 IRELAND. A proclamation ... 22 November 1693. **Dublin, A. Crook.** 1693. Brs. WI511.

1694 ATKYNS, Sir ROBERT. The lord Chief Baron Atkyn's speech to Sir William Ashhurst. **Dublin, reprinted for M. Gunn.** 1694. Fol. WA4143.

1694 H[OPKINS], C[HARLES]. Epistolary poems. **Dublin.** 1694. 8°. WH2722.

1694 IRELAND. A proclamation ... 16 February 1693. **Dublin, A. Crook.** 1693[4]. Brs. WI512.

1694 IRELAND. A proclamation ... 23 May 1694. **Dublin, A. Crook.** 1694. Brs. WI513.

1694 IRELAND. A proclamation ... 2 July 1694. **Dublin, A. Crook.** 1694. Brs. WI514.

1694 IRELAND. A proclamation ... 19 October 1694. **Dublin, A. Crook.** 1694. Brs. WI515.

1694 IRELAND. A proclamation ... 10 December 1694. **Dublin, A. Crook.** 1694. Fol. WI516.

1695 Answers the Corporation of weavers. [**Dublin.** 1695]. Brs. WA3291.

1695 CONGREVE, WILLIAM. The mourning nurse of Alexis. "Third" edition. **Dublin, for William Norman and Jacob Milner.** 1695. Fol. WC5862.

1695 CORKER, SAMUEL. The great necessity. **Dublin: by Joseph Ray.** 1695. Fol. WC6307.

1695 DIONYSIUS SYRUS. A clear and learned exposition of. **Dublin: by Samuel Lee.** 1695. 4°. WD1524.

1695 ENGLAND. PARLIAMENT. Two acts I. An act for reviving two statutes. **Dublin, by Andrew Crook.** 1695. Fol. WE2383.

1695 ENGLAND. PARLIAMENT. Two acts, I. an act for taking away the writt. **Dublin, by Andrew Crook.** 1695. Fol. WE2384.

1695 ENGLAND. PARLIAMENT. Two acts I. An act to take away damage clear. **Dublin, reprinted by Andrew Crook.** 1695. Fol. WE2385.

1695   IRELAND.   An act concerning fines in the County Palatine of Tipperary.   **Dublin, by Andrew Crook.** 1695.   Fol.   WI298.

1695   IRELAND.   An act declaring which days.   **Dublin, by Andrew Crook.**   1695.   Fol.   WI299.

1695   IRELAND.   An act for continuing the statute. **Dublin, by Andrew Crook.**   1695.   Fol.   WI302.

1695   IRELAND.   An act for granting tales on tryals. **Dublin, by Andrew Crook.**   1695.   Fol.   WI306.

1695   IRELAND.   An act for granting unto His Majesty. **Dublin, by Andrew Crook.**   1695.   Fol.   WI307.

1695   IRELAND.   An act for prevention of frauds. **Dublin, by Andrew Crook.**   1695.   Fol.   WI308.

1695   IRELAND.   An act for taking special bails. **Dublin, by Andrew Crook.**   1695.   Fol.   WI309.

1695   IRELAND.   An act for the better observation of the Lords-Day.   **Dublin, by Andrew Crook.**   1695. Fol.   WI310.

1695   IRELAND.   An act for the better regulating of measures.   **Dublin, by Andrew Crook.**   1695.   Fol. WI311.

1695   IRELAND.   An act for the better securing the government.   **Dublin, by Andrew Crook.**   1695. Fol.   WI312.

1695   IRELAND.   An act for the better settleing. **Dublin, by Andrew Crook.**   1695.   Fol.   WI313.

1695   IRELAND.   An act for the better suppressing Tories.   **Dublin, by Andrew Crook.**   1695.   Fol. WI314.

1695   IRELAND.   An act for the more easy discharging. **Dublin, by Andrew Crook.**   1695.   Fol.   WI318.

1695   IRELAND.   An act for the more effectual suppressing.   **Dublin, by Andrew Crook.**   1695.   Fol. WI319.

1695   IRELAND.   An act for the more speedy and effectual proceeding.   **Dublin, by Andrew Crook.** 1695.   Fol.   WI320.

1695   IRELAND.   An act for the prevention of vexatious. **Dublin, by Andrew Crook.**   1695.   Fol.   WI322.

1695   IRELAND.   An act to restrain foreign education. **Dublin, by Andrew Crook.**   1695.   Fol.   WI327.

1695   IRELAND.   A declaration . . . 18 January 1694[5]. **Dublin, A. Crook.**   1694[5].   Brs.   WI517.

1695   IRELAND.   A declaration . . . 22 February 1694/5.   **Dublin, A. Crook.**   1694[5].   Brs.   WI518.

1695   IRELAND.   A declaration . . . 9 December 1695. **Dublin, A. Crook.**   1695.   Brs.   WI519.

1695   IRELAND.   A proclamation concerning a Parliament.   **Dublin, A. Crook.**   1695.   Brs.   WI603.

1695   IRELAND.   A proclamation for a general fast. **Dublin, A. Crook.**   1695.   Brs.   WI611.

1695   IRELAND.   A proclamation for a publick thanksgiving.   **Dublin, A. Crook.**   1695.   Brs.   WI614.

1695   IRELAND.   A proclamation for a solemn and publick thanksgiving.   **Dublin, B. Tooke.**   1695. Fol.   WI615.

1695   IRELAND.   A proclamation for the raising of coyn. **Dublin, A. Crook.**   1695.   Fol.   WI636.

1695   The rector's case.   **London: for Edward Mory, and sold by M. Gunne, Dublin.**   1695.   4°.   WR655.

1695   The state of the English and foreign weavers case. [**Dublin.**   1695].   Brs.   WS5317.

1696   IRELAND.   By His Highness the Lord Protector's council . . . A declaration and Commission for the assessment.   [**Dublin?**   1696].   Fol.   WI337A.

1696   IRELAND.   A declaration . . . 20 January 1695/6. **Dublin, A. Crook.**   1695[6].   Brs.   WI520.

1696   IRELAND.   A declaration . . . 11 February 1695/6.   **Dublin, A. Crook.**   1695[6].   Brs.   WI521.

1696   IRELAND.   A declaration . . . 11 February 1695/6.   **Dublin, A. Crook.**   1695[6].   Brs.   WI522.

1696   IRELAND.   A declaration . . . 4 March 1695[6]. **Dublin, A. Crook.**   1695[6].   Brs.   WI523.

1696   IRELAND.   A declaration . . . 16 March 1695[6]. **Dublin, A. Crook.**   1695[6].   Brs.   WI524.

1696   IRELAND.   A proclamation . . . 25 April 1696. **Dublin, A. Crook.**   1696.   WI525.

1696   IRELAND.   A proclamation . . . 29 June 1696. **Dublin, A. Crook.**   1696.   Brs.   WI526.

1696   IRELAND.   A proclamation . . . 16 July 1696. **Dublin, A. Crook.**   1696.   Brs.   WI527.

1696   IRELAND.   A proclamation . . . 21 August 1696. **Dublin, A. Crook.**   1696.   Brs.   WI528.

1696   IRELAND.   A proclamation . . . 16 November 1696.   **Dublin, A. Crook.**   1696.   Brs.   WI529.

1696   IRELAND.   A proclamation . . . 4 December 1696.   **Dublin, A. Crook.**   1696.   Fol.   WI530.

1696   IRELAND.   A proclamation for a general fast . . . 17 June 1696.   **Dublin, A. Crook.**   1696.   Brs. WI612.

1696   IRELAND.   A proclamation for a thanksgiving. **Dublin, A. Crook.**   1696.   Brs.   WI618.

1696   IRELAND.   A proclamation for the publishing. **Dublin, A. Crook.**   1695[6].   Brs.   WI635.

1697   ENGLAND. PARLIAMENT.   An act for making the collectors receipts.   **Dublin: by Andrew Crook.** 1697.   Fol.   WE1048.

1697   IRELAND.   An act for avoiding of vexatious delays. **Dublin: by Andrew Crook.**   1697.   Fol.   WI300.

1697   IRELAND.   An act for banishing all Papists. **Dublin, by Andrew Crook.**   1697.   Fol.   WI301.

1697   IRELAND.   An act for dividing the parish of Saint Michan's.   **Dublin, by Andrew Crook.**   1697.   Fol. WI302A.

1697   IRELAND.   An act for granting a supply.   **Dublin: by Andrew Crook.**   1697.   Fol.   WI304.

1697   IRELAND.   An act for granting an additional duty upon tobacco.   **Dublin: by Andrew Crook.**   1697. Fol.   WI305.

1697   IRELAND.   An act for reforming abuses in making of butter-cask.   **Dublin, by Andrew Crook.**   1697. Fol.   WI308A.

1697   IRELAND.   An act for the confirmation of articles. **Dublin: by Andrew Crook.**   1697.   Fol.   WI315.

1697   IRELAND.   An act for the more easy, and speedy securing.   **Dublin: by Andrew Crook.**   1697.   Fol. WI317.

1697   IRELAND.   An act for the preventing frivolous . . . law-sutes.   **Dublin: Andrew Crook.**   1697.   Fol. WI321.

1697   IRELAND.   An act to hinder the reversal. **Dublin; by Andrew Crook.**   1697.   Fol.   WI324.

1697   IRELAND.   An act to prevent frauds.   **Dublin: by Andrew Crook.**   1697.   Fol.   WI325.

1697 IRELAND. An act to prevent Protestants inter-marrying. **Dublin, by Andrew Crook**. 1697. Fol. WI326.

1697 IRELAND. An act to supply the defects. **Dublin: by Andrew Crook**. 1697. Fol. WI328.

1697 IRELAND. Acts and statutes made in a Parliament. **Dublin, by Andrew Crook**. 1697. Fol. WI329A.

1697 IRELAND. By the honourable the Commissioners, appointed to hear ... 19 September 1697. **Dublin, A. Crook**. 1697. Brs. WI344.

1697 IRELAND. A proclamation ... 12 January 1696[7]. **Dublin, A. Crook**. 1696[7]. Fol. WI531.

1697 IRELAND. A proclamation ... 29 March 1697. **Dublin, A. Crook**. 1697. Fol. WI532.

1697 IRELAND. A proclamation ... 18 June 1697. **Dublin, A. Crook**. 1697. Brs. WI533.

1697 IRELAND. A proclamation ... 22 June 1697. **Dublin, A. Crook**. 1697. Brs. WI534.

1697 IRELAND. A proclamation ... 26 July 1697. **Dublin, A. Crook**. 1697. Brs. WI535.

1697 IRELAND. A proclamation ... 13 August 1697. **Dublin, A. Crook**. 1697. Brs. WI536.

1697 IRELAND. A proclamation ... 20 August 1697. **Dublin, A. Crook**. 1697. Brs. WI537.

1697 IRELAND. A proclamation ... 21 August 1697. **Dublin, A. Crook**. 1697. Brs. WI538.

1697 IRELAND. A proclamation ... 24 September 1697. **Dublin, A. Crook**. 1697. Brs. WI539.

1697 IRELAND. A proclamation ... 14 October 1697. **Dublin, A. Crook**. 1697. Brs. WI540.

1697 IRELAND. A proclamation ... 3 November 1697. **Dublin, A. Crook**. 1697. Brs. WI541.

1697 IRELAND. A proclamation ... 10 December 1697. **Dublin, A. Crook**. 1697. Brs. WI542.

1697 IRELAND. A proclamation ... 18 December 1697. **Dublin, A. Crook**. 1697. Brs. WI543.

1697 IRELAND. A proclamation for a thanksgiving. **Dublin, A. Crook**. 1697. Brs. WI619.

1697 IRELAND. Rules and orders to be observed. **Dublin, A. Crook**. 1697. Brs. WI644.

1697 IRELAND. Rules, orders and declarations. **Dublin, A. Crook**. 1697. WI645.

1697 IRELAND. Rules to be observed ... 9 October 1690. **Dublin, A. Crook**. 1697. Fol. WI651.

1697 IRELAND. Whereas by our proclamation ... 2 September 1697. **Dublin, A. Crook**. 1697. Fol. WI740.

1697 JAMES II, king of England. The late king James's second manifesto. **Dublin, re-printed by Andrew Crooke, for William Norman, Eliphal Dobson, Patrick Campbell and Jacob Milner**. 1697. 4°. WJ386A.

1697 [M., C.] The case of the coin fairly represented. [**Dublin?** 1697]. 4°. WM10.

1698 An answer to a letter from a gentleman in the country. **Dublin, by Andrew Crook, and are to be sold by William Norman and Eliphet Dobson**. 1698. 4°. WA3315.

1698 C[ROWLEY], R[OBERT]. The school of vertue. **Dublin**. 1698. 12°. WC7371.

1698 IRELAND. Acts and statutes made in a Parliament. **Dublin, by Andrew Crook**. 1698. Fol. WI329B.

1698 IRELAND. A proclamation ... 3 January 1697[8]. **Dublin, A. Crook**. 1697[8]. Brs. WI544.

1698 IRELAND. A proclamation ... 8 January 1697/8. **Dublin, A. Crook**. 1697[8]. Brs. WI545.

1698 IRELAND. A proclamation ... 27 January 1697[8]. **Dublin, A. Crook**. 1697[8]. Brs. WI546.

1698 IRELAND. A proclamation ... 5 February 1697[8]. **Dublin, A. Crook**. 1697[8]. Brs. WI547.

1698 IRELAND. A proclamation ... 21 February 1697/8. **Dublin, A. Crook**. 1697[8]. Brs. WI548.

1698 IRELAND. A proclamation ... 21 February 1697/8. **Dublin, A. Crook**. 1697[8]. Brs. WI549.

1698 IRELAND. A proclamation ... 1 April 1698. **Dublin, A. Crook**. 1698. Brs. WI550.

1698 IRELAND. A proclamation ... 27 April 1698. **Dublin, A. Crook**. 1698. Brs. WI551.

1698 IRELAND. A proclamation ... 7 May 1698. **Dublin, A. Crook**. 1698. Brs. WI552.

1698 IRELAND. A proclamation ... 7 May 1698. **Dublin, A. Crook**. 1698. Brs. WI553.

1698 IRELAND. A proclamation ... 23 May 1698. **Dublin, A. Crook**. 1698. Brs. WI554.

1698 IRELAND. A proclamation ... 2 June 1698. **Dublin, A. Crook**. 1698. Brs. WI555.

1698 IRELAND. A proclamation ... 16 June 1698. **Dublin, A. Crook**. 1698. Brs. WI556.

1698 IRELAND. A proclamation ... 27 June 1698. **Dublin, A. Crook**. 1698. Brs. WI557.

1698 IRELAND. A proclamation ... 27 June 1698. **Dublin, A. Crook**. 1698. Brs. WI558.

1698 IRELAND. A proclamation ... 30 June 1698. **Dublin, A. Crook**. 1698. Brs. WI559.

1698 IRELAND. A proclamation ... 12 July 1698. **Dublin, A. Crook**. 1698. Brs. WI560.

1698 IRELAND. A proclamation ... 14 July 1698. **Dublin, A. Crook**. 1698. Fol. WI561.

1698 IRELAND. A proclamation ... 14 July 1698. **Dublin, A. Crook**. 1698. Fol. WI562.

1698 IRELAND. A proclamation ... 14 July 1698. **Dublin, A. Crook**. 1698. Fol. WI563.

1698 IRELAND. A proclamation ... 22 August 1698. **Dublin, A. Crook**. 1698. Brs. WI564.

1698 IRELAND. A proclamation ... 29 August 1698. **Dublin, A. Crook**. 1698. Brs. WI565.

1698 IRELAND. A proclamation ... 12 September 1698. **Dublin, A. Crook**. 1698. Brs. WI566.

1698 IRELAND. A proclamation ... 7 October 1698. **Dublin, A. Crook**. 1698. Brs. WI567.

1698 IRELAND. A proclamation ... 8 October 1698. **Dublin, A. Crook**. 1698. Brs. WI568.

1698 IRELAND. A proclamation ... 19 October 1698. **Dublin, A. Crook**. 1698. Brs. WI569.

1698 IRELAND. A proclamation ... 29 October 1698. **Dublin, A. Crook**. 1698. Fol. WI570.

1698 IRELAND. A proclamation ... 18 November 1698. **Dublin, A. Crook**. 1698. Brs. WI571.

1698 IRELAND. A proclamation ... 24 November 1698. **Dublin, A. Crook**. 1698. Brs. WI572.

1698 IRELAND. A proclamation ... 3 December 1698. **Dublin, A. Crook**. 1698. Brs. WI573.

1698 IRELAND. A proclamation ... 7 December 1698. **Dublin, A. Crook**. 1698. Brs. WI574.

1698 IRELAND. A proclamation for preventing disorders. **Dublin, A. Crook.** 1697[8]. Brs. WI623.

1698 IRELAND. Whereas it hath pleased . . . 23 June 1688. **Dublin, Crook & Helsham.** 1698. Fol. WI842.

1698 MOLYNEUX, WILLIAM. The case of Ireland's being bound. **Dublin, by and for J. R. and are to be sold by R. Clavel and A. and J. Churchil.** 1698. 8°. WM2403.

1698 PENN, WILLIAM. Truth further clear'd. **Dublin, printed.** 1698. 8°. WP1391.

1699 [PULLEN, TOBIAS], bp. A vindication of Sir Robert King's designs. [**Dublin**]. 1699. 8°. WP4196.

1699 H., J. An essay concerning liberty of conscience. **Dublin, printed; to be sold by John Foster.** 1699. 4°. WH64.

1699 IRELAND. An act for the relief and release of poor distressed prisoners. **Dublin, by Andrew Crook.** 1699. Fol. WI322A.

1699 IRELAND. Acts and statutes made in a Parliament. **Dublin, by Andrew Crook.** 1699. Fol. WI330.

1699 IRELAND. A proclamation . . . 23 January 1698[9]. **Dublin, A. Crook.** 1698[9]. Fol. WI575.

1699 IRELAND. A proclamation . . . 7 February 1698[9]. **Dublin, A. Crook.** 1698[9]. Fol. WI576.

1699 IRELAND. A proclamation . . . 3 April 1699. **Dublin, A. Crook.** 1699. Fol. WI577.

1699 IRELAND. A proclamation . . . 5 April 1699. **Dublin, A. Crook.** 1699. Brs. WI578.

1699 IRELAND. A proclamation . . . 17 April 1699. **Dublin, A. Crook.** 1699. Fol. WI579.

1699 IRELAND. A proclamation . . . 1 May 1699. **Dublin, A. Crook.** 1699. Brs. WI580.

1699 IRELAND. A proclamation . . . 4 May 1699. **Dublin, A. Crook.** 1699. Brs. WI581.

1699 IRELAND. A proclamation . . . 12 May 1699. **Dublin, A. Crook.** 1699. Brs. WI582.

1699 IRELAND. A proclamation . . . 14 June 1699. **Dublin, A. Crook.** 1699. Brs. WI583.

1699 IRELAND. A proclamation . . . 5 July 1699. **Dublin, A. Crook.** 1699. Brs. WI584.

1699 IRELAND. A proclamation . . . 19 July 1699. **Dublin, A. Crook.** 1699. Fol. WI585.

1699 IRELAND. A proclamation . . . 14 August 1699. **Dublin, A. Crook.** 1699. Brs. WI586.

1699 IRELAND. A proclamation . . . 13 September 1699. **Dublin, A. Crook.** 1699. Fol. WI587.

1699 IRELAND. A proclamation . . . 5 October 1699. **Dublin, A. Crook.** 1699. Brs. WI588.

1699 IRELAND. A proclamation . . . 20 October 1699. **Dublin, A. Crook.** 1699. Fol. WI589.

1699 IRELAND. A proclamation . . . 30 October 1699. **Dublin, A. Crook.** 1699. Brs. WI590.

1699 IRELAND. A proclamation . . . 29 November 1699. **Dublin, A. Crook.** 1699. Brs. WI591.

1699 IRELAND. A proclamation . . . 29 December 1699. **Dublin, A. Crook.** 1699. Fol. WI592.

1699 IRELAND. Rules, orders and directions. **Dublin, A. Crook.** 1699. Fol. WI648.

1699 IRELAND. William . . . Whereas it has been humbly . . . 17 April 1699. **Dublin, A. Crook.** 1699. Fol. WI1015.

1700 Account concerning the fire and burning of Edenbourgh. **Dublin.** 1700. Brs. WA170.

1700 CLAYTON, JOHN. A sermon preached . . . February the 23d, 1700. **Dublin; by Joseph Ray.** [1700]. 4°. WC4611.

1700 ENGLAND. PARLIAMENT. The report of the commissioners appointed by Parliament to enquire into the Irish forfeitures. **By Edw. Jones; and reprinted in Dublin by John Brocas.** 1700. Fol. WE2232.

1700 [HUMFREY, THOMAS]. A true narrative of God's gracious dealing with the soul of Shalome ben Shalomoh. Third edition. **Dublin, by John Brocas, for John Ware.** 1700. 8°. WH3718A.

1700 IRELAND. By the Lords Justices general, . . . for the better preserving good order . . . 30 September 1700. **Dublin, A. Crook.** 1700. Fol. WI349.

1700 IRELAND. By the Lords Justices general, . . . whereas in and by . . . 26 January 1699. **Dublin, A. Crook.** 1699[1700]. Fol. WI350.

1700 IRELAND. A proclamation . . . 19 February 1699[1700]. **Dublin, A. Crook.** 1699[1700]. Fol. WI593.

1700 IRELAND. A proclamation . . . 18 March 1699[1700]. **Dublin, A. Crook.** 1699[1700]. Fol. WI594.

1700 IRELAND. A proclamation . . . 26 April 1700. **Dublin, A. Crook.** 1700. Brs. WI595.

1700 IRELAND. A proclamation . . . 17 May 1700. **Dublin, A. Crook.** 1700. Fol. WI596.

1700 IRELAND. A proclamation . . . 24 June 1700. **Dublin, A. Crook.** 1700. Brs. WI597.

1700 IRELAND. A proclamation . . . 26 June 1700. **Dublin, A. Crook.** 1700. Fol. WI598.

1700 IRELAND. A proclamation . . . 12 December 1700. **Dublin, A. Crook.** 1700. Brs. WI599.

1700 IRELAND. Rules, orders and instructions. **Dublin, A. Crook.** 1700. Fol. WI649.

1700 MELFORT, JOHN DRUMMOND, earl of. A letter directed to the Right Honourable the Earl of Perth. **Dublin.** 1700. Brs. WM1643.

1700 WILLIAM III, king of England. Most gracious speech to both Houses — 11th day of February. **Dublin.** 1700. Fol. WW2424.

DURHAM

1655 HOBSON, PAUL. Fourteen queries and ten absurdities. **By Henry Hills for William Hutchison in Durham.** 1655. 8°. WH2273.

EAST MOLESEY

1588 MARPRELATE, MARTIN, pseud. Oh read ouer D. Iohn Bridges for it is a worthy worke, Or an epitome of the fyrste booke of that right worshipfull volume written against the Puritanes. **Printed overseas in Europe.** [East Molesey? R. Waldegrave. October 1588]. 4°. STC17453.

1588 PENRY, JOHN. An exhortation vnto the gouernours and people of Wales. **Moulsey.** 1588. 8°. STC19605.

1588 UDALL, JOHN. A demonstration of the trueth of that discipline which Christe hath prescribed, etc. [**East Molesey, R. Waldegraue.** 1588]. 8°. STC24499.

EDINBURGH

1540 BOETHIUS, HECTOR. Heir beginnis the hystory and croniklis of Scotland. Translated by J. Bellenden. **Edinburgh, T. Davidson.** [1540?]. Fol. STC3203.

1569 LAUDER, WILLIAM. Ane godlie tractate, quhairuntill may be easilie perceauit quho thay be that ar ingraftit in to Christ. Compyld in meter. [**Edinburgh, R. Lekpreuik.** 1569?]. 4°. STC15315.

1570 SCOTLAND, CHURCH OF. GENERAL ASSEMBLY. The determination of the General Assemblie anent the obedience to the Kingis Maiestie his authoritie. [7 July 1570]. [**Edinburgh, R. Lekpreuik.** 1570]. Brs. STC22046.

1573 HOTMAN, FRANÇOIS. De furoribus gallicis, horrenda amirallij Castillionei cæde, inaudita piorum strage passim edita per complures Galliæ ciuitates. [E. Varamundus, pseud.] **Edimburgi.** 1573. 8°. STC13845.

1574 BARNAUD, NICOLAUS. Dialogi in Gallorum gratiam compositi per Eusebium Philadelphum. [Anon]. **Edimburgi ex typ. J. Jamæi.** [Geneva?]. 1574. 2 vols. 8°. STC1463.

1574 BARNAUD, NICOLAUS. La réveille-matin des François composé par Eusebe Philadelphe en forme de dialogues. [Anon]. **Edimbourg, J. James** [Geneva?]. 1574. 8°. STC1464.

1578 Maddeis proclamatioun. [A ballad]. **Edinburgh, R. Lekpreuik.** 1578. STC17177.

1580 SCOTLAND. PROCLAMATIONS. Ane proclamatioun for publischeing of the Actis of Parliament [23 Jan., 1579 o.s.]. [**Edinburgh, J. Ros.** 1580]. Fol. STC21946.

1583 BUCHANAN, GEORGE. Rerum Scoticarum historia. [**London?**], **Ad ex. A. Arbuthneti, Edinburgi.** 1583. Fol. STC3992.

1590 DANEAU, LAMBERT. The judgement of L. Danæus, touching certaine points now in controuersie. [**Edinburgh, R. Waldegrave,** 1590?]. 4°. STC6228.

1591 BRUCE, ROBERT. Sermons vpon the sacrament. **Edinburgh, R. Waldegrave.** [1591?]. 8°. STC3924.

1592 PERKINS, WILLIAM. A case of conscience. **Edinburgh, R. Walde-graue.** 1592. 8°. STC19666.

1594 NAPIER, JOHN. A plaine discouery of the whole Reuelation of Saint John. Newlie imprinted. [**Edinburgh, R. Waldegrave for**] **J. Norton,** [**London**]. 1594. 4°. STC18355.

1596 BUREL, JOHN. To the richt high, Lodwick duke of Lenox, J. Burel wisheth lang life. [Poems]. [**Edinburgh.** 1596?]. 4°. STC4105.

1596 SCOTLAND, CHURCH OF. Ane shorte and generall confession, etc. **Edinburgh, H. Charteris.** 1596. Brs. STC22024.

1597 SKENE, Sir JOHN. De verborum significatione. **Edinburgh, R. Walde-graue.** 1597. Fol. STC22622.

1597 A table of all the kinges of Scotland (a table of the moveable feastes for 50 yeires to cum). [**Edinburgh?** 1597?]. Fol. STC22014.

1598 WENTWORTH, PETER. A pithie exhortation to her majestie for establishing her successor. [**Edinburgh, R. Waldegrave**]. 1598. 2 vols. 8°. STC25245.

1599 A briefe and true declaration of the sicknes and death of Phillip the Second. Translated into English. **Edinburgh, R. Walde-graue.** 1599. 4°. STC19834.

1599 SCOTLAND. PROCLAMATIONS. Ane acte anent the registring of saisings, etc. [31 July, 1599]. **Edinburgh, R. Waldegraue.** 1599. Brs. STC21956.

1600 BLAKE, DAVID. An exposition vppon the thirtie two psalme. **Edinburgh, R. Waldegraue.** 1600. 8°. STC3122.

1600 SALUSTE DU BARTAS, GUILLAUME DE. Hadriani Dammanis a Bysterveldt Bartasias; de mundi creatione libri septem liberius tralati et acuti [sic]. **Edinburgi, R. Walde-graue.** 1600. 8°. STC21657.

1600 SCOTLAND. PROCLAMATIONS. Ane act made be his hienes, etc. [30 June, 1600]. **Edinburgh, R. Waldegraue.** 1600. Brs. STC21957.

1603 ENGLAND. PROCLAMATIONS. Forasmuch etc. [Proclamation of James I. 24 March. 1603]. **Edinburgh, R. Waldegrave.** 1603. Brs. STC8300.

1603 JAMES I, king of England. The copie of K. Maiesties letter to the L. Maior of London. [28 Mar. 1603]. [**Edinburgh.** 1603]. Brs. STC14362.

1603 JAMES I, king of England. The true lawe of free monarchies. **Edinburgh, R. Waldegraue.** 1603. 8°. STC14411.

1604 COLVILLE, JOHN. The palinod of J. Coluill, wherein he doth recant his former offences. **Edinburgh, R. Charteris.** 1604. 4°. STC5588.

1604 SCOTLAND. PROCLAMATIONS. Ane act of counsell anent the insertings of the clause of registration in seasings, etc. [5 Jan., 1604]. **Edinburgh, Widow Waldegraue.** 1604. Brs. STC21959.

1604 SCOTLAND. PROCLAMATIONS. Whereas B. Bulmer, etc. [An order of Council for search for mines. 16 Feb., 1604]. **Edinburgh, Widdowe Waldegraue.** 1604. Brs. STC21960.

1606 SCOTLAND. PROCLAMATIONS. Whereas divers of the ministerie, etc. [Prohibiting prayers for the imprisoned ministers. 26 Sept., 1606]. **Edinburgh, R. Charteris.** 1606. Brs. STC21964.

1606 SCOTLAND. PROCLAMATIONS. Whereas dureing oure stay, etc. [Enforcing laws against Jesuits, etc. 26 Sept. 1606]. **Edinburgh, R. Charteris.** 1606. Brs. STC21965.

1607 YOUNG, ANDREW. Theses philosophiæ præs. A. Young. **Edinburgi, R. Charteris.** 1607. 4°. STC26106.

1608 SCOTLAND. PROCLAMATIONS. James, etc. [Proclamation for better inbringing of the land tax. For the third instalment due 1 Feb., 1609. Filled in for Aberdeen]. [**Edinburgh, R. Charteris.** 1608]. Brs. STC21963.

1609 SCOTLAND. The xvi-xx parliament of King James the sext, extracted foorth of the Acts of Parliament. [By Sir J. Skene]. [**Edinburgh.** 1609]. Fol. STC21892.

1613 BECON, THOMAS. The sicke mans salue. **Edinburgh, A. Hart.** 1613. 8°. STC1771.

1614 DRUMMOND, WILLIAM, of Hawthornden. Poems. [**Edinburgh, A. Hart.** 1614?]. 4°. STC7253.

1614 JULIUS, ALEXANDER. Paraphrasis prophetiae Ieschahiae. **Edinburgi.** 1614. 4°. STC14856.

1615 BUCHANAN, GEORGE. Poemata castigata & aucta addito miscellaneorum libro. **Edinburgi, A. Hart.** 1615. 12°. STC3990.

1616 The speech of a Fife laird. [**Edinburgh?** 1616?]. Brs. STC10864.

1618   Rudimenta grammatices in gratiam juventutis
        Scoticæ conscripta. Prioribus edit. longe
        emendatior. **Edinburgi, A. Hart.** 1618. 8°.
        STC21438.

1620   SCOTLAND. PROCLAMATIONS. A proclamation
        for keeiping the Actes of the last Assemblies, etc.
        [8 June, 1620]. **Edinburgh, T. Finlason.** [1620].
        Brs. STC21966.

1622   REID, JAMES. Theses philosophicæ præs.
        J. Reido. **Edinburgi, hær A. Hart.** 1622. 4°.
        STC20859.

1623   FAIRLEY, JAMES. Theses philosophicæ. Praes.
        J. Fairlaeo. **Edinburgi, A. Hart.** 1623. 4°.
        STC10671.

1626   HAMILTON, FRANCIS. King James, his
        encomium. **Edinburgh, J. Wreittoun.** 1626. 4°.
        STC12726.

1626   REID, JAMES. Theses philosophicæ præs.
        J. Reido. **Edinburgi, J. Wreittoun.** 1626. 4°.
        STC20860.

1628   KING, WILLIAM. Theses philosophicæ præs.
        G. Regio. **Edinburgi, J. Wreittoun.** 1628. 4°.
        STC14997.

1628   SCOTLAND. PROCLAMATION. Charles etc.
        [Anent the yearly certification of Papists, 10 July,
        1628]. **Edinburgh, T. Finlason.** [1628]. Brs.
        STC21977.

1628   SCOTLAND. PROCLAMATIONS. Charles etc.
        [Concerning teinds. 14 July, 1628]. **Edinburgh,
        T. Finlason.** [1628]. Brs. STC21978.

1628   SCOTLAND. PROCLAMATIONS. Charles etc.
        [Lords of erections to produce their titles. 8 Aug.
        1628]. **Edinburgh, T. Finlason.** [1 ?8]. Brs.
        STC21981.

1628   SCOTLAND. PROCLAMATIONS. [A proclama-
        tion by the Commissioners of teinds concerning
        sellers and buyers. 3 Dec. 1628]. **Edinburgh,
        heirs of T. Finlason.** [1628]. Fol. STC21983.

1629   The confession and conversion of my lady
        C[ountess] of L[inlithgow]. **Edinburgh, J. Wreit-
        toun.** 1629. 8°. STC16610.

1629   KENNEDY, JOHN. A theological epitome, or divine
        compend. **Edinburgh, J. Wreittoun.** 1629. 8°.
        STC14931.

1629   SCOTLAND. PROCLAMATIONS. Anent the prop-
        osition, etc. [concerning teinds. 5 June 1629].
        Edinburgh, heirs of T. Finlason. [1629].
        Brs. STC21985.

1629   SCOTLAND. PROCLAMATIONS. Charles etc.
        [Publication of decrees on the generall submis-
        sions. 18 Sept., 1629]. **Edinburgh, heires of
        T. Finlason.** [1629]. Fol. STC21987.

1629   SCOTLAND. PROCLAMATIONS. Forasmeekle,
        etc. [Concerning wages of valuers, etc. 1 July,
        1629]. **Edinburgh, heirs of T. Finlason.** [1629].
        Brs. STC21986.

1629   SCOTLAND. PROCLAMATIONS. Forsomeekle,
        etc. [Sub-commissioners to meet at once. 24
        Mar., 1629]. **Edinburgh, heirs of T. Finlason.**
        [1629]. Brs. STC21984.

1631   Rudimenta grammatices in gratiam juventutis
        Scoticæ conscripta. Prioribus edit. longe
        emendatior. **Edinburgi, A. Hart.** 1631. 8°.
        STC21439.

1632   COWPER, WILLIAM, bp. The triumph of a
        christian. Ninth impression with two prayers.
        Edinburgh, Heirs of A. Hart. 1633. 8°.
        STC5941.

1633   Rudimenta grammatices in gratiam juventutis
        Scoticæ conscripta. Prioribus edit. longe
        emendatior. **Edinburgi, J. Wreittoun.** 1633. 8°.
        STC21440.

1633   SCOTLAND. PROCLAMATIONS. Charles, etc.
        [For collecting the tax for the College of Justice.
        28 June, 1633]. [**Edinburgh, R. Young.** 1633]. Brs.
        STC21993.

1634   The practice of christianity, gathered out of holy
        scripture, in Perkins, and other learned writers.
        Edinburgh, J. Wreittoun. 1634. 8°. STC5150.

1634   RALEIGH, Sir WALTER. Sir Walter Raleighs
        Instructions to his sonne and to posteritie.
        Edinburgh, J. Wreittoun. 1634. 8°. STC20645.

1636   Kirk patronage the peoples privilege. **Edinburgh,**
        1636. 12°. STC22035.

1638   Answers to some brethren of the ministerie; also
        Duplies of the ministers and professors.
        R. Y[oung], H. M. Printer for Scotland. 1638.
        2 vols. 4°. STC70.

1638   BURTON, ROBERT. The anatomy of melancholy.
        Fifth ed. **Oxford, for H. Cripps [printed by
        R. Young, Edinburgh, L. Lichfield, Oxford, and
        W. Turner, Oxford, with cancels by M. Flesher,
        London].** 1638. Fol. STC4163.

1638   Generall demands concerning the late covenant
        propounded by the ministers and professors in
        Aberdeen; with the answers: also the replies.
        Edinburgh, R. Young. 1638. 4°. STC67.

1640   BAILLIE, ROBERT. Ladensium $\alpha\upsilon\tau o\kappa\alpha\tau\acute{\alpha}\kappa\rho\iota\sigma\iota\varsigma$.
        The Canterburians self-conviction. [Anon].
        [Edinburgh, J. Bryson]. 1640. 2 vols. 4°.
        STC1205.

1640   MOORE, Sir WILLIAM. A counter-buff to
        Lysimachus Nicanor [i.e. John Corbet].
        [Edinburgh, R. Bryson]. 1640]. 4°. STC18062.

1640   SCOTLAND. ACTS. Act anent the out comming
        of horses. **Edinburgh.** 1640. Fol. STC21913.

1641   A catechisme for young children. [**Edinburgh?**]
        printed. 1641. Brs. WC1473.

1641   CHARLES I, king of England. His Majesties
        declaration to all his loving subjects. **Edinburgh.**
        1641. 4°. WC2252.

1641   CURRIEHILL, Sir JOHN SKENE, lord. De
        verborum significatione. **Edinburgh.** 1641. Fol.
        WC7682.

1641   ENGLAND. PARLIAMENT. Acts made in the
        second Parliament of ... Charles. **Edinburgh,
        by Robert Young and Evan Tyler.** 1641. Fol.
        WE1165.

1641   ENGLAND. PARLIAMENT. The heads of several
        proceedings in this present Parliament.
        **Imprinted first at London, re-imprinted by R.Y.
        and E.T. in Edinburgh.** 1641. 4°. WE1550.

1641   ENGLAND. PARLIAMENT. HOUSE OF
        COMMONS. It is this day ordered by the House.
        **Printed at London by Robert Barker and reprinted
        at Edinburgh by Robert Bryson.** 1641. Brs.
        WE2610.

1641   FALCONER, PATRICK. The anatomie of the
        messe. **Edinburgh, by James Bryson.** 1641.
        12°. WF299.

1641   GILLESPIE, GEORGE. An assertion of the
        government of the Church of Scotland.
        [**Edinburgh**], **printed.** 1641. 4°. WG746.

1641 HAMILTON, JAMES, duke. The Marqves Hamiltons speech before the Kings ... Novem. 6. 1641. **Printed at Edinburgh, by James Brison, reprinted for T.B.** 1641. 4°. WH484.

1641 His Maiesties passing through the Scots armie. [**Edinburgh?**] printed. 1641. 4°. WH2085.

1641 L[AUDER], G[EORGE]. Caledonias covenant. [**Edinburgh?**]. 1641. 8°. WL603.

1641 The recantation, and hvmble svbmission of two ancient prelates. [**Edinburgh**], **printed.** 1641. 4°. WR611.

1641 Reformation no enemie. [**Edinburgh**]. 1641. 12°. WR741.

1641 SCOTLAND. ESTATES. Eight articles of the Scots demands. I. Iuly 1641. [**Edinburgh?**] **printed.** 1641. 4°. WS1233.

1641 SCOTLAND. ESTATES. In the nationall Assemble at Edinburgh the 4 day of August, 1641. [**Edinburgh.** 1641]. Fol. WS1245.

1641 SCOTLAND. ESTATES. In the nationall Assemble at Edinburgh the 6 day of August, 1641. [**Edinburgh**. 1641]. Fol. WS1246.

1641 SCOTLAND. ESTATES. Questions exhibited by the Parliament now in Scotland. [**Edinburgh**], **printed.** 1641. 4°. WS1328.

1642 ENGLAND. PARLIAMENT. Returne from the Parliament of England ... to the Lords. **Edinburgh.** 1642. 4°. WE2281.

1642 A relation of divers remarkable proceedings. [**London**]. **Reprinted at Edinburgh.** 1642. 4°. WR804.

1642 SCOTLAND. PRIVY COUNCIL. Acts of Councell, concerning Iesuits..... 5 July, 1642. **Edinburgh, Young & Tyler.** 1642. 4°. WS1474.

1642 SCOTLAND. PRIVY COUNCIL. Apud Edinburgh ultima die mensis Maii, Anno Domini, 1642. The which day in presence. [**Edinburgh.** 1642]. Brs. WS2007A.

1642 SCOTLAND. PRIVY COUNCIL. Charges against Iesuits ... 5 July, 1642. **Edinburgh, Young & Tyler.** 1642. 4°. WS1482.

1642 SCOTLAND. PRIVY COUNCIL. Commissions against Iesuits, ... 5 July 1642. **Edinburgh, Young & Tyler.** 1642. 4°. WS1489.

1642 SCOTLAND. PRIVY COUNCIL. Forasmekle as by the crueltie... 1 February 1642. [**Edinburgh.** 1642]. Brs. WS1501.

1642 To the Kings most excellent maiesty: the humble petition of the Major, alderman, ... of London. [**Edinburgh**], **printed.** 1642. Brs. WT1542A.

1642 A true copie of the petition of the gentlewomen. **Printed at Edinburgh.** 1642. 4°. WT2657B.

1643 CHARLES I, king of England. Charles by the grace of God ... to our lovits [blank] messengers. [**Edinburgh.** 1643]. Brs. WC2826.

1643 CHARLES I, king of England. His Majesties declaration to his loving subjects ... 21 April 1643. **Edinburgh, E. Tyler.** 1643. 4°. WC2274.

1643 CHURCH OF SCOTLAND. The principall acts of the Generall Assembly. **Edinburgh, by Evan Tyler.** 1643. 4°. WC4234.

1643 CHURCH OF SCOTLAND. The remonstrance of the commissioners of the General Assembly. **Edinburgh, by Evan Tyler.** 1643. 4°. WC4253.

1643 A declaration against a crosse petition. **Edinburgh, by Evan Tyler.** 1643. 4°. WD517.

1643 SCOTLAND. COMMISSIONERS OF THE TREATY. The Commissioners ... doe find that the petition ... 18 January 1643. **Edinburgh, by E. Tyler.** 1643. 4°. WS1007.

1643 SCOTLAND. ESTATES. Act of the Committee of Estates for contriving the severall troupes. [**Edinburgh.** 1643]. Brs. WS1129A.

1643 SCOTLAND. ESTATES. The Estates ... having read and considered the ... 27 June 1643. **Edinburgh, by Evan Tyler.** 1643. 4°. WS1234.

1643 SCOTLAND. ESTATES. Forsameikle ... that by the promiscuous ... 27 September 1643. [**Edinburgh.** 1643]. WS1242.

1643 SCOTLAND. ESTATES. It is now, we suppose, knowne ... 10 November 1643. **Edinburgh, by Evan Tyler.** 1643. 4°. WS1243.

1643 SCOTLAND. SECRET COUNCIL. Forasmeikle... the necessities of the Scottish ... 11 May 1643. **Edinburgh, by Evan Tyler.** 1643. Brs. WS2013.

1643 A solemne league and covenant, for reformation. **Edinburgh, by Evan Tyler.** 1643. 4°. WS4441.

1644 CHURCH OF SCOTLAND. The principall acts of the Generall Assembly. **Edinburgh, by Evan Tyler.** 1644. 4°. WC4236.

1644 CHURCH OF SCOTLAND. The principall acts of the Generall Assembly. **For Evan Tyler of Scotland.** [1644]. 4°. WC4238.

1644 LEVEN, ALEXANDER LESLIE, 1st earl of. A letter from Generall Leven, the Lord Fairfax **Reprinted at Edinburgh by Evan Tyler.** 1644. 4°. WL1468.

1644 LEVEN, ALEXANDER LESLIE, 1st earl of. A letter from Generall Leven. **Re-printed at Edinburgh by Evan Tyler.** 1644. 4°. WL1817.

1644 RUTHERFORD, SAMUEL. Lex, Rex: the law and the prince. **Edinburgh.** 1644. 4°. WR2387.

1644 SCOTLAND. ESTATES. An act and ordinance of the convention of estates. **Edinburgh.** 1644. 4°. WS1034.

1644 SCOTLAND. ESTATES. Forsamekle as Alaster McDonald ... 17 September 1644. [**Edinburgh.** 1644]. WS1239.

1644 SCOTLAND. ESTATES. Forsameikle as James Earle of Montrose ... 12 September 1644. **Edinburgh, by Evan Tyler.** 1644. Brs. WS1240.

1645 CHURCH OF SCOTLAND. The causes of the fast, appointed ... last Wednesday of March. **Edinburgh.** 1645. Brs. WC4201I.

1645 CHURCH OF SCOTLAND. The principall acts of the Generall Assembly. **Edinburgh: by Evan Tyler.** 1645. 4°. WC4239.

1645 R[OLLOCK], R[OBERT]. Lectures upon the 1st and 2nd epistles of Paul to the Thessalonians. **Edinburgh.** 1645. 4°. WR1886.

1645 SCOTLAND. ESTATES. Act anent the in-bringing of the loane ... 1 February 1645. **Edinburgh, by E. Tyler.** 1645. Brs. WS1047.

1645 SCOTLAND. ESTATES. Act of Parliament anent the excise. **Edinburgh: by Evan Tyler.** 1645. Fol. WS1122.

1646 CHURCH OF SCOTLAND. The causes of a publike fast. **Printed at Edinburgh by Evan Tyler.** 1646. Brs. WC4201A.

1646 CHURCH OF SCOTLAND. The Kirk of Scotlands conclusion. **Edinburgh.** 1646. WC4202A.

1646 CHURCH OF SCOTLAND. The principall acts of the Generall Assembly. **Edinburgh: by Evan Tyler.** 1646. 4°. WC4240.

1646 KER, ANDREW. A solemne and seasonable warning to all estates. **Edinburgh: by Evan Tyler.** 1646. 4°. WK336.

1646 [LILBURNE, JOHN] An vnhappy game at Scotch and English. **Edinburgh, by Evan Tyler.** 1646. 4°. WL2195.

1646 SCOTLAND. ESTATES. Act anent officers. **Edinburgh, by E. Tyler.** 1646. Brs. WS1039.

1646 SCOTLAND. ESTATES. Act anent the excise ... 1 May 1646. **Edinburgh, by Evan Tyler.** 1646. Brs. WS1046.

1646 SCOTLAND. ESTATES. Charles ... Forsameikle as James Grahame ... [8 January 1646]. **[Edinburgh, by E. Tyler.** 1646.]. Brs. WS1191.

1647 CHURCH OF SCOTLAND. The principall acts of the Generall Assembly. **Edinburgh: by Evan Tyler.** 1647. 4°. WC4241.

1647 A directory for church-government. **Edinburgh: by Evan Tyler.** 1647. 4°. WD1542.

1647 [DOUGLAS, ROBERT]. Copie of a letter from the commission of the General Assembly. **Printed at Edinburgh by Evan Tyler.** 1647. 4°. WD2025.

1647 SCOTLAND. ESTATES. Act and Commission anent the excise ... 10. March 1647. **Printed at Edinburgh by Evan Tyler.** 1647. Fol. WS1031.

1647 SCOTLAND. ESTATES. At Edinburgh, the 15 of October, 1647. The Committee of Estates being frequently met. **Printed at Edinburgh, by Evan Tyler.** 1647. Brs. WS1192A.

1647 SCOTLAND. ESTATES. A letter from the Parliament of Scotland to both Houses. **Edinburgh, by Evan Tyler.** [1647]. 4°. WS1283.

1647 WESTMINSTER ASSEMBLY OF DIVINES. The humble advice of the Assembly ... concerning a larger catechisme. **Re-printed at Edinburgh by Evan Tyler.** 1647. 4°. WW1437A.

1648 CHURCH OF SCOTLAND. A declaration of the commissioners of the Generall Assembly. **Printed at Edinburgh by Evan Tyler.** 1648. 4°. WC4217.

1648 CHURCH OF SCOTLAND. The principall acts of the Generall Assembly. **Edinburgh, by Evan Tyler.** 1648. 4°. WC4242.

1648 An humble remonstrance of the citizens of Edenbvrgh to the convention of the Estates of Scotland. March 1. 1648. **by E. T. for the use of the inhabitants of the city of Edenburgh.** 4°. WH3617.

1648 A letter from Edinburgh, containing a true ... relation. **[Edinburgh].** 1648. 4°. WL1462.

1648 Mercurius Caledonius, presenting. **[Edinburgh], printed.** 1648. 4°. WM1759.

1648 Reasons of the dissenting brethren. **Re-printed at Edinburgh by Evan Tyler.** 1648. 4°. WR574.

1648 SCOTLAND. ESTATES. Act of the Committee of Estates for ordering the quarterings ... 15 July 1648. **[Edinburgh.** 1648]. Brs. WS1130.

1648 SCOTLAND. ESTATES. Acts done and past in the first session of the second trienniel Parliament. **Edinburgh, by Evan Tyler.** 1648. Fol. WS1165.

1648 SCOTLAND. ESTATES. At Edinburgh, 22 September 1648. Whereas divers persons in the iles and highlands. **[Edinburgh], by Evan Tyler.** 1648. Brs. WW1617A.

1648 SCOTLAND. ESTATES. At Edinburgh, the 6 of October 1648. Whereas upon disbanding. **Edinburgh, by Evan Tyler.** 1648. Brs. WW1635A.

1648 SCOTLAND. ESTATES. The Committee of Estates taking into their consideration. At Edinburgh the 9th of November 1648. **Edinburgh, by Evan Tyler.** 1648. Brs. WS1195.

1648 SCOTLAND. ESTATES. Edinburgh, 22 September 1648. Whereas many within this Kingdom. **Edinburgh, by Evan Tyler.** 1648. Brs. WW1627A.

1648 SCOTLAND. ESTATES. Edinburgh, October 20. 1648. The Committee of Estates considering how necessary. **Edinburgh, by Evan Tyler.** 1648. Brs. WS1192B.

1648 SCOTLAND. ESTATES. Edinburgh, October 20. 1648. The Committee of estates taking into their consideration. **[Edinburgh], by Evan Tyler.** 1648. WS1193A.

1648 SCOTLAND. ESTATES. Edinburgh, 9 November 1648. The Committee of Estates taking into their consideration. **[Edinburgh], by Evan Tyler.** 1648. Brs. WS1194.

1648 SCOTLAND. ESTATES. The last declarations of the General Assembly. **Edinburgh.** 1648. 4°. WS1249.

1648 SCOTLAND. ESTATES. Whereas divers persons in the Iles ... 22 September 1648. **[Edinburgh], by Evan Tyler.** 1648. Brs. WS1355.

1648 SCOTLAND. ESTATES. Whereas the honorable Houses of the ... 11 October 1648. **Edinburgh, by Evan Tyler.** 1648. Brs. WS1357.

1648 A solemne league and covenant, for reformation. **Edinburgh, by Evan Tyler.** 1648. 4°. WS4451.

1649 CHARLES II, king of England. The declaration and resolution of His Highnesse the Prince of Wales, upon the death of his royall father. **Edinburgh, by Evan Tyler.** 1649. 4°. WC2956.

1649 CHURCH OF SCOTLAND. Edinburgh, Aug. 6, 1649. Causes of a solemn public humiliation. **[Edinburgh].** 1649. Brs. WC4201G.

1649 CHURCH OF SCOTLAND. The principall acts of the Generall Assembly. **Edinburg, by Evan Tyler.** 1649. 4°. WC4243.

1649 ENGLAND. PARLIAMENT. Acts done and past in the third session of the second triennial Parliament. **Edinburgh, by Evan Tyler.** 1649. Fol. WE1162A.

1649 The forms of the commission for a new valuation. **Edinburgh, by Evan Tyler.** 1649. 4°. WF1573.

1649 FORRESTER, DUNCAN. Theses philosophicæ. **Edinburgh, Lithgow.** 1649. Brs. WF1593.

1649 GILLESPIE, GEORGE. A treatise of miscellany questions. **Printed at Edinburgh, to be sold at London, by Thomas Whitaker.** 1649. 4°. WG762.

1649 [HART, JOHN]. The fort-royal. **Edinburgh, by the heires of George Anderson, for Andrew Wilson.** 1649. 12°. WH951.

1649 R[OLLOCK], R[OBERT]. Select works of. **Edinburgh.** 1649. 4°. WR1887.

1649 SCOTLAND. ESTATES. Act for redress of the complaints ... 5 July 1649. **[Edinburgh.** 1649]. Fol. WS1097.

1649 SCOTLAND. ESTATES. The Estates of Parliament presently ... 5 February 1649. **Edinburgh, by Evan Tyler.** 1649. Brs. WS1236.

1649 The vindication and declaration of the Scots nation. [**Edinburgh?** 1649]. 4°. WV463A.

1650 A declaration of the army of England upon their march into Scotland ... 19 Julii, 1650. **London, reprinted at Edinburgh, E. Tyler.** 1650. 4°. WD636.

1650 DELL, WILLIAM. Right reformation. **London, reprinted Edinburgh.** 1650. 4°. WD928.

1650 An examination of the seasonable and necessarie warning concerning present dangers and duties. **Printed at Edinburgh by Evan Tyler, London, by William Du-gard.** 1650. 4°. WE3729.

1650 The humble remonstrance and supplication. **Edinburgh.** 1650. Fol. WH3609.

1650 KING, DANIEL. A way to Sion sovght ovt. Second edition. **London, reprinted Edinburgh.** 1650. 4°. WK491.

1650 SCOTLAND. ESTATES. Act act ⌊sic⌋ for putting the Kingdome in a posture of defence ... 3 July, 1650. [**Edinburgh.** 1650]. Fol. WS1094.

1650 SCOTLAND. ESTATES. Articles and ordinances of warre. **Edinburgh.** 1650. 4°. WS1188.

1650 SCOTLAND. ESTATES. Declaratio deputatorum. **Edinburgh, excudit Erasmus Tyler.** 1650. 4°. WS1198.

1650 SCOTLAND. ESTATES. A declaration of the Committee of the Estates of the Parliament of Scotland. [**Edinburgh**], **by Evan Tyler.** 1650. 4°. WS1214.

1650 SCOTLAND. ESTATES. The Estates of Parliament now presently ... 4 June 1650. **Edinburgh, by Evan Tyler.** 1650. Brs. WS1235.

1650 SCOTLAND. ESTATES. The Estates of Parliament understanding ... July 1650. [**Edinburgh**], **by Evan Tyler.** 1650. 4°. WS1237.

1650 SHEPARD, THOMAS. The sound beleever. **Edinburgh, by George Lithgow.** 1650. 12°. WS3134A.

1650 To the right honourable the Lords and others of the Committee of Estates, the humble remonstrance ... 15 August 1650. **Edinburgh, E. Tyler.** 1650. Brs. WT1701.

1651 The remonstrance of the presbyterie of Sterling. **Edinburgh, by Evan Tyler.** 1651. 4°. WR1009.

1651 WHALLY, HENRY. There is a young man. **Edinburgh, by Evan Tyler.** 1651. Brs. WW1535A.

1652 A fight at Dunin at Scotland. **Edinburgh.** 1652. 4°. WF894.

1652 GUARNA, ANDREAS. Bellum grammaticale. **Edinburgi.** 1652. 8°. WG2179.

1653 [GUTHRIE, JAMES]. A humble acknowledgement of the sins. **Edinburgh, printed.** 1653. 4°. WG2262.

1652 [GUTHRIE, JAMES]. A treatise of ruling elders. [**Edinburgh**], **printed.** 1652. 12°. WG2265.

1653 A letter from the protesters, with an answer. [**Edinburgh**], **printed** [**by Andrew Anderson**]. 1653. 4°. WL1538.

1654 The great sin, and chief guiltines of Scotland. [**Edinburgh?**] **printed.** 1654. 4°. WG1753.

1655 The covenant of life opened. **Edinburgh, by A. A. for Robert Broun.** 1655. 4°. WC6619.

1655 SCOTLAND. COMMISSIONERS FOR VISITING UNIVERSITIES IN SCOTLAND. By the Commissioners ... Whereas by our former proclamation. **Printed at Edinburgh.** 1655. Brs. WS1001A.

1655 SCOTLAND. COUNCIL IN SCOTLAND. Council for the government of Scotland. **Edinburgh.** 1655. Fol. WS1012.

1655 SCOTLAND. COUNCIL IN SCOTLAND. Declaration of His Highnes Council in Scotland election of magistrates for the government thereof. **Edinburgh, by Christopher Higgins.** 1655. Brs. WS1015.

1655 SCOTLAND. COUNCIL IN SCOTLAND. It having pleased the Lord to visit ... 17 October 1655. **Edinburgh, C. Higgins.** 1655. Brs. WS1017.

1656 SCOTLAND. COUNCIL IN SCOTLAND. Although the said Council have with some trouble ... 21 day of March 1655/6. **Edinburgh, by Christopher Higgins.** 1656. Brs. WS1010A.

1656 SCOTLAND. COUNCIL IN SCOTLAND. Declaration of His Highnes Council in Scotland election of magistrates ... 22 May 1656. **Edinburgh, C. Higgins.** 1656. Fol. WS1014.

1656 SCOTLAND. COUNCIL IN SCOTLAND. An order and declaration ... for the more equal raising the assessment. **Edinburgh, by Christopher Higgins.** 1656. Fol. WS1019A.

1656 SCOTLAND. LORD PROTECTOR AND COUNCIL. Ordered by ... 15 April 1656. **Edinburgh, C. Higgins.** 1656. Brs. WS1364.

1657 CAMPBELL, Sir WILLIAM. Theses philosophicæ. **Edinburgh.** 1657. 4°. WC404.

1657 CROMWELL, OLIVER. A proclamation by ... 26 June 1657. **Edinburgh, Christopher Higgins.** 1657. Brs. WC7137A.

1657 ENGLAND. PARLIAMENT. An act for an assessment ... upon England ... for three years. **Edinburgh, re-printed by Christopher Higgins.** 1657. Fol. WE999.

1657 ENGLAND. PARLIAMENT. An act for continuing and establishing the subsidie. **Edinburgh: reprinted by Christopher Higgins.** 1657. Fol. WE1017.

1657 ENGLAND. PARLIAMENT. An act for limiting and setling the price for vvines. **Edinburgh, reprinted by Christopher Higgins.** 1657. Fol. WE1047.

1657 ENGLAND. PARLIAMENT. An act for quiet enjoying of sequestred parsonages. **Edinburgh, re-printed by Christopher Higgins.** 1657. Fol. WE1052.

1657 ENGLAND. PARLIAMENT. An act for the taking away of purveyance. **Edinburgh, re-printed by Christopher Higgins.** 1657. Fol. WE1132.

1657 ENGLAND. PARLIAMENT. An act giving licence for transporting fish. **Edinburgh, re-printed by Christopher Higgins.** 1657. Fol. WE1139.

1657 ENGLAND. PARLIAMENT. The humble petition and advice presented unto His Highness ... by ... Parliament. **Edinburgh, reprinted for Christopher Higgins.** 1657. Fol. WE1567.

1657 [NEWTON, ARCHIBALD]. Uldericus veridicus. **Eleutheropoli Nataliæ** [**Edinburth**], **excudebat Calabricus Neapolitanus.** 1657. 4°. WN1042.

1657 SCOTLAND. AUDITOR-GENERAL. By the Auditor-general of the revenues of Scotland. Whereas. **Edinburgh, by Christopher Higgins.** 1657. Brs. WS967A.

1657   SCOTLAND. COMMISSIONERS. Edinburgh the
        8. day of November, 1656. By the Commissioners
        for ... Scotland. Whereas divers debitors.
        Edinburgh, by Christopher Higgins. 1657. Brs.
        WS972A.

1657   SCOTLAND. COMMITTEE FOR AUDITING. By
        the Committee appointed for auditing and stating
        the accompts ... 12 October 1657. **Edinburgh,
        C. Higgins.** 1657. Brs. WS1008.

1657   SCOTLAND. ESTATES. An additional act for the
        better improvement & advancing. **Edinburgh, re-
        printed by Christopher Higgins.** 1657. Fol.
        WS1175.

1658   CROMWELL, OLIVER. A declaration of ... for a
        day of publick thanksgiving. **Edinburgh, by
        Christopher Higgins.** 1658. Fol. WC7068.

1659   DURHAM, JAMES. Of scandal. **Edinburgh.**
        1659. 8°. WD2820.

1659   FERGUSON, DAVID. Nine hundred and forty
        Scottish proverbs. [**Edinburgh, C. Higgins**].
        1659. 8°. WF768.

1659   [MACKAILE, MATTHEW]. Fons Moffetensis.
        Edinburgi, by Higgins for R. Brown. 1659. 12°.
        WM145.

1659   The pedegree and descent of His Excellency,
        General George Monck. **Edinburgh.** 1659. 4°.
        WP1049.

1659   A testimony and warning of the Presbyterie of
        Edinburgh, ... Octob. 5 ... 1659. [**?Edinburgh**]
        printed. 1659. WT807.

1660   ASHMOLE, ELIAS. Sol in ascendente: or, the
        glorious appearance of Charles the Second.
        Edinburgh, reprinted by Christopher Higgins.
        1660. 4°. WA3986.

1660   CHARLES II, king of England. His Majesties
        gracious proclamation concerning the government
        of ... Scotland. **Edinburgh, by the Society of
        Stationers.** 1660. Brs. WC3039A.

1660   CHARLES II, king of England. The Kings
        Majesties proclamation, concerning the carriage.
        Edinburgh, by Evan Tyler. 1660. Brs. WC3264.

1660   CHURCH OF SCOTLAND. The national covenant.
        Edinburgh, by a Society of Stationers. 1660. 8°.
        WC4231C.

1660   ENGLAND. PARLIAMENT. A proclamation
        against all seditious railers. **Edinburgh, by a
        Society of Stationers.** 1660. Brs. WE2189.

1660   ENGLAND. PARLIAMENT. A proclamation of
        both Houses ... for proclaiming of His Majesty
        king. **Edinburgh, by Christopher Higgins.** 1660.
        Brs. WE2197.

1660   ENGLAND. PARLIAMENT. HOUSE OF
        COMMONS. A letter to the kings most excellent
        Majesty from the Commons. **Edinburgh reprinted
        by Christopher Higgins.** 1660. Brs. WE2623.

1660   [GILLESPIE, GEORGE]. A dispute against the
        English-Popish ceremonies. [**Edinburgh**], **printed.**
        1660. 4°. WG748.

1660   The royal pilgrimage. **Re-printed at Edinburgh
        by a Society of Stationers.** 1660. 4°. WR2142A.

1660   SCOTLAND. ESTATES. An act of free and
        general pardon. **Edinburgh.** 1660. Fol. WS1117.

1660   [SYMSON, MATTHIAS]. Mephibosheth; or, the
        lively picture. **Edinburgh, by Ch. Higgins.** 1660.
        4°. WS6373.

1660   To his excellency the Lord General Monck, ...
        the humble address of the officers. **Edinburgh,
        re-printed by Christopher Higgins.** 1660.
        Brs. WT1358.

1661   ARGYLE, ARCHIBALD CAMPBELL, marquis.
        The Marques of Argyll his defences.
        [**Edinburgh?**]. Anno 1661. 4°. WA3652.

1661   DOUGLAS, ROBERT. Master Dowglasse his
        sermon. [**Edinburgh.** 1661]. 4°. WD2036.

1661   I., J. A short treatise comprising a brief survey.
        Edinburgh. 1661. 4°. WI7[A].

1661   SCOTLAND. COMMISSIONERS OF EXCISE.
        Instructions by the Commissioners of Excise, to
        Robert Petrie ... 19 January 1661. [**Edinburgh.**
        1661]. Brs. WS1004.

1661   SCOTLAND. ESTATES. Act and proclamation
        that none come from Ireland. **Edinburgh, by Evan
        Tyler.** 1661. Brs. WS1037.

1661   SCOTLAND. ESTATES. An act for ordering the
        payment of debts. **Edinburgh, by Evan Tyler.**
        1661. Fol. WS1091.

1661   SCOTLAND. PRIVY COUNCIL. Act against thefts
        and robberies. **Edinburgh, by Evan Tyler.** 1661.
        Brs. WS1380.

1662   ENGLAND. PARLIAMENT. An act for the
        uniformity of publick prayers. **London, printed,
        Edinburgh re-printed.** 1662. 4°. WE1136.

1662   ENGLAND. PARLIAMENT. At the Parliament
        begun at Westminster the eighth day of May, anno
        Dom. 1661. **Printed at London, and re-printed at
        Edinburgh.** 1662. 4°. WE1249.

1662   HINDE, SAMUEL. Iter lusitanicum. **Re-printed
        at Edinburgh.** 1662. 4°. WH2059.

1662   HORACE. Opera. **Edinburgi, excudebat Gideon
        Lithgo.** 1662. 12°. WH2762.

1662   SCOTLAND. PRIVY COUNCIL. The Lords ...
        that notwithstanding that ... 1 October 1662.
        Edinburgh, by Evan Tyler. 1662. Brs. WS1523.

1662   SCOTLAND. PRIVY COUNCIL. A proclamation
        prohibiting all ecclesiastical meetings. **Edinburgh,
        by Evan Tyler.** 1662. Brs. WS1966.

1663   ALMANACS. CORSS, JAMES. Mercurius cœlicus
        ... 1663. **Edinburgh, by a Society of Stationers.**
        1663. 8°.

1663   CHARLES II, king of England. His Majesties
        declaration to all his loving subjects, December
        26, 1662. **Edinburgh, by Evan Tyler.** 1663. Brs.
        WC2988A.

1663   [MACKENZIE, Sir GEORGE]. Religio stoici.
        Edinburgh, for R. Broun. 1663. 8°. WM197.

1663   SCOTLAND. ESTATES. Act for a new imposi-
        tion upon English commodities. **Edinburgh, by
        Evan Tyler.** 1663. Brs. WS1081.

1663   SCOTLAND. ESTATES. Act rescinding two acts.
        Edinburgh, by Evan Tyler. 1663. Fol. WS1158.

1663   SCOTLAND. ESTATES. Additional act concern-
        ing the declaration ... 4 August 1663. **Edinburgh,
        by Evan Tyler.** 1663. Brs. WS1174.

1664   CHARLES II, king of England. Articles of peace
        between ... , Charles the II and the city and
        kingdom of Algiers. **Edinburgh, reprinted.** 1664.
        4°. WC2908.

1664   CULPEPER, NICHOLAS. Physick for the common
        people. **Edinburgh.** 1664. 8°. WC7538.

1664   ENGLAND. PRIVY COUNCIL. Whereas it is informed ... 8 July 1664. [**Edinburgh, E. Tyler. 1664**]. Brs. WE2925.

1664   KENT, ELIZABETH GREY, countess of. A choice manuall. Fifteenth edition. **Edinburgh, by a society of stationers.** 1664. 12°. WK315.

1664   MANCHESTER, EDWARD MONTAGU, earl of. The speech of ... 1st Dec. 1664. **Edinburgh, reprinted.** 1664. 4°. WM398A.

1664   PRÉVOST, JEAN. Medicaments for the poor. "Second edition". **Edinburgh, by a Society of Stationers.** 1664. 12°. WP3326.

1664   SCOTLAND. PRIVY COUNCIL. Forasmuch as it hath pleased ... 18 February 1664. **Edinburgh, by Evan Tyler.** 1664. Brs. WS1495.

1664   The young clerk's companion. **Edinburgh.** 1664. 12°. WY98.

1665   MACKENZIE, Sir GEORGE. A moral essay. **Edinburgh, for Robert Brown.** 1665. 8°. WM171.

1665   NASMYTH, ARTHUR. Divine poems. **Edinburgh, for James Miller.** 1665. 8°. WN233A.

1665   SCOTLAND. PRIVY COUNCIL. Proclamation, discharging trade and commerce. 21 December 1665. **Edinburgh, by Evan Tyler.** 1665. Brs. WS1778.

1665   A short relation of the happy victory, obtained by His Majesties fleet against the Dutch. **Edinburgh, by Evan Tyler.** 1665. Brs. WS3621.

1665   WILD, ROBERT. Gratulatory verse upon our late glorious victory. **Printed at London, and reprinted at Edinburgh.** Brs. WW2128A.

1666   Advertisement be Agnes Campbell, relict. [**Edinburgh.** 1666]. Brs. WA608.

1666   CHARLES II, king of England. A proclamation for a publick general fast ... 28 June 1666. **Edinburgh, E. Tyler.** 1666. WC3311.

1666   SCOTLAND. PRIVY COUNCIL. Act discharging the vending of any goods ... 14 August 1666. **Edinburgh, by Evan Tyler.** 1666. Brs. WS1414.

1666   SCOTLAND. PRIVY COUNCIL. A proclamation discharging the receipt of the rebells. **Edinburgh, by Evan Tyler.** 1666. Brs. WS1775.

1666   SCOTLAND. PRIVY COUNCIL. A proclamation for procuring obedience. **Edinburgh, by Evan Tyler.** 1666. Brs. WS1889.

1667   CHARLES II, king of England. A proclamation for publishing the peace ... Netherlands. **Edinburgh, E. Tyler.** 1667. Brs. WC3391.

1667   MACKENZIE, Sir GEORGE. A moral paradox. **Edinburgh, for Robert Broun.** 1667. 8°. WM181.

1667   SCOTLAND. PRIVY COUNCIL. The Lords ... in pursuance of His Majesty's gracious ... 9 October 1667. [**Edinburgh, by Evan Tyler.** 1667]. Brs. WS1525.

1667   SCOTLAND. PRIVY COUNCIL. Proclamation against the importation of Irish cattle. **Edinburgh, by Evan Tyler.** 1667. Brs. WS1610.

1667   SCOTLAND. PRIVY COUNCIL. Proclamation, for bringing in arms. **Edinburgh, by Evan Tyler.** 1667. Brs. WS1842.

1667   [STIRLING, JAMES]. Naphtali, or the wrestlings. [**Edinburgh**], printed. 1667. 8°. WS5683.

1668   MORISON, JAMES. The everlasting Gospel. [**Edinburgh**]. 1668. 8°. WM2769.

1668   SCOTLAND. PRIVY COUNCIL. A proclamation anent the late horrid attempt. **Edinburgh, by Evan Tyler.** 1668. Brs. WS1667.

1669   A full and true relation of the taking of Cork. **Reprinted Edinburgh.** 1669. Brs. WF2332.

1669   LAUDERDALE, JOHN MAITLAND, duke of. The speech of ... nineteenth day of October, 1669. [**London**], in the Savoy by Tho: Newcomb: and re-printed in Edinburgh by Andrew Anderson. 1669. Fol. WL613A.

1669   SCOTLAND. PRIVY COUNCIL. Advertisement anent stollen goods. **Edinburgh, by Evan Tyler.** 1669. Brs. WS1475.

1669   [WINCHELSEA, HINEAGE FINCH, earl.] A true and exact relation of the late prodigious earthquake. **Edinburgh, re-printed.** 1669. 4°. WT2451.

1669   WINCHELSEA, HINEAGE FINCH, earl. A true and exact relation of the late prodigious earthquake. **Edinburgh.** 1669. 4°. WW2968.

1671   ANNAND, WILLIAM. Mysterium pietatis. **Edinburgh, by Andrew Anderson.** 1671. 8°. WA3220A.

1671   The confession of faith approved. **Edinburgh.** 1671. 4°. WC5777.

1671   DICKSON, DAVID. The summe of saving know-ledge. **Edinburgh, by George Swintoun, and Thomas Brown, to be sould by James Glen, and David Trench.** 1671. 4°. WD1405.

1671   A further account of East-New-Jersey. **Edinburgh, John Reid.** [1671]. 4°. WF2543.

1671   GRAY, ANDREW. The mystery of faith. **Edinburgh, by George Swintoun, James Glen, to be sold by them, and by David Trench and Thomas Brown.** 1671. 12°. WG1618.

1671   RUTHERFORD, SAMUEL. Joshua redivivus. Second edition. [**Edinburgh?**], printed. 1671. 8°. WR2382.

1671   SCOTLAND. PRIVY COUNCIL. Proclamation anent copper coyn. **Edinburgh, by Evan Tyler.** 1671. Brs. WS1629.

1671   SIMONS, WILLIAM. The true Christians path way to Heaven. **Edinburgh, by Andrew Anderson.** 1671. 12°. WS3806.

1672   CHARLES II, king of England. His Majesties declaration to all his loving subjects, ... 14 March. **Edinburgh, E. Tyler.** 1672. Brs. WC2991.

1672   CHARLES II, king of England. His Majesties gracious declaration for the encouraging the subjects of the United Provinces. **Reprinted Edinburgh, [A. Anderson].** 1672. Brs. WC3012.

1672   Devout meditations. **Edinburgh.** 1672. 12°. WD1245.

1672   ENGLAND. KING IN COUNCIL. Whereas His Majesty did the ... 15 May 1672. **Edinburgh, E. Tyler.** 1672. Brs. WE844.

1672   GRAY, ANDREW. The spiritual warfare. **Edinburgh, by George Swinton, James Glen and Thomas Brown.** 1672. 12°. WG1619A.

1672   SCOTLAND. PRIVY COUNCIL. Proclamation anent the making use of forreign salt. **Edinburgh, by His Majesties printers.** 1672. Brs. WS1669.

1672   [STEWART, Sir JAMES]. An accompt of Scotlands grievances. [**Edinburgh.** 1672]. 4°. WS5532.

1673   ENGLAND. KING IN COUNCIL. At the Court at Whitehall ... whereas by the late address of ... 6 June 1673. **Edinburgh, reprinted A. Anderson.** 1673. Brs. WE836.

1673   SCOTLAND. COMMISSIONERS OF THE TREASURY. Act [of the Commissioners of] His Majesties Thesaury ... 11 July 1673. **Edinburgh, His Majesties printers.** 1673. Brs. WS1005.

1673   SCOTLAND. ESTATES. Act concerning the importation and excise of brandy. **Edinburgh, by A. Anderson.** 1673. Brs. WS1068.

1673   SCOTLAND. PRIVY COUNCIL. A proclamation against conventicles. [**Edinburgh, by His Majesties printers.** 1673]. Brs. WS1582.

1673   SCOTLAND. PRIVY COUNCIL. A proclamation against Papists. **Edinburgh, by His Majesties printers.** 1673. Fol. WS1593.

1674   Edinburgh, first May one thousand six hundred and seventy four. The which day. [**Edinburgh.** 1674]. Fol. WE172.

1674   Morning and evening prayers. **Edinburgh, by His Majestie's printers.** 1674. 8°. WM2803.

1674   SCOTLAND. PRIVY COUNCIL. A proclamation, containing His Majesties grace. **Edinburgh, by Andrew Anderson.** 1674. Brs. WS1727.

1674   SCOTLAND. PRIVY COUNCIL. A proclamation, containing His Majesties grace. **Edinburgh, by His Majesties printers.** [1674]. Brs. WS1728.

1674   SCOTLAND. PRIVY COUNCIL. A proclamation, containing His Majesties grace. **Edinburgh, by His Majesties printers.** 1674. Brs. WS1729.

1674   SCOTLAND. PRIVY COUNCIL. A proclamation, oblidging heritors and masters ... 18 June. **Edinburgh, by His Majesties printers.** 1674. Brs. WS1952.

1675   COCKBURN, ALEXANDER. Theses philosophicae. **Edinburgi, excudebat Andreas Andersonus.** 1675. 4°. WC4799.

1675   COLLINGES, JOHN. The weavers pocket-book. **Edinburgh.** [1675?]. 8°. WC5350.

1675   [HEAD, RICHARD]. O-Brazile. **Edinburgh, re-printed.** 1675. 4°. WH1270.

1675   A list of the persons intercommuned. [**Edinburgh.** After 1674]. Brs. WL2483.

1675   RUTHERFORD, SAMUEL. Mr. Rutherfoord's letters. [**Edinburgh?**], **printed.** 1675. 8°. WR2384.

1675   SCOTLAND. PRIVY COUNCIL. Letters of inter-communing. **Edinburgh, by A. Anderson.** 1675. Fol. WS1510.

1676   DURHAM, JAMES. The law unsealed. Fourth edition. **Edinburgh, by the heir of Andrew Anderson.** 1676. 8°. WD2818.

1676   DURHAM, JAMES. A practical exposition of the X. commandments. Third edition. **Edinburgh, Andrew Anderson.** 1676. 8°. WD2824.

1676   GRANT, ALEXANDER. Clarrissimis, generosis de summum spem ... Davidi Haliburton. **Edinburgi, excudebat Georgius Swintoun, & Jacobus Glen.** 1676. 4°. WG1515.

1676   The impeachment of the Duke and Dutchess of Lauderdale. [**Edinburgh?** 1676]. Brs. WI98.

1676   SCOTLAND. ESTATES. Act concerning the keeping of conventicles. **Edinburgh, by Andrew Anderson.** 1676. Brs. WS1070.

1676   SCOTLAND. LORDS OF COUNCIL AND SESSION. Act concerning the re-entry of some advocats. **Edinburgh, A. Anderson.** 1676. Brs. WS1369.

1676   SCOTLAND. PRIVY COUNCIL. Act anent the indulged ministers. **Edinburgh, by A. Anderson.** 1676. Brs. WS1397.

1676   SCOTLAND. PRIVY COUNCIL. Advertisement, anent stolen goods. [**Edinburgh, by A. Anderson.** 1676]. Brs. WS1477.

1678   SCOTLAND. PRIVY COUNCIL. Charles ... forasmuch as upon consideration ... 13 March 1678. **Edinburgh, by the heir of A. Anderson.** 1678. WS1485.

1676   SCOTLAND. PRIVY COUNCIL. A proclamation for setling of the staple-port. **Edinburgh, by the heir of A. Anderson.** 1676. WS1921.

1677   CHARLES II, king of England. A treaty marine between the most serene ... Charles II ... and ... Lewis XIV. **Edinburgh, reprinted by the heir of Andrew Anderson.** 1677. 8°. WC3618.

1677   SCOTLAND. PRIVY COUNCIL. A proclamation anent passes. **Edinburgh, by the heir of A. Anderson.** 1677. Brs. WS1639.

1678   Articles and rules for the better government of His Majesties forces. **Edinburgh, by the heir of Andrew Anderson.** 1678. 8°. WA3813.

1678   [CALDERWOOD, DAVID]. The true history of the church of Scotland. [**Edinburgh?**] **printed.** 1678. Fol. WC279.

1678   CHARLES II, king of England. A proclamation commanding all persons being Popish recusants. **Reprinted Edinburgh, heir of A. Anderson.** 1678. Brs. WC3243.

1678   CHARLES II, king of England. Proclamation prohibiting the nobility, ... third day of January, 1678. **Edinburgh, by the heir of Andrew Anderson.** 1678. Brs. WC3551.

1678   GRAY, ANDREW. Great and precious promises. **Edinburgh.** 1678. 12°. WG1611.

1678   MACKENZIE, Sir GEORGE. The laws and cus-tomes of Scotland. **Edinburgh, by James Glen.** 1678. 4°. WM166.

1678   Samsons riddle. [**Edinburgh?**] **printed.** [1678?]. 4°. WS544.

1678   SCOTLAND. ESTATES. Act anent drovers. **Edinburgh, by the heir of Andrew Anderson.** 1678. Brs. WS1038.

1678   SCOTLAND. PRIVY COUNCIL. A proclamation for securing the peace of the Highlands. **Edinburgh, by the heir of Andrew Anderson.** 1678. WS1913.

1678   SCOTLAND. PRIVY COUNCIL. Proclamation prohibiting the nobility, and others to withdraw. **Edinburgh, by the heir of A. Anderson.** 1678. Brs. WS1969.

1679   CHARLES II, king of England. His Majesties most gracious speech, together ... 30th of April, 1679. **Edinburgh, re-printed by the heir of Andrew Anderson.** 1679. 4°. WC3187.

1679   CHARLES II, king of England. A proclamation about dissolving ... Parliament. **Edinburgh, reprinted, heir of A. Anderson.** 1679. Brs. WC3211.

1679   CHARLES II, king of England. A proclamation against the resetting of tenents ... Feb. 11. **Edinburgh, by the heir of Andrew Anderson.** 1678[9]. Brs. WC3224.

1679 COCKBURN, ALEXANDER. Theses philosophicae. **Edinburgi, excudebant Thomas Brown, & Ioannes Swintoun.** 1679. 4°. WC4800.

1679 The great victory obtain'd by His Majesties army under ... Monmouth. **Edinburgh.** 1679. Brs. WG1778.

1679 M[URRAY], M[UNGO]. On the death and horrid murther of ... James [Sharp]. [**Edinburgh.** 1679]. Brs. WM3108.

1679 M[URRAY], M[UNGO]. On the death of the illustrious David, Earl of Wemyss. [**Edinburgh.** 1679]. Brs. WM3110.

1679 A relation of the birth as well as several remarkable passages. [**Edinburgh.** 1679]. Fol. WR816.

1679 SCOTLAND. ESTATES. The laws and acts of the second Parliament. **Edinburgh, re-printed by the heir of Andrew Anderson.** 1679. Fol. WS1272.

1679 SCOTLAND. PRIVY COUNCIL. A proclamation anent the rebels. **Edinburgh, by the heir of A. Anderson.** 1679. Brs. WS1681.

1679 SCOTLAND. PRIVY COUNCIL. A proclamation appointing the officers and souldiers. [**Edinburgh, by the heir of A. Anderson.** 1679]. Brs. WS1709.

1679 The Scots demonstration. [**Edinburgh?** 1679]. Brs. WS2025.

1679 SMITH, SAMUEL. The great assize. "Twenty-third" edition. **Edinburgh, by the heir of Andrew Anderson.** 1679. 12°. WS4182.

1679 TERENTIUS AFER, PUBLIUS. Comoediæ sex. **Edinburgi, excudebat Ioannes Swinton.** 1679. 12°. WT743.

1680 [CALDERWOOD, DAVID]. The true history of the church of Scotland. [**Edinburgh?**]. 1680. Fol. WC280.

1680 CARGILL, DONALD. A true and exact copy of a treasonable and bloody paper ... taken from. **Edinburgh, by the heir of Andrew Anderson.** 1680. Fol. WC569.

1680 The Catholick gamesters or a dubble match of bowleing. [**Edinburgh**], **printed.** February 14, 1680. Brs. WC1493A.

1680 [DYKE, JEREMIAH]. A worthy communicant. **Edinburgh.** 1680. WD2965.

1680 Heads and conclusions of the policie of the kirk. [**Edinburgh**], **reprinted.** 1680. 8°. WH1280.

1680 LINDSAY, Sir DAVID. Information for the Earl of Crawfurd. [**Edinburgh.** 1680?]. WL2323.

1680 L[IVINGSTON], M[ICHAEL]. Albion's elegie. **Edinburgh, by the heir of Andrew Anderson.** 1680. 4°. WL2601.

1680 QUARLES, FRANCIS. Enchiridion miscellaneum. **Edinburgh, by J. Cairnes for G. Shaw.** 1680. 24°. WQ95.

1680 SCOTLAND. ESTATES. Additional instructions for the militia ... eight day of July 1680. [**Edinburgh.** 1680]. Brs. WS1177.

1680 SCOTLAND. PRIVY COUNCIL. Act appointing a voluntary contribution ... 24 February 1680. [**Edinburgh, by the heir of A. Anderson.** 1680]. Brs. WS1400.

1680 SCOTLAND. PRIVY COUNCIL. Act appointing a voluntary contribution ... 13 July 1680. [**Edinburgh, heir of A. Anderson.** 1680]. Brs. WS1401.

1680 SCOTLAND. PRIVY COUNCIL. A proclamation appointing all passes to ships. **Edinburgh, by the heir of A. Anderson.** 1680. Brs. WS1700.

1680 SCOTLAND. PRIVY COUNCIL. A proclamation for securing the peace of ... Caithness. **Edinburgh, by the heir of A. Anderson.** 1680. Brs. WS1912.

1680 SCOTLAND. PRIVY COUNCIL. A proclamation, regulating the prices of ale ... 7 Dec. **Edinburgh, by the heir of A. Anderson.** 1680. Brs. WS1977.

1680 [STIRLING, JAMES]. Naphtali, or the wrestlings. [**Edinburgh**], **printed.** 1680. 8°. WS5683A.

1681 An apostrophe from the loyal party. **Edinburgh, reprinted by the heir of Andrew Anderson.** 1681. Fol. WA3563.

1681 CARGILL, DONALD. A lecture and sermon. [**Edinburgh.** 1681?]. 4°. WC568.

1681 CURRIEHILL, JOHN SKENE, lord. De verborum significatione. [**Edinburgh**], **A. Smellie.** 1681. Fol. WC7684.

1681 MAC WARD, ROBERT. The poor man's cup. [**Edinburgh**], **printed.** 1681. 4°. WM234.

1681 OVID. Heroidum epistolarum liber. **Edinburgi, excudebat Thomas Brown & Jacobus Glen.** 1681. Sixes. WO675.

1681 RUSSELL, JAMES. A true and exact copy of a prodigious and traiterous libel. **Edinburgh, printed.** 1681. Fol. WR2342.

1681 SCOTLAND. ESTATES. Act acknowledging and asserting, the right of succession. **Edinburgh, by the heir of A. Anderson.** 1681. Brs. WS1023A.

1681 SCOTLAND. ESTATES. Act, ratifying all former laws. **Edinburgh, by the heir of A. Anderson.** 1681. Brs. WS1155.

1681 SCOTLAND. PRIVY COUNCIL. Act for a voluntary contribution. [**Edinburgh, by the heir of A. Anderson**]. 1681. Brs. WS1422.

1681 SCOTLAND. PRIVY COUNCIL. A proclamation, anent the Earl of Argyl. **Edinburgh, by the heir of Andrew Anderson.** 1681. Brs. WS1661.

1681 SCOTLAND. PRIVY COUNCIL. A proclamation imposing a further custom upon wines. **Edinburgh, by the heir of A. Anderson.** 1681. Brs. WS1938.

1681 SCOTLAND. PRIVY COUNCIL. A proclamation, offering a reward ... 12 March. **Edinburgh, by the heir of A. Anderson.** 1681. Brs. WS1956.

1682 CHURCH OF SCOTLAND. A true copy of the whole printed acts. [**Edinburgh?**] **printed.** 1682. 8°. WC4272.

1682 DESPAUTÈRE, JEAN. Ioan. Despauterii Ninivitæ grammaticæ institutionis. **Edinburgi, excudebat hæres Andreæ Anderson.** 1682. 12°. WD1204.

1682 DURHAM, JAMES. The blessedness of death. Second edition. [**Edinburgh, Anderson**], **printed.** 1682. 8°. WD2796.

1682 GREG, Mother. The burgess ticket of Buckhaven. **Edinburgh, printed.** 1682. Fol. WG1876.

1682 MONTGOMERIE, ALEXANDER. The cherrie and the slae. **Edinburgh, by the heirs of Andrew Anderson.** 1682. 12°. WM2500.

1682 SCOTLAND. PRIVY COUNCIL. Act, for a voluntar contribution ... 7 July 1682. **Edinburgh, by the heir of A. Anderson.** 1682. Brs. WS1420.

1682   SCOTLAND. PRIVY COUNCIL. Act of Council, dispensing with circuit courts. **Edinburgh.** 1682. Brs. WS1446.

1682   SCOTLAND. PRIVY COUNCIL. Charles ... forasmuch as wee having for the ... 9 August 1682. **Edinburgh, by the heir of A. Anderson.** 1682. Fol. WS1487

1682   WEDDERBURN, ALEXANDER. Believers priviledges. Part first. [**Edinburgh?**], **printed.** 1682 12°. WW1238.

1683   An account how the Earl of Essex killed himself in the Tower. **Edinburgh, reprinted by the heir of Andrew Anderson.** 1683. Fol. WA176.

1683   Advertisement concerning East-New-Jersey. **Edinburgh, by John Reid.** 1683. Brs. WA609A.

1683   CHARLES II, king of England. A proclamation, for the apprehending James Duke of Bucclough ... 4 July, 1683. **Edinburgh, by the heir of Andrew Anderson.** 1683. Brs. WC3436A.

1683   DURHAM, JAMES. Christ crucified. **Edinburgh, by the heir of Andrew Anderson.** 1683. 4°. WD2799.

1683   The hue and cry after J____ Duke of M____. **Edinburgh, reprinted by the heir of Andrew Anderson.** 1683. Brs. WH3280.

1683   LONDON. Address to the Lord Mayor, aldermen ... of London, ... 2 July 1683. **Edinburgh reprinted, by the heir of Andrew Anderson.** 1683. Brs. WL2867.

1683   MASSIE, ANDREW. Decermina hæc philosophica. **Edinburgi, excudebat Ionnes Reid.** 1683. Brs. WM1041.

1683   No Popery, or a catechism. **Edinburgh.** 1683. 12°. WN1188.

1683   PITCAIRNE, ARCHIBALD. Exempla additionis, subtrationis. **Edinburgi.** Martii 1 1683. Brs. WP2290.

1683   The proceedings to execution of the sentence awarded against Captain Thomas Walcot. [**London**], **for Langley Curtis, Edinburgh, reprinted by the heir of Andrew Anderson.** 1683. Fol. WP3625.

1683   REID, JOHN. The gard'ner's kalendar. **Edinburgh, by David Lindsay.** 1683. 4°. WR763.

1683   SCOTLAND. PRIVY COUNCIL. His Majesties gracious proclamation, for ordering. **Edinburgh, by the heir of A. Anderson.** 1683. Fol. WS1504.

1683   SCOTLAND. PRIVY COUNCIL. A proclamation anent the rendezvouses ... 23 March. [**Edinburgh, by the heir of A. Anderson.** 1683]. Brs. WS1685.

1683   SCOTLAND. PRIVY COUNCIL. A proclamation, discharging merchants. **Edenburgh, by the heir of Andrew Anderson.** [1683]. Brs. WS1750.

1683   SCOTLAND. PRIVY COUNCIL. A proclamation, indicting a solemn and publick thanksgiving. **Edinburgh, by the heir of Andrew Anderson.** 1683. Brs. WS1948.

1684   DICK, JOHN. A testimony to the doctrine. [**Edinburgh**], **printed.** 1684. 4°. WD1381.

1684   DICKSON, DAVID. Truths victory over error. **Edinburgh.** 1684. 12°. WD1412.

1684   [DRUMMOND, WILLIAM]. Breviuscula, & compendiuscula, tellatio. **Edinburgi, reprintat.** 1684. 4°. WD2194.

1684   DURHAM, JAMES. The blessedness of the death. Third edition. **Edinburgh, heir of Andrew Anderson.** 1684. 12°. WD2797.

1684   Factum comitis Argatheliae seu de Argyll. [**Edinburgh?**]. 1684. 4°. WF80.

1684   HOLLOWAY, JAMES. The free and voluntary confession and narrative. **Edinburgh, re-printed by the heir of Andrew Anderson.** 1684. Fol. WH2510.

1684   PARTRIDGE, JOHN. Mr. John Partrige's new prophesie of ... 1684. **Edinburgh, reprinted by the heir of Andrew Anderson.** 1684. Fol. WP624.

1684   S., T. The second part of the Pilgrims progress. **Edinburgh, by the heir of Andrew Anderson.** 1684. 12°. WS181.

1684   SCOTLAND. PRIVY COUNCIL. Act in favours of the afflicted inhabitants of ... Kelso. **Edinburgh, by the heir of A. Anderson.** 1684. Brs. WS1436.

1684   SCOTLAND. PRIVY COUNCIL. Charles ... forasmuch as we considering ... 5 May 1684. **Edinburgh, by the heir of A. Anderson.** 1684. WS1486.

1684   SCOTLAND. PRIVY COUNCIL. Letters of intercommuning against Mr. James Rennick. **Edinburgh, by the heir of A. Anderson.** 1684. Brs. WS1512.

1684   SCOTLAND. PRIVY COUNCIL. A proclamation, anent the sumptuary act. **Edinburgh, by the heir of Andrew Anderson.** 1684. Brs. WS1693.

1684   SCOTLAND. PRIVY COUNCIL. A proclamation discharging all persons. **Edinburgh, by the heir of A. Anderson.** 1684. Brs. WS1739.

1684   SCOTLAND. PRIVY COUNCIL. A proclamation for discovering and apprehending some rebels. **Edinburg, by the heir of Andrew Anderson.** 1684. Brs. WS1864.

1684   SCOTLAND. PRIVY COUNCIL. A proclamation for discovering such as own ... 30 Dec. **Edinburgh, by the heir of Andrew Anderson.** 1684. Brs. WS1866

1685   CANARIES, JAMES. A sermon preacht at Selkirk ... 29th of May, 1685. **Edinburgh, heirs of A. Anderson.** [1685]. 4°. WC422.

1685   CHARLES II, king of England. His Majesties gracious letter to the Parliament of Scotland. **By Thomas Newcomb in the Savoy; and reprinted at Edinburgh, by the heir of Andrew Anderson.** 1685. Fol. WC3033.

1685   ENGLAND. PRIVY COUNCIL. Whereas it hath pleased Almight God ... [6 February, 1684/5]. **Edinburgh, by the heir of Andrew Anderson.** 1685. Brs. WE2922A.

1685   The form of the proceeding to the coronation of ... King James the Second. **Edinburgh, by the heir of A. Anderson.** 1685. Brs. WF1579A.

1685   IRELAND. Whereas it hath pleased Almighty God. **Edinburgh, reprinted, by the heir of A. Anderson.** 1685. Brs. WI840.

1685   JAMES II, king of England. A proclamation requiring all herefors and freeholders. **Edinburgh, by the heir of Andrew Anderson.** 1685. Brs. WJ368A.

1685   JAMES II, king of England. A proclamation requiring all herefors and freeholders. **Edinburgh, by the heir of Andrew Anderson.** 1685. Brs. WJ368B.

1685   JAMES II, king of England. A proclamation signifying His Majesties pleasure. **London, printed 1684. Edinburgh [re]printed, by the heir of Andrew Anderson.** 1685. Brs. WJ370.

1685   [SARDI, ALESSANDRO]. Johannis Seldeni Angli Liber de nummis. **Edinburgense.** 1685. 4°. WS689.

1685   SCOTLAND. COMMISSIONERS FOR ADMINISTRING OF JUSTICE IN SCOTLAND. Whereas His Highness ... 8 November 1655. **Edinburgh, C. Higgins.** 1685. Fol. WS996.

1685   SCOTLAND. ESTATES. Acts of supply. **Edinburgh.** 1685. Brs. WS1172.

1685   SCOTLAND. PRIVY COUNCIL. Act explaining a former act. **Edinburgh, by the heir of A. Anderson.** 1685. Brs. WS1415.

1685   SCOTLAND. PRIVY COUNCIL. Act in favours of the undertakers. **Edinburgh, by the heir of Andrew Anderson.** 1685. Brs. WS1440.

1685   SCOTLAND. PRIVY COUNCIL. Act taking off the restraint. **Edinburgh, by the heir of Andrew Anderson.** 1685. Brs. WS1473.

1685   SCOTLAND. PRIVY COUNCIL. A proclamation, against all persons. **Edinburgh, by the heir of A. Anderson.** 1685. Brs. WS1580.

1685   SCOTLAND. PRIVY COUNCIL. A proclamation anent runawayes. **Edinburgh, by the heir of A. Anderson.** 1685. Brs. WS1649.

1685   SCOTLAND. PRIVY COUNCIL. A publication, of the royal authority. **Edinburgh, by the heir of Andrew Anderson.** 1685. Brs. WS1993

1685   [SCOTT, GEORGE]. The model of the government of the province of East-New-Jersey. **Edinburgh, by John Reid.** [1685]. 8°. WS2035.

1685   Severeal addresses to His Majesty. **Edinburgh, heirs of A. Anderson.** [1685]. Fol. WS2747.

1685   SHIPTON, URSULA. The wonderful prophesies of. **Edinburgh, printed.** 1685. 4°. WS3456.

1685   [TYLER, ALEXANDER]. Signal dangers and deliverance. **Edinburgh.** 1685. 8°. WT3559.

1685   Whitehall, April 23. This day being the festival of St. George. **[London], by Thomas Newcomb in the Savoy: and re-printed at Edinburgh by the heir of Andrew Anderson.** 1685. Fol. WT925.

1686   [COMBER, THOMAS]. Friendly and seasonable advice to the Roman Catholicks. Fifth edition. **For Charles Brome, 1685, reprinted Edinburgh.** 1686. 12°. WC5471.

1686   DURHAM, JAMES. Christ crucified. Second edition. **Edinburgh, by the heir of Andrew Anderson.** 1686. 4°. WD2800.

1686   JAMES II, king of England. His Majesties most gracious letter to the Parliament of Scotland. [**Edinburgh.** 1686]. Fol. WJ219A.

1686   KINNAIRD, CHARLES. Reverendissimo in Christi patri Arthuro. [**Edinburgh.** 1686]. Brs. WK618.

1686   [MACKENZIE, Sir GEORGE]. A representation to the high court of Parliament. [**Edinburgh?** 1686]. WM203.

1686   MONRO, JOHN. Illustrissimo & nobilissimo domino D. Georgio Vicecomiti de Tarbat. **Edinburgi, excudebat Joannes Reid.** 1686. Brs. WM2449.

1686   MONRO, JOHN. Positiones hasce philosophicas. **Edinburgi, excudebat Joannes Reid.** 1686. WM2451.

1686   PATERSON, NINIAN. On the lamentable death of the Lady Lee, younger. [**Edinburgh?** 1686]. Brs. WP701.

1686   PATERSON, NINIAN. To the memory of ... Thomas Lord Napier. [**Edinburgh.** 1686]. Brs. WP704.

1686   Positiones philosophicæ quas ad lauream magisterialem. **Edinburgh.** 1686 Brs. WP3013.

1686   SCOTLAND. ESTATES. Act for setling the orders in the Parliament-House. **Holy-rude-House printed,** 28 April 1686. **Edinburgh re-printed by the heir of A. Anderson.** 1686. Brs. WS1103.

1686   SCOTLAND. ESTATES. Act in favours of John Addir. **Edinburgh, by the heir of A. Anderson.** 1686. Brs. WS1111.

1686   SCOTLAND. PRIVY COUNCIL. A proclamation continuing the adjournment ... 22 March 1686. **Edinburgh, by the heir of A. Anderson.** 1686. Brs. WS1732.

1687   IRELAND. Whereas we are informed ... 21 February 1686[7]. **Edinburgh, by the heir of A. Anderson.** 1687. Brs. WI983.

1687   M., G. Morality represented. **Edinburgh, by the heir of Andrew Anderson.** 1687. 8°. WM27.

1687   MAC QUEEN, JOHN. Gods interest in the King. **London, by Nath. Thompson. And sold by Alexander Ogston ... at Edingurgh** [sic]. 1687. 4°. WM226.

1687   MELFORT, JOHN DRUMMOND, earl of. The Earle of Melfort's letter. [**Edinburgh?** 1687]. 4°. WM1641.

1687   Protestancy destitute of scripture-proofs. **London, by H. Hills,** 1687. **Edinburgh re-printed James Watson.** 1687. 4°. WP3818.

1687   SCOTLAND. ESTATES. Act for burying in Scots linen. **Edinburgh, by the heir of A. Anderson.** 1687. Brs. WS1088.

1687   [SHIELDS, ALEXANDER]. A hind let loose. [**Edinburgh?**], printed. 1687. 8°. WS3431.

1687   VINCENT, THOMAS. An explicatory catechism. **Edinburgh.** 1687. 8°. WV435.

1688   Catalogue of excellent and rare books. **Edinburgh.** 1688. 4°. WC1324.

1688   The confession of faith, and the larger and shorter catechism. **Edinburgh.** 1688. 12°. WC5773.

1688   [DUNBAR, WILLIAM]. Cogitations upon death. Sixth edition. **Edinburgh, printed.** 1688. 8°. WD2599.

1688   ENGLAND. PARLIAMENT. HOUSE OF LORDS. A declaration of the Lords ... 11 December 1688. **Reprinted at Edinburgh.** 1688. Brs. WE2795.

1688   ESPAGNE, JEAN D'. The use of the Lord's Prayer. **Edinburgh, by the heir of Andrew Anderson.** 1688. 8°. WE3274.

1688   [HALIFAX, GEORGE SAVILE, marquis of]. The lady's New-Years gift. Third edition. **Edinburgh, by John Reid, for James Glen, and Walter Cunningham.** 1688. 8°. WH306.

1688   JAMES II, king of England. A proclamation commanding the return. **Edinburgh, by the heir of Andrew Anderson.** 1688. Brs. WJ317A.

1688   A letter from the Arch-bishops and Bishops. **Edinburgh, by the heir of Andrew Anderson.** 1688. Brs. WL1513A.

1688 PATERSON, NINIAN. To the memory of the incomparable Sir Andrew Ramsay. [**Edinburgh.** 1688]. Brs. WP705.

1688 RENWICK, JAMES. Antipas. [**Edinburgh.** 1688]. 4°. WR1043.

1688 SCOTLAND. PRIVY COUNCIL. Act appointing a voluntary contribution. **Edinburgh**, the 17th day of Aprill. 1688. Brs. WS1399.

1688 SCOTLAND. PRIVY COUNCIL. Act for inbringing of His Majesties excise. **Edinburgh, by the heir of A. Anderson.** 1688. Brs. WS1426.

1688 SCOTLAND. PRIVY COUNCIL. Act in favours of His Majesties printer. **Edinburgh, by the heir of A. Anderson.** 1688. Brs. WS1435.

1688 SCOTLAND. PRIVY COUNCIL. Act of His Majesties Privy Council for suppressing tumults. **Edinburgh, by the heir of A. Anderson.** 1688. Brs. WS1452.

1688 SCOTLAND. PRIVY COUNCIL. Act of Privy Council, in favours of the officers. **Edinburgh, by the heir of Andrew Anderson.** 1688. Brs. WS1465.

1688 SCOTLAND. PRIVY COUNCIL. Act of Privy Council, ordering probation. **Edinburgh, by the heir of Andrew Anderson.** 1688. Brs. WS1466.

1688 SCOTLAND. PRIVY COUNCIL. The following depositions ... 9 November 1688. [**Edinburgh, by the heir of Andrew Anderson.** 1688]. Brs. WS1492.

1688 [SHIELDS, ALEXANDER]. An elegie upon the death of that famous ... minister ... Mr. James Renwick. [**Edinburgh**]. 1688. 12°. WS3430.

1688 [SHIELDS, ALEXANDER]. March 11, 1688. Some notes or heads of a preface. [**Edinburgh.** 1688?]. 4°. WS3435.

1688 TILLOTSON, JOHN, abp. A persuasive to frequent communion. **Edinburgh, by John Reid.** 1688. 8°. WT1209.

1688 TILLOTSON, JOHN, abp. A persuasive to frequent communion. **Edinburgh, by the heir of Andrew Anderson.** 1688. 8°. WT1210.

1689 An account of a second victory obtained over the Turks. **Edinburgh, reprinted.** 1689. Brs. WA192.

1689 An account of the last Thursdays sea engagement. **Edinburgh, reprinted.** 1689. Brs. WA306.

1689 An address to the nobility, clergy and gentlemen of Scotland. **Edinburgh.** 1689. 4°. WA568.

1689 Answers for the Duke of Gordon. [**Edinburgh.** 1689]. Fol. WA3466.

1689 CHATEILLON, SEBASTIEN. Dialogorum sacrorum. **Edinburgi, ex officina Societatis bibliopolarum.** 1689. 12°. WC3734.

1689 ENGLAND. PARLIAMENT. The address of the Lords spiritual and temporal ... 16 April 1689. **Printed at London, and re-printed at Edinburgh.** 1689. 4°. WE1190.

1689 ENGLAND. PARLIAMENT. A declaration [13 February 1688/9]. **Edinburgh, reprinted** [heir of A. Anderson]. 1689. Brs. WE1294.

1689 ENGLAND. PARLIAMENT. Die Sabbathi [13 February 1689]. **Edinburgh, reprinted.** 1689. Brs. WE2188.

1689 Four questions debated. [**Edinburgh**], re-printed. 1689. 4°. WF1669.

1689 JAMES II, king of England. His Majesty's letter to the Lords ... 1 March. [**Edinburgh.** 1689]. 4°. WJ209.

1689 [KER, WILLIAM]. The sober conformists answer. [**Edinburgh**], printed. 1689. 4°. WK346.

1689 A letter to a member of the convention of states in Scotland. [**Edinburgh**], printed. 1689. 4°. WL1684.

1689 A letter to a reverend minister of the Gospel. [**Edinburgh.** 1689]. 4°. WL1696.

1689 The names of the lords spiritual and temporal, who deserted. **Edinburgh, re-printed.** 1689. Brs. WN141A.

1689 [PARK, ROBERT]. To the right reverend, the ministers ... the following defence of the rights and liberties of the church. [**Edinburgh.** 1689]. 8°. WP364.

1689 Popery banished. **Edinburgh, reprinted.** 1689. 4°. WP2924.

1689 SCHOMBERG, FREDERICK. A proclamation by ... 1 September 1689. **Edinburgh, reprinted** [heir of A. Anderson]. 1689. Brs. WS871.

1689 SCHOMBERG, FREDERICK. A third proclamation, by. **Edinburgh reprinted** 1689. Brs. WS876.

1689 SCOTLAND. ESTATES. Act. approving the address, made by the noblemen. **Edinburgh, printed.** 1689. Brs. WS1057.

1689 SCOTLAND. ESTATES. Act, concerning the militia. **Edinburgh** [heir of A. Anderson]. 1689. Brs. WS1071.

1689 SCOTLAND. ESTATES. Act declaring the meeting of Estates. **Edinburgh, by the heir of Andrew Anderson.** 1689. Brs. WS1076.

1689 SCOTLAND. ESTATES. Act of the meeting of the Estates, for inbringing. **Edinburgh.** 1689. Brs. WS1143.

1689 SCOTLAND. ESTATES. Act ordaining the members. **Edinburgh, printed** [heir of A. Anderson]. 1689. Brs. WS1150.

1689 SCOTLAND. ESTATES. Additional warrand for the proclamation of the king. **Edinburgh** [heir of A. Anderson]. 1689. Brs. WS1178.

1689 SCOTLAND. ESTATES. Order for an embargo. **Edinburgh,** [heir of A. Anderson]. 1689. Brs. WS1296.

1689 SCOTLAND. PRIVY COUNCIL. Act for furnishing of baggage-horse. **Edinburgh, by the heir of Andrew Anderson.** 1689. Brs. WS1425.

1689 SCOTLAND. PRIVY COUNCIL. Act for the better regulating. **Edinburgh, by the heir of A. Anderson.** 1689. Brs. WS1434.

1689 SCOTLAND. PRIVY COUNCIL. Act of His Majesties Privy Council, reviving the foresaid act. **Edinburgh, by the heir of Andrew Anderson.** 1689. Brs. WS1455.

1689 Several queries relating to the present proceedings in Parliament. [**Edinburgh.** 1689]. 4°. WS2806.

1689 USSHER, JAMES, abp. The reduction of Episcopacie. [**Edinburgh**], printed. 1689. 4°. WU220.

1689 WILLIAM III, king of England. A declaration by ... 6 February 1689. **Edinburgh.** 1689. Brs. WW2314.

1689 WILLIAM III, king of England. A declaration by ... 6 February 1689. [**Edinburgh.** 1689]. Brs. WW2315.

1689 WILLIAM III, king of England. The declaration of His Highnes William Henry, ... of the reasons. [**Edinburgh**], **printed.** 1689. 4°. WW2330.

1689 WILLIAM III, king of England. His Highness the Prince of Orange his letter to the Lords ... January 22. 1688/9. **Edinburgh, re-printed.** 1689. WW2359.

1689 WILLIAM III, king of England. His Majesties reason for withdrawing himself. [**Edinburgh**], **printed.** 1689. Brs. WW2477.

1689 WILLIAM III, king of England. The only reason which induced. [**Edinburgh**]. 1689. Brs. WW2426.

1689 WILLIAM AND MARY, king and queen of England. Their Majesties declaration against the French king. **Reprinted Edinburgh, by the heir of A. Anderson.** 1689. Brs. WW2503.

1689 WILLIAM AND MARY, king and queen of England. The declaration of ... 4 April, 1689. **Edinburgh, reprinted.** 1689. Brs. WW2510.

1690 An account of the ceremony of investing. **London, reprinted Edinburgh.** 1690. 4°. WA262.

1690 ENGLAND. PARLIAMENT. An act for recognizing King William and Queen Mary. [**Edinburgh**], **reprinted.** 1690. Brs. WE1058.

1690 An exact and faithful relation of the process pursued by Dame Margaret Areskine. **Edinburgh, at the Society of Stationers.** [1690]. 4°. WE3598.

1690 GREGORY, JAMES. Nobilissimo viro Georgio. **Edinburgi, ex officina typographica societatis bibliopolarum.** 1690. Brs. WG1911.

1690 Information for the heritors, elders, ... against Mr. William Veatch. [**Edinburgh.** 1690]. 4°. WI166.

1690 LOTHIAN, ROBERT KERR, earl. His discourse to the Lords, ... January the 27th, 1690. **Edinburgh.** 1690. Fol. WL3082.

1690 SCOTLAND. ESTATES. Laws ... first Parliament ... (first session) ... William and Mary. **Edinburgh, by the heir of Andrew Anderson.** 1690. Fol. WS1255.

1690 SCOTLAND. ESTATES. Laws ... second session ... first Parliament. **Edinburgh, by the heir of Andrew Anderson.** 1690. Fol. WS1256.

1690 SCOTLAND. ESTATES. Laws ... third session. **Edinburgh, by the heir of A. Anderson.** 1690. Fol. WS1257.

1690 SCOTLAND. LORDS OF COUNCIL AND SESSION. Act against solicitation. **Edinburgh, by the heir of A. Anderson.** 1690. Brs. WS1365.

1690 SCOTLAND. PRIVY COUNCIL. Act for raising a supply. **Edinburgh, by the heir of Andrew Anderson.** 1690. Fol. WS1430.

1690 SCOTLAND. PRIVY COUNCIL. A proclamation, for choosing the additional representatives. **Edinburgh, by the heir of A. Anderson.** 1690. Brs. WS1856.

1690 WILLIAM AND MARY, king and queen of England. A proclamation for a general fast ... twentieth day of February 1689[90]. **Edinburgh, reprinted by the Society of Stationers.** 1690. Brs. WW2571.

1690 A wish for peace. **Eirenopoli** [**Edinburgh**]. 1690. 4°. WW3116.

1691 CARSTAIRS, JOHN. A song for this sad times. **Edinburgh, by John Reid.** 1691. 8°. WC647.

1691 CHURCH OF SCOTLAND. The principall acts of the Generall Assembly. **Edinbvrgh, by George Mosman.** 1691. Fol. WC4245.

1691 Copy of a paper presented ... in the year, 1681, to the then Duke of York. **Edinburgh, by the heir of Andrew Anderson.** 1691. 4°. WC6183B.

1691 HOPE, Sir WILLIAM. The sword-man's vademecum. **Edinburgh, by John Reid.** 1691. 12°. WH2716.

1691 A list of the princes present at the congress at the Hague. **Edinburgh, re-printed.** 1691. Brs. WL2495.

1691 Monsieur in a mouse-trap. [**Edinburgh?**]. Re-printed. 1691. Brs. WM2459.

1691 MONTGOMERIE, ALEXANDER. The cherry and the slae. **Edinburgh, by John Reid.** 1691. WM2501.

1691 SCOTLAND. PRIVY COUNCIL. A proclamation, prorogating the dyet. **Edinburgh, by the heir of A. Anderson.** 1691. Brs. WS1970.

1691 TARRAS, WALTER SCOTT, earl. To the right reverend, the moderator, ... the humble representation of. [**Edinburgh.** 1691]. Fol. WT168.

1691 The tryal and condemnation, together with thee [sic] execution of Capt. Ashtoun. **Printed at London, and re-printed at Edinburgh.** 1691. Brs. WT2159.

1692 ADVOCATES LIBRARY. Catalogus librorum bibliothecæ juris utriusque. **Edinburgi, ex officind typographied Georgee Mosman.** 1692. 4°. WA672.

1692 An elegie upon the Earl of Angus. [**Edinburgh?** 1692]. Brs. WE480.

1692 ENGLAND. PARLIAMENT. HOUSE OF COMMONS. The address of the House of Commons to the king. **Edinburgh, re-printed by the heir of Andrew Anderson.** 1692. Brs. WE2516.

1692 A further account of the victory obtained. **London, Edinburgh reprinted.** 1692. Brs. WF527.

1692 A further account of the victory obtained by the English and Dutch fleet. **London, Edinburgh, reprinted.** 1692. Brs. WF2548.

1692 JAMES II, king of England. His Majesties most gracious declaration to his good people. [**Edinburgh.** 1692]. Fol. WJ218.

1692 The resolution taken by the confederate princes. **Edinburgh, re-printed.** 1692. Brs. WR1161.

1692 RYSSEN, LEONARD VAN. Summa theologiæ. **Edinbvrgi, excudebat George Mosman.** 1692. 12°. WR2436.

1692 S., M. T. The coppy of a letter written by a friend to the laird of Blaikwood. [**Edinburgh.** 1692]. Fol. WS119.

1692 SCOTLAND. LORDS OF COUNCIL AND SESSION. Act concerning the minut-books. **Edinburgh, by the heir of A. Anderson.** 1692. Brs. WS1368.

1692 TILLY, JOHANN TSERCLAES, graf. A relation of the late action. **Reprinted Edinburgh.** 1692. Brs. WT1273.

1692 The touch stone of the A, B, C. **Edinburgh, by John Reid.** 1692. 12°. WT1957.

1693 CHAMBERLEN, HUGH. Papers relating to a bank of credit. [**Edinburgh.** 1693]. 4°. WC1877A.

1693 C[LARK], I[AMES]. Plain truth or, a seasonable discourse of the duties of people. **Edinburgh, J: Reid, to be sold by James Wardlaw.** 1693. 4°. WC4465.

1693 [FORRESTER, THOMAS]. A counter-essay. **Edinburgh.** 1693. 4°. WF1595.

1693 A letter from a Presbyterian minister. [**Edinburgh.** 1693?]. 4°. WL1429.

1693 MACKENZIE, SIMON. Disputatio juridica. **Edinburgi, apud Joannem Reid.** 1693. 4°. WM217.

1693 MONRO, ROBERT. Disputatio juridica. **Edinburgi, apud successores Andreæ Anderson.** 1693. 4°. WM2452.

1693 SCOTLAND. ESTATES Act adjourning the session ... 30 May 1693. **Edinburgh, by the heir of A. Anderson.** 1693. Brs. WS1024.

1693 SCOTLAND. ESTATES. Act anent the loyal curing ... of herring. **Edinburgh, by the heir of A. Anderson.** 1693. Brs. WS1048.

1693 SCOTLAND. ESTATES. Act for a new supply. **Edinburgh, by the heir of A. Anderson.** 1693. Brs. WS1084.

1693 SCOTLAND. ESTATES. Act for an additional excise. **Edinburgh, by the heir of A. Anderson.** 1693. Brs. WS1087.

1693 SCOTLAND. ESTATES. Act for levying of seamen. **Edinburgh, by the heir of A. Anderson.** 1693. Brs. WS1089.

1693 SCOTLAND. ESTATES. Act for the levy. **Edinburgh, by the heir of A. Anderson.** 1693. Brs. WS1107.

1693 SCOTLAND. ESTATES Acts for settling the orders. [**Edinburgh.** 1693]. Brs. WS1168.

1693 SCOTLAND. LORDS OF COUNCIL AND SESSION. Act concerning tutors. **Edinburgh, by the heir of A. Anderson.** 1693. Brs. WS1370.

1693 SCOTLAND. PRIVY COUNCIL. Act against tumults. **Edinburgh, by the successors of A. Anderson.** 1693. Brs. WS1381.

1693 SCOTLAND. PRIVY COUNCIL. Act in favours of the synod of Lothian. **Edinburgh.** 1693. Brs. WS1439.

1693 SCOTLAND. PRIVY COUNCIL. A proclamation anent beggars ... 29 Aug. [**Edinburgh, by the heir of A. Anderson**]. 1693. Brs. WS1628.

1693 WISHART. Catalogue of excellent and rare books. **Edinburgh.** 1693. 4°. WW3117.

1694 An account of a most horrid and barbarous murther ... Captain Brown. **Edinburgh, reprinted.** 1694. Brs. WA187.

1694 CHURCH OF SCOTLAND. The principall acts of the Generall Assembly. **Edinbvrgh, by George Mosman.** 1694. Fol. WC4247.

1694 DURHAM, JAMES. The blessedness of the death. **Edinburgh, by the heirs and successors of Andrew Anderson.** 1694. 12°. WD2798.

1694 PORTERFIELD, JAMES. A choice jewel for children. **Edinburgh, by John Reid.** 1694. WP3000.

1694 SCOTLAND. PRIVY COUNCIL. Act anent the deficients. **Edinburgh, by the heirs & successors of A. Anderson.** 1694. Brs. WS1395.

1694 SCOTLAND. PRIVY COUNCIL. Letters of publication, of a commission. **Edinburgh, by the heirs of Andrew Anderson** 1694. Brs. WS1516.

1694 TAYLOR, THOMAS. Jacob wrestling with God. **Edinburgh.** 1694. 8°. WT557.

1695 CHURCH OF SCOTLAND. The principall acts of the Generall Assembly. **Edinbvrgh, by George Mosman.** 1695. Fol. WC4247A.

1695 FLAVELL, JOHN. An exposition of the Assemblies catechism. **Edinburgh, re-printed by the heirs and successors of Andrew Anderson.** 1695. 12°. WF1161.

1695 In luctrosissimum Mariae ... obitum. **Edinburgi.** 1695. Brs. WI113.

1695 Instructions given by the commissioners and trustees for improving the fisheries. [**Edinburgh.** 1695]. Brs. WI251.

1695 SCOTLAND. ESTATES. Act against irregular baptisms. **Edinburgh, by the heirs & successors of A. Anderson.** 1695. Brs. WS1026.

1695 SCOTLAND. ESTATES. Act and commission by the general meeting. **Edinburgh: printed.** 1695. 4°. WS1032.

1695 SCOTLAND. ESTATES. Act for setling the orders in the Parliament-House. **Edinburgh by the heirs & successors of A. Anderson.** [1695]. WS1104.

1695 SCOTLAND. PRIVY COUNCIL. Act for a company trading to Africa. [**Edinburgh.** 1695]. Brs. WS1417.

1695 SCOTLAND. PRIVY COUNCIL. A proclamation for the more effectual uplifting. **Edinburgh, by the heirs & successors of A. Anderson.** 1695. Brs. WS1935.

1695 SCOTLAND. PRIVY COUNCIL. A proclamation, prorogating the dyets. **Edinburgh, by the heirs & successors of A. Anderson.** 1695. Brs. WS1971.

1695 SCOTLAND. PRIVY COUNCIL. A proclamation prorogating the dyets. **Edinburgh, by the heirs & successors of A. Anderson.** 1695. Brs. WS1972.

1695 TWEEDDALE, JOHN HAY, marquis. The speech of. **Edinburgh.** 1695. Fol. WT3391.

1695 Unto His Grace, Their Majesties High Commissioner. [**Edinburgh?** 1695]. Brs. WU101.

1696 Answer for the African Company. [**Edinburgh.** 1696]. Brs. WA3277.

1696 A[RBUTHOT], J[OHN]. Theses medicæ. [**Edinburgh**], **ex officina Georgii Mosman.** 1696. 4°. WA3603.

1696 A character of Mr. Blow's book entitled Suadela victrix. [**Edinburgh?** 1696]. 4°. WC2021A.

1696 CHURCH OF SCOTLAND. The principall acts of the Generall Assembly. **Edinbvrgh, by George Mosman.** 1696. 4°. WC4248.

1696 COCKBURN, JOHN. Jacobs vow. **Edinburgh, for Alexander Ogston; to be sold by William Keblewhite.** 1696. 8°. WC4813.

1696 COMPANY OF SCOTLAND TRADING TO AFRICA AND THE INDIES. At a meeting of the committee. [**Edinburgh.** 1696]. Brs. WC5589.

1696 COMPANY OF SCOTLAND TRADING TO AFRICA AND THE INDIES. Constitutions agreed upon by the committee. [**Edinburgh?** 1696]. Brs. WC5593A.

1696 COMPANY OF SCOTLAND TRADING TO AFRICA AND THE INDIES. A perfect list of the several persons residenters. **Edinburgh, printed and sold by the heirs and successors of Andrew Anderson.** 1696. Fol. WC5599.

1696 D[ONALDSON], J[AMES]. Husbandry anatomized. **Edinburgh.** 1696. 12°. WD1852.

1696 DURHAM, JAMES. The unsearchable riches of Christ. Third edition. **Edinburgh, heirs and successors of Andrew Anderson.** 1696. 12°. WD2829.

1696 FLAVELL, JOHN. A saint indeed. **Edinburgh, by the heirs and successors of Andrew Anderson.** 1696. 12°. WF1193.

1696 HENDERSON, ALEXANDER. The government and order. **Edinburgh, for the Society of Stationers.** 1696. 4°. WH1435.

1696 HOPE, Sir WILLIAM. A supplement of horsemanship. **Printed at Edinburgh.** 1696. Fol. WH2715.

1696 Insignia præ lustris societatis Scoticanæ, ... explicata. [**Edinburgh**? 1696]. Brs. WI225A.

1696 K., C. Some seasonable and modest thoughts. [**Edinburgh**], printed. 1696. 4°. WK5.

1696 K., C. Some seasonable and modest thoughts. **Edinburgh, reprinted by George Mosman.** 1696. 4°. WK6.

1696 Octupla; hoc est octo paraphrases poeticæ Psalmi 104. **Edinburgi,** 1696. 12°. WO130.

1696 S., T. The second part of the Pilgrims progress. **Edinburgh, by the heirs and successors of Andrew Anderson.** 1696. 12°. WS182.

1696 SCOTLAND. PRIVY COUNCIL. A proclamation for rouping of His Majesties customs. **Edinburgh, by the heirs & successors of A. Anderson.** 1696. Brs. WS1906.

1696 SCOTLAND. PRIVY COUNCIL. A proclamation for securing the kingdom. **Edinburgh, by the heirs & successors of A. Anderson.** 1696. Brs. WS1910.

1697 Advice to the electors of Great Britain. **Edinburgh, reprinted by the heirs and successors of Andrew Anderson.** [1697?]. 4°. WA654.

1697 ARBUTHNOTT, ALEXANDER. Disputatio juridica. **Edinburgi, ex officina typographica haeredum Andreae Anderson.** 1697. 4°. WA3604.

1697 CHURCH OF SCOTLAND. The principall acts of the Generall Assembly. **Edinbvrgh, by George Mosman.** 1697. 4°. WC4248A.

1697 ENGLAND. LORDS JUSTICES. A proclamation for publishing the peace ... French. **Edinburgh, by the heirs & successors of A. Anderson.** 1697. Brs. WE953.

1697 GRAY, ANDREW. The spiritual warfare. **Edinbvrgh, by the heirs and successors of Andrew Anderson.** 1697. 12°. WG1622.

1697 A memorial given in to the Senate of the city of Hamburgh. [**Edinburgh.** 1697]. Brs. WM1688.

1697 SCOTLAND. PRIVY COUNCIL. Act discharging any person to go abroad. **Edinburgh, by the heirs & successors of A. Anderson.** 1697. Brs. WS1408.

1697 Some principal heads of Christian religion. **Edinbvrgh, by G. Mosman.** 1697. Brs. WS4556.

1697 WILLIAM III, king of England. His Majesties gracious answer ... 30 November, 1967. **Edinburgh, by the heirs & successors of A. Anderson.** 1697. Brs. WW2333.

1698 A call to Scotland. **Edinburgh, printed.** 1698. 8°. WC298.

1698 CHURCH OF SCOTLAND. The principall acts of the Generall Assembly. **Edinbvrgh, by George Mosman.** 1698. Fol. WC4249.

1698 In the act of raising two millions. [**Edinburgh**? 1698]. Brs. WI123.

1698 MACKENZIE, Sir GEORGE. Observations upon the 28. [sic] act, 23. Parl. Second edition. **Edinburgh, by the heirs and successors of Andrew Anderson. For Mr. Andrew Symson.** 1698. 8°. WM188.

1698 MATHER, COTTON. Eleutheria; or, an idea of the reformation. **For J. R. and sold by John Mackie in Edinburgh.** 1698. 8°. WM1102.

1698 MATHER, COTTON. Eleutheria; or, an idea of the reformation. **For J. R. and sold by John Mackie in Edinburgh.** 1698. 8°. WM1103A.

1698 SCOTLAND. ESTATES. A proclamation of Parliament, for a solemn national fast. **Edinburgh, by the heirs & successors of A. Anderson.** 1698. Brs. WS1325.

1698 SCOTLAND. PRIVY COUNCIL. Act additional to the proclamation. **Edinburgh, by the heirs & successors of A. Anderson.** 1698. Brs. WS1379.

1698 SCOTLAND. PRIVY COUNCIL. A proclamation against prophaneness ... 25 Jan. **Edinburgh, by the heirs & successors of A. Anderson.** 1698. Brs. WS1600.

1698 A true account of the types of His Majesties Printing-House. **Edinburgh, by the heirs and successors of Andrew Anderson.** 1698. Brs. WT2407.

1698 WILLIAM III, king of England. A proclamation discharging the transporting of persons ... America. **Edinburgh, by the heirs and successors of Andrew Anderson.** 1698. Brs. WW2453A

1699 ALMANACS. A prognostication for the year 1699. **Edinburgh.** 1699. 12°. WA2221.

1699 Caledonia triumphans: a panegyrick. [**Edinburgh.** 1699]. Brs. WC286.

1699 CHURCH OF SCOTLAND. The principal acts of the Generall Assembly. **Edinburgh, by George Mosman.** 1699. Fol. WC4250.

1699 COMPANY OF SCOTLAND TRADING TO AFRICA AND THE INDIES. At a council-general of the company of Scotland. [**Edinburgh.** 1699]. Brs. WC5584.

1699 A defence of Dr. Oliphant's short discourse. **Edinburgh by J. W. for Thomas Carruthers.** 1699. 12°. WD813.

1699 An exact list of all the men, woman, and boys that died. **Edinburgh, G. Mosman.** 1699. Brs WE3653.

1699 [FOYER, ARCHIBALD]. A defence of the Scots settlement at Darien. With an answer. **Edinburgh, printed.** 1699. 8°. WF2047A.

1699 [HENDERSON, JO.] Mr. Clanny's Character. [**Edinburgh**]. 1699. 4°. WH1445.

1699 MACKENZIE, Sir GEORGE. The institutions of the law of Scotland. "Third edition". **Edinburgh, for Thomas Broun.** 1699. 8°. WM161.

1699 MACKENZIE, Sir GEORGE. Observations upon the XVIII. act. **Edinburgh, by the heirs and successors of Andrew Anderson. For Mr. Andrew Symson.** 1699. Fol. WM189.

1699 MAKEMIE, FRANCIS. Truths in a true light. **Edinbvrgh, by the successors of Andrew Anderson.** 1699. 12°. WM308.

1699 [MONCRIEF, JO.] A seasonable admonition and exhortation. **Edinbvrgh, by George Mosman.** 1699. 8°. WM2411.

1699 ROYAL COLLEGE OF PHYSICIANS. Pharmacopoeia Collegii Regalis Londini. **Edinburgi.** 1699. 12°. WR2110.

1699 SCOTLAND. COMMISSION OF TRADE. Act of the Commission for communication of trade. **Edinburgh, by the heirs & successors of Andrew Anderson.** 1699. Brs. WS968.

1699 SCOTLAND. PRIVY COUNCIL. Act and intimation anent this currant Parliament ... 11 October 1694. **Edinburgh, by the heirs & successors of A. Anderson.** 1699. Brs. WS1390.

1699 SETON, Sir ALEXANDER. A treatise of mutilation and demembration. **Edinburgh, by the heirs and successors of Andrew Anderson. For Mr. Andrew Symson.** 1699. Fol. WS2649.

1699 [SHIELDS, ALEXANDER]. A proper project for Scotland. **[Edinburgh], printed.** 1699. 4°. WS3433.

1700 An advice concerning the communication of trade. **Edinburgh, by the heirs of Andrew Anderson.** 1700. Fol. WA630A.

1700 ALMANACS. MAN, JOHN. Edinburghs true almanack ... for ... 1700. **Edinburgh.** 1700. 8°. WA1934.

1700 ALMANACS. [SYMSON, MATTHJAS.] The Caledonian almanack. **Edinburgh, printed.** 1700. 4°. WA2492.

1700 ANDERSON, JAMES. An historical essay. **Edinburgh.** 1700. 8°. WA3097.

1700 C., H. Remarks on the giving vomits. **Edinburgh.** 1700. 8°. WC46.

1700 CATO, DIONYSIUS. Catonis disticha de moribvs. **Edinburgi.** 1700. 8°. WC1511.

1700 CATO, DIONYSIUS. His four books of moral precepts. **Edinburgh, printed.** 1700. 8°. WC1512.

1700 The causes of Scotland's miseries. A poem. **Edinburgh, by James Watson.** 1700. 4°. WC1538.

1700 CHAMBERLEN, HUGH. A few proposals. **Edinburgh, printed.** 1700. 4°. WC1872.

1700 CHAMBERLEN, HUGH. Proposal, by. [**Edinburgh.** 1700?] Brs. WC1881.

1700 CHAMBERLEN, HUGH. Several matters, relating to the improvement of the trade. [**Edinburgh**? 1700.] 4°. WC1889.

1700 CHATEILLON, SEBASTIEN. Dialogorum sacrorum. **Edinburgi, ex typographæo Georgii Mosman.** 1700. 12°. WC3734A.

1700 COMPANY OF SCOTLAND TRADING TO AFRICA AND THE INDIES. A full and exact collection of all the considerate addresses. [**Edinburgh**]. **printed.** 1700. 8°. WC5597B.

1700 COMPANY OF SCOTLAND TRADING TO AFRICA AND THE INDIES. The original papers and letters. [**Edinburgh**], **printed.** 1700. 8°. WC5598A.

1700 COMPANY OF SCOTLAND TRADING TO AFRICA AND THE INDIES. The representation and petition of the Council-General. **Edinburgh, printed.** 1700. 8°. WC5599A.

1700 COMPANY OF SCOTLAND TRADING TO AFRICA AND THE INDIES. Scotland's right to Caledonia. [**Edinburgh**], **printed.** 1700. WC5599B.

1700 COMPANY OF SCOTLAND TRADING TO AFRICA AND THE INDIES. A short proposal for. [**Edinburgh**?] 1700. 4°. WC5599C.

1700 COMPANY OF SCOTLAND TRADING TO AFRICA AND THE INDIES. A supplement of original papers. [**Edinburgh**?] 1700. 8°. WC5599D.

1700 COMPANY OF SCOTLAND TRADING TO AFRICA AND THE INDIES. The three following memorials. [**Edinburgh**? 1700]. 4°. WC5599E.

1700 COMPANY OF SCOTLAND TRADING TO AFRICA AND THE INDIES. To His Grace, His Majesty's High Commissioner ... The humble representation. [**Edinburgh.** 1700]. Brs. WC5601.

1700 COMPANY OF SCOTLAND TRADING TO AFRICA AND THE INDIES. To His Grace, His Majesty's High Commissioner ... The humble representation [**Edinburgh.** 1700]. Fol. WC5602.

1700 Coppy of the addres; of a great number of the members. **Edinburgh, reprinted by John Reid.** 1700. Brs. WC6201.

1700 CORBET, JOHN. Self-imployment in secret. **Edinburgh, by George Mosman.** [1700?]. 8°. WC6267.

1700 [CULLEN, FRANCIS GRANT, lord]. A brief account of the nature. **Edinburgh, by George Mosman.** 1700. 4°. WC7474A.

1700 [CULLEN, FRANCIS GRANT, lord]. A discourse, concerning the execution of the laws. **Edinburgh, by George Mosman.** 1700. 8°. WC7474B.

1700 [DEMPSTER, GEORGE]. The prodigal returned to Scotland. **Edinburgh, in June 1700 by John Reid, and are to be sold at John Vallange's Mrs Ogstoun's and Thomas Carruther's.** 4°. WD984.

1700 D[ONALDSON], J[AMES]. The undoubted art of thriving. **Edinburgh, by John Reid.** 1700. 4°. WD1856.

1700 [DOUGLAS, ROBERT]. The form and order of the coronation ... Januarie, 1651. **Aberdeen, printed, and Edinburgh reprinted by John Reid.** 1700. 8°. WD2033.

1700 DURHAM, JAMES. Christ crucified. Third edition. **Edinburgh.** 1700. 4°. WD2801.

1700 The emblem of our King. **Edinburgh, by John Reid.** 1700. 4°. WE702.

1700 ENGLAND. PARLIAMENT. At a Parliament. **Printed at London, and re-printed at Edinburgh.** 1700. 4°. WE1253.

1700 ENGLAND. PARLIAMENT. HOUSE OF LORDS. The humble address of the right honourable the Lords spiritual and temporal. **Edinburgh, re-printed by the heirs and successors of Andrew Anderson.** 1700. Brs. WE2805.

1700 [FLETCHER, ANDREW]. Overtures offered to the Parliament. **Edinburgh, by John Reid.** 1700. 4°. WF1296.

1700 [FOYER, ARCHIBALD]. Scotland's present duty. [**Edinburgh**], **printed.** 1700. 4°. WF2048.

1700 A further explication of the proposal relating to the coyne. [**Edinburgh.** 1700?]. 4°. WF2557.

1700 [GORDON, JAMES], bp. Some observations on the Fables of AEsop. **Edinburgh, for Mr. Andrew Symson and are to be sold by him and by Mr. Henry Knox.** 1700. WG1284.

1700 [GRANT, PATRICK]. The Nonconformists vindication. [**Edinburgh**?] **printed.** 1700. 4°. WG1522.

1700 Helter Skelter. [**Edinburgh.** 1700?]. Fol. WH1408.

1700 [HODGES, JAMES]. A defence of the Scots abdicating Darien. [**Edinburgh**?] **printed.** 1700. 8°. WH2298.

1700 The humble representation and petition of the Council-General of the company of Scotland. **Edinburgh.** 1700. 8°. WH3632.

1700 A letter from the nobility. **Impressum juxta typum nuper Edinburgi excusum anno.** 1700. 4°. WL1534.

1700 A letter to a member of Parliament, occasioned, by the growing poverty of the nation. **Edinburgh, printed.** 1700. 4°. WL1677.

1700 LINDEMAN, MICHEL. A prophesie, of a country-man. **Edinburgh, re-printed.** 1700. Brs. WL2309

1700 MARCHMONT, PATRICK, earl. The speech of ... 21. Mar. 1700. **Edinburgh, by the heirs and successors of Andrew Anderson.** 1700. Fol. WM587.

1700 MARCHMONT, PATRICK, earl. The speech of ... 29 October, 1700. **Edinburgh, by the heirs and successors of Andrew Anderson.** 1700. Brs. WM588.

1700 [MIDDLETON, JOHN MIDDLETON, earl]. For the good of the publick. **Edinburgh, for the author.** [1700?] 4°. WM1975.

1700 [MONRO, GEORGE]. The first measures of the pious institution of youth. **Edinburgh, by John Reid.** 1700. 12°. WM2448.

1700 MURRAY, JANET. Unto the lords of council and session, the petition of. [**Edinburgh.** 1700]. Brs. WM3107.

1700 NISBET, ALEXANDER. An essay on additional figures. **Edinburgh.** 1700. 12°. WN1167.

1700 OGILVY, ARCHIBALD. Disputatio juridica. **Edinburgi, ex officina hæredum Andræ Anderson.** 1700. 4°. WO185.

1700 Overtures for correcting and amending the laws. [**Edinburgh**?] 1700. Fol. WO644.

1700 [PENNECUIK, ANDREW]. The tragedy of Gray-Beard. [**Edinburgh**], **printed.** 1700. 8°. WP1397

1700 The probable reasons why the fire. **Edinburgh,** 1700. Fol. WP3542.

1700 QUEENSBERRY, JAMES DOUGLAS, duke of. The speech of. [**Edinburgh.** 1700]. Brs. WQ160.

1700 QUEENSBERRY, JAMES DOUGLAS, duke of. The speech of ... 30. of May. **Edinburgh, by the heirs and successors of Andrew Anderson.** 1700. Brs. WQ161.

1700 [RIDPATH, GEORGE]. Scotland's grievances. [**Edinburgh**?] **printed.** 1700. 4°. WR1464.

1700 ROSS, JAMES. Origo gentis Hayorum. **Edinburgi,** Anno Dom. 1700. 8°. WR1987.

1700 SCOTLAND. COMMISSION OF TRADE. Act of the Commission of Parliament for settling. [**Edinburgh.** 1700]. Brs. WS969.

1700 SCOTLAND. PRIVY COUNCIL. Act for publishing His Majesties most gracious letter. **Edinburgh, by the heirs and successors of Andrew Anderson.** 1700. Brs. WS1429.

1700 SCOTLAND. PRIVY COUNCIL. Proclamation, adjourning the Parliament ... 16 January 1700. **Edinburgh, by the heirs & successors of A. Anderson.** 1700. Brs. WS1575.

1700 SCOTLAND. PRIVY COUNCIL. Proclamation, adjourning the Parliament ... 7 May 1700. **Edinburgh, by the heirs & successors of A. Anderson.** 1700. Brs. WS1576.

1700 SCOTLAND. PRIVY COUNCIL. Proclamation, adjourning the Parliament ... 17 June 1700. **Edinburgh, by the heirs & successors of A. Anderson.** 1700. Brs. WS1577.

1700 SCOTLAND. PRIVY COUNCIL. Proclamation, adjourning the Parliament ... 15 October 1700. **Edinburgh, by the heirs & successors of A. Anderson.** 1700. Brs. WS1578.

1700 SCOTLAND. PRIVY COUNCIL. Proclamation against a late resolve. **Edinburgh, by the heirs & successors of A. Anderson.** 1700. Brs. WS1579.

1700 SCOTLAND. PRIVY COUNCIL. Proclamation discharging bonfires. **Edinburgh, by the heirs & successors of A. Anderson.** 1700. Brs. WS1742.

1700 SCOTLAND. PRIVY COUNCIL. A proclamation, for a solemn national fast ... 20 February 1700. **Edinburgh, by the heirs & successors of A. Anderson.** 1700. WS1797.

1700 SCOTLAND. PRIVY COUNCIL. A proclamation, for a solemn national fast .. 2 August 1700. **Edinburgh, by the heirs & successors of A. Anderson.** 1700. Brs. WS1798.

1700 SCOTLAND. PRIVY COUNCIL. A proclamation, for adjourning the Parliament ... 1 July 1700. **Edinburgh, by the heirs & successors of A. Anderson.** 1700. Brs. WS1826.

1700 SCOTLAND. PRIVY COUNCIL. A proclamation, for adjourning the Parliament ... 6 August 1700. **Edinburgh, by the heirs & successors of A. Anderson.** 1700. Brs. WS1827.

1700 SCOTLAND. PRIVY COUNCIL. Proclamation, for apprehending Captains Gavine Hamilton. **Edinburgh, by the heirs and successors of Andrew Anderson.** 1700. Brs. WS1828.

1700 SCOTLAND. PRIVY COUNCIL. Proclamation for discovering and apprehending house-breakers. **Edinburgh, by the heirs & successors of A. Anderson.** 1700. Brs. WS1863.

1700 SCOTLAND. PRIVY COUNCIL. A proclamation for preventing and punishing. **Edinburgh, by G. Mossman.** 1700. Fol. WS1886.

1700 Serious advice and direction to all. **Edinburgh, printed.** 1700. 8°. WS2601.

1700 The sett or decreet arbitral of King James VI. **Edinburgh.** 1700. 8°. WS2648.

1700 A short survey of a pamphlet. [**Edinburgh.** 1700?] Fol. WS3331.

1700 Speech in Parliament touching communication of trade. [**Edinburgh**? 1700]. Brs. WS4852A.

1700 [STEEL, G.] Robert the III ... his answer to a summonds. **Edinburgh, printed.** 1700. 8°. WS5377.

1700 Unto His Grace, His Majesty's High Commissioner ... the representation of the button makers. [**Edinburgh**? 1700]. Brs. WU100.

1700 W., R. A letter to an honourable member of Parliament, concerning the great growth of Popery. **Edinburgh, reprinted.** 1700. 4°. WW96.

1700 W., T. An essay concerning inland and foreign ... trade. [**Edinburgh.** 1700?] 4°. WW118.

1700 WEDDERBURN, DAVID. A short introduction to grammar. **Edinburgh, by George Mosman.** 1700. 12°. WW1242.

1700 WEDDERBURN, DAVID. Vocabula. **Edinburgi, apud Andrea Anderson hæredes & successores.** 1700. WW1244.

1700 WILLIAM III, king of England. His Majesties most gracious letter to the Parliament of Scotland. **Edinburgh, by the heirs and successors of Andrew Anderson.** 1700. Brs. WW2370.

1700 WILLIAM III, king of England. A proclamation for apprehending Captains Gavine Hamilton. **Edinburgh, by the heirs and successors of Andrew Anderson.** 1700. Brs. WW2462.

1700 The world's infection. [**Edinburgh**? 1700]. 4°. WW3590.

EDINBURGH
HOLYROODHOUSE

1687 [ARNAULD, ANTOINE.] The faith of the Cathelick church. **Printed at Holy-Rood-House.** 1687. 8°. WA3722.

1687 JAMES II, king of England. His Majestie's gracious declaration ... April 27th, 1688. **By Charles Bill, Henry Hills, and Thomas Newcomb, 1687. Edinburgh, re-printed at Holy-Rood-House by James Watson.** 1687. Fol. WJ192.

1687 Resolutions of a penitent soul. **Holy-Rood-House.** 1687. 12°. WR1165.

1688 DRYDEN, JOHN. Britannia rediviva: a poem. **Holy-Rood-House, reprinted by Mr. P. B. Enginier.** 1688. 4°. WD2252.

1688 JAMES II, king of England. A declaration. James R. having already signified ... one and twentieth day of September, 1688. **Holy-Rood-House, by Mr. P. B.** 1688. Brs. WJ160.

1688 JAMES II, king of England. His Majesties gracious declaration ... seventh day of April, 1688. **Holy-Rood-House, reprinted by Mr. P. B.** 1688. Fol. WJ193.

ETON

1607 DIONYSIUS, PERIEGETES. Διονυσίου οἰκουμένης π εριηγησις. **Etonæ.** [1607?]. 8°. STC6899.

1610 GREGORY OF NAZIANZUS. Sancti Gregorii Nazianzeni in Julianum invectivae duae. **Etonæ, J. Norton.** 1610. 4°. STC12346.

1610 JOANNES, Metropolitanus Euchaitensis. Versus iambici: editi cura M. Busti. **Etonæ, J. Norton.** 1610. 4°. STC14622.

1610 JOHN, CHRYSOSTOM, Saint. τοῦ ἐν 'αγιοις Πατρος ημων 'Ιωαννοῦ τοῦ χρυσοστόμου τὰ εὑρισκομευα. **Etonæ, J. Norton.** 1610-12. 8 vols. Fol. STC14629.

1613 XENEPHON. Xenephontis de Cyri institutione libri octo. **Etonæ, in Coll. Regali.** 1613. 4°. STC26065.

1615 GREGORY OF NAZIANZUS. Γρηγορίου Ναξαυξηνοῦ λογος εἰς τα θεοφανια τοῦ σωτηρος. **Etonæ, in Collegio Regali.** 1615. 8°. STC12347.

EXETER

1594 TASSO, TORQUATO. Godrey of Bulloigne, or the recouerie of Hierusalem. Tr. R. C[arew]. **J. Windet for C. Hunt of Exeter.** 1594. 4°. STC23697.

1631 MICO, JOHN. Spirituall food a. physick. Fourth edition. **For J. Boler, sold by T. Hunt in Exeter.** 1631. 8°. STC17863.

1640 JOHNSON, THOMAS, Minister. Stand up to your beliefe. [In verse.] **London, E. G[riffin], sold by T. Hunt, Exeter.** 1640. Brs. STC14706.

1645 CHARLES II, king of England. By His Highnesse, the Prince of Great Britain, ... a proclamation, for all persons within our quarters. **Imprinted at Exeter by Robert Barker and John Bill.** 1645. Brs. WC3314.

1645 CHURCH OF ENGLAND. Certain prayers fitted to severall occasions. **Exeter, by Robert Barker and John Bill.** 1645. 4°. WC4091C.

1645 A copy of a petition, commended to the peace-making association in the West. **Exeter, imprinted.** 1645. 4°. WC6186.

1645 FANSHAWE, RICHARD. A proclamation for all persons within our quarters in ... Devon. **Imprinted at Exeter by Robert Barker, and John Bill.** 1645. Brs. WF418.

1645 [FULLER, THOMAS]. Good thoughts in bad times. **Exeter, for Thomas Hunt.** 1645. 12°. WF2425.

1647 JELINGER, CHRISTOPHER. The usefulnesse and excellency of Christ. **For F. Eglesfield, to be sold by Tho. Hunt in Exeter.** 1647. 12°. WJ548.

1648 [ANTHONY, EDWARD.] Practicall law, controlling. **Printed at Exeter.** 1648. 4°. WA3478.

1648 HERRICK, ROBERT. Hesperides: or the works. **For John Williams, and Francis Eglesfield, to be sold by Tho. Hunt in Exon.** 1648. 8°. WH1595.

1655 TICKELL, JOHN. The sum and substance of religion. **Exeter.** [1655?] Brs. WT1158.

1663 V[ILVAIN], R[OBERT]. Theoremata theologica. **For the author, and are to be sold by Michael Hide, in Excester.** 1663. 4°. WV398. ♭8.

1666 WARD, SETH, bp. A sermon preached ... October 10th. M.DC.LXVI. Third edition. **By E. C. for James Collins, and are to be sold by Abisha Brocas in Exon.** 1666. 4°. WW829.

1667 [FULLWOOD, FRANCIS]. The General Assembly. **By E. Cotes for James Collins, and are to be sold by Abisha Brocas in Exon.** 1667. 4°. WF2503.

1668 WETENHALL, EDWARD, bp. Miserere cleri. A sermon. **In the Savoy, by T. N. for James Collins, and are to be sold by Abisha Brocas in Exon.** 1668. 4°. WW1505.

1668 F[ORD]. T[HOMAS]. Αγτοκατακριτος. Or the sinner condemned. **For Edward Brewster, and are to be sold by Anne Dwight, in Exon.** 1668. 8°. WF1511.

1668 MALL, THOMAS. Of holy living. **London, for William Grantham, to be sold by Robert Eveleigh in Exon.** 1668. 12°. WM334.

1668 MALL, THOMAS. A serious exhortation to holy living. **London, for William Grantham, to be sold by Robert Eveleigh, in Exon.** 1668. 12°. WM335.

1668 [STODDON, SAMUEL]. The voice of the rod. **London, for Walter Dight, in Exeter.** 1668. 12°. WS5715.

1670 HOLE, MATTHEW. Our Saviours passion. **For Richard Royston, to be sold by Abisha Brocas in Exon.** 1670. 4°. WH2411.

1672 [FULLWOOD, FRANCIS]. Toleration not to be abused. **For John Martyn, to be sold by Abisha Brocas, in Exeter.** 1672. 4°. WF2518.

1672 GOULD, WILLIAM. Domus mea, domus orationis, a sermon. **For R. Royston, to be sold by Abisha Brocas, in Exeter.** 1672. 4°. WG1439.

1673 A sermon preach'd on May the 29th, 1673. In one of His Majesties licens'd meetings in Devon. **London, by T. P. and are to be sold by Michael Hyde, in Exon.** 1673. 4°. WS2640.

1674 GOULD, WILLIAM. Conformity according to canon justified. **By A. Maxwell, for R. Royston, and are to be sold by Abisha Brocas, in Exon.** 1674. 4°. WG1438.

1674 PRINCE, JOHN. A sermon preached at Exon. **London, by A. Maxwell for R. Royston, and are to be sold by Abisha Brocas, in Exon.** 1674. 4°. WP3478.

1678 REYNOLDS, JOHN. Vituli labiorum. Or, a thanksgiving sermon. **London, for Tho. Cockeril: and Walter Dight in Exceter.** 1678. 4°. WR1318.

1680 LONG, THOMAS. A sermon against murmuring. **For Richard Royston, to be sold by George May, in Exon.** 1680. 4°. WL2982.

1682 A key to catechisms. **For Richard Chiswell, to be sold by Robert Eveleigh in Exon.** 1682. 8°. WK385.

1682 A trve and impartial account of the informations against three witches. **London, by Freeman Collins, and are to be sold by T. Benskin, and C. Yeo in Exon.** 1682. 4°. WT2502.

1683 An essay on hypocrisie. By J. C. and **Freeman Collins, for Charles Yeo in Exon.** 1683. 4°. WE3288.

1688 A form of prayer. **Exeter, by J. B.** 1688. 4°. WF1570.

1688 The general association, of the gentlemen of Devon, to ... Prince of Orange. **Exon, printed.** 1689. [but 1688]. Brs. WG489.

1688 O., W. H. P. A letter, &c. Gentlemen and friends, we have given. [**Exeter**? 1688]. Brs. WO12.

1688 WILLIAM III, king of England. A speech of the Prince of Orange, ... 15th of Nov., 1688. **Exeter, by J. B.** 1688. Brs. WW2480.

1689 [FULLWOOD, FRANCIS]. Agreement betwixt the present and the former government. **For A. C. and are to be sold by Charles Yeo, in Exon.** 1689. 4°. WF2495.

1689 The general association, of the gentlemen of Devon to ... Prince of Orange. **Exon, printed.** 1689. Brs. WG490.

1689 WILLIAM III, king of England. The Prince of Orange's letter to the King. **Exon: printed.** 1689. Brs. WW2354.

1693 HALLETT, JOSEPH. Christ's ascension. **For John Salusbury, and Robert Osborne, in Exon.** 1693. 12°. WH450.

1693 MAYNE, ZACHARY. Sanctification by faith vindicated. **London, by W. O. for John Salusbury, and sold by Walter Dight in Exon.** 1693. 4°. WM1486.

1693 T[ROSSE], G[EORGE]. The pastor's care and dignity. **London, for John Salusbury, and R. Osborn in Exon.** 1693. 8°. WT2304.

1694 [STODDON, SAMUEL] Ποιμνη φυλακιον. The pastors charge. **London, for Jonath. Robinson: and are to be sold by Robert Osborne in Exon.** 1694. 12°. WS5714.

1696 A sermon preached in a congregation in ... Exon. **For Robert Osborne, in Exon.** 1696. 4°. WS2638.

1698 CHILCOT, WILLIAM. A practical treatise concerning evil thoughts. **Exon, by Samuel Darker, for Charles Yeo, John Pearce, and Philip Bishop.** 1698. 8°. WC3847.

1698 CHURCH OF ENGLAND. A form of prayer for married persons. **Exeter.** 1698. 8°. WC4136.

1698 D[UNNING], R[ICHARD]. Bread for the poor. **Exeter, by Samuel Darker, for Charles Yeo, John Pearse and Philip Bishop.** 1698. 4°. WD2613.

1698 KING, JOSIAH. Mr. Blount's oracles of reason, examined. **Exeter: by Samuel Darker, for Philip Bishop, Charles Yeo, John Pearce, sold by the booksellers of London and Westminster.** 1698. 8°. WK512.

1698 KING, JOSIAH. Mr. Blount's oracles of reason, examined. **Exeter, by S. Darker for Philip Bishop.** 1698. WK512A.

1698 SMITH, HUMPHRY. A sermon preached ... July 24th, Anno Dom. 1698. **Exon. by Sam Darker and Sam Farley, for Charles Yeo, John Pearce and Philip Bishop.** 1698. 4°. WS4086.

1699 CHANDLER, SAMUEL. An impartial account of the Portsmouth disputation. **Exon: by Sam. Darker and Sam. Farley, for Philip Bishop.** 1699. 4°. WC1932.

1699 GILBERT, JOHN. A sermon on the sin of stealing custom. **Exon: by Sam. Darker, and Sam. Farley, for Charles Yeo.** 1699. 4°. WG709.

1699 GILBERT, JOHN. A sermon preached ... January 30th, 1698/9. **Exon: by Sam. Darker, and Sam. Farley, for Charles Yeo.** 1699. 4°. WG710.

1700 R[OSSINGTON], J[AMES]. Infant baptism; or, infant sprinkling. **London, printed, and are to be sold by J. Taylor, Philip Bishop at Exon, and Benjamin Smithurst at Launceston in Cornwall.** 1700. 8°. WR1993.

FALMOUTH

1678 SAMBLE, RICHARD. Richard Samble's testimony concerning Christopher Bacon. [**Falmouth.** 1678]. 4°. WS529.

FAWSLEY

1588 MARTIN, MARPRELATE. Oh read ouer D. Iohn Bridges, for it is worthy worke, etc. **Printed on the other hand of some of the priests.** [Fawsley, R. Waldegrave. Nov. 1588.] 4°. STC17454.

GATESHEAD

1653 [COLE, WILLIAM.] The perfect Pharisee. **Gateside, by S. B. to be sould by Will: London, in Newcastle.** 1653. WC5045.

1653 [GILPIN, JOHN]. The Qvakers shaken . **Gateside, by S. B. to [be] sould by Will London, in Newcastle.** 1653. 4°. WG769.

1654   WELDE, THOMAS. A further discovery of that generation of men called Qvakers. **Gateside, by S. B.** 1654. 4°. WW1268.

1657   WEYCOE, ELLIS. Publick sorrow. **Gateshead, by Stephen Bulkley.** 1657. 4°. WW1524.

1658   HAMMOND, SAMUEL. The Quaker's house. **Gateside, by Stephen Bulkley.** 1658. 4°. WH623 [A].

1660   ASTELL, RALPH. Vota non bella. Newcastle's heartie gratulation. **Gateshead, by Stephen Bulkley,** 1660. 4°. WA4068.

GLASGOW

1645   The copie of the letter, sent from the commissioners of the G. A. [n.p.], for **George Anderson in Glasgow.** 1645. 4°. WC4203.

1646   STAIR, JAMES DALRYMPLE, viscount. Theses logicæ. **Glasguae, excudebat Georgius Andersonus** 1646. 4°. WS5180.

1656   LINDSAY, Sir DAVID. The vvorkes of. **Glasgow, by Robert Sanders.** 1656. 12°. WL2314.

1662   ALMANACS. CORSS, JAMES. Mercurius cœlicus ... 1662. **Glasgow, by Robert Sanders.** 1662. 8°. WA1470.

1662   SCOTLAND. PRIVY COUNCIL. Glasgow. The first day of October 1662. The Lords of His Majesties Privie Councill. **By Robert Sanders, Glasgow.** 1662. Brs. WS1503.

1663   Theses philosophicæ quas (Deo favente). **Excudebat Robertus Sanders, Glascuensis.** 1663. Brs. WT884.

1664   ALMANACS. CORSS, JAMES. A new prognostication for the year ... 1664. **Printed by Robert Sanders. Glasgow.** 1664. 8°. WA1474.

1664   HAMMOND, CHARLES. Gods eye from heaven. **Glasgow, by Robert Sanders.** 1664. 8°. WH493.

1665   ALMANACS. CORSS, JAMES. A new prognostication for the year 1665. **Printed by Robert Sanders, Glasgow.** 1665. 8°. WA1476.

1666   The testament of the twelve patriarchs. **Glasgow, R. Sanders.** 1666. 12°. WT795A.

1667   DESPAUTÈRE, JEAN. Artis versificatoriæ compendium. **Glasguae, excudebat Robertus Sanders.** 1667. 12°. WD1199.

1667   DESPAUTÈRE, JEAN. Ioan. Despauterii Ninivitae grammaticæ institutionis. **Glasguae, excudebat Robertus Sanders.** 1667. 12°. WD1201.

1667   DESPAUTÈRE, JEAN. Syntaxis. **Glasguae, excudebat Robertus Sanders.** 1667. 12°. WD1205.

1667   FERGUSON, DAVID. Nine hundred and forty Scottish proverbs. [**Glasgow?**] printed. 1667. 8°. WF769.

1668   The frier and the boy. **Glasgow, printed.** 1668. 8°. WF2205.

1668   The history of Adam Bell. **Glasgow, by Robert Sanders.** 1668. 8°. WH2111.

1668   [SIMPSON]. An edifying wonder of two children. **Glasgow, by Robert Sanders.** 1668. 12°. WS3808.

1669   GUTHRIE, WILLIAM. The Christian's great interest. **At Glasgow, by Robert Sanders.** 1669. 8°. WG2271.

1669   The history of Sir Eger. **Glasgow, by Robert Sanders.** 1669. 4°. WH2139.

1671   Catechesis religionis. **Glasguae, excudebat Robertus Sanders.** [1671]. 4°. WC1468.

1672   CRAUFORD, MATTHEW. Popery anatomized. **Glasgow, by Robert Sanders.** 1672. 8°. WC6855.

1672   DESPAUTÈRE, JEAN. Artis versificatoriæ compendium. **Glasguae, excudebat Robertus Sanders.** 1672. 12°. WD1200.

1672   DESPAUTÈRE, JEAN. Syntaxis. **Glasguae, excudebat Robertus Sanders.** 1672. 12°. WD1206.

1672   MEAD, MATTHEW. Εν. ολιγω χριστιανος. The almost Christian discovered. **Glasgow, by Robert Sanders.** 1672. 12°. WM1550.

1673   DOWNAME, JOHN. Spiritual physick. **Glasgow, by Robert Sanders.** 1673. 12°. WD2076.

1674   CICERO. M. Tullii Cicerouis epistolarum libri IV. **Glasguae, ex typographeo Roberti Sanders.** 1674. 8°. WC4303.

1674   ERASMUS, DESIDERIUS. Epitome colloquiorum. **Glascuae, excudebat Robertus Sanders.** 1674. Sixes. WE3202.

1676   [ALLESTREE, RICHARD.] The art of contentment. **Glasgow, by Robert Sanders.** 1676. 8°. WA1088.

1678   [ALLESTREE, RICHARD.] the whole dvty of man. **Glasgow.** 1678. 12°. WA1184.

1678   MEAD, MATTHEW. Εν ολιγω χριστιανος. The almost Christian discovered. **Glasgow, by Robert Sanders.** 1678. 12°. WM1552.

1678   SCOTLAND. PRIVY COUNCIL. A proclamation. For removing of horses. **Glasgow, by R. Sandars.** 1678. Brs. WS1903.

1679   DYER, WILLIAM. A cabinet of jewels. **Glasgow.** 1679. 12°. WD2934.

1679   DYER, WILLIAM. Christ's voice to London. **Glasgow.** 1679. 12°. WD2945.

1679   DYER, WILLIAM. Desire of all nations. **Glasgow, [Sanders.** 1679]. 12°. WD2946.

1680   FLAVELL, JOHN. Sacramental meditations. **Glasgow. By Robert Sanders.** 1680. 12°. WF1184.

1680   VINCENT, THOMAS. The true Christians love. **Glasgow, by Robert Sanders.** 1680. 8°. WV448.

1681   FLAVELL, JOHN. The seamans companion. **Glasgow, by Robert Sanders.** 1681. 12°. WF1196.

1683   LINDSAY, Sir DAVID. The history of the noble and valiant Squyer William Meldrum. **Glasgow, by Robert Sanders.** 1683. 4°. WL2322.

1684   SCOTLAND. COMMITTEE OF THE WEST. Forasmuch as His Majestie by a ... 3 October 1684. **Glasgow, R. Sanders.** 1684. Brs. WS1009.

1684   SCOTLAND. PRIVY COUNCIL. The Lords ... command all the kings ... 7 October 1684. **Glasgow, R. Sanders.** 1684. Brs. WS1519.

1685   DURHAM, JAMES. The unsearchable riches of Christ. **Glasgow, by Robert Sanders.** 1685. 12°. WD2827.

1686   LINDSAY, Sir DAVID. The vvorkes of. **Glasgow, by Robert Sanders.** 1686. 12°. WL2319.

1687   The history of Sir Eger. [**Glasgow, Robert Sanders?**], printed. 1687. 24°. WH2140.

1690 The confession of faith, and the larger and shorter catechism. **Glasgow, by Robert Sanders.** 1690. 12°. WC5775.

1691 Vocabula cum aliis nonnullis Latinæ linguae subsidiis. **Glasguae, excudebat Robertus Sanders.** 1691. 8°. WV673.

1692 TRENCHFIELD, CALEB. A cap of gray hairs. Fifth edition. **Glasgow, by Robert Sanders.** 1692. 12°. WT2120.

1692 VINCENT, THOMAS. An explicatory catechism. **Glasgow, by Robert Sanders.** 1692. 12°. WV436.

1693 CATO, DIONYSIUS. Catonis disticha de moribvs. **Glasguae, ex typis Roberti Sanders.** 1693. 8°. WC1510.

1693 ERASMUS, DESIDERIUS. Dicta sapientum, e Graecis. **Glasguae, ex typis Roberti Sanders.** 1693. 4°. WE3199.

1693 GUTHRIE, WILLIAM. Two sermons preached by. **Glasgow, printed.** 1693. 8°. WG2276.

1693 K., P. Rudimenta grammatices. **Glasguae. Excudebat Robertus Sanders.** 1693. 8°. WK17.

1693 Rudimenta pietatis. **Glasguae, ex typis Roberti Sanders.** 1693. 8°. WR2172.

1693 SULPITZIO, GIOVANNI ... De moribus & civilitate puerorum. **Glasguae, ex typis Roberti Sanders.** 1693. 4°. WS6165.

1695 D., P. The Meir of Collingtoun. **[Glasgow].** 1695. 12°. WD79.

1695 SCOTLAND. PRIVY COUNCIL. Proclamation, discharging the base copper money ... 7 March. **Glasgow, R. Sanders.** 1695. Brs. WS1757.

1696 A record of auncient histories ... gesta Romanorum. **Glasgow, by R. Sanders.** 1696. 8°. WR639.

1699 Caledonia. The declaration of the council constituted by the Indian and African company of Scotland. **Boston, printed and reprinted at Glasgow by Robert Sanders.** 1699. Brs. WC284.

1698 CRAGHEAD, ROBERT. Advice to communicants. **Glasgow, Robert Sanders.** 1698. Sixes. WC6792.

1698 Relation of six seamen. **London, reprinted Glasgow.** 1698. Brs. WR809.

1698 ROBINS, THOMAS. Mans chief guide. **Glasgow, by Robert Sanders.** 1698. 8°. WR1655.

1700 Certain propositions relating to the Scots plantations. **Glasgow, printed.** 1700. Brs. WC1732.

1700 An enquiry into the causes of the miscarriage of the Scots colony at Darien. **Glasgow.** 1700. [sic]. 8°. WI213.

1700 A new wife of Beath much better reformed. **Glasgow, by Robert Sanders.** 1700. 12°. WN796.

1700 The VVelch-mans warning-piece. **Glasgow.** 1700. 4°. WW1340.

1700 WILLIAMSON, DAVID. A sermon. **Glasgow.** 1700. 4°. WW2798.

GLOUCESTER

1646 WORKMAN, GILES. Private-men no pulpit-men. **By F. N. for Toby Langford, in Gloucester.** 1646. 4°. WW3584.

1656 H., W. A perfect and most usefull table to compute the year. **For the use of W. H. the author, to be sold by Master Michell, and by Tobias Jorden in Gloucester.** 1656. Brs. WH158.

GRANTHAM

1674 WALKER, WILLIAM. The royal grammar, commonly called Lylly's grammar, explained. Second edition. **For Robert Powlet [sic], and Edward Pawlet, in Grantham.** 1674. 8°. WW434.

HALIFAX

1694 SMITH, JOHN. The doctrine of the Church of England. Second edition. **London, for Edw. Mory, Francis Bentley in Hallifax; and Ephr. Johnson in Manchester.** 1694. 8°. WS4112.

HEREFORD

1674 [GOOD, THOMAS]. Firmianus and Dubitantius. **Oxford, by L. Lichfield, for Tho. Hancox, in Hereford.** 1674. 8°. WG1029.

HULL

1654 HIBBERT, HENRY. Waters of Marah. **By W. Hunt, to be sold by Francis Coles, and by John Awdsley at Hull.** 1654. 8°. WH1794.

1685 L., N. The way to good success. **York, by John White, to be sold by Thomas Clark in Hull.** 1685. 4°. WL49.

IPSWICH

1541 MELANCTHON, PHILIPP. A very godly defense, defending the mariage of preistes. **Lipse, U. Hoff, [Ipswich, J. Oswen. 1541].** 8°. STC17798.

1548. BALE, JOHN, bp. Illustrium majoris Britanniæ scriptorum summariũ. **[Wesel, D. van den Straten] Gippiswici per J. Overton.** 1548. 4°. STC12695.

1548 BALE, JOHN, bp. Illustrium majoris Britanniæ scriptorum summariũ. **Wesaliae per T. Plateanum; Gippeswici per J. Overton.** 1549 [1548]. 4°. STC1296.

1548 CALVIN, JEAN. The mynde of M. J. Caluyne, what a faithful man ought to do. **Ippyswiche, J. Oswen.** 1548. 8°. STC4435.

1548 HEGENDORFF, CHRISTOPHER. Domestycal or housholde sermons. **Ippiswich, J. Oswē.** 1548. 8°. STC13021.

1548 HERMAN V, abp. of Cologne. The right institutiõ of baptisme. **Ippeswich, A. Scoloker.** 1548. 8°. STC13210.

1548 An invectyve against dronkennes. **Ippiswiche, J. Oswen.** [1548?] 16°. STC14126.

1548 LUTHER, MARTIN. A ryght notable sermon vppon the twenteth chapter of Johan. **Ippeswich, A. Scoloker.** 1548. 8°. STC16992.

1548 MARCORT, ANTOINE. A declaration of the masse; trãslated newly out of French. **Ippyswyche, J. Oswen.** 1548. 8°. STC17316.

1548 MOONE, PETER. A short treatyse of certayne thinges abused in the popysh church, long used. **Ippyswyche, J. Oswen.** [1548]. 4°. STC18055.

1548 A new boke conteyninge an exhortatiõ to the sycke. **Ippyswiche, John Oswen.** 1548. 8°. STC3362.

1548   OCHINO, BERNARDINO. Sermons. **Ippeswych, A. Scoloker.** 1548. 8°. STC 18765.

1548   RAMSEY, JOHN. A plaister for a galled horse. **Ippyswitche, J. Oswen.** 1548. 4°. STC 20663.

1548   ZWINGLI, ULRICH. Certeyne precepts. **Ippeswich, A. Scoloker.** 1548. 8°. STC 26136.

1636   PRYNNE, WILLIAM. Newes from Ipswich: discovering practises of domineering lordly prelates. **Ipswich.** [Edinburgh, G. Anderson. 1636?]. 4°. STC 20469.

1636   PRYNNE, WILLIAM. Newes from Ipswich: discovery practises of domineering lordly prelates. **Ipswich** [London?] 1636. STC 20470.

1650   WESTUP, WILLIAM. Gentil-congregations. [London], by John Clowes, **to be sold in Ipswich.** 1650. 4°. WW 1485.

1656   HUBBARD, BENJAMIN. Orthodoxal navigation. **By Thomas Maxey, for William Weekley of Ipswich, to be sold by John Rothwell.** 1656. 8°. WH 3206.

1657   BECK, CAVE. Le charactere universel. **Imprimé à Londres, chez A. Maxey, pour Guillaume Weekly, en Ipswich.** 1657. 8°. WB 1646.

1657   BECK, CAVE. The universal character. **By Tho. Maxey, for William Weekley, and and** [sic] **... in Ipswich.** 1657. 8°. WB 1647.

1657   LAWRENCE, MATTHEW. The use and practice of faith. **By A. Maxey for William Weekly at Ipswich, and are to be sold by John Rothwel; and by Robert Littleberry.** 1657. 4°. WL 673.

1657   PRINGLE, ALEXANDER. [Hebrew]. A stay in trouble. **London, by Anne Maxey, for William Weekly at Ipswich, to be sold by John Rothwel,** [London]. 1657. 8°. WP 3500.

1658   NEWCOMEN, MATTHEW. A sermon preached at the funerals of ... Samvel Collins. **London, by D. Maxwell for W. Weekley at Ipswich to be sold by J. Rothwel, and Rich. Tomlins.** 1658. 8°. WN 912.

1659   WARREN, EDMUND. The Jevvs Sabbath antiquated. **By David Maxwel, for W. Weekly of Ipswich, to be sold by John Rothwel, and also by Nath. Web, and Will. Grantham.** 1659. 4°. WW 955.

1660   BRUNING, BENJAMIN. Βλαστ ημα'εξ ῦΨους, or, the best wisdome. **By D. Maxwell, for W. Weekley of Ipswich, to be sold by John Rothwell.** 1660. 4°. WB 5231.

1692   DAVIS, RICHARD. Truth and innocency vindicated. **For Nath. and Robert Ponder, to be sold by Randal Taylor, by Mr. Coolidge at Cambridge, Mr. Prior at Colchester, Mr. Noble at St. Edmund's Bury, Mr. Haworth at Ipswich, Northampton, Wellingborow, Kettering, Oundle, Harborow, Litterworth, Upingham, Bedford, Kimbolton and Canterbury.** [1692?] 4°. WD 435.

1693   P., J. The new Westminster wedding. [London], **for the inhabitants of Ipswich.** 1693. 4°. WP 61.

KENDAL

1661   EUSEBIUS PAMPHILI, bp. An abridgement or a compendious commemoration of. [Rotterdam], **for the author; to be enquired of at Tho. Simmons, and Rob. VVilsons in London, and at Tho. VVillans in Kendall.** 1661. 8°. WE 3419.

KETTERING

1692   DAVIS, RICHARD. Truth and innocency vindicated. **For Nath. and Robert Ponder, to be sold by Randal Taylor, by Mr. Coolidge at Cambridge, Mr. Prior at Colchester, Mr. Noble at St. Edmund's Bury, Mr. Haworth at Ipswich, Northampton, Wellingborow, Kettering, Oundle, Harborow, Litterworth, Upingham, Bedford, Kimbolton and Canterbury.** [1692?] 4°. WD 435.

KIDDERMINSTER

1655   BAXTER, RICHARD. Making light of Christ. **By R. White, for Nevil Simmons in Kederminster.** 1655. 8°. WB 1303.

1655   BAXTER, RICHARD. A sermon of judgment. **By R. W. for Nevil Simmons in Kidderminster.** 1655. 12°. WB 1408.

1655   [BAXTER, RICHARD.] True Christianity. **For Nevill Simmons in Kidderminster, and are to be sold by William Roybould.** 1655. 12°. WB 1436.

1656   The agreement of divers ministers of Christ ... **By R. W. for Nevil Simmons at Kidderminster, and are to be sold there by him, and at London by William Roybould.** 1656. 8°. WA 773.

1656   BAXTER, RICHARD. Gildus Salvianus. **By Robert White for Nevil Simmons at Kederminster.** 1656. 8°. WB 1274.

1656   BAXTER, RICHARD. A sermon of judgment. **By R. W. for Nevill Simmons in Kidderminster.** 1656. 8°. WB 1409.

1656   BAXTER, RICHARD. True Christianity. **For Nevil Simmons in Kidderminster.** 1656. 8°. WB 1437.

1657   BAXTER, RICHARD. A treatise of conversion. **By R. W. for Nevil Simmons in Kederminster, and are to be sold by Joseph Nevil.** 1657. 4°. WB 1423.

1657   BAXTER, RICHARD. A vvinding sheet for popery. **By Robert White, for Nevil Simmons in Kederminster.** 1657. 8°. WB 1454.

1658   BAXTER, RICHARD. A call to the unconverted. **By R. W. for Nevill Simmons in Kederminster, to be sold by him there, and by Nathaniel Ekins.** 1658. 12°. WB 1196.

1658   BAXTER, RICHARD. Certain disputations. Second edition. **By R. W. for Nevil Simmons in Kederminster, to be sold by him there; and by Nathaniel Ekins.** 1658. 4°. WB 1212.

1658   BAXTER, RICHARD. Confirmation and restauration. **By A. M. for Nevil Simmons in Kederminster, and are to be sold by Joseph Cranford.** 1658. 8°. WB 1232.

1658   BAXTER, RICHARD. The crucifying of the world. **By R. W. for Nevill Simmons, and are to be sold by him in Kederminster, and by Nathaniel Ekins.** 1658. 4°. WB 1233.

1658   BAXTER, RICHARD. Directions and perswasions. **By A. M. for Nevil Simmons in Kederminster and are to be sold by him ... and by N. Ekins.** 1658. 8°. WB 1243.

1658   BAXTER, RICHARD. Directions and perswasions. **By A. M. for Nevil Simmons in Kederminster, to be sold by Joseph Cranford.** 1658. 8°. WB 1244.

1658   BAXTER, RICHARD. The Grotian religion discovered. **By R. W. for Nevill Simmons in Kederminster, and are to be sold by him there and by Tho. Brewster, and by John Starkey.** 1658. 8°. WB 1280.

1658 BAXTER, RICHARD. Of justification. **By R.W. for Nevil Simmons, in Kederminster, and are to be sold by him ... and by Nathaniel Ekins.** 1658. 4°. WB1328.

1658 BAXTER, RICHARD. Of saving faith. **By R.W. for Nevill Simmons, and are to be sold by him in Kederminster and by Nathaniel Ekins.** 1658. 4°. WB1330.

1658 BAXTER, RICHARD. A treatise of conversion. **By R.W. for Nevill Simmons in Kederminster and by Nathaniel Ekins.** 1658. 4°. WB1424.

1659 BAXTER, RICHARD. Five disputations. **By R.W. for Nevil Simmons, and are to be sold by him in Kederminster, and by Thomas Johnson.** 1659. 4°. WB1267.

1659 BAXTER, RICHARD. Five disputations. **By R.W. for Nevil Simmons in Kederminster, and are to be sold by him there, and by N. Ekins, and by J. Baker.** 1659. 4°. WB1268.

1660 BAXTER, RICHARD. The life of faith, as it is. **By R.W., for Francis Tyton, and are to be sold in [London]: and by Nevil Simmons at Kederminster.** 1660. 4°. WB1300.

1660 BAXTER, RICHARD. A treatise of death. **By R.W. for Nev. Simmons in Kederminster, to be sold by him there, and by Tho. Johnson.** 1660. 12°. WB1425.

1660 BAXTER, RICHARD. A treatise of self-denyall. **By Robert White, for Nevil Simmons in Kederminster, and are to be sold by him ... and by William Gilbertson, and by Joseph Nevil.** 1660. 4°. WB1430.

1663 BAXTER, RICHARD. A call to the unconverted. Tenth edition. **By R.W. for N. Simmons at Kederminster, to be sold by John Daniel.** 1663. 12°. WB1198.

1664 BAXTER, RICHARD. The divine life. **For Francis Tyton, and Nevil Simmons in Kederminster.** 1664. 4°. WB1254.

1665 BAXTER, RICHARD. The second sheet for poor families. **By Robert White, for Francis Tyton; and for Nevill Simmons in Kederminster.** 1665. 8°. WB1403.

1665 BAXTER, RICHARD. Two sheets for poor families. **By Robert White for Francis Tyton: and for Nevill Simmons, in Kederminster.** 1665. 8°. WB1441.

1665 G[EARING], W[ILLIAM]. The love-sick spouse. **For Nevill Simmons, in Kederminster.** 1665. 4°. WG436.

1666 BYRDALL, THOMAS. The profit of godliness. **For Nevil Simmons in Kederminster.** 1666. 8°. WB6406.

KILKENNY

1646 By the ecclesiastical congregation of the clergy of Ireland, for avoyding. [Kilkenny. 1646.] Brs. WB6363A.

1646 A declaration of the council and congregation against plundering. [Kilkenny. 1646.] Brs. WD657.

1646 ENOS, WALTER. The second part of the survey. **Printed at Kilkenny.** 1646. 4°. WE3130.

1646 ENOS, WALTER. A survey of the late rejected peace concluded. **Printed at Kilkenny.** 1646. 4°. WE3131.

1646 IRELAND. By the councell and congregation. **Kilkenny.** 1646. Brs. WI342.

1646 IRELAND. By the General Assembly of the confederate Catholicks. **Waterford 1645, reprinted Kilkenny.** 1646. Brs. WI343.

1646 IRELAND. By the General Assembly of the confederate Catholicks. **Printed at Kilkenny.** 1646. 4°. WI343A.

1646 IRELAND. A declaration of the general assemblie of the Confederate Catholicks. Second edition. [**Kilkenny.** 1646.] Brs. WD672A.

1646 IRELAND. Whereas severall declarations and protestations ... 4 July 1645. **Waterford printed, Kilkenny reprinted.** 1646. Brs. WI867.

1646 IRELAND. Whereas such of the Roman ... 28 September 1646. **Kilkenny.** 1646. Brs. WI885.

1646 [KEARNIE, P.] By the generall assemblie of the confederate Catholics. **Kilkenny.** 1646. 4°. WK111.

1646 The Marques of Clanrickards engagement. [**Kilkenny.** 1646]. 4°. WM707.

1646 ORMONDE, JAMES BUTLER, duke of. Articles of peace agreed upon July 30, 1646 ... **Kilkenny, printed.** 1646. 4°. WO439.

1646 [PRESTON, T.] The declaration of the Lord General of the army. [**Kilkenny.**] 1646. Brs. WP3314.

1646 RINUCCINI, JOHN BAPTIST. By ... a degree of excommunication ... 5 October 1646. [**Kilkenny.** 1646]. Brs. WR1522.

1647 [KEARNIE, P.] By the generall assemblie of the confederate Catholics. **Kilkenny.** 1647. 4°. WK111A.

1648 The copie of a letter from a gentleman in London to his friend in Dublin. [**Kilkenny.**] 1648. 4°. WC6115A.

1648 The copy of the major and baylifs of the towne of Weixford their letter. [**Kilkenny.** 1648.] 4°. WC6212.

1648 A declaration made by the maior, towne council, ... Galway. **Kilkenny.** 1648. 4°. WD600A.

1648 The ensuing declaration of the Lord Muncio. **Kilkenny.** 1648. Brs. WE3132.

1648 IRELAND. Although wee find ourselves much afflicted ... 28 July 1648. **Kilkenny.** 1648. Brs. WI334.

1648 IRELAND. By the supreame Councell of the confederate Catholicks. **Kilkenny.** 1648. Brs. WI355.

1648 IRELAND. Declaration by the general assemblie of the confederate Catholiques. [**Kilkenny**]. 1648. Brs. WD563A.

1648 IRELAND. Declaration of the supreme council of the Confederate Catholicks ... admonishing. [**Kilkenny.** 1648.] Brs. WD769B.

1648 IRELAND. Declaration of the supreme council ... withdrawing. [**Kilkenny, by Thomas Bourke.** 1648.] Brs. WD769C.

1648 IRELAND. The deepe sense which wee have of the sadd conditions ... 3 June 1648. **Kilkenny.** 1648. Brs. WI393.

1648 IRELAND. It cannot be expressed ... 7 July 1648. **Kilkenny.** 1648. Brs. WI419.

1648   IRELAND. Manifesto by the supreme council ...
        against the Lord Nuncio. [**Kilkenny.** 1648]. Brs.
        WM427.

1648   IRELAND. Order of the General Assemblie of
        the Confederate Catholiques. [**Kilkenny.** 1648.]
        Brs. WO388.

1648   IRELAND. A proclamation by the General
        Assemblie of the Confederate Catholiques ... of
        Pardon. [**Kilkenny.** 1648]. Brs. WP3632.

1648   IRELAND. Proclamation of the supreme council
        of the Confederate Catholicks ... against
        malitious reports. [**Kilkenny.** 1648]. Brs.
        WP3637.

1648   IRELAND. Proclamation of the supreme council
        of the Confederate Catholiques ... complaining
        of the Nuntio. [**Kilkenny.** 1648]. Brs. WP3638.

1648   IRELAND. This assembly taking seriously into
        consideration ... 30 September 1648. **Kilkenny.**
        [1648]. Brs. WI654.

1648   IRELAND. Wee the supreame Councell of the
        said Confederate Catholickes ... 27 May 1648.
        Kilkenny. 1648. Brs. WI698.

1648   IRELAND. Whereas by our late proclamation
        ... 13 August 1648. **Kilkenny, Thomas Bourke.**
        [1648]. Brs. WI735.

1648   IRELAND. Whereas divers ill affected to the
        government ... 14 September 1648. **Kilkenny.**
        1648. Brs. WI767.

1648   [KEARNIE, P.] By the generall assemblie of
        the confederate Catholics. **Kilkenny.** [1648]. Brs.
        WK112.

1648   O'NEILL, OWEN. The declaration of. [**Kilkenny.**
        1648]. 4°. WO338.

1648   Queries concerning the lawfulnesse of the present
        cessation. **Printed at Kilkenny.** 1648. 4°.
        WQ166.

1649   CHARLES I, king of England. A proclamation
        declaring Iames Marqves of Ormond. **Printed
        at Kilkenny.** 1649. Brs. WC3285.

1649   IRELAND. Whereas articles of peace are made
        ... 17 January 1648 [9]. **Kilkenny, William
        Smith.** 1648 [9]. Brs. WI713.

1649   ORMONDE, JAMES BUTLER, duke of. Proclama-
        tion by ... 17th of January. **Printed at Kilkenny,
        by William Smith.** 1649. Brs. WO455.

1649   ORMONDE, JAMES BUTLER, duke of. Proclama-
        tion by ... 22nd January. **Printed by Kilkenny,
        by William Smith.** 1649. Brs. WO456.

1649   ORMONDE, JAMES BUTLER, duke of. By the
        Lord Lievtenant Generall of Ireland. Ormonde.
        Whereas wee have graunted. **Printed at Kilkenny.**
        1649. Brs. WO464.

KIMBOLTON

1692   DAVIS, RICHARD. Truth and innocency
        vindicated. **For Nath. and Robert Ponder, to be
        sold by Randal Taylor, by Mr. Coolidge at Cam-
        bridge, Mr. Prior at Colchester, Mr. Noble at St.
        Edmund's Bury. Mr. Haworth at Ipswich, North-
        ampton, Wellingborow, Kettering, Oundle,
        Harborow, Litterworth, Upingham, Bedford,
        Kimbolton and Canterbury.** [1692?] 4°. WD435.

KNUTSFORD

1684   FORENESS, E. A sermon preached ... July 11,
        1684. **For Peter Swinton, at Knutsford.** 1684.
        4°. WF1555.

LAUNCESTON

1694   HILL, JOHN, of St. Mabyn. Ishbibenob defeated
        and David succoured. **For W. Crooke, and are
        to be sold by Benj. Smithurst, at Launceton.**
        1694. 4°. WH1995.

1700   GASCOYNE, JOEL. Map of the county of Corn-
        wall. [n.p.] **sold by J. Thorn, by Charles Blith,
        in Launceston.** 1700. Fol. WG283.

1700   R[OSSINGTON], J[AMES]. Infant-baptism; or
        infant sprinkling. **London, printed, and are to
        be sold by J. Taylor, Philip Bishop at Exon, and
        Benjamin Smithurst at Launceston in Cornwall.**
        1700. 8°. WR1993.

LEEDS

1700   SHARP, THOMAS. [Hebrew]. Or divine
        comforts. **London, for The Parkhurst; and John
        Whitworth in Leeds.** 1700. 8°. WS3007.

LEICESTER

1639   FOXLE, GEORGE. The groanes of the spirit.
        Oxford, & Lichfield, sold by J. Allen, Lecester.
        1639. 12°. STC11252.

1689   SAWBRIDGE, THOMAS. A sermon preached ...
        July the 25th, 1689. **By C.B. for Francis Ward,
        in Leicester, to be sold by R. Taylor in London.**
        1689. 4°. WS782.

LEITH

1643   A declaration by the Lord Generall and his
        councel ... shewing the grounds. **London,
        reprinted Leith.** 1643. 4°. WD702.

1651   CROMWELL, OLIVER. Forasmuch as divers of
        this nation, ... 15 March 1651. **Leith, E. Tyler.**
        1651. Brs. WC7087.

1651   A discovery after some search of the sinnes
        of the ministers. [**Leith**], printed [by E. Tyler].
        1651. 4°. WD1631.

1651   SCOTLAND. COMMISSIONERS AT LEITH.
        Forasmuch as by the blessing ... 1 March 1651.
        Leith, by Evan Tyler. 1651. Brs. WS994.

1652   [GUTHRIE, JAMES]. The nullity of the pretended-
        assembly. [**Leith**], printed. 1652. 4°.
        WG2263.

1652   LOCKYER, NICHOLAS. A little stone, out of
        the mountain. **Printed at Leith by Evan Tyler.**
        1652. 12°. WL2796.

1652   PITTILOH ROBERT. Examination of a sermon.
        Leith. 1652. 4°. WP2309.

1652   SCOTLAND. COMMISSIONERS FOR VISITING
        UNIVERSITIES IN SCOTLAND. By the
        commissioners for visiting and regulating the
        universities. **Printed at Leith by Evan Tyler.**
        1652. Brs. WS1000.

1653   The commissioners for administration of justice
        to the people in Scotland considering ...
        8 January 1653. **Leith.** 1653. Brs. WC5557.

1653   ENGLAND. PRIVY COUNCIL. A letter from the
        Councel of officers at Whitehall to Colonel
        Lilburne. **Leith.** 1653. 4°. WE2909.

1653   The humble remonstrance of the General-Council of officers met at Dalkeith. **Leith.** 1653. 4°. WH3621.

1653   Observations upon the chief acts of the two late P. Assemblies. [**Leith**], **printed.** 1653. 4°. WO114.

1653   A reply to late printed ansvver given to the letter. [**Leith**] **printed** [**by E. Tyler**]. 1653. 4°. WR1076.

1654   CROMWELL, OLIVER. An ordinance for erecting courts Baron ... 12 April 1654. **Leith, reprinted.** 1654. Brs. WC7129.

1654   CROMWELL, OLIVER. An ordinance for settling of the estates ... 12 April 1654. **Leith reprinted.** 1654. Brs. WC7132.

1654   CROMWELL, OLIVER. His Highness speech to the Parliament ... 22nd. of January, 1654. **Reprinted Leith.** 1654. 4°. WC7172.

1654   Orders for regulating of the prices ... 14. day of January, 1654. **Printed at Leith.** 1654. Brs. WO400.

1656   These are to give notice, that the commissioners of customs. [**Leith.** 1656]. Brs. WT877.

LICHFIELD

1680   [BRINLEY, JOHN.] A discovery of the impostures of witches. **For John Wright, and sold by Edward Milward, in Leitchfield.** 1680. 8°. WB4698.

1687   FLOYER, Sir JOHN. $\phi\alpha\rho\mu\alpha\kappa o$-$\beta\alpha\sigma\alpha\upsilon os$: or, the touchstone of medicines. **For Michael Johnson in Litchfield: to be sold by Robert Clavel.** 1687. 2 vols. 8°. WF1388.

1687   SHAW, SAMUEL. Grammatica Anglo-Romana: or. **London, for Michael Johnson to be sold at his shops in Litchfield and Uttoxeter: and Ashby-de-la-Zouch.** 1687. 12°. WS3035.

1690   ADDISON, LANCELOT. The primitive institution. Second edition. **For William Crook and W. Baylie in Litchfield.** 1690. 12°. WA531.

1691   CROMWEL, RICHARD. The happy sinner. **For R. Clavell to be sold by Mich. Johnson, in Leichfield.** 1691. 4°. WC7035.

LINCOLN

1681   NICOLS, DANIEL. A sermon preach'd ... July XVIII. 1681. **London, by A. G. and J. P. for Joseph Lawson, in Lincoln; and sold by Richard Chiswell; and Thomas Sawbridge.** 1681. 4°. WN1142.

1681   SELDEN, JOHN ... Of the judicature in Parliaments. **London, for Joseph Lawson, in Lincoln; and sold in London.** [1681?] 8°. WS2433.

1682   METFORD, JAMES. A general discourse of simony. **London, for Joseph Lawson, in Lincoln; and sold by R. Chiswel, and T. Sawbridge.** 1682. 8°. WM1938.

1683   [STRATFORD, NICHOLAS], bp. A sermon preached ... Christmas-day, 1682. **London, by J. R. for Joseph Lawson, in Lincoln, and sold by Richard Chiswel, and Tho. Guy.** 1683. 4°. WS5940.

1684   CURTOIS, JOHN. A sermon preach'd ... July XXIX. 1683. **By J. Playford, for Joseph Lawson in Lincoln, and sold by Thomas Sawbridge, and Richard Chiswel.** 1684. 4°. WC7702.

1697   CURTOIS, JOHN. An essay to persuade Christian parents. **For John Knight, in Lincoln.** 1697. 8°. WC7701.

LITTLEBURY

1688   WINSTANLEY, HENRY. To the most excellent majesty of James ... book of the ground (platts) ... [**Littlebury.** 1688]. Brs. WW3057A.

LLANFYLLIN

1671   [EDWARDS, CHARLES]. Y Ffydd ddiffuant. Second edition. **Rhydychen [Oxford] by H. Hall, sold in Wrexham, Llanfyllin, &c.** 1671. 8°. WE193.

LUDLOW

1686   SMITH, WILLIAM. A just account of the horrid contrivance of John Cupper. **London, for Edw. Robinson, in Ludlow.** 1686. 4°. WS4261.

1691   An answer to the call to humiliation. **Ludlow, Robinson.** 1691. 4°. WA3394.

LUTTERWORTH [?]

1692   DAVIS, RICHARD. Truth and innocency vindicated. **For Nath. and Robert Ponder, to be sold by Randal Taylor, by Mr. Coolidge at Cambridge, Mr. Prior at Colchester, Mr. Noble at St. Edmund's Bury, Mr. Haworth at Ipswich, Northampton, Wellingborow, Kettering, Oundle, Harborow, Litterworth, Upingham, Bedford, Kimbolton and Canterbury.** [1692?] 4°. WD435.

MANCHESTER

1653   [MARTINDALE, ADAM]. An antidote against the poyson of the times. **London, for Luke Fawn, to be sold by Thomas Smith in Manchester.** 1653. 8°. WM853.

1656   HOLLINGSWORTH, RICHARD, elder. The Holy Ghost on the bench. **For Luke Fawn, to be sold by Ralph Shelmerdine, in Manchester.** 1656. 8°. WH2494.

1657   MOORE, WILLIAM. The grand inquiry who is the righteous man. **London, by E. Cotes, for Ralph Shelmerdine in Manchester.** 1657. 8°. WM2611.

1661   HEYRICK, RICHARD. Sermon preached ... 23. of April 1661. **For Ralph Shelmerdine in Manchester.** 1661. 4°. WH1750.

1673   S[ERGEANT], I[OHN]. The mysterie of rhetorique unveil'd. **London, by E. T. and R. H. for George Eversden, and Ralph Shellmerdin in Manchester.** 1673. 8°. WS2582.

1685   BAGSHAW, WILLIAM. The riches of grace displayed in the instances. **For Ralph Shelmardine in Manchester.** 1685. 8°. WB433C.

1694   SMITH, JOHN. The doctrine of the Church of England. Second edition. **London, for Edw. Mory, Francis Bentley in Hallifax; and Ephr. Johnson in Manchester.** 1694. 8°. WS4112.

1696   CHORLTON, JOHN. The glorious reward of faithful ministers declared. **For T. P. to be sold by Zachary Whitworth in Manchester.** 1696. 4°. WC3927.

1696   G[RIPPS], T[HOMAS]. Tentamen novum: proving. **For E. Johnson, in Manchester; and sold by Hen. Mortlock.** 1696. 8°. WG2052.

1696   PENDLEBURY, HENRY. The books opened. **London, by J. D. for Ann Unsworth of Manchester; and sold by Jonathan Robinson, [London].** 1696. 12°. WP1139.

1696 PENDLEBURY, HENRY. Invisible realities.
**London, by J. D. for Ann Unsworth of Manchester:
and sold by Jonathan Robinson,** [London]. 1696.
12°. WP1140.

1697 GIPPS, THOMAS. A sermon against corrupting
the word. **For Ephraim Johnston, in Manchester.**
1697. 4°. WG781.

1697 OWEN, JAMES. Remarks on a sermon, about
corrupting. **London, for Zachary Whitworth,
in Manchester.** 1697. 4°. WO709.

1697 OWEN, JAMES. Tutamen evangelicum: or, a
defence. **London, for Zachary Whitworth, in
Manchester.** 1697. 8°. WO710.

1697 TAYLOR, ZACHARY. The Surey impostor.
**London, for John Jones, and Ephraim Johnson,
in Manchester.** 1697. 4°. WT601.

1698 GIPPS, THOMAS. Remarks on remarks.
For Ephraim Johnston, in Manchester. 1698. 4°.
WG780.

1698 LEIGH, CHARLES. Remarks on Mr. Richard
Bolton's piece. **Printed; and sold by John
Shelmerdine in Manchester.** 1698. 8°. WL977.

1698 LEIGH, CHARLES. A reply to John Colebatch.
**Printed; and sold by John Shelmerdine, in
Manchester.** 1698. Sixes. WL978.

1699 GIPPS, THOMAS. Tentamen novum continuatum.
Or, an answer to Mr. Owen's plea. **By Tho.
Warren, for Ephraim Johnson in Manchester.**
1699. 4°. WG782.

MANSFIELD

1689 Melius inquirendum: or a further modest and
impartial enquiry. **London, for Jonathan
Robinson. Sold by Clement Elis, in Mansfield.**
1689. 4°. WM1647.

1691 ELLIS, CLEMENT. Religion & loyalty
inseperable. **For William Rogers; and Clement
Elis, in Mansfield.** 1691. 4°. WE571.

1692 ELLIS, CLEMENT. The folly of atheism
**Printed, and are to be sold by William Rogers,
and Thomas Elis in Mansfield.** 1692. 8°.
WE555.

1692 ELLIS, CLEMENT. The lambs of Christ.
**Printed, to be sold by W. Rogers; and Tho. Elis
in Mansfield.** 1692. 12°. WE564.

MARLBOROUGH

1694 [HALL, JOHN]. An answer to some queries.
propos'd by W. C. **Oxford, by Leon. Lichfield,
for John Buckeridge in Marleborough.** 1694. 4°.
WH343.

MARKET HARBOROUGH

1654 TIMSON, JOHN. The bar to free admission ...
removed. **London, by E. Cotes, to be sold by
Will. Tompson in Harborough.** 1654. 8°.
WT1293.

1655 TIMSON, JOHN. To receive the Lords supper.
**London, by E. C. for Tho. Williams and Will.
Tomson at Harborough in Leicesshire.** 1655. 8°.
WT1296.

1661 GODDARD, THOMAS. Miscellanea. **By E. C. for
Tho. William, and Will Thompson, at Harborough.**
1661. 4°. WG916.

1669 BENTHAM, JOSEPH. A disswasive from error.
**Printed, and are to be sold by William Thompson,
in Harborow.** 1669. 4°. WB1909.

1692 DAVIS, RICHARD. Truth and innocency
vindicated. **For Nath. and Robert Ponder, to be
sold by Randal Taylor, by Mr. Coolidge at
Cambridge, Mr. Prior at Colchester, Mr. Noble
at St. Edmund's Bury, Mr. Haworth at Ipswich,
Northampton, Wellingborow, Kettering, Oundle,
Harborow, Litterworth, Upingham, Bedford, Kimbolton and Canterbury.** [1692?] 4°. WD435.

NANTWICH

1684 [CAWDREY, ZACHARY.] The certainty of
salvation. **For Peter Gillworth in Newcastle in
Staffs. and James Thurston, in Nantwich.** 1684.
4°. WC1645.

NEWCASTLE UNDER LYME

1684 [CAWDREY, ZACHARY.] The certainty of
salvation. **For Peter Gillworth in Newcastle in
Staffs. and James Thurston in Nantwich.** 1684.
4°. WC1645.

NEWCASTLE UPON TYNE

1639 CHARLES I, king of England.
By the king [allowing export of butter to Northern
ports. 9 May 1639]. **Newcastle, R. Barker and
assigns of J. Bill].** 1639. Brs. STC9143.

1639 ENGLAND. STATUTES. Lawes and ordinances
of warre. **Newcastle, R. Barker and assignes of
J. Bill.** 1639. 4°. STC9335.

1639 MORTON, THOMAS. A sermon preached in the
cathedrall church of Durham. **Newcastle upon
Tyne, R. Barker and assignes of J. Bill.** 1639.
4°. STC18196A.

1646 CHARLES I, king of England. A message from
His Majestie to the Speaker. **Newcastle, by
Stephen Bulkley.** 1646. 4°. WC2433.

1646 DIODATE, GIOVANNI. An answer sent to the
ecclesiastical assembly. **Genevah** [Newcastle.]
Printed. 1646. 4°. WD1504.

1647 CHARLES I, king of England. The King's
possessions. **Newcastle: by Stephen Bulkley.**
1647. 4°. WC2360.

1647 DIODATE, GIOVANNI. An answer sent to the
ecclesiastical assembly. **Newcastle: by Stephen
Bulkley.** 1647. 4°. WD1505.

1647 The Kings possessions. **Newcastle, S. Bulkley.**
1647. 4°. WK604.

1649 [GREY, WILLIAM]. Chorographia, or a survey
of Newcastle-upon-Tyne. **Newcastle, by S. B.**
1649. WG1975.

1649 [JENISON], R[OBERT]. The faithfull depositary.
Newcastle, by S. B. 1649. 4°. WJ558.

1650 A declaration of the army of England upon their
march into Scotland. **Newcastle, by S. B.** 1650.
4°. WD637.

1650 Musgrave muzzled: or the traducer gagg'd.
Newcastle, by S. B. 1650. 4°. WM3156.

1651 FENWICKE, Sir JOHN. Englands deliverer.
Newcastle, by S. B. 1651. 4°. WF721.

1651 The true state of the case of Josiah Primatt.
Newcastle. 1651. WT3112.

1652 SHAW, JONATHAN. The povrtraictvre of the
primitive saints. **Newcastle, by S. B.** 1652.
4°. WS3033.

1653 [COLE, WILLIAM] of Newcastle. The perfect
Pharisee. **Gateside, by S. B. to be sould by Will.
London in Newcastle.** 1653. WC5045.

1653 [GILPIN, JOHN]. The Qvakers shaken. **Gateside, by S. B. to [be] sould by Will. London, in Newcastle.** 1653. 4°. WG769.

1653 WELDE, THOMAS. A false Jew. **For William London in Newcastle, [by Stephen Bulkley].** 1653. 4°. WW1266.

1655 WILLIS, THOMAS. Proteus vinctus. **By E. Cotes, to be sold by Will London in Newcastle.** 1655. 8°. WW2819.

1659 A conference between two soldiers. The first part. **Printed at Newcastle.** 1659. 4°. WC5729.

1659 SHAW, JONATHAN. A catalogue of the Hebrevv saints. **Newcastle, by S. B.** 1659. WS3032.

1660 THOMSON, R. The loyall subject. **Newcastle, by Stephen Bulkley.** 1660. 4°. WT1032.

1661 [HOOKE, RICHARD]. The bishop's appeale. **Newcastle, by Stephen Bulkley.** 1661. 4°. WH2606.

1662 THOMSON, R. The loyall subject. Second edition. **Newcastle, by Stephen Bulkley.** 1662. 4°. WT1034.

1677 [GILPIN, RICHARD]. Dæmonologia sacra. Or, a treatise. **By J. D. for Richard Randel, and Peter Maplisden, in New Castle upon Tine.** 1677. 4°. WG777.

1677 MARCH, JOHN. A sermon preached ... 30th of January, 1676/7. **London, by Thomas Hodgkin, for Richard Randell, and Pet. Maplisden, in Newcastle upon Tyne.** 1677. 4°. WM581.

1680 The famous and renowned history of the two unfortunate ... lovers, Hero. **Newcastle, John White.** [1680?]. 4°. WF361.

1682 MARCH, JOHN. Th' encænia of St. Ann's Chappel. **London, for Richard Randal and Peter Maplisden, in Newcastle upon the Tyne.** 1682. 4°. WM579.

1683 MARCH, JOHN. The false prophet unmask't. **London, by J. R. for Richard Randell, and Peter Maplesden, in New-Castle upon Tyne.** 1683. 4°. WM580.

1683 WERGE, RICHARD. A sermon preached ... May 29. anno Dom. 1683. **London, by Henry Clark, for Joseph Hall, Newcastle upon Tyne, and Robert Clavel.** 1683. 4°. WW1366.

1685 WERGE, RICHARD. The trouble and cure of a wounded conscience. **London: for Joseph Hall, at New-Castle upon Tine.** 1685. 4°. WW1367.

1686 STUART, GEORGE. A joco-serious discourse. **London, for Benjamin Tooke and John Story, in New-Castle.** 1686. 4°. WS6026.

1688 DAVISON, THOMAS. A sermon preached on the 8 of January. **York: by J. White, for Joseph Hall, in New-Castle upon Tine.** 1688. 4°. WD441.

1691 TULLY, GEORGE. A sermon, preached October, the 19, 1690. **York: by J. White: to be sold by Joseph Hall, New-Castle upon Tyne.** 1691. 4°. WT3242.

1693 MARCH, JOHN. Sermons. **For Robert Clavell, sold by Joseph Hall in New Castle upon Tine.** 1693. 8°. WM582.

1695 S., J. Europe's tears for the present war. **Newcastle** [1695?] 12°. WS57.

1700 ELLISON, NATHANAEL. The magistrates obligation. **By W. B. for Richard Randell, in Newcastle upon Tyne; and sold by Luke Meredith.** 1700. 4°. WE610.

1700 [GILPIN, RICHARD]. An assize-sermon preach'd ... September the 10th ann. 1660. **For Tho. Parkhurst; and Sarah Burton at Newcastle.** 1700. 4°. WG775.

1700 [GILPIN, RICHARD]. The comforts of divine love. **For Tho. Parkhurst. And Sarah Button at Newcastle upon Tyne.** 1700. 8°. WG776.

1700 [HART, JOHN]. Christ's last sermon. Twenty-first edition. **Newcastle; printed and sold by John White.** [1700?] 8°. WH942.

NEWPORT, CORNWALL

1697 MEAGER, LEONARD. The mystery of husbandry. **London: by W. Onley, to be sold by Will Majore, in Newport, Cornwall.** 1697. 12°. WM1573.

NEWPORT, ISLE OF WIGHT

1648 The commencement of the treaty between the kings Majesty and the commissioners of Parliament at Newport. A prayer, drawne by his Majesties speciall direction and dictates, for a blessing on the treaty at Newport. **Newport, Septemb. 6 1648.** Brs. WC5546.

NEWPORT PAGNELL

1657 BUNYAN, JOHN. A vindication of the book called Some gospel-truths opened. **For Matthias Cowley, in Newport.** 1657. 4°. WB5606.

1659 BUNYAN, JOHN. A doctrine of the lavv and grace unfolded. **For Matthias Cowley in Newport-Pannell.** 1659. 8°. WB5514.

1677 TANNER, THOMAS. [Hebrew] Or wisdome and prudence. **London, for William Keblewhite at Newport.** [1677]. 4°. WT148.

1698 GIBBS, JOHN. A funeral sermon preached March 13, 1697/8. For Mr. William Hartley. **For Mark Conyers, at Newport-Pagnel: and sold by A. Roper, and G. Conyers** 1698. In twos. WG663.

1700 HARRISON, MICHAEL. A gospel church describ'd. **Printed, and sold by T. Pashum in Northampton, and M. Conyers in Newport-Pagnal.** 1700. 12°. WH904.

NORTHAMPTON

1651 COMENIUS, JOHANN AMOS. A patterne of universall knowledge. **By T. H. to be sold by Thomas Collins in Notthampton** [sic]. 1651. 8°. WC5527.

1655 AINSWORTH, SAMUEL. A sermon preached Decemb. 16. 1654. **For William Gilbertson, to be sold by Thomas Collins in Northampton.** 1655. 4°. WA817.

1657 HOWES, JOHN. Christ, God-man, set out. **For Joseph Nevill, and William Cockrain, in Northampton.** 1657. 4°. WH3148.

1677 [FORD, SIMON]. The fall and funeral of Northampton. **For John Wright, to be sold by William Cockrain, in Northampton.** 1677. 4°. WF1486.

1691 PIERCE, EDWARD. Christ alone our life. **For Jonathan Robinson, to be sold by Thomas Pasham in Northampton.** 1691. 12°. WP2161.

1692   DAVIS, RICHARD.   Truth and innocency
       vindicated.   **For Nath. and Robert Ponder, to be
       sold by Randal Taylor, by Mr. Coolidge at
       Cambridge, Mr. Prior at Colchester, Mr. Noble
       at St. Edmund's Bury, Mr. Haworth at Ipswich,
       Northampton, Wellingborow, Kettering, Oundle,
       Harborow, Litterworth, Upingham, Bedford,
       Kimbolton and Canterbury.**   [1692?]   4°.   WD435.

1700   HARRISON, MICHAEL.   A gospel church
       describ'd.   **Printed and sold by T. Pashum in
       Northampton, and M. Conyers in Newport-Pagnal.**
       1700.   12°.   WH904.

NORWICH

1568   BIBLE. DUTCH.   De C. L. Psalmen Davids in
       Nederlantschen.   **Norwich, A. de Solemne.**
       1568.   8°.   STC2741.

1569   CORRO, ANTONIO DE.   Tableau de l'oeuure
       de Dieu.   **[Norwich, A. de Solempne].**   1569.
       Fol.   STC5792.

1569   GONSALVIUS, MONTANUS, REGINALDUS.
       Der Heyliger Hispanischer Inquisitie etlicke
       listighe consten int licht ghebracht.   **[Norwich?
       A. Solempne?]**   1569.   8°.   STC12001.

1570   BROOKE, THOMAS.   Certayne versis, writtene
       by T. Brooke, in the tyme of his imprysoment.
       Norwich, A. de Solempne.   1570.   Fol.   STC3835.

1570   CORRO, ANTONIO DE.   Diuinorum operum
       tabula.   **[London? or Norwich? 1570?]**   Fol.
       STC5793.

1578   ADRIANS, CORNELIUS.   Het tweede boeck van
       de sermoenen des predicants B. Cornelis
       Adriaennsen.   **Noirdwitz [Norwich, A. de Solempne]**
       1578.   8°.   STC151.

1586   DELONEY, THOMAS.   A proper newe sonet
       declaring the lamentation of Beckles.   **R. Robin-
       son, for N. Colman of Norwich.**   1586.   Brs.
       STC6564.

1586   STERRIE, D.   A briefe sonet declaring the
       lamentation of Beckles, in Suffolke.
       R. Robinson for N. Colman of Norwich.   [1586].
       Brs.   STC23259.

1631   KNEVET, RALPH.   Rhodon and Iris, a pastorall.
       For M. Sparke, sold by E. Causon at Norwich.
       1631.   STC15036A.

1640   FLETCHER, GILES.   Christs victorie, and
       triumph.   **For A. Atfend, bookeseller in Norwich.**
       1640.   STC11061A.

1646   An hve and cry after Vox Popvli.   **[London], for
       Edward Martin, in Norwich.**   1646.   4°.   WH3296.

1647   CARTER, JOHN.   The nail and the vvheel.   **By
       J. Macock for M. Spark and are to be sold by
       William Franklin in Norwich.**   1647.   4°.
       WC654A.

1647   COLLINGES, JOHN.   A memorial for posteritie.
       For William Franklin, in Norwich.   1647.
       WC5326.

1647   HOPKINS, MATTHEW.   The discovery of vvitches.
       **For R. Royston, and are to sold by Edward
       Martin, in Norwich.**   1647.   4°.   WH2751.

1650   ARMITAGE, TIMOTHY.   Eight sermons.
       Norwich.   [c1650].   WA3701.

1650   ROUS, THOMAS.   Christ the Saviour.   **London,
       for W. Franklin, in Norwich.**   [1650].   4°.
       WR2046.

1653   CARTER, JOHN.   The tomb-stone, and a rare
       sight.   **By Tho: Roycroft, for E. D. and N. E. to
       be sold by John Sprat in Norwich.**   1653.   8°.
       WC656.

1654   HUBBERTHORN, RICHARD.   The testimony of
       the everlasting gospel.   **[Norwich? 1654].**   4°.
       WH3237.

1655   Certain propositions tending to the reformation
       of the parish-congregations.   **For William
       Frankling, in Norwich.**   1655.   4°.   WC1733.

1659   The agreement of the associated ministers in
       the county of Norfolk ...   **For Joseph Cranford
       and are to be sold [by him] in Norwich.**   1659.
       4°.   WA778.

1660   BRABOURNE, THEOPHILUS.   A defence of the
       kings authority.   **For the author, to be sold by
       William Nowell, in Norwich.**   1660.   4°.
       WB4090.

1660   BRABOURNE, THEOPHILUS.   A defence of the
       kings authority.   Second edition.   **For the
       author, to be sold in London and by William
       Nowell, in Norwich.**   1660.   4°.   WB4091.

1660   BRABOURNE, THEOPHILUS.   God save the king,
       and prosper him.   **For the author, to be sold
       in London and by Wm. Nowell, in Norwich.**   1660.
       4°.   WB4092.

1661   BRABOURNE, THEOPHILUS.   Svndry particulars
       concerning bishops.   **[London], for the author, to
       be sold by William Nowell in Norwich,** 1661.   4°.
       WB4097.

1663   WINTER, JOHN.   Ἁπλως καὶ καλως, honest plain
       dealing.   **By A. M. and are to be sold by William
       Oliver, in Norwich.**   1663.   4°.   WW3080.

1672   BOYS, EDWARD.   Sixteen sermons.   **By Richard
       Hodgkinson, for William Oliver, in Norwich.**
       1672.   4°.   WB4065.

1675   CONOLD, ROBERT.   A sermon preached ...
       January 31, 1674/5.   **For George Rose in Norwich,
       to be sold by him there, and by Nath. Brook.**
       1675.   4°.   WC5893.

1676   [HARRIS, BENJAMIN].   The divine physician.
       **[London], for George Rose, in Norwich, to be sold
       by him there, and by Nath. Brook, and Will.
       Whitwood, in London.**   1676.   8°.   WH848.

1676   [HARRIS, BENJAMIN].   The divine physician.
       **By H. B. for Will Whitwood, sold by George Rose
       in Norwich.**   1676.   8°.   WH849.

1677   CONOLD, ROBERT.   The notion of schism
       stated according to the antients.   Second edition.
       **For W. Oliver in Norwich, sold by Richard
       Chiswell,** 1677.   8°.   WC5892.

1677   RIVELEY, BENEDICT.   A sermon preach'd ...
       July 28, 1676.   **London, for Sam. Lowndes and
       William Oliver in Norwich.**   1677.   4°.   WR1548.

1677   SCAMLER, ROBERT.   The state or the condition
       of the religious man on earth.   **Printed, and are
       to be sold by George Rose, in Norwich.**   1677.
       4°.   WS808.

1678   COLLINGES, JOHN.   Several discourses.   **For
       Tho. Parkhurst, sold by E. Giles in Norwich.**   1678.
       4°.   WC5335.

1680   COLLINGES, JOHN.   Defensative armour.
       **For Benjamin Alsop, and Ewdard [sic] Giles in
       Norwich.**   1680.   8°.   WC5312.

1680   Whereas in the London Gazzette.   **[Norwich?
       1680].**   Brs.   WW1620A.

1683 ALLEN, THOMAS. The glory of Christ. **By A. M. and R. R. for E. Giles in Norwich.** 1683. 8°. WA1046.

1683 ASTY, ROBERT. A treatise of rejoycing. **For E. Giles in Norwich, sold in London.** 1683. 8°. WA4086.

1683 CLAPHAM, JONATHAN. Obedience to magistrates recommended. **By T. S. for Edward Giles, in Norwich.** 1683. 4°. WC4408.

1683 COLLINGES, JOHN. The intercourses of divine love. **By T. Snowden for Edward Giles in Norwich.** 1683. 4°. WC5324.

1683 HILDYARD, JOHN. A sermon preached at the funeral of ... Viscount Yarmouth. **By S. Roycroft, for George Rose in Norwich, and Robert Clavel, in London.** 1683. 4°. WH1982.

1684 CLAPHAM, JONATHAN. Obedience to magistrates recommended. **By T. S. for Edward Giles, in Norwich.** 1684. 4°. WC4409.

1684 COLLINGES, JOHN. Thirteen sermons. **By T. S. for Edward Giles in Norwich.** 1684. 8°. WC5344.

1684 KIDDER, RICHARD, bp. Convivium cæleste. A plain and familiar discourse. Second edition. **By John Richardson, for Tho. Parkhurst; to be sold by Edward Giles, in Norwich.** 1684. 8°. WK401.

1685 JEGON, WILLIAM. The damning nature of rebellion. **For Will. Oliver, in Norwich.** 1685. 4°. WJ530.

1686 BATT, MICHAEL. A sermon preached ... May 5th. 1668 [sic]. **For William Oliver in Norwich; to be sold by B. Aylmer in London.** 1686. 4°. WB1145.

1686 BUGG, FRANCIS. The Quakers detected. **For the author, and are to be sold by Edward Gyles in Norwich, and Ralph Watson in St. Edmund's-Bury.** 1686. 4°. WB5387.

1687 OLDFIELD, JAMES. Sincerity of the upright mans walk to Heaven. **London, for Edward Giles in Norwich.** 1687. 8°. WO218.

1689 COLLINGES, JOHN. The happiness of brethrens. **By T. S. for Edward Giles, in Norwich.** 1689. 4°. WC5318.

1691 A discovery of audacious insolence. **By Tho. Snowden for Edward Giles in Norwich.** 1691. 4°. WD1638.

1691 FINCH, MARTIN. An answer to Mr. Thomas Grantham's book. **By T. S. for Edward Giles in Norwich.** 1691. 8°. WF942.

1691 PETTO, SAMUEL. Infant baptism vindicated. **London, by Thos. Snowden, for Edward Giles, in Norwich.** 1691. 8°. WP1899.

1692 A brief and plain discourse upon the decrees of God. **By T. S. for Edw. Giles in Norwich.** 1692. 4°. WB4530.

1692 SKELTON, BERNARD. Christus Deus. The divinity. **London, for Jonathan Robinson and Samuel Oliver in Norwich.** 1692. 4°. WS3933.

1692 WARREN, ERASMUS. Divine rules. **London, for Samuel Oliver in Norwich to be sold by J. Robinson.** 1692. 4°. WW964.

1693 A catalogue of ancient and modern books ... tenth of July, 1693. [Norwich]. 1693. 4°. WC1273.

1693 JEFFERY, JOHN. The duty & encouragement of religious artificers. **Cambridge, by John Hayes, for Samuel Oliver in Norwich.** 1693. 4°. WJ515.

1694 RUSSELL, JOHN. A sermon preached at the assizes at Norwich ... fifth day of August 1693. **Cambridge, by John Hayes, for Samvel Oliver in Norwich.** 1694. 4°. WR2344.

1695 FINCH, MARTIN. A sermon preach'd ... 25th day of January, 1690. **For Edward Giles in Norwich.** 1695. 4°. WF945.

1695 [SNOWDEN, SAMUEL]. A sermon preached upon the thirtieth of Janueary 1694/5. **London, by J. Heptinstall for Edward Giles in Norwich.** 1695. 4°. WS4397.

1698 STACKHOUSE, JOHN. The mutual desires of elders and people. **London, by Tho. Snowden, for Edward Giles, in Norwich.** 1698. 4°. WS5104.

1700 A catalogue of ancient and modern books ... December 2nd. 1700. [Norwich]. 1700. 4°. WC1275.

1700 JEFFERY, JOHN. Proposals made. **For Tho. Goddard, in Norwich.** 1700. 12°. WJ517.

1700 PENDLEBURY, HENRY. The barren fig-tree. **London, by R. Janeway, jun., for Ed. Giles in Norwich.** 1700. 8°. WP1138.

NOTTINGHAM

1669 REYNER, EDWARD. The beginning and well being of a Christian. **London, by R. W. for Henry Mortlock: and Samuel Richards in Nottingham.** 1669. 8°. WR1220.

1674 ELLIS, CLEMENT. A catechism wherein the learner. **For Sam. Richards in Nottingham.** 1674. 8°. WE550.

1675 BARRET, JOHN. Good will towards men. **For Sam. Richards in Nottingham, and Tho. Guy.** 1675. 8°. WB909.

1678 BARRET, JOHN. The Christian temper. **For Jonathan Robinson, and Samuel Richards in Nottingham.** 1678. 8°. WB907.

1686 D., J. Feed my lambs. **By J. H. for Samuel Richards in Nottingham, and sold by Luke Meredith.** 1686. 8°. WD34.

1698 CHADWICK, DANIEL. A sermon preached ... to the Society for reformation of manners. **For John Richards in Nottingham.** 1698. 8°. WC1788B.

OUNDLE

1692 DAVIS, RICHARD. Truth and innocency vindicated. **For Nath. and Robert Ponder, to be sold by Randal Taylor, by Mr. Coolidge in Cambridge, Mr. Prior at Colchester, Mr. Noble at St. Edmund's Bury, Mr. Haworth at Ipswich, Northampton, Wellingborow, Kettering, Oundle, Harborow, Litterworth, Upingham, Bedford, Kimbolton and Canterbury.** [1692?]. 4°. WD435.

OXFORD

1517 OPUSCULUM. Compilatū est hoc opusculum insolibilium ī alma vniversitati Oxonie. [**Oxford, J. Scolar.** 1517?]. 4°. STC18833.

1585 De philosophia; panathenaicæ duæ: in comitiis Oxonii habitæ. [**Oxford?** 1585]. 8°. STC19887.

1585 DUDLEY, ROBERT, earl of Leicester. In illustrissimi comitis Leicestrensis Oxoniensis Academiæ Cancellarii aduentum. **Oxoniæ, ex æd, J. Barnes.** 1585. Brs. STC7287.

1585 PARRY, WILLIAM. In Guil. Parry proditorem odæ et epigrammata. **Oxoniæ, ex off. J. Barnesii.** 1585. 8°. STC19340.

1586   CORRO, ANTONIO DE. Reglas grammaticales
       para aprender la lengua Española y Francesa.
       Paris, [Oxford], J. Barnes. 1586. STC5789A.

1586   D., H. Anglia querens. **Oxford, J. Barnes.** 1586.
       8°. STC6167.

1586   In Catalinarias proditiones, ac proditores domes-
       ticos, odae 6. **Oxoniae, ex off. J. Barnesii. 1586.**
       8°. STC4838.

1589   HENRY III, king of France. De caede Gallorum
       Regis. [Verses]. **Oxonii, ex off. Josephi Barnesii.**
       1589. 4°. STC13099.

1589   MISOPHONUS, pseud. De caede et interitu
       Gallorum regis Henrici tertii epigrammata.
       Oxoniae, ex off. J. Barnesij. 1589. 4°.
       STC17984.

1595   BILSON, THOMAS, bp. The true difference
       between Christian subjection and unchristian
       rebellion. **Oxford, J. Barnes.** 1595. 4°.
       STC3073.

1598   BÈZE, THÉODORE DE. Theod. Bezae ad J. G.
       Stuckium epistola. Et pastorum Genevensium
       responsio. **Oxoniae, ex off. J. Barnesii.** 1598. 8ᵛ.
       STC1997.

1599   AUNGERVILE, RICARDUS D'. Philobiblon
       Richardi Dunelmensis sive de amore librorum.
       Oxoniae, J. Barnesius. 1599. 4°. STC959.

1601   OVERTON, WILLIAM, bp. Oratio and praeben-
       darios. **Oxoniae, J. Barnesius.** 1601. 4°.
       STC18926.

1602   BUNNY, FRANCIS. An exposition of the Lordes
       praier. **Oxford, Jos. Barnes, for John Barnes.**
       1602. 8°. STC4098A.

1602   OXFORD UNIVERSITY. Questiones. **[Oxford].**
       1602. 16°. STC19015.

1602   Quaestiones in vesperiis discutiendae. Iul 10.
       1602. **[Oxford. 1602].** 16°. STC20525.

1603   R., R. Post nubila sudum. (In obitum Elisabethae,
       etc.) **Oxoniae, ap. J. Barnesium.** 1603. 4°.
       STC20587.

1604   THEOPHRASTUS. Θεοφράστου ηθικοι'
       χαρακτῆρες. Theophrasti notationes morum.
       Oxoniae, exc. Jos. Barnesius. 1604. 4°.
       STC23947.

1605   BRIMELLUS, ISRAEL. Viri generosissimi R.
       Barnabii vita atꝙ obitus. **[Oxford? 1605?].**
       Brs. STC3757.

1605   OXFORD UNIVERSITY. Quaestiones. **Oxford,
       L. Lichfield.** 1605-1640. Fol. STC19017.

1605   OXFORD UNIVERSITY. Quaestiones discutiendae.
       Oxford. 1605. Brs. STC19016.

1606   VORSTIUS, CONRAD. Enchiridion controuer-
       siarum, seu index errorum Ecclesiae Romanae.
       Oxoniae, J. Barnesius. 1606. 8°. STC24881.

1610   D., D. Xenia regia ad Jacobum Britanniae regem
       conscripta. **[Oxford? 1610?].** 4°. STC6163.

1612   RIDER, JOHN, bp. Riders dictionarie. (A dic-
       tionarie etymologicall by F. Holyoke. Lat.-Eng.)
       Oxford, Joseph Barnes. 1612. 4°. STC21033.

1613   BENEFIELD, SEBASTIAN. A sermon preached
       March 24, 1612. **Oxford, Joseph Barnes for John
       Barnes, London.** 1613. 4°. STC1871.

1613   PRICE, DANIEL. Sorrow for the sinnes of time.
       A sermon. (Tears shed over Abner). **Oxford,
       J. Barnes.** 1613. 2 vols. 4°. STC20303.

1614   OXFORD. Orders made by the Justices of peace,
       etc. [11 Jan. 1614]. **[Oxford. 1614].** Fol.
       STC19003.

1615   SMITH, SAMUEL. Aditus ad logicam. Autore
       S.S. artium magistro. Editio secunda. **Oxoniae,
       J. Barnesius.** 1615. 12°. STC22826.

1625   ENGLAND. PROCLAMATIONS. By the King.
       Commanding Captaines to attend their charge.
       [4 Sept. 1625]. **Oxford, J. L[ichfield] and
       W. T[urner] for B. Norton and J. Bill.** 1625.
       Brs. STC8801.

1625   ENGLAND. PROCLAMATIONS. By the King.
       For adjournement of Michaelmas terme. [4 Sept.
       1625]. **Oxford, J. L[ichfield] and W. T[urner] for
       B. Norton and J. Bill.** 1625. Brs. STC8799.

1625   ENGLAND. PROCLAMATIONS. By the King.
       For adjournement of Michaelmas terme. **Oxford,
       J. L[ichfield] and W. T[urner] for B. Norton and
       J. Bill.** 1625. Brs. STC8800.

1625   ENGLAND. PROCLAMATIONS. By the King.
       For avoiding intercourse, etc. [17 Oct. 1625].
       **Oxford, J. L[ichfield] and W. T[urner] for
       B. Norton and J. Bill.** 1625. Brs. STC8805.

1625   ENGLAND. PROCLAMATIONS. By the King.
       For further adjournement of Michaelmas terme.
       [11 Oct. 1625]. **Oxford, J. L[ichfield] and
       W. T[urner] for B. Norton and J. Bill.** 1625.
       Brs. STC8803.

1625   ENGLAND. PROCLAMATIONS. By the King.
       For further adjournement of Michaelmas terme.
       **Oxford, J. L[ichfield] and W. T[urner] for
       B. Norton and J. Bill.** 1625. Brs. STC8804.

1625   ENGLAND. PROCLAMATIONS. By the King.
       For making currant certaine French coyne.
       [4 Sept. 1625]. **Oxford, J. L[ichfield] and W.
       T[urner] for B. Norton and J. Bill.** 1625. Brs.
       STC8797.

1625   ENGLAND. PROCLAMATIONS. By the King.
       For making currant certaine French coyne.
       **Oxford, J. L[ichfield] and W. T[urner] for B.
       Norton and J. Bill.** 1625. Brs. STC8798.

1625   ENGLAND. PROCLAMATIONS. By the King.
       For recalling subjects, etc. [14 Aug. 1625].
       **Oxford, J. L[ichfield] and W. T[urner] for
       B. Norton and J. Bill.** 1625. Brs. STC8795.

1625   ENGLAND. PROCLAMATIONS. By the King.
       For recalling subjects, etc. [14 Aug. 1625].
       **Oxford, J. L[ichfield] and W. T[urner] for
       B. Norton and J. Bill.** 1625. Brs. STC8796.

1625   ENGLAND. PROCLAMATIONS. By the King.
       For removing the receipt of Exchequer. [31 July
       1625]. **Oxford, J. L[ichfield] and W. T[urner]
       for B. Norton and J. Bill.** 1625. Brs. STC8789.

1625   ENGLAND. PROCLAMATIONS. By the King.
       For remooving the receipt of Exchequer. [31 July
       1625]. **Oxford, J. L[ichfield] and W. T[urner]
       for B. Norton and J. Bill.** 1625. STC8790.

1625   ENGLAND. PROCLAMATIONS. By the King.
       For the calling home of subjects in the service
       of the Emperor. [11 Sept. 1625]. **Oxford,
       J. L[ichfield] and W. T[urner] for B. Norton and
       J. Bill.** 1625. Brs. STC8802.

1625   ENGLAND. PROCLAMATIONS. By the King.
       Prohibiting Bartholomew Faire. [4 Aug. 1625].
       **Oxford, J. L[ichfield] and W. T[urner] d. B. Norton
       and J. Bill.** 1625. Brs. STC8792.

1625   ENGLAND. PROCLAMATIONS. By the King.
       Prohibiting Bartholomew Faire. [4 Aug. 1625].
       **Oxford, J. L[ichfield] and W. T[urner] for
       B. Norton and J. Bill.** 1625. STC8793.

1625   ENGLAND. PROCLAMATIONS. Charles, etc.
       [Collection for poor. 11 Aug. 1625]. **Oxford.**
       1625. Brs. STC8794.

1625 TAYLOR, JOHN. The fearefull sommer. [Second edition enlarged]. **Oxford, J. L[ichfield] and W. T[urner]**. 1625. 8°. STC23755.

1626 TERRY, JOHN. Theologicall logicke: or the third part of the Tryall of truth, etc. **Oxford, J. Lichfield and W. Turner** for W. T[urner] and **H. Curtaine**. 1626. 4°. STC23915.

1627 GUMBLEDEN, JOHN. Three sermons. **A. Mathewes for H. Crips of Oxford**. 1626[1627]. 4°. STC12515.

1628 PEMBLE, WILLIAM. Five godly and profitable sermons. **Oxford, J. Lichfield**. 1628. 4°. STC19576.

1629 CAMDEN, WILLIAM. Annales-Tomus alter & idem. Translated by T. Browne. (Bk. 4.). **T. Harper, sold by W. Web, Oxford**. 1629. 4° STC4498.

1629 A catechisme in briefe questions and answeres. **Oxford, J. L[ichfield]**. 1629. STC4800.

1629 OXFORD UNIVERSITY. Ordinationes decreta et statuta de munere procuratorio. **Oxford**. 1629. Brs. STC19008.

1629 SPARKE, WILLIAM. The mystery of godlinesse. **Oxford, J. Lichfield for W. Webb**. 1629. 4°. STC23027.

1630 BIBLE. LATIN. PSALMS. Psalmi aliquot Davidici in metrum Lat. trad. **Oxoniæ, J. Lichfield**. 1630. 8°. STC2365.

1631 ENGLAND. CHURCH OF. VISITATION ARTICLES. Gloucester. **Oxford, J. Lichfield**. 1631. 4°. STC10210.

1631 ENGLAND, CHURCH OF. VISITATION ARTICLES. Peterborough. **Oxford, W. Turner**. 1631. 4°. STC10316.

1631 MARKHAM, GERVASE. Markhams faithfull farrier. **Oxford, W. Turner for M. Sparke**. 1631. 8°. STC17368.

1634 SMITH, SAMUEL. Aditus ad logicam. Autore S.S. artium magistro. Editio quinta. **Oxford**. 1634. 8°. STC22832.

1636 EVANS, WILLIAM. The christian conflict and conquest. **Oxford, L. Lichfield, sold by W. Webb**. 1636. 4°. STC10595.

1637 AIRAY, CHRISTOPHER. Fasciculus præceptorum logicorum. Editio tertia. **Oxoniæ, Guil. Turner**. 1637. 8°. STC243.

1637 WRIGHT, ABRAHAM. Delitiæ delitiarum. **Oxoniæ, L. Lichfield, imp. G. Webb**. 1637. 12°. STC26017.

1638 ENGLAND, CHURCH OF VISITATION ARTICLES. Worcester. Archdeaconry. **Oxford, L. Lichfield**. [1638]. 4°. STC10373.

1639 SCHEIBLER, CHRISTOPH. Philosophia compendiosa. Editio sexta. **Oxoniæ, G. Turner, pro H. Curteine**. 1639. 8°. STC21815.

1641 BROAD, TH. Three questions answered. **Oxford**. 1641. 4°. WB4829.

1641 Certain treatises written by learned men concerning the government of the church. **Oxford**. 1641. 4°. WC1761.

1641 OXFORD, CITY OF. Civitas Oxon: a bill of all the burials. [**Oxford**. 1641]. Brs. WO853.

1641 OXFORD, UNIVERSITY OF. To the high court of Parliament, the humble petition of all colledges and halls. [**Oxford**. 1641]. Brs. WO987.

1642 BOROUGH, Sir JOHN. Burrh: impetus juveniles. **Oxoniæ, excudebat L. Lichfield**. 1642. 12°. WB3772.

1642 CHARLES I, king of England. An agreement betwixt his Majesty and the inhabitants of the county of Oxford. **At Oxford by Leonard Lichfield**. Decemb. 21, 1642. 4°. WC2080.

1642 CHARLES I. king of England. His Majesties royall declaration and protestation to all his loving subjects. **Oxford, Leonard Lichfield**. [1642?]. 4°. WC2763.

1642 Petition of the Commons of Kent. **York printed, reprinted Oxford**. 1642. 4°. WP1791.

1642 RUPERT, prince. Prince Rupert his reply. **Oxford, by Leonard Lichfield**. 1642. 4°. WR2305.

1642 To the King, the humble petition of the mayor. **Oxford**. 1642. 4°. WT1496.

1642 WILDE, GEORGE. A sermon preached in St. Maries. **Oxford**. 1642. 4°. WW2159.

1643 BOGAN, ZACHARY. Clavis. **Oxford, Henry Hall**. 1643. 8°. WB3438.

1643 BURROUGHS, Sir JOHN. Burrhi impetus juveniles. **Oxoniæ, excudebat Leonardus Lichfield**. 1643. 12°. WB6128A.

1643 CHARLES I, king of England. The collection of all the particular papers that passed. **Oxford, by Leonard Lichfield**. 1643. 4°. WC2157.

1643 CHARLES I, king of England. His Majesties answer to a late petition ... 16 March 1643. **Oxford, L. Lichfield**. 1642[3]. 4°. WC2097.

1643 CHARLES I, king of England. His Maiesties declaration to all his loving subjects, in answer to a declaration ... 3 June, 1643. **Printed at Oxford by Leonard Lichfield**. 1643. 30 pp. 4°. WC2233.

1643 CHARLES I, king of England. His Maiesties gracious message to both his Houses ... February the 20th. [**Oxford**. 1642/3]. Brs. WC2328.

1643 CHARLES I, king of England. Orders, by the king. To our trusty & well beloved our Colonells. **Printed at Oxford by Leonard Lichfield**. [1643]. Brs. WC2531.

1643 CHARLES I, king of England. We are so highly sensible of the extra. **Printed at Oxford, by Leonard Lichfield**. 1643. Brs. WC2874.

1643 ENGLAND. PARLIAMENT. An act for the confirmation of the treaty ... between ... England and Scotland. **Oxford, by Leonard Lichfield**. 1643. 4°. WE1101.

1643 ENGLAND. PARLIAMENT. A copy of a letter, from the members of both Houses ... to the Earle of Essex. **Oxford, by Leonard Lichfield**. 1643. 4°. WE1285.

1643 ENGLAND. PARLIAMENT. A paper received by His Maiesty from the Committee of both Houses. **Printed at Oxford, by Leonard Lichfield**. 1643. WE2118.

1643 F., H. The unlavvfulnesse of the new covenant. **Oxford, by Leonard Lichfield**. I. March 1643. 4°. WF24.

1643 HAMMOND, HENRY. The Scriptures plea for magistrates. **Oxford, by Leonard Lichfield**. 1643. 4°. WH598A.

1643 MANCHESTER, EDWARD MONTAGU, earl of. Letter. **Oxford, L. Lichfield**. 1643. Brs. WM391.

1643   MARSHALL, STEPHEN. A letter of spirituall advice. **Oxford, Henry Hall.** 1643. 4°. WM760.

1643   Moribus epidemicus anni 1643. Englands new disease. **Oxford, L. Lichfield.** 1643. 8°. W**M**2760.

1643   An oath taken by the gentry ... of York. [**Oxford.** 1643]. Brs. WO76.

1643   The opinions of certaine reverend and learned divines. [**London and Oxford**], for Ch. **Downes.** 1643. 4°. WO356.

1644   A bill of all that deceased. **Oxford.** 1644. 4°. WB2891.

1644   A briefe answer to the declaration of the king-domes of England and Scotland. **Oxford, by H. Hall.** 1644. 4°. WB4545.

1644   CHARLES I, king of England. Trusty. Whereas the members of both Houses. [**Oxford, L. Lichfield.** 1644]. Brs. WC2849.

1644   Devotions for the helpe and assistance. [**Oxford**], **printed.** 1644. 8°. WD1238.

1644   [DIGGES, DUDLEY, younger]. The vnlavvfvl-nesse of subjects taking up armes. [**Oxford**], **printed.** 1644. 4°. WD1463.

1644   ENGLAND. LORDS COMMISSIONERS. An order for the observance and execution of the statute. **Oxford, L. Lichfield.** 1644. Brs. WE928.

1644   FEATLEY, DANIEL. The gentle lash. [**Oxford**], **imprinted.** 1644. 4°. WF582.

1644   HALL, JOSEPH, bp. A modest offer of some meet considerations. [**Oxford**], **imprinted.** 1644. 4°. WH394.

1644   WHARTON, Sir GEORGE. Naworth 1644. **Printed at Oxford by Henry Hall.** 1644. 8°. WA2673.

1645   ENGLAND. LORDS COMMISSIONERS. An order for the observance and execution of the statute. **Oxford, L. Lichfield.** 1645. Brs. WE929.

1645   ENGLAND. PRIVY COUNCIL. Whereas by a for-mer order of the second of July ... 19 August 1645. **Oxford, L. Lichfield.** [1645]. Brs. WE2920.

1645   QUARLES, FRANCIS. The loyall convert. **Oxford, printed.** 1645. 4°. WQ108.

1645   WHARTON, Sir GEORGE. Wharton. 1645. An almanack. **Printed at Oxford, by Henry Hall.** 1645. 8°. WA2650.

1646   TAYLOR, JOHN. The complaint of Christmas. [**Oxford, by H. Hall.** 1646]. **Printed at the charges of the author.** 4°. WT442.

1647   A declaration from His Excellencie Sr Thomas Fairfax, and his councell of warre. Concerning their proceeding. **Oxford, by J. Harris and H. Hills.** 1647. 4°. WD580.

1647   HAMMOND, HENRY. Of the povver of the keyes. **For Richard Royston and Richard Davis in Oxford.** 1647. 4°. WH568.

1648   POLYCARP, Saint, bp. of Antioch. Polycarpi et Ignatii epistolae. **Oxoniae, Henry Hall.** 1648. 4°. WP2790.

1649   HAMMOND, HENRY. A practicall catechisme. "Fifth" edition. **For R. Royston, and for R. Davis in Oxford.** 1649. 4°. WH584A.

1650   FORD, STEPHEN. An epistle to the Church of Christ. **Oxford.** 1650. 4°. WF1506.

1650   M., M. V. Satyra Manneiana [**Oxford?**]. 1650. 4°. WM61.

1651   GREENWOOD, DANIEL. Whereas the right honourable the Councell of State. **Oxford, L. Lichfield.** 1651. Brs. WG1866.

1651   The receiver undeceived: or an answer. **Oxford, printed.** 1651. 4°. WR626.

1652   BIBLE. GREEK. Musae sacrae: seu Jonas, Jeremias ... reddibe carmine. **Oxoniae, L. Lichfield & veneunt apud Jos. Godwin & Ric. Davis.** 1652. 8°. WB2727.

1652   CATO, DIONYSIUS. Catonis disticha de moribvs. **Oxoniae, excudebant L. L. & H. H.** 1652. 8°. WC1504.

1652   DOWNAME, GEORGE, bp. A briefe summe of divinitie. Third edition. [**Oxford, by H. Hall**], for **W. Webb in Oxford and W. Graves in Cambridge.** 1652. 8°. WD2058.

1652   OUGHTRED, WILLIAM. Elementi decimi Euclidis declaratio. **Oxoniae, excudebat Leon. Lichfield, veneunt apud Tho. Robinson.** 1652. 8°. WO580.

1652   OUGHTRED, WILLIAM. Horologiorum. **Oxoniae, excudebat Leon Lichfield, veneunt apud Tho. Robinson.** 1652. 8°. WO581.

1652   OUGHTRED, WILLIAM. Theorematum. **Oxoniae, excudebat Leon. Lichfield, veneunt apud Tho. Robinson.** 1652. 8°. WO588.

1652   OXFORD, UNIVERSITY OF. Quæstiones in S. theologia. **Oxoniae, excudebat Leon. Lichfield.** 1652. Brs. WO944.

1653   HAUSKINS, THOMAS. A sermon preached at Hievvorth ... 24. of August 1649. **Oxford, by H. Hall.** 1653. 12°. WH1153.

1653   HOFFMAN, JOHN. The principles of Christian religion. **Oxford, by L. Lichfield.** 1653. 8°. WH2348.

1655   HAMMOND, HENRY. An account of Mr. Cawdry's Triplex diatribe. **By J. Flesher, for Richard Royston, and for Richard Davis in Oxford.** 1655. 4°. WH511.

1655   HAMMOND, HENRY. The baptizing of infants. **By J. Flesher, for Richard Royston, and for Richard Davis in Oxford.** 1655. 4°. WH516.

1655   LYFORD, WILLIAM. The plain mans senses exercised. **London, for Richard Royston, and Edward Forrest in Oxford.** 1655. 4°. WL3550.

1656   WALLIS, JOHN. Johannis Wallisii ... operum mathematicorum pars altera. **Oxonii, typis Leon. Lichfield, veneunt apud Octav. Pullein.** 1656. 4°. WW598A.

1657   HAMMOND, HENRY. Δευτεραι φροντιδες, or a review. **By J. Flesher for R. Royston, and R. Davis in Oxford.** 1657. 8°. WH535.

1657   OWEN, JOHN. Of communion with God. **Oxford, by A. Lichfield, for Tho: Robinson.** 1657. 4°. WO778.

1658   BARON, ROBERT, of Aberdean. Rob. Baronii ... metaphysica generalis. **Ex officina R. Danielis, & veneunt apud Tho. Robinson & Ri. Davis ... Oxonienses.** 1658. 12°. WB883.

1658   BARON, ROBERT, of Aberdean. Philosophia theologiæ ancillans. [**Oxford**], **impensis T. Robinson & R. Davis.** 1658. 12°. WB887.

1658   [BOBART, JAKOB]. Catalogue horti botanici Oxoniensis. **Oxonii, typis Gulielmi Hall.** 1658. 8°. WB3375A.

1688   HIGFORD, WILLIAM. Institutions: or, advice. **By Tho. Warren, for Edmund Thorn of Oxford.** 1658. 8°. WH1947.

1658 A tract to prove, that true grace. **Oxford.** 1658. 8°. WT2003.

1658 ZOUCHE, RICHARD. Ivris et ivdicii fecialis. **Oxoniæ.** 1658. 4°. WZ21.

1659 HAMMOND, HENRY. A paraphrase, and annotations upon all the books of the New Testament. "Second edition". **By J. Flesher for Richard Davis in Oxford.** 1659. Fol. WH573B.

1659 [JEANES, HENRY]. A treatise concerning the indifference of hvmane actions. **Oxford, by Hen: Hall, for Tho: Robinson.** 1659. 4°. WJ509.

1660 BRADSHAW, WILLIAM. Several treatises of worship. [London], **printed for Cambridge and Oxford, to be sold** [London]. 1660. 4°. WB4161.

1660 HAMMOND, HENRY. 'Αιεν 'αληθεδειν, or, a brief account. **For Richard Davis, in Oxfor** [sic]. 1660. 4°. WH512.

1660 JEANES, HENRY. Uniformity in humane doctrinall ceremonies. **Oxford, by A. Lichfield, for Tho. Robinson.** 1660. 4°. WJ510.

1660 A New-Years-gift for the Rump. [**Oxford?** 1660]. Brs. WN809.

1660 OXFORD, UNIVERSITY OF. Mariæ principis Arausionensis. **Oxoniæ, typis Lichfieldianis.** 1660. 4°. WO877.

1660 PEARSON, JOHN, bp. Critici sacri. **Londini, excudebat Jacobus Flesher**, 1660. **Prostant apud** {**Cornelium Bee, Richardum Royston, Guilielmum Wells, Samuelem Thomson**} **Londini. Thomam Robinson, Oxonii. Guilielmum Morden, Cantabrigiæ.** Fol. WP994A.

1661 OXFORD, UNIVERSITY OF. Quæstiones in S. theologia. **Oxoniæ, typis Lihfieldianis** [sic]. 1661. Brs. WO943.

1661 THEYER, JOHN. Aerio-mastix, or, a vindication. **Oxford By William Hall, for John Forrest.** 1661. 4°. WT890.

1662 [CALAMY, EDMUND, elder]. Eli trembling for fear of the ark. **Oxford, printed.** 1662. WC231.

1662 FELL, JOHN, bp. The life and death of that reverend divine ... Doctor Thomas Fuller. **Oxford: printed.** 1662. 8°. WF615.

1662 [GLANVILL, JOSEPH]. Lux orientalis, or an enquiry. **Printed, are to be sold at Cambridge, and Oxford.** 1662. 8°. WG814.

1662 KENDALL, GEORGE. Fur pro tribunali. **Oxoniæ.** 1662. 16°. WK285.

1662 NEWCASTLE, WILLIAM CAVENDISH, duke of. Being commanded by ... to publish the following articles for his new course. [Oxford. 1662]. Brs. WN876.

1662 OWEN, JOHN. Animadversions on a treatise intituled Fiat lux. **By E. Cotes, for Henry Cripps and George West in Oxford.** 1662. 8°. WO713.

1662 WHEAR, DEGORY. Relectiones Hyemales. "Fourth edition". **Oxoniæ, excudebat W. Hall, impensis Jos. Godwin.** 1662. 8°. WW1595A.

1663 [CALAMY, EDMUND, elder]. Eli trembling for fear of the ark. **Oxford, printed.** 1663. 4°. WC232.

1663 F., D. Reason and judgement. **Oxford: by J. W. for Will. Thorne.** 1663. 4°. WF9.

1663 The fanatick barber. **Oxford.** 1663. Brs. WF393.

1663 OXFORD, UNIVERSITY OF. Quæstiones in S. theologia. **Oxoniæ, typis Lichfieldianis.** 1663. Brs. WO945.

1663 A vindication of the degree of gentry. **London, printed, and are to be sold at Oxford and Cambridge.** 1663. 8°. WV503.

1664 BARKSDALE, CLEMENT. Apanthismata. Memorials ... two new decads. **Oxford, A. and L. Lichfield, for E. Thorn.** 1664. WB790.

1664 RIDLEY, Sir THOMAS. A view of the civile and ecclesiasticall law. **Oxford, by W. Hall for Edw. Forrest.** 1664. 8°. WR1455.

1666 Cum per nuperam dispensandi hac in Acedemiâ licentiam. [**Oxford.** 1666]. Brs. WC7574.

1667 The case truly stated betwixt the Dean and chapter of Christs Church in Oxford. [**Oxford?** 1667]. Brs. WC1207.

1667 [EDWARDS, CHARLES]. Y Ffydd ddiffuant. **Oxford,** 1667. 8°. WE192.

1667 In nobile admodum inter gallos. **Oxonii.** 1667. 4°. WI119.

1668 MAYOW, JOHN. Tractatvs duo. **Oxon: excudebat Hen: Hall impensis Ric. Davis.** 1668. WM1535.

1668 OXFORD, UNIVERSITY OF. Ordo baccalavreorum [**Oxford.** 1668]. Brs. WO904.

1668 PEMBLE, WILLIAM. De sensibus internis. **Oxoniæ.** 1668. 16°. WP1116.

1669 BARON, ROBERT, of Aberdean. Rob. Baronii ... Metaphysica generalis. **Ex officina R. Danielis, & veneunt apud Th. Robinson & Ri. Davis. Oxon.** [1669?]. WB884.

1669 BOYLE, ROBERT. Origo formarum et qualitatum. **Oxoniæ, R. Davis.** 1669. 12°. WB4016.

1669 [KÖRNMANN, HEINRICH]. Sibylla trigAndriana, seu de virginitate. **Prostant venales apud Ed. Forrest, Oxon.** 1669. 12°. WK749.

1669 OXFORD, UNIVERSITY OF. Quæstiones in S. theologia. **Oxoniæ, typis Lichfieldianis.** 1669. Brs. WO946.

1670 BOYLE, ROBERT. Tracts written by. **Oxford, by W. H. for Ric. Davis.** 1670. 8°. WB4056.

1670 HEYLYN, PETER. Ærivs redivivvs: or, the history. **Oxford, for John Crosley and are to be sold in London by Thomas Basset.** 1670. Fol. WH1681A.

1670 OXFORD, UNIVERSITY OF. Ordo baccalavreorum. **Oxonii, e theatro Sheldoniano, excudebat Hen. Hall.** [1670]. Brs. WO905.

1670 ROUS, FRANCIS. Archaeologiæ Atticae. Seventh edition. **Oxford, by Henry Hall for John Adams.** 1670. 4°. WR2038.

1671 [BLOME, RICHARD]. Proposals for printing a geographical description. [**Oxford**]. 1671. Fol. WB3216.

1671 BOYLE, ROBERT. Three tracts written by. **Oxford, by W. H. for Ric. Davis.** 1671. 8°. WB4049.

1671 [GODWYN, THOMAS]. Romanæ historiæ anthologia. **Oxford.** 1671. 4°. WG992.

1671 OXFORD, UNIVERSITY OF. Ordo baccalavreorum **Oxonii e theatro Sheldoniano.** 1671. Brs. WO906

1671 OXFORD, UNIVERSITY OF. Quæstiones in S. theologia. **Oxonii, ex officina Leonardi Lichfield.** 1671. Brs. WO947

1671 OXFORD, UNIVERSITY OF. Statuta selecta. **Oxon.** 1671. 8°. WO967.

1671 TOZER, HENRY. Directions for a godly life.
Eighth edition. **Oxford, by L. Lichfield, for
Richard Davis.** 1671. 12°. WT1998.

1672 HEYLYN, PETER. Ærivs redivivvs. Second
edition. **By Robert Battersby for Christopher
Wilkinson, and Thomas Archer, and John Crosley
in Oxford.** 1672. Fol. WH1682.

1673 BOYLE, ROBERT. Tracts written by ... containing new experiments. **For Richard Davis, in Oxon.**
1673. 8°. WB4061.

1673 OXFORD. UNIVERSITY OF. Quæstiones in
S. theologia. **Oxonii, ex officina Leonardi
Lichfield.** 1673. Brs. WO948.

1673 PRIDEAUX, MATHIAS. An easy and compendious
introdvction for reading. "Fifth" edition. **Printed
at Oxford, by Leon. Lichfield, to be sold by James
Good.** 1673. 4°. WP3444A.

1673 [WHEELER, MAURICE]. The Oxford almanack
for ... 1674. **Printed at the theater in Oxford.**
[1673]. 12°. WA2677.

1673 [WOOD, ANTHONY]. Historia et antiquitates
universitatis Oxoniensis. **Oxonii, e theatro
Sheldoniano.** 1673. Fol. WW3384.

1674 CHURCH OF ENGLAND. Articles of visitation.
Oxford, by L. Lichfield. 1674. 4°. WC4076.

1674 HAMMOND, HENRY. The vvorkes of. The first
volume. **By Elizabeth Flesher for Richard
Royston, and Richard Davis of Oxford.** 1674. Fol.
WH506.

1674 HICKES, WILLIAM. Oxford drollery. **Oxford,
for J. C. to be sold by Thomas Palmer, [London].**
1674. 8°. WH1889.

1674 HILDEBRAND, FRIEDRICH. Dissertatio
theologica. **Oxoniæ, excudebat H. Hall impensis
authorem.** 1674. WH1973.

1674 OXFORD, UNIVERSITY OF. Ordo baccalavreorum
[Oxford], ex officina Leonardi Lichfield. [1674].
Brs. WO907.

1674 OXFORD, UNIVERSITY OF. Quæstiones in
S. theologia. **Oxonii, ex officina Leonardi
Lichfield.** 1674. Brs. WO949.

1674 OXFORD, UNIVERSITY OF. Theatri Oxoniensis
encaenia ... Jul. 10. **Oxon, e theatro Sheldoniano.**
1674. Brs. WO971.

1674 TULLY, THOMAS. Dissertativncla de sententia.
**Oxon, Typis L. Lichfield, prostant venales apud
Fran. Oxlad sen.** 1674. 4°. WT3243.

1675 BIBLE. ENGLISH. NEW TESTAMENT. **Oxford,
at the theater.** 1675. 8°. WB2673.

1675 BOYLE, ROBERT. Experiments and notes about
... corrosiveness. **By E. Flesher, for R. Davis in
Oxford.** 1675. 8°. WB3969.

1675 BOYLE, ROBERT. Experiments, and notes about
... volatility. **By E. Flesher, for R. Davis in
Oxford.** 1675. 8°. WB3973.

1675 BOYLE, ROBERT. Experiments, and observations
about ... odours. **By E. Flesher, for R. Davis in
Oxford.** 1675. 8°. WB3974.

1675 BOYLE, ROBERT. Experiments, and observations
about ... taste. **By E. Flesher, for R. Davis in
Oxford.** 1675. 8°. WB3975.

1675 BOYLE, ROBERT. Of the imperfection of the
chymist's doctrine. **By E. Flesher, for R. Davis
in Oxford.** 1675. 8°. WB4010.

1675 BOYLE, ROBERT. Of the mechanical causes of
chymical precipitation. **By E. Flesher, for
R. Davis in Oxford.** 1675. 8°. WB4011.

1675 BOYLE, ROBERT. Of the mechanical origine of
heat. **By E. Flesher, for R. Davis in Oxford.**
1675. 8°. WB4012.

1675 BOYLE, ROBERT. Reflections upon the hypothesis
of alcali. **By E. Flesher, for R. Davis.** 1675.
8°. WB4020.

1675 HAMMOND, HENRY. A paraphrase, and annota-
tions upon all the books of the New Testament.
Fourth edition. **By E. F. T. R. and J. M. for Ric.
Davis in Oxford.** 1675. Fol. WH575.

1675 [JACK, GILBERT]. Grammatica rationis.
Oxonii, e theatro Sheldoniano. 1675. 12°. WJ56.

1675 OXFORD, UNIVERSITY OF. Ordo baccalavreorum
[Oxford], ex officina Leonardi Lichfield. [1675].
Brs. WO908.

1675 OXFORD, UNIVERSITY OF. Quæstiones in
S. theologia ... **Oxonii, ex officina Leonardi
Lichfield.** 1675. Brs. WO950.

1675 OXFORD, UNIVERSITY OF. Theatri Oxoniensis
encaenia ... Jul. 9. **Oxon, e theatro Sheldoniano.**
1675. Brs. WO972.

1675 [WHEELER, MAURICE]. The Oxford almanack
for ... 1675. **Printed at the theater in Oxford.**
[1675]. Brs. WA2678.

1676 BOYLE, ROBERT. Experiments and notes about
... magnetism. **By E. Flesher, for R. Davis in
Oxford.** 1676. 8°. WB3971.

1676 OXFORD, UNIVERSITY OF. Ordo baccalaureorum
[Oxford], ex officina Lichfieldiana. 1676. Brs.
WO909.

1676 OXFORD, UNIVERSITY OF. Quæstiones in
S. theologia. **Oxonii, ex officina Leonardi
Lichfield.** 1676. Brs. WO951.

1676 OXFORD, UNIVERSITY OF. Theatri Oxoniensis
encaenia ... Jul. 7. **Oxon, e theatro Sheldoniano.**
1676. Brs. WO973.

1676 PLOT, ROBERT. The natural history of Oxford-
shire. **Printed at the Theater in Oxford, and are
to be had there; and in London at Mr. Moses Pits,
and Mr. S. Millers.** [1676]. Fol. WP2585.

1676 Proposals for printing a catalogue of books.
Oxford. [1676]. Fol. WP3731.

1676 [WHEELER, MAURICE]. The Oxford almanack
for ... 1676. **Printed at the theater in Oxford.**
[1676]. Brs. WA2679.

1677 ISOCRATES. Orationes duæ. **Oxonii, Excudit
H. H., sumptibus authoris.** 1677. 4°. WI1076.

1677 OXFORD, UNIVERSITY OF. Ordo baccalavreorum
[Oxford], ex officina Lichfieldiana. 1677. Brs.
WO910.

1677 OXFORD, UNIVERSITY OF. Quæstiones in
S. theologia. **Oxonii, ex officina Leonardi
Lichfield.** 1677. Brs. WO952.

1677 OXFORD, UNIVERSITY OF. Theatri Oxoniensis
encaenia ... Julii 6. **Oxon, e theatro Sheldoniana.**
1677. Brs. WO977.

1677 [WHEELER, MAURICE]. The Oxford almanack
for ... 1677. **Printed at the theater in Oxford.**
[1677]. Brs. WA2680.

1678 OXFORD, UNIVERSITY OF. Ordo baccalavreorum
[Oxford], ex officina Leonardi Lichfieldiana. 1678.
Brs. WO911.

1678 OXFORD, UNIVERSITY OF. Quæstiones in
S. theologia. **Oxoni, ex officina Leonardi
Lichfield.** 1678. Brs. WO953.

1678 [WHEELER, MAURICE]. The Oxford almanack for ... 1678. **Printed at the theater in Oxford.** [1678]. Brs. WA2681.

1679 BIBLE. ENGLISH. NEW TESTAMENT. **Printed at the theater in Oxford, to be sold by Moses Pitt, Peter Parker, Thomas Guy and William Leake, London.** 1679. 8°. WB2682.

1679 A brief account of the Pope's pretences. **Oxford.** 1679. Brs. WB4513.

1679 COWLEY, ABRAHAM. Songs for one, two, and three voyces. Second edition. **Oxford, for Ric Davis.** 1679. Fol. WC6691.

1679 OXFORD, UNIVERSITY OF. Quæstiones in S. theologia. **Oxonii, ex officina Leonardi Lichfield.** 1679. Brs. WO954.

1679 OXFORD, UNIVERSITY OF. Theatri Oxoniensis encaenia ... Jul, 11. **[Oxford], e theatro Sheldoniano.** 1679. Brs. WO978.

1679 PIERCE, THOMAS. A seasonable caveat against the dangers. **London, by E. F. for R. Davis, in Oxford.** 1679. 4°. WP2196.

1679 Trial and memoirs of Isaac Darkin. **Oxford.** [1679]. Fol. WT2169.

1679 [WHEELER, MAURICE]. The Oxford almanack for ... 1679. **Printed at the theater in Oxford.** [1679]. Brs. WA2682.

1680 GREENWOOD, DANIEL. Two sermons. **Oxford, Printed.** 1680. 4°. WG1865.

1680 GREGORY, FRANCIS. 'Επιφανια, or a discourse. **Oxford, by L. L. for Thomas Bowman.** 1680. 4°. WG1891A.

1680 OXFORD, UNIVERSITY OF. Ordo baccalavreorum. **Oxonii, ex officina Leonardi Lichfield.** 1680. Brs. WO912.

1680 OXFORD, UNIVERSITY OF. Quæstiones in S. theologia. **Oxonii, ex officina Leonardi Lichfield.** 1680. Brs. WO955.

1680 OXFORD, UNIVERSITY OF. Theatri Oxoniensis encaenia ... Jul. 9. **[Oxford], e theatro Sheldoniano.** 1680. Brs. WO979.

1680 [PARSONS, ROBERT]. A sermon preached ... July 26. 1680. **Oxford, at the Theater for R. Davis & Tho. Bowman.** 1680. 4°. WP570.

1680 [WHEELER, MAURICE]. The Oxford almanack for ... 1680. **Printed at the theater in Oxford.** [1680]. Brs. WA2683.

1681 ANTHONY, M. Animae humanae non præexistunt. Jul. 4. 1681. **[Oxford? 1681].** Brs. WA3481.

1681 BENNION, JOHN. Moses's charge. **Printed at Oxford, to be sold by Francis Dollit.** 1681. 4°. WB1890.

1681 BIBLE. ENGLISH. **Oxford, at the theatre, for T. Guy, London.** 1681. 12°. WB2318.

1681 BURY, ARTHUR. The constant communicant. **Oxford, by Leon. Lichfield, for Stephen Bolton.** 1681. 8°. WB6191.

1681 CHARLES II, king of England. His Majesties most gracious speech to both Houses ... 21st of March, 1680/1. **Oxford, at the theatre.** [1681]. Fol. WC3163.

1681 CYPRIAN, saint. Of the unity of the church. **Printed at the theater in Oxford.** 1681. 4°. WC7714.

1681 DRYDEN, JOHN. The epilogue spoken to the king. **[Oxford, by L. Lichfield, jun.** 1681]. Brs. WD2271.

1681 DUGDALE, Sir WILLIAM. A short view of the late troubles in England. **Oxford, at the theater for M. Pitt, London.** 1681. Fol. WD2492.

1681 The great case put home. **Oxford, for R. Davis, and are to be sold by R. Taylor, London.** 1681. 4°. WG1674.

1681 HAMMOND, HENRY. A paraphrase, and annotations upon all the books of the New Testament. Fifth edition. **For R. Royston and R. Davis in Oxford.** 1681. Fol. WH576.

1681 [HUMFREY, JOHN]. Materials for union. **Printed, and are to be sold in Oxford.** 1681. 4°. WH3685.

1681 JOANNES, Scotus, Erigena. Joannis Scoti Erigenae de divisione naturae. **Oxonii, e Theatro Sheldoniano.** 1681. Fol. WJ747.

1681 LITURGIES. BOOK OF COMMON PRAYER. The book of common prayer. **At the theater in Oxford, to be sold by Moses Pitt, Peter Parker, William Leak, Thomas Guy, London.** 1681. 8°. WB3664.

1681 [NORTHLEIGH, JOHN]. Exercitationes philologicæ tres. **Oxonii, typis, L. L. prostant venales apud J. Crosley.** 1681. 4°. WN1299.

1681 OXFORD, CITY OF. The Oxford list of the names of the knights ... of the Cinque-Ports. **Oxford, by L. Lichfield, for John Starkey.** 1681. Brs. WO857.

1681 OXFORD, UNIVERSITY OF. Ordo baccalavreorum. **Oxonii, ex officina Leonardi Lichfield.** [1681]. Brs. WO913.

1681 OXFORD, UNIVERSITY OF. Quæstiones in S. theologia. **Oxonii, ex officina Leonardi Lichfield.** 1681. Brs. WO956.

1681 OXFORD, UNIVERSITY OF. Theatri Oxoniensis encaenia ... Jul. 8. **[Oxford], e theatro Sheldoniano.** 1681. Brs. WO980.

1681 PITT, MOSES. The English atlas. Volume II. **Oxford, at the theater, for Moses Pitt, London.** 1681. Fol. WP2306A.

1681 PRIDEAUX, JOHN, bp. A synopsis of councels. **Oxford, by Leonard Lichfield, for R. Davis.** 1681. 4°. WP3437.

1681 [WHEELER, MAURICE]. The Oxford almanack for ... 1681. **Printed at the theater in Oxford.** [1681]. Brs. WA2684.

1681 WILLIAMS, Sir WILLIAM. The speech of. **Oxford; by Leo. Lichfield, for Gabriel Kunholt, London.** 1681. Fol. WW2782.

1681 [WRIGHT, WILLIAM]. The Oxford alderman's speech to the D. of M. **[Oxford?** 1681]. Brs. WW3716.

1682 [ALLESTREE, RICHARD]. The lively oracles. **Oxford.** 1682. 12°. WA1153.

1682 ATHENAGORAS. Τον ... Αθεναγορου ... Opera. **Oxonii, e theatro Sheldoniano.** 1682. Sixes. WA4111.

1682 BIBLE. ENGLISH. **Oxford, at the theater, to be sold by Ann Leake, London.** 1682. Fol. WB2324.

1682 BIBLE. ENGLISH. **Printed at ye theater in Oxford, sold by P. Parker, [London.** 1682]. 12°. WB2326.

1682 BIBLE. ENGLISH. **Printed at ye theater in Oxford, sold by M. Pitt.** [1682]. 4°. WB2327.

1682 BIBLE. ENGLISH. **Oxford, at the theatre for T. Guy, London.** 1682. 8°. WB2328.

1682 BIBLE. ENGLISH. NEW TESTAMENT. **Oxford, at the theater, to be sold by Moses Pitt, Peter Parker, William Leake, Thomas Guy, London.** 1682. Fol. WB2686.

1682 BIBLE. ENGLISH. PSALMS. **Printed at the theater in Oxford, and are to be sold by Moses Pitt, Peter Parker, William Leake, Thomas Guy, London.** 1682. Fol. WB2547.

1682 BIBLE. ENGLISH. PSALMS. **Printed at the theater in Oxford, to be sold by Moses Pitt, Peter Parker, Ann Leake, Thomas Guy, London.** 1682. 4°. WB2548.

1682 BIBLE. ENGLISH. PSALMS. **Oxford, at the theater, to be sold by Peter Parker, London.** 1682. 8°. WB2549.

1682 BOYLE, ROBERT. A continvation of nevv experiments, the second part. **By Miles Flesher, for Richard Davis, in Oxford.** 1682. 4°. WB3935.

1682 BUTLER, CHARLES. Monarchia fœminarum. **Oxon typis Lichfieldianis.** 1682. 8°. WB6263.

1682 CLARK, GILBERT. Astronomica specimina. **Typis Milonis Flesher, veneunt apud Ric. Davis, Oxoniensem.** 1682. 8°. WC446.

1682 CYPRIAN, saint. Opera. **Oxonii, e theatro Sheldoniano.** 1682. Fol. WC7711.

1682 DODWELL, HENRY. Dissertationes Cyprianicæ. [**Oxon.** 1682]. Fol. WD1809.

1682 DRYDEN, JOHN. Absalon et Achitophel.Carmine Latino heroico. **Oxon, typis Lichfieldianis prostant apud Ricardum Davis.** 1682. 4°. WD2221.

1682 DRYDEN, JOHN. Absalon et Achitophel. Poema Latino ... carmine donatum. **Oxon, typis Lichfieldianis, prostant apud Johannem Crosley.** 1682. 4°. WD2222.

1682 DUGDALE, Sir WILLIAM. The antient usage. **Oxford, at the theater, for Rich. Davis.** 1682. 8°. WD2477.

1682 DUGDALE, Sir WILLIAM. The antient usage. Second edition. **Oxford, at the theater for Moses Pitt, and Samuel Smith.** 1682. 12°. WD2478.

1682 EUSEBIUS PAMPHILI, bp. A meditation of life and death. **Oxford, by L. L. for Tho. Fickus.** 1682. 4°. WE3425.

1682 [HARRISON, ROBERT]. A strange relation of the suddain and violent tempest. **For Richard Sherlock in Oxford.** 1682. 4°. WH908.

1682 HIEROCLES. Hierocles upon the golden verses of Pythagoras. **By M. Flesher, for Thomas Fickus, in Oxford.** 1682. 8°. WH1939.

1682 LITURGIES. BOOK OF COMMON PRAYER. Book of common prayer. **Oxford, sold by M. Pitt, London.** [1682?]. 4°. WB3666.

1682 LITURGIES. BOOK OF COMMON PRAYER. Book of common prayer. **Oxford, at the theater, to be sold by Ann Leake, London.** 1682. Fol. WB3667.

1682 LITURGIES. BOOK OF COMMON PRAYER. Book of common prayer. **Printed at the theater in Oxford, to be sold by Peter Parker, London.** 1682. Fol. WB3668.

1682 MANNINGHAM, THOMAS, bp. Praise and adoration. **London: for William Crooke, and William Cadman, also sold by R. Davis in Oxford.** 1682. 4°. WM497.

1682 Mysogynus: or, a satyr upon women. **London, for John Langly, in Oxford.** 1682. 4°. WM3178.

1682 NIEREMBERG, JUAN. EUSEBIO. A meditation of life and death. **Oxford, by L. L., for Tho. Fickus.** 1682. 8°. WN1150.

1682 OXFORD, UNIVERSITY OF. Ordo baccalavreorum. **Oxonii, ex officina Leonardi Lichfield.** [1682]. Brs. WO914.

1682 OXFORD, UNIVERSITY OF. Parecbolæ sive excerpta è corpore statutorum. **Oxoniæ, e theatro Sheldoniano.** 1682. 8°. WO931.

1682 OXFORD, UNIVERSITY OF. Quæstiones in S. theologia. **Oxonii, ex officina Leonardi Lichfield.** 1682. Brs. WO957.

1682 OXFORD, UNIVERSITY OF. Statuta selecta. **Oxon.** 1682. 8°. WO968.

1682 OXFORD, UNIVERSITY OF. Theatri Oxoniensis encaenia ... Jul 7. [**Oxford**], e theatro Sheldoniano. 1682. Brs. WO981.

1682 PENTON, STEPHEN. A discourse concerning the worship of God. **By J. G. to be sold by James Good, in Oxon.** 1682. 8°. WP1438.

1682 PITT, MOSES. The English atlas. Volume IV. **Oxford, at the Theater, for Moses Pitt, London.** 1682. Fol. WP2306C.

1682 PRIDEAUX, MATHIAS. An easy and compendious introdvction for reading. Sixth edition. **Printed at Oxford, by Leon. Lichfield, and are to be sold by Richard Davis.** 1682. 4°. WP3445.

1682 PTELOMAEUS, CLAUDIUS ... Αρμονικων ... harmonicorum libri tres. **Oxonii, e Theatro Sheldoniano.** 1682. 4°. WP4149.

1682 [WALKER, OBADIAH]. Some instructions concerning the art of oratory. Second edition. **Oxford, by L. Lichfield for the author, to be sold by Jo. Crosley.** 1682. 8°. WW411.

1682 [WALKER, OBADIAH]. Some instructions concerning the art of oratory. "Second edition". **Oxford, by L. Lichfield for T. A. and are to be sold by Ed. Forrest.** 1682. 8°. WW412.

1682 [WHEELER, MAURICE]. The Oxford almanack for ... 1682. **Printed at the theater in Oxford.** [1682]. Brs. WA2685.

1682 WILSON, THOMAS. A sermon on the martyrdom. **By Miles Flesher, for Richard Davis in Oxford.** 1682. 4°. WW2937A.

1683 ANACREON. Anacreon done into English. **Oxford, by L. Lichfield, for Anthony Stephens.** 1683. 8°. WA3046.

1683 BIBLE. ENGLISH. **Oxford, at the theater.** 1683. 4°. WB2324.

1683 BURY, ARTHUR. The constant communicant. **Oxford, by L. Lichfield, to be sold by Henry Bonwick.** 1683. 8°. WB6192.

1683 BURY, ARTHUR. Not feare, but love. **Oxford, by L. Lichfield.** 1683. 8°. WB6203.

1683 CHURCH OF ENGLAND. Certain sermons or homilies. **Oxford, at the theatre, and are to be sold by Thomas Guy, London.** 1683. 12°. WC4091H.

1683 CLEMENS, TITUS FLAVIUS, Alexandria. Κλημεγτος Λογος. liber. **Oxoniæ, e theatro Sheldoniano.** 1683. 12°. WC4628.

1683 DOWELL, JOHN. The Leviathan heretical. **Oxon, by L. Lichfield, to be sold by A. Stephens.** 1683. Sixes. WD2056.

1683 ELLIS, TOBIAS. The Kingdom of God opened. **Oxford, by Leon. Lichfield, to be sold by Francis Oxlad and Robert Gibs.** 1683. 8°. WE609.

1683 ERASMUS, DESIDERIUS. Witt against wisdom. **Oxford, by L. Lichfield, for Anthony Stephens.** 1683. 8°. WE3215.

1683 HAMMOND, HENRY. A paraphrase and annotations upon the books of the Psalms. Second edition. **By T. Newcomb and M. Flesher, for Richard Royston, and Richard Davis, in Oxford.** 1683. Fol. WH580.

1683 [HOY, THOMAS]. Agathocles the Sicilian usurper. **For John Crosley in Oxford.** 1683. Fol. WH3199[A].

1683 JEMMAT, SAMUEL. A sermon preached ... March the nineteenth, 1682/3. **Oxford, by Leonard Lichfield, for George Teonge, in Warwick.** 1683. 4°. WJ550.

1683 KUHLMANN, QUIRIN. Quinarius sacrum lapidum. **Londoni, Oxoniique, pro Authore excudebatur.** 1683. 8°. WK756.

1683 KUHLMANN, QUIRIN. His quinary of slingstones. **London and Oxford, for the Author.** 1683. 8°. WK757.

1683 LITURGIES. BOOK OF COMMON PRAYER. Book of common prayer. **Oxford, at the theatre, sold by Thomas Guy, London.** 1683. Fol. WB3672.

1683 LITURGIES. BOOK OF COMMON PRAYER. Book of common prayer. **Oxford, for Moses Pitt.** [1683?]. Fol. WB3671.

1683 [MARSHALL, THOMAS]. The catechism set forth. Fifth edition. **At the Theater in Oxford.** 1683. 8°. WM802.

1683 OXFORD, UNIVERSITY OF. The judgment and decree of the ... July 21, 1683. **[Oxford], at the theater.** 1683. Fol. WO891.

1683 OXFORD, UNIVERSITY OF. Judicium & decretum ... Jul. 21, An. 1683. **[Oxford], e theatro Sheldoniano.** 1683. Fol. WO893.

1683 OXFORD, UNIVERSITY OF. Ordo baccalavreorum. **Oxonii, ex officina Leonardi Lichfield.** [1683]. Brs. WO915.

1683 OXFORD, UNIVERSITY OF. Quæstiones in S. theologia. **Oxonii, ex officina Leonardi Lichfield.** 1683. Brs. WO958.

1683 OXFORD, UNIVERSITY OF. Theatri Oxoniensis encaenia ... Jul. 6. **[Oxford], e theatro Sheldoniano.** 1683. Brs. WO982.

1683 PIERCE, THOMAS. Pacificatorium orthodoxae. **Londini, typis Milonis Flesher, prostat apud Ric. Davis, Oxoniensem.** 1683. 8°. WP2187.

1683 PITT, MOSES. The English atlas. Volume III. **Oxford, at the Theater, for Moses Pitt, London.** 1683. Fol. WP2306B.

1683 RODERICK, RICHARD. A sermon preached ... December the 19th 1682. **London, by M. Flesher for Henry Clements, in Oxford.** 1683. 4°. WR1770.

1683 [WALKER, OBADIAH]. Of education especially of young gentlemen. Fourth edition. **Oxford, for A. Curteyne.** 1683. 12°. WW402.

1683 WALLIS, JOHN. A proposal about printing a treatise of algebra. **[Oxford. 1683].** Brs. WW600.

1683 [WHEELER, MAURICE]. The Oxford almanack for ... 1683. **Printed at the theater in Oxford.** [1683]. Brs. WA2686.

1683 [WHEELER, MAURICE]. The Oxford almanack for ... 1684. **Printed at the theater in Oxford.** [1683]. Brs. WA2687.

1684 [ALLESTREE, RICHARD]. Forty sermons. **Printed at the theater in Oxford and in London, for R. Scott, G. Wells, T. Sawbridge, R. Bentley.** 1684. 2 vols. Fol. WA1114.

1684 [ALLESTREE, RICHARD]. The works. **Printed at the theater in Oxford, and in London, by Roger Norton, for George Pawlett.** 1687. 2 vols. Fol. WA1082.

1684 BIBLE. ENGLISH. **Oxford, at the theater, sold by Thomas Guy, London.** 1684. Fol. WB2338.

1684 BIBLE. ENGLISH. PSALMS. The psalter or psalms. Second edition. **Oxford by L. Litchfield, for Jo. Crosley.** 1684. 8°. WB2554.

1684 BREREWOOD, EDWARD. Elementa logicae. **Excudebat Milo Flesher, impensis Ric. Davis, Oxoniensis.** 1684. 12°. WB4377.

1684 CORBET, JOHN. The epistle congratulatory of Lysimachus Nicanor. **Oxford, by Leon Lichfield, to be sold by Tho. Fickus.** 1684. 4°. WC6247.

1684 COSIN, RICHARD. Ecclesiæ Anglicanæ politeia. **Oxonii, excudebat L. Lichfield, impensis Tho. Fickus, & Joh. Howel.** 1684. Fol. WC6365.

1684 DODWELL, HENRY. Dissertationes Cyprianicæ. **Oxoniæ, e theatro Sheldoniano.** 1684. 8°. WD1810.

1684 ELLIS, TOBIAS. The poors English spelling book. **Oxford, by Leon. Lichfield, for the author.** 1684. 4°. WE609A.

1684 [FULMAN, WILLIAM]. Rerium Anglicarum Scriptores veteres. **Oxoniæ, e theatro Sheldoniano.** 1684-91. 3 vols. Fol. WF2525.

1684 HAMMOND, HENRY. The vvorkes of. Fourth volume. **By T. Newcomb and M. Flesher, for Richard Royston, and Richard Davis, in Oxford.** 1684. Fol. WH507.

1684 HAMMOND, HENRY. The vvorkes of. Second volume. **For R. Royston; and R. Davis, in Oxford.** 1684. Fol. WH509.

1684 HAMMOND, HENRY. A practicall catechisme. "Twelfth" edition. **By M. Flesher, for Richard Davis, in Oxford.** 1684. 8°. WH594.

1684 HODY, HUMFREY. Contra historiam Aristeae. **Oxonii, typis Leon. Lichfield, impensis Ant. Stephens.** 1684. 8°. WH2340.

1684 JOCELINE, ELIZABETH The mother's legacy. **Oxford, at the Theater, and are to sold by Jo. Wilmot.** 1684. 8°. WJ756.

1684 JUSTINUS, MARCUS JUNIANUS. Iustini historiarum ex Trogo Pompeio. **[Oxford], e teatro Sheldoniano.** 1684. 12°. WJ1269.

1684 LITURGIES. BOOK OF COMMON PRAYER. Book of common prayer. **Printed at the theatre in Oxford, to be sold by Thomas Guy, London.** 1684. 12°. WB3674.

1684 [MARSHALL, THOMAS]. The catechism set forth. Sixth edition. **At the Theater in Oxford.** 1684. 8°. WM803.

1684 [NEPOS, CORNELIUS]. The lives of illustrious men. **Oxon, for Hen. Crultenden, to be sold by Anth. Stephens.** 1684. 8°. WN428.

1684 OXFORD, UNIVERSITY OF. Ordo baccalavreorum. **Oxonii, ex officina Leonardi Lichfield.** [1684]. Brs. WO916.

1684   OXFORD, UNIVERSITY OF. Quaestiones in
        S. theologia. **Oxonii, ex officina Leonardi**
        Lichfield. 1684. Brs. WO959.

1684   OXFORD, UNIVERSITY OF. Statuta legenda in
        admissione ... baccalaureorum in medicina.
        [**Oxford.** 1684]. Brs. WO963.

1684   OXFORD, UNIVERSITY OF. Statuta legenda in
        admissione ... baccalaureorum in theologia.
        [**Oxford.** 1684]. Brs. WO964.

1684   OXFORD, UNIVERSITY OF. Statuta legenda in
        admissione baccalaureorum in theologia.
        [**Oxford.** 1684]. Brs. WO965

1684   OXFORD, UNIVERSITY OF. Theatri Oxoniensis
        encaenia ... Jul 11. [**Oxford**], **e theatro**
        Sheldoniano. 1684. Brs. WO983.

1684   PLOT, ROBERT. De origine fontium. **Oxonii,**
        for H. Clements. 1684. 8°. WP2582.

1684   [PUDSEY, Sir GEORGE]. The speech of ...
        eighth day of January 1683/4. **London, for Anthony**
        Stephens, Oxford, and are to be sold by Thomas
        Sawbridge. 1684. Fol. WP4166.

1684   [PUDSEY, Sir GEORGE]. The speech of ...
        eighth day of January 1683/4. **Oxon for Anthony**
        Stephens. 1684. Fol. WP4167.

1684   RODERICK, RICHARD. A sermon preached
        August the 19th, 1684. **London, by Miles Flesher,**
        for Henry Clements in Oxford: and sold by Walter
        Davis in London. 1684. 4°. WR1771.

1684   THEOCRITUS. The idylliums of Theocritus.
        Oxford: for Anthony Stephens, and are to be sold
        in London by Abel Swalle. 1684. 8°. WT854.

1684   THEOCRITUS. The idylliums of Theocritus.
        Oxford, by L. Lichfield, for Anthony Stephens.
        1684. 8°. WT855.

1684   THEOPHILUS, abp. Του εν Θεοφιλου ... ad
        autolycum. **Oxonii, e Theatro Sheldoniano.** 1684.
        12°. WT859.

1684   [WALKER, OBADIAH]. A paraphrase and annota-
        tions upon all the epistles of Saint Paul. **Oxford,**
        for J. Wilmot. 1684. 8°. WW406.

1684   WALLIS, JOHN. Cono-cuneus or, the ship-
        wright's circular vvedge. **By John Playford, for**
        Richard Davis, in Oxford. 1684. Fol. WW565.

1684   WALLIS, JOHN. The life of faith. **By James**
        Rawlins, for Thomas Parkhurst and are to be sold
        by Amos Curteine, in Oxford. 1684. 4°.
        WW592.

1684   WALLIS, JOHN. A treatise of angular sections.
        By John Playford, for Richard Davis, in Oxford.
        1684. Fol. WW614.

1684   [WHEELER, MAURICE]. The Oxford almanack
        for ... 1685. **Printed at the theater in Oxford.**
        [1684]. Brs. WA2688.

1684   WHITBY, DANIEL. Ethices compendium. **Oxonii,**
        typis Lichfieldianis, prostat apud Joannem Langley.
        1684. 8°. WW1726.

1684   [WOOD, ANTHONY]. Historia et antiquitates uni-
        versitatis Oxoniensis. **Oxonii, e theatro**
        Sheldoniano. 1684. Fol. WW3386.

1685   [ALLESTREE, RICHARD]. A sermon preach'd
        ... 26th. of July 1685. **Oxford, for Henry**
        Clements, and sold by Joseph Hindmarsh, London.
        1685. 4°. WA1081.

1685   BARNABAS, saint. PP. App. Barnabae et Hermæ
        epistola. **Oxoniæ, e theatro Sheldoniano.** 1685.
        12°. WB849.

1685   BIBLE. ENGLISH. **Oxford, printed at the theater.**
        1685. Fol. WB2341.

1685   BIBLE. ENGLISH. **Printed at the theater in**
        Oxford, to be sold by Thomas Guy, London.
        1685. 12°. WB2342.

1685   BIBLE. ENGLISH. PSALMS. The psalter or
        psalms. Third edition. **Oxford.** 1685. 8°. WB2556.

1685   BIBLE. ENGLISH. PSALMS. The whole book of
        psalms. **Oxford, at the theatre.** 1685. 12°.
        WB2557.

1685   Britain reviv'd in a panegyrick to William and
        Mary. **For N. Cox in Oxon.** [1685]. Brs.
        WB4803.

1685   BULL, GEORGE, bp. Defensio fidei Nicaenae.
        Oxonii, e theatro Sheldoniano. 1685. 4°.
        WB5414.

1685   CASWELL, JOHN. A brief (but full) account of
        the doctrine of trigonometry. **By John Playford,**
        for Richard Davis, in Oxford. 1685. Fol. WC1252.

1685   CAVE, JOHN. Daphnis. A pastoral elegy.
        Oxford, by Leonard Lichfield, for the author.
        1685. Brs. WC1581.

1685   A century of sacred disticks. **Oxford.** 1685. 8°.
        WC1672.

1685   DAVIS, RICHARD. On Thursday the 26. of ...
        November, 1685. at the Auction-House; ... part
        of the stock of Mr. Richard Davis. [**Oxford**].
        1685. Fol. WD431.

1685   DERHAM, SAMUEL. Hydrologia philosophica; or.
        Oxford, by L. Lichfield for J. Howell. 1685. 8°.
        WD1098.

1685   EUCLID. The elements of Euclid. **Oxford, by**
        L. Lichfield for Anthony Stephens. 1685. 8°.
        WE3400.

1685   FREZER, AUGUSTINE. The divine original and
        the supreme dignity of kings. **Oxford, by**
        L. Lichfield, and are to be sold by Nicholas Cox.
        1685. 4°. WF2203.

1685   G[RIFFITH], G[EORGE], bp. Gueddist-arglwydd
        wedi ei hegluro. **Printiedig yn y theater yn**
        Rhydychen. 1685. 4°. WG1997.

1685   HODY, HUMFREY. Contra historiam Aristeæ.
        Oxonii, typis Leon. Lichfield prostant venales
        Londini apud Sam. Smith. 1685. 8°. WH2341.

1685   IRONSIDE, GIEBERT, bp. A sermon preached ...
        November 23. 1684. **Oxford, by Leonard Lichfield,**
        for James Good. 1685. 4°. WI1049.

1685   LITURGIES. BOOK OF COMMON PRAYER.
        Book of common prayer. **Printed at the theater**
        in Oxford, to be sold by Thomas Guy, London.
        1685. 12°. WB3676.

1685   MAYOW, JOHN. Ραχιτιδολογια or a tract.
        Oxford, by L. L. for Th. Fickus. 1685. 12°.
        WM1534.

1685   Miscellany poems and translations. **London, for**
        Anthony Stephens, in Oxford. 1685. 8°. WM2232.

1685   MUNDY, HENRY. Βιοχρηστολογια seu commen-
        tairii de aere vitali. **Oxoniae.** 1685. 12°.
        WM3078.

1685   NORRIS, JOHN. A sermon preach'd ... March
        29. 1685. **Oxford, by Leonard Lichfield, for**
        Thomas Fickus. 1685. 4°. WN1269.

1685   ORIGENES. Libellus de oratione. **Oxoniae.**
        1685. 12°. WO428.

1685   OXFORD, UNIVERSITY OF. Comitia habita in
        universitate Oxoniensi ... Ap. 23. [**Oxford**], **e**
        theatro Sheldoniano. 1685. Brs. WO866.

1685 OXFORD, UNIVERSITY OF. Ordo baccalavreorum. **Oxonii, ex officina Leonardi Lichfield.** [1685]. Brs. WO917.

1685 OXFORD, UNIVERSITY OF. Pietas universitatis Oxoniensis ... Caroli II. **Oxonii, e theatro Sheldoniano.** 1685. Fol. WO936.

1685 OXFORD, UNIVERSITY OF. Supplex recognitio et gratulatio solennis. **Oxonii, e theatro Sheldoniano.** 1685. Fol. WO970.

1685 OXFORD, UNIVERSITY OF. To the right worship- ful the heads of the respective colleges ... You are desired to signify. [**Oxford**]. 1685. Brs. WO988.

1685 PEMBLE, WILLIAM. A briefe introduction to geography. **Oxford, by Leonard Lichfield for Edward Forrest.** 1685. 4°. WP1113.

1685 PIERCE, THOMAS. Pacificatorium orthodoxae. Second edition. **Londini, typis S. Roycroft, impensis R. Davis Oxonii, & R. Clavell Londini.** 1685. 8°. WP2188.

1685 A Pindarick ode upon the death of his late Sacred Majesty King Charles the second. **Oxford, by Leonard Lichfield, for Anthony Stephens.** 1685. Fol. WP2257.

1685 PLINY, the younger. An address of thanks. **London, by M. Flesher, for Tho. Fickus, in Oxford.** 1685. 8°. WP2573.

1685 PLOT, ROBERT. De origine fontium. **Oxonii, e Theatro Sheldoniano 1685. Prostant apud Hen. Clements.** 8°. WP2583.

1685 POCOCKE, EDWARD. A commentary of the prophecy of Hosea. **Oxford, at the Theater.** 1685. Fol. WP2660.

1685 ROUS, FRANCIS. Archeologiæ Atticæ. Ninth edition. **London, by Miles Flesher, for Richard Davis, and to be sold by Henry Clements, in Oxford.** 1685. 4°. WR2041.

1685 WALLIS, JOHN. A treatise of algebra. **By John Playford, for Richard Davis, in Oxford.** 1685. Fol. WW613.

1685 WASE, CHRISTOPHER. Stricturae nonianæ. **Oxonii, excudebat L. Lichfield.** 1685. 4°. WW1024.

1685 [WOODHEAD, ABRAHAM]. An historical narra- tion of the life and death of Our Lord Jesus Christ. **Printed at the theater in Oxford.** 1685. Fol. WW3448.

1686 BIBLE, ENGLISH. **Oxford, at the theatre, for P. Parker, London.** 1686. 4°. WB2344.

1686 BIBLE, ENGLISH. **Oxford, at the theatre, for T. Guy in London.** 1686. 12°. WB2345.

1686 [CHAMBERLAYNE, EDWARD]. Angliæ notitia, sive. **Oxonii, typis Leon Lichfield, impensis Henric. Clements.** 1686. 12° in sixes. WC1837.

1686 DAVIS, RICHARD. Catalogus variorum in quavis lingua & facultate insignium. Pars secunda. **Oxford.** 4 October, 1686. Fol. WD427.

1686 DICKENSON, EDMUND. Epistola. **Oxoniae, e theatro Sheldoniano.** 1686. 8°. WD1386.

1686 LITURGIES. BOOK OF COMMON PRAYER. Book of Common prayer. **Printed at the theatre in Oxford, to be sold by Peter Parker, London.** 1686. 12°. WB3677.

1686 LITURGIES. BOOK OF COMMON PRAYER. Book of common prayer. **Oxford.** 1686. 8°. WB3678.

1686 ORIGENES ... Περι ευχης συνταγμα. Εν τη Oxoniae, Θεατρω Σκηλδηνου. 1686. 8°. WO429.

1686 OXFORD, UNIVERSITY OF. Ordo baccalavreorum. **Oxonii, ex officina Leonardi Lichfield.** [1686]. Brs. WO918.

1686 PLINY, the younger. An address of thanks. **London, for Tho. Fickus and W. Hart, in Oxford.** 1686. 8°. WP2575.

1686 PLINY, the younger. C Plinii Secundi epistolae et Panegyricus. **Oxonii, e Theatro Sheldoniano.** 1686. 8°. WP2578.

1686 RANDOLPH, BERNARD. The present state of the Morea. **Printed at Oxford.** 1686. 4°. WR236.

1686 [WHEELER, MAURICE]. The Oxford almanack for ... 1686. **Printed at the theater in Oxford.** [1686]. Brs. WA2689.

1686 WILLUGHBY, FRANCIS. De historia piscium. **Oxonii, e theatro Sheldoniano.** 1686. Fol. WW2877.

1686 WILLUGHBY, FRANCIS. Ichthyographia. **Oxonii.** 1686. Fol. WW2878.

1687 [ALDRICH, HENRY]. A reply to two discourses. Lately printed at Oxford. **Oxford, at the theater.** 1687. 4°. WA899.

1687 [ALLESTREE, RICHARD]. The works. Second edition. **Printed at the theater in Oxford, and in London, by Roger Norton for George Pawlett.** 1687. Fol. WA1083.

1687 AMYDENUS, THEODORUS. Pietas romana et parisiensis, or, a faithful relation. **Printed at Oxford.** 1687. 4°. WA3033.

1687 [ATTERBURY, FRANCIS, bp]. An answer to some considerations on the spirit of Martin Luther. **Oxford, at the theater.** 1687. Fol. WA4146.

1687 BIBLE. ENGLISH. **Oxford, at the theatre, for T. Guy, London.** 1687. 4°. WB2347.

1687 Catalogus librorum in omni facultate ... insignium. [**Oxford?** 1687]. 4°. WC1439.

1687 Catalogus librorum tam antiquorum quam recentium. **Oxford.** Feb. 28, 1686/7. 4°. WC1448.

1687 [COMBER, THOMAS]. The plausible arguments of a Romish priest answered. **For R. Clavell, to be sold by John Crosly in Oxford.** 1687. 8°. WC5482.

1687 HELWICH, CHRISTOPHER. The historical and chronological theatre of. **By M. Flesher, for George West and John Crosley, in Oxford.** 1687. Fol. WH1411.

1687 [HOWELL, WILLIAM]. The Common-prayer-book the best companion. Second edition. **Oxford, at the theater, for John Howell.** 1687. 8°. WH3131.

1687 [HOWELL, WILLIAM]. The Common-prayer-book the best companion. Third edition. **Oxford, at the theater, for John Howell.** 1687. 8°. WH3131A.

1687 LITURGIES. BOOK OF COMMON PRAYER. Book of common prayer. **Printed at the theater in Oxford, to be sold by Peter Parker, London.** 1687. 12°. WB3681.

1687 MAYOW, JOHN. The mothers family physician. **Oxford, by L. Lichfield for J. Cox.** 1687. 12°. WM1533.

1687 [NEPOS, CORNELIUS]. Cornelii Nepotis vitæ excellentium imperatorum. **Oxonii, e theatro Sheldoniano.** 1687. 12°. WN432.

1687 NORRIS, JOHN. A collection of miscellanies. **Oxford, at the Theater for John Crosley.** 1687. 8°. WN1248.

1687 OXFORD, UNIVERSITY OF. Advertisement from the delegates of convocation for His Majesties reception. [**Oxford.** 1687]. Brs. WO860.

1687 OXFORD, UNIVERSITY OF. Doctors in all faculty's appointed to meet the king. [**Oxford.** 1687]. Brs. WO874.

1687 OXFORD, UNIVERSITY OF. Ordo baccalavreorum. **Oxonii ex officina Leonardi Lichfield.** [1687]. Brs. WO919.

1687 [PUDSEY, Sir GEORGE]. The speech of ... Sept. 3. 1687. **Oxon., by Henry Cruttenden.** 1687. Fol. WP4170.

1687 RANDOLPH, BERNARD. The present state of the islands in the archipelago. **Printed at the Theater in Oxford.** 1687. 4°. WR234.

1687 RANDOLPH, BERNARD. The present state of the Morea. **Oxford, at the theater** [by J. Venn]. 1687. 4°. WR237.

1687 [WALKER, OBADIAH]. Of education especially of young gentlemen. Fifth edition. **Oxford, at the theater for Amos Curteyne.** 1687. 12°. WW403.

1687 WALLIS, JOHN. Institutio logicae. **Oxonii, e theatro Sheldoniano.** 1687. **Prostant apud Amos Curteyne.** 8°. WW590.

1687 WASE, CHRISTOPHER. Chr. Wasi Senarius, sive de legibus. **Oxonii, e theatro Sheldoniano.** 1687. 4°. WW1023.

1687 [WHEELER, MAURICE]. The Oxford almanack for ... 1687. **Printed at the theater in Oxford.** [1687]. Brs. WA2690.

1687 [WOODHEAD, ABRAHAM]. The Catholicks defence, for their adoration. **At Oxford, printed.** 1687. 4°. WW3439.

1687 [WOODHEAD, ABRAHAM]. Church-government. Part V. **Printed at Oxford.** 1687. 4°. WW3440.

1687 [WOODHEAD, ABRAHAM]. A discourse concerning the celibacy of the clergy. **At Oxford, printed.** 1687. 4°. WW3445.

1687 [WOODHEAD, ABRAHAM]. Pietas Romana et Parisiensis. **Oxford.** 1687. 8°. WW3450.

1687 [WOODHEAD, ABRAHAM]. Two discourses concerning the adoration. **At Oxford, printed.** 1687. 4°. WW3459.

1687 [WOODHEAD, ABRAHAM]. Two discourses, the first, concerning the spirit of Martin Luther. **Printed at Oxford.** 1687. 4°. WW3460.

1688 An account of the late persecution of the Protestants in the vallys of Piemont. **Oxford, at the theatre for John Crosley.** 1688. 4°. WA315.

1688 [ALDRICH, HENRY]. A vindication of the Oxford reply. [**Oxford.** 1688]. 4°. WA901.

1688 [ALLESTREE, RICHARD]. The lively oracles. "Third" edition. **Printed at the theatre in Oxford to be sold by George Monke, and William Ewrey.** 1688. 8°. WA1154.

1688 An answer to the city ministers letter from his country friend. [**Oxford?**] printed. 1688. Fol. WA3400.

1688 ARISTARCHUS, SAMIUS. Ἀριστάρχου Ἐαμιου περι μεγε θων ... De magnitidinibus. **Oxoniae, e theatro Sheldoniano.** 1688. 8°. WA3681.

1688 BERNARD, EDWARD. Edvardi Bernardi de mensuris et ponderibus. **Oxoniae, e theatro Sheldoniano.** 1688. 8°. WB1987.

1688 BIBLE. ENGLISH. **Oxford, at the theater, to be sold by Thomas Guy, London.** 1688. Fol. WB2350.

1688 BIBLE. ENGLISH. **Printed at the theater in Oxford, to be sold by Thomas Guy, London.** 1688. 12°. WB2351.

1688 BROWN, THOMAS. Heraclitus ridens redivivus. Second edition. **Oxford; printed.** 1688. 4°. WB5060.

1688 BULL, GEORGE, bp. Defensio fidei Nicaenae. Second edition. **Oxonii, e theatro Sheldoniano.** 1688. 4°. WB5415.

1688 CHURCH OF ENGLAND. Articles to be enquired of ... Sarum. **Oxford, printed.** 168[8?]. 4°. WC4084B.

1688 [COMBER, THOMAS]. The plausible arguments of a Romish priest answered. **For R. Clavell, to be sold by John Crosly in Oxford.** 1688. 8°. WC5483.

1688 CUDWORTH, JOHN. Fides ecclesiae Anglicanae. **Oxonii, typis Sheldonianis, impensis Hen. Clements.** 1688. 4°. WC7464.

1688 DAVIS, RICHARD. Catalogus variorum in quavis lingua & facultate insignium. Pars tertia. **Oxford.** June 25: 1688. Fol. WD428.

1688 [DEANE, THOMAS]. The religion of Mar. Luther. **Oxon, by Henry Cruttenden.** 1688. 4°. WD499.

1688 [GRASCOMBE, SAMUEL]. The resolution of a case of conscience. [**Oxford.** 1688]. 4°. WG1577.

1688 [HARRINGTON, JAMES]. Some reflexions upon a treatise call'd Pietas romana. **Oxford, at the theater.** 1688. 4°. WH834.

1688 [HARRINGTON, JAMES]. A vindication of Protestant charity. **Oxford.** 1688. 4°. WH836.

1688 HELLIER, HENRY. A sermon preached ... December 4, 1687. **Oxford, at theater for Richard Chiswell.** 1688. 4°. WH1380.

1688 HELLIER, HENRY. A sermon preached ... December 4, 1687. **Oxford, at the theater for John Crosley.** 1688. 4°. WH1380A.

1688 LITURGIES. BOOK OF COMMON PRAYER. Book of common prayer. **Oxford, at the theater, to be sold by Thomas Guy, London.** 1688. Fol. WB3683.

1688 A new litany for the holy time of Lent. **Oxford, by H. Cruttenden.** [c1688]. Brs. WN655.

1688 NORRIS, JOHN. The theory and regulation of love. **Oxford, at the theatre for Hen. Clements.** 1688. 8°. WN1272.

1688 OXFORD, UNIVERSITY OF. At a meeting of the heads of houses. Mar. 22. 1688. Whereas the gowns. [**Oxford.** 1688]. Brs. WO861.

1688 OXFORD, UNIVERSITY OF. Ordo baccalavreorum. **Oxonii, ex officina Leonardi Lichfield.** [1688]. WO920.

1688 OXFORD, UNIVERSITY OF. The prices of provision, appointed by the rev. G. Fronsyde. [**Oxford.** 1688?]. Brs. WO939.

1688 OXFORD, UNIVERSITY OF. Strenae natalitiae academiae Oxoniensis. **Oxonii, e theatro Sheldoniano.** 1688. Fol. WO969.

1688 PARKER, GEORGE. A treatise of japanning. **Oxford, printed for, and sold by the authors, George Parker in Oxford; or by John Stalker, London.** 1688. Fol. WP390.

1688 RIDLEY, NICHOLAS, bp. An account of a disputation. **Oxford, at the Theater.** 1688. 4°. WR1451.

1688 [TULLY, GEORGE]. An answer to A discourse concerning the celibacy of the clergy. **Oxford, at the theater, for Richard Chiswell.** 1688. 4°. WT3235.

1688 Twenty-one conclusions further demonstrating the schism. **Oxon. H. Cruttenden.** 1688. 4°. WT3413.

1688 [WALKER, OBADIAH]. Five short treatises. [**Oxford.** 1688]. 4°. WW396A.

1688 [WALKER, OBADIAH]. Of faith necessary to salvation. **Oxford, printed.** 1688. 4°. WW404B.

1688 [WHEELER, MAURICE]. The Oxford almanack for ... 1688. **Printed at the theater in Oxford.** [1688]. Brs. WA2691.

1688 [WOODHEAD, ABRAHAM]. A compendious discourse on the Eucharist. **Oxford, printed.** 1688. 4°. WW3440A.

1688 [WOODHEAD, ABRAHAM]. Motives to holy living. **Oxford, printed.** 1688. 4°. WW3449.

1689 [ALLESTREE, RICHARD]. The art of contentment. **At the theater in Oxford.** 1689. 8°. WA1092.

1689 BERNARD, EDWARD. Orbis eruditi literaturam a charactere Samaritico. **Oxoniæ, apud theatrum.** 1689. Brs. WB1989.

1689 BERNARD, EDWARD. Private devotion and a brief explication. **Oxon, at the theater for Henry Clements.** 1689. 8°. WB1991.

1689 BIBLE. ENGLISH. **Oxford, at the theater to be sold by Thomas Guy, London.** 1689. 8°. WB2353.

1689 COLE, WILLIAM. A physico-medical essay. **Oxford, at the theater.** 1689. 8°. WC5043.

1689 DODWELL, HENRY. Dissertationes in Irenæum. **Oxoniæ, e theatro Sheldoniano.** 1689. 8°. WD1812.

1689 [HICKES, GEORGE]. Institutiones grammaticæ. **Oxoniæ, e theatro Sheldoniano.** 1689. 4°. WH1851.

1689 [HOWELL, WILLIAM]. The Common-prayer-book the best companion. Fourth edition. **Oxford, at the theater, for John Howell.** 1689. 8°. WH3132.

1689 [HOWELL, WILLIAM]. Prayers in the closet. **Oxford, at the theatre, for John Howell.** 1689. 8°. WH3143.

1689 [HOWELL, WILLIAM]. The word of God the best guide. **Oxford, at the Sheldonian Theatre, sold by T. Bennet.** 1689. 8°. WH3145.

1689 [HYDE, THOMAS]. De historia Shahiludii. **Oxonii, e theatro Sheldoniano.** 1689. 4°. WH3873.

1689 [MARSHALL, THOMAS]. The catechism set forth. Eighth edition. **At the Theater in Oxford.** 1689. 4°. WM804.

1689 Officium viri sapientiæ studiosi. **Oxonii.** 1689. 8°. WO159.

1689 OXFORD, UNIVERSITY OF. Comitia habita in universitate Oxoniensi ... Apr. 11. [**Oxford**], e **theatro Sheldoniano.** 1689. Brs. WO867.

1689 OXFORD, UNIVERSITY OF. Ordo baccalavreorum **Oxonii, ex officina Leonardi Lichfield.** [1689]. Brs. WO921.

1689 OXFORD, UNIVERSITY OF. Vota Oxoniensia. **Oxonii, e theatro Sheldoniano.** 1689. **Prostant venales apud Th. Bennet, London.** Fol. WO992.

1689 [PEERS, RICHARD]. A catalogue of all graduats in divinity. **Oxford, at the Theater for Henry Clement.** 1689. 8°. WP1055.

1689 POND, BENJAMIN. A new almanack for ... 1689. **Oxford, at the theatre for Thomas Guy, London.** 1689. 8°. WA2126.

1689 [RAWLET, JOHN]. Y rhybudd. wr Christnogawl. **Rhydychen.** 1689. 4°. WR360.

1689 [WHEELER, MAURICE]. The Oxford almanack for ... 1689. **Printed at the theater in Oxford.** [1689]. Brs. WA2692.

1689 [WOODHEAD, ABRAHAM]. Catholick theses. [**Oxford.** 1689]. 4°. WW3438.

1689 [WOODHEAD, ABRAHAM]. Concerning images and idolatry. **Oxford, printed.** 1689. 4°. WW3441.

1690 [ALDRICH, HENRY]. Dr. Aldrich his service in G. [**Oxford?** 1690?]. Fol. WA900.

1690 BIBLE. WELSH. **Rydychain, yn y theatr.** 1690. Fol. WB2816.

1690 The case of the vniversity of Oxford. **Oxford, at the theater.** 1690. WC1174.

1690 The case of the vniversity of Oxford. [**Oxford.** 1690?]. Fol. WC1175.

1690 Ecclesiæ Anglicanæ filii collatio. **Oxonii, typis Lichfieldianis.** 1690. 8°. WE135.

1690 ELLIS, CLEMENT. The Gentile Sinner. Seventh edition. **Oxford, for Ric. Davis, to be sold by L. Meredith.** 1690. 12°. WE562.

1690 [ELYS, EDMUND]. Dominus est Deus. **Oxford.** 1690. 8°. WE670.

1690 FARISOL, ABRAHAM BEN MORDECAI. Tractatus de Turcarum liturgia. **Oxon.** 1690. 4°. WF439.

1690 [HARRINGTON, JAMES]. An account of the proceedings of the right reverend Jonathan ... Exeter. **Oxford, at the theatre.** 1690. **Sold by Tho. Bennet, London.** 4°. WH826.

1690 [HYDE, THOMAS]. Specimen libri more Nerochim Maimonidis. [**Oxford.** 1690]. 4°. WH3879.

1690 [MARTIN, THOMAS]. Historia. descriptio camplectens vitam, ... Gulielmi Wicami. **Oxoniæ, e theatro Sheldoniano.** 1690. 4°. WM852.

1690 MISHNAH. Misnæ pars: ordinis primi. **Oxoniæ, e theatro Sheldoniano.** 1690. 4°. WM2250.

1690 MOSES BEN MAIMON. Specimen libri more norochim. [**Oxford.** 1690]. 4°. WM2856.

1690 OXFORD, UNIVERSITY OF. Academiæ Oxoniensis gratulatio. **Oxoniæ, e theatro Sheldoniano.** 1690. Fol. WO858.

1690 OXFORD, UNIVERSITY OF. Gratulatio pro exoptato. **Oxoniæ, e theatro Sheldoniano.** 1690. Fol. WO886.

1690 OXFORD, UNIVERSITY OF. Judicium & decretum ... August 19. Anno Dom. 1690. **Oxonii, e theatro Sheldoniano anno, 1690. Sold by Tho. Bennet, London.** Fol. WO894.

1690 OXFORD, UNIVERSITY OF. Ordo baccalavreorum **Oxonii, ex officina Leonardi Lichfield.** [1690]. Brs. WO922.

1690 [PROAST, JONAS]. The argument of the letter concerning toleration. **Oxford, at the Theatre, for George West, and Henry Clements.** 1690. 4°. WP3538.

1690 TOZER, HENRY. Directions for a godly life. Eleventh edition. **Oxford, by L. Lichfield, for Richard Davis.** 1690. 12°. WT2001.

1690 W[ELLWOOD], J[AMES]. An answer to the vindication of the letter concerning the profession. **Oxford, printed.** 1690. 4°. WW1305.

1690 [WHEELER, MAURICE]. The Oxford almanack for ... 1690. **Printed at the theater in Oxford.** [1690]. Brs. WA2693.

1690 [WILLES, JOHN]. Brevissimum metaphysicae. **Oxonii, typis L. Lichfield, sumptibus Hen. Clements.** 1690. 12°. WW2301.

1690 WILLIS, FRANCIS. Synopsis physicae. **Prostant venales apud Joh. Place, & N. Cox, Oxon.** 1690. 8°. WW2804.

1690 [WRIGHT]. The case of the city of Oxford. **[Oxford.** 1690-91]. Fol. WW3683.

1690 XENEPHON. Ἀπομνηονευμα των βιβλια δ'. **Oxford.** 1690. 8°. WX3.

1691 [ALDRICH, HENRY]. Artis logicae compendium. **Oxonii, e theatro Sheldoniano.** 1691. 8°. WA896.

1691 Anglicani novi schismatis redargutio. **Oxonii, e theatro Sheldoniano.** 1691. 4°. WA3184.

1691 Articuli religionis xxxix. **Oxon.** 1691. 12°. WA3892.

1691 BIBLE. ENGLISH. **Printed at the theater in Oxford, to be sold by Thomas Guy, London.** 1691. 12°. WB2357.

1691 [DRUMMOND, WILLIAM]. Polemo-Midinia carmen maccoronicum. **Oxonii, e theatro Sheldoniano.** 1691. 4°. WD2204.

1691 FARISOL, ABRAHAM BEN MORDECAI. [Hebrew] id est. Itinera mundi. **Oxonii, e theatro Sheldoniano.** 1691. 4°. WF438.

1691 FORDUN, JOHN. Historiae Brittanicae. **Oxoniae. e theatro Sheldoniano.** 1691. WF1551.

1691 FROMMAN, ANDREAS. Synopsis metaphysica. **Oxoniae, typis L. Lichfield, impensis Tho. Gilbert, et Elis. Gilbert.** 1691. 12°. WF2244.

1691 GALE, THOMAS. Historiae Britannicae. **Oxoniae, e theatro Sheldoniano.** 1691. 2 vols. Fol. WG154.

1691 [GRASCOMBE, SAMUEL]. A farther account of the Baroccian manuscript. **[Oxford?** 1691]. 4°. WG1571.

1691 HODY, HUMFREY. Anglicani novi schismatis redargutio. **Oxonii, e theatro Sheldoniano.** 1691. 4°. WH2337.

1691 HOLDER, WILLIAM. Introductio ad chronologiam. **Oxoniae, typis L. Lichfield, Sumptibus Geo. West.** 1691. 8°. WH2388.

1691 [JANE, WILLIAM]. A sermon preached ... the 26th of November, 1691. **Oxford, at the theater, for Thomas Bennet, London.** 1691. 4°. WJ457.

1691 JOANNES, Malalas. Ιωαννου ... Joannis. Antiocheni cognomento Malalae historia chronica. **Oxonii, e Theatro Sheldoniano.** 1691. 8°. WJ745.

1691 LITURGIES. BOOK OF COMMON PRAYER. Book of common prayer. **Printed at the theater in Oxford, to be sold by Peter Parker, London.** 1691. 12°. WB3684.

1691 OXFORD, UNIVERSITY OF. Ordo baccalavreorum. **Oxonii, ex officina Leonardi Lichfield.** [1691]. Brs. WO923.

1691 OXFORD, UNIVERSITY OF. Parecbolae sive excerpta è corpore statutorum. **Oxoniae, e theatro Sheldoniano.** 1691. 8°. WO932.

1691 POCOCKE, EDWARD. A commentary on the prophecy of Joel. **Oxford, at the Theater.** 1691. Fol. WP2661.

1691 [PROAST, JONAS]. A third letter concerning toleration. **Oxford, by L. Lichfield, for George West and Henry Clements.** 1691. 4°. WP3539.

1691 [WHEELER, MAURICE]. The Oxford almanack for ... 1691. **Printed at the theater in Oxford.** [1691]. Brs. WA26941.

1691 WHITBY, DANIEL. Tractatus de vera Christi deitate. **Oxoniae, typis L. Lichfield, sumptibus Joh. Howel.** 1691. 4°. WW1738.

1691 XANTHOPOULLOS, NICEPHORUS CALLISTOS. Anglicani Novi schismatis redargutio. **Oxonii, e theatro Sheldoniano.** 1691. 4°. WX1.

1691 XENOPHON. Ξενοφωντυς λογος. Εκ Θεατρου εν Οξονια. [1691]. 8°. WX12.

1692 [ALDRICH, HENRY]. Artis logicae compendium. **Oxonii, e theatro Sheldoniano.** 1692. 8°. WA897.

1692 ANGLO-SAXON CHRONICLE. Chronicon Saxonicum. **Oxonii, e theatro Sheldoniano.** 1692. 4°. WA3185.

1692 Appendix librorum. **Oxford.** 28 Nov. 1692. 4°. WA3570.

1692 ARISTEAS. Aristeae historia LXXII interpretum. **Oxonii, e theatro Sheldoniano.** 1692. 8°. WA3683.

1692 BIBLE. ENGLISH. PSALMS. The whole book of psalms. **Oxford, for the university printers.** 1692. 12°. WB2581.

1692 Catalogus librorum tam antiquorum quam recentium. Novemb. 9. 1692. **Oxford.** 1692. Fol. WC1449.

1692 CHISHULL, EDMUND. Gulielmo tertio. **Oxonii, e theatro Sheldoniano. Prostant apud Joh. Crosley.** 1692. 4°. WC3900.

1692 CHURCH OF ENGLAND. Articles to be enquired of within the diocess of Hereford. **Oxford, printed.** 1692. 4°. WC4049.

1692 DAVIS, RICHARD. Catalogus variorum in quavis lingua & facultate insignium. Pars quarta. **Oxford.** 1692. 4°. WD429.

1692 DODWELL, HENRY. Praelectiones academicae. **Oxonii, e theatro Sheldoniano: væneunt in officina Benj. Tooke, Londinensis.** 1692. 8°. WD1815.

1692 EDWARDS, THOMAS. Dialling made easy. **Oxford, by L. Lichfield, for Sam. Clarke.** 1692. 8°. WE226.

1692 HODY, HUMFREY. A letter from Mr. **Oxford. by L. Lichfield, for Ant. Pisly.** 1692. 4°. WH2342.

1692 [JANE, WILLIAM]. A sermon preached ... in November, 1692. **Oxford, at the theater for Thomas Bennet.** 1692. 4°. WJ458.

1692 [JOYNER, EDWARD]. Armante Gulielmo. **[Oxford.** 1692]. Brs. WJ1156.

1692 [JOYNER, EDWARD]. Poema. **[Oxford].** 1692. Fol. WJ1158.

1692 [MARSHALL, THOMAS]. The catechism set forth. Ninth edition. **At the Theater in Oxford.** 1692. 4°. WM805.

1692 [MONTGOMERY, JAMES]. Great Britain's just complaint. Second edition. **Oxford: printed.** 1692. 4°. WM2505.

1692 [MORGAN, MATTHEW]. An elegy on the death of the Honourable Mr. Robert Boyle. **Oxford, by L. Lichfield.** 1692. Fol. WM2732.

1692 [MORGAN, MATTHEW]. An elegy on the death of the Honourable Mr. Robert Boyle. **Oxford, by L. Lichfield, for Chr. Coningsby, London.** 1692. Fol. WM2733.

1692 Musarum Anglicanarum analecta: ... Vol. 1. **Oxon e theatro Sheldoniano. Impensis Joh. Crosley & Sam. Smith.** 1692. 8°. WM3135.

1692 OXFORD, UNIVERSITY OF. Librorum manuscriptorum in duabus. **Oxonii, e theatro Sheldoniano.** 1692. 4°. WO896.

1692 OXFORD, UNIVERSITY OF. Musarum Anglicanarum analecta. **Oxon, e theatro Sheldoniano, impensis Joh. Crosley, & Sam. Smith, Lond.** 1692. WO898.

1692 OXFORD, UNIVERSITY OF. Ordo baccalavreorum. **Oxonii, ex officina Leonardi Lichfield.** [1692]. Brs. WO924.

1692 OXFORD, UNIVERSITY OF. Prælectiones academicae in schola historices Camdeniana. **Oxonii, e theatro Sheldoniano: væneunt in officina Benj. Tooke.** 1692. 8°. WO938.

1692 POCOCKE, EDWARD. A commentary on the prophecy of Malachi. Second edition. **Oxford, at the theater.** 1692. Fol. WP2662.

1692 POCOCKE, EDWARD. A commentary on the prophecy of Micah. Second edition. **Oxford, at the Theater.** 1692. Fol. WP2663A.

1692 QUINTILIAN, MARCUS FABIUS. M. Fab. Quintiliani declamationum liber. **Oxonii, e Theatro Sheldoniano.** 1692. 8°. WQ223.

1692 WALLIS, JOHN. A defense of the Christian Sabbath. **Oxford, by L. Lichfield, to be sold by Chr. Coningsby, London.** 1692. 4°. WW569.

1692 [WHEELER, MAURICE]. The Oxford almanack for ... 1693. **Printed at the theater in Oxford.** [1692]. Brs. WA2695.

1692 WHITING, CHARLES. A sermon preached July 19, 1692. **Oxford, at the theater for Jo. Crosley.** 1692. 4°. WW2017.

1693 ABENDANO, ISAAC. An almanack for the year of Christ, 1693. **Oxford, at the theater.** [1693]. Sixes. WA1233.

1693 [ALLESTREE, RICHARD]. The ladies calling. Sixth edition. **At the theater in Oxford.** 1693. 4°. WA1147.

1693 ASHWELL, GEORGE. De socino et socinianismo dissertatio. **Oxoniæ impressi, prostant autem venales Londini apud J. Adamson.** 1693. 8°. WA3996.

1693 EDWARDS, JONATHAN. A preservative against Socinianism. The first part. **Oxon. At the theater for Henry Clements.** 1693. 4°. WE216.

1693 EDWARDS, JONATHAN. A preservative against Socinianism. The first part. Second edition. **Oxon. At the theater for Henry Clements.** 1693. 4°. WE217.

1693 ERASMUS, DESIDERIUS. Des. Erasmi Roterodami. Dialogus, cui titulus Ciceronianus. **Oxoniæ, typis L. Lichfield.** 1693. **Prostant venales apud Christoph. Coningsby ... Londinensem.** 8°. WE3198.

1693 FELL, JOHN, bp. Specimen. **Oxford, at the theater.** 1693. 8°. WF622.

1693 LITURGIES. BOOK OF COMMON PRAYER. Book of Common prayer. **Oxford, by the university-printers.** 1693. Fol. WB3689.

1693 N., N. A letter from Oxford, concerning Mr. Samuel Johnson's late book. **Oxford, printed.** 1693. 4°. WN40.

1693 OUGHTRED, WILLIAM. Clavis mathemeticæ. Fifth edition. **Oxoniæ, excudebat Leon. Lichfield.** 1693. 12°. WO576.

1693 OXFORD, UNIVERSITY OF. Ordo baccalavreorum. **Oxonii, ex officina Leonardi Lichfield.** [1693]. Brs. WO925.

1693 OXFORD, UNIVERSITY OF. Parecbolae sive excerpta è corpore statutorum. **Oxoniæ, e theatro Sheldoniano.** 1693. 8°. WO933.

1693 OXFORD, UNIVERSITY OF. Quæstiones in S. theologia. **[Oxford], e theatro Sheldoniano.** 1693. Brs. WO960.

1693 OXFORD, UNIVERSITY OF. Theatri Oxoniensis encaenia ... **Oxonii, e theatro Sheldoniano.** 1693. Fol. WO984.

1693 QUINTILLIAN, MARCUS FABIUS. M. Fabii Quinctiliani de institutione oratoria. **Oxoniæ, e theatro Sheldoniano, impensis H. Cruttenden.** 1693. 4°. WQ221.

1693 VELLEIUS PATERCULUS. Quae supersunt. **Oxonii, e teatro Sheldoniano. Prostant venales apud Joh. Crosley, Geor. West, Hen. Clements, & Joh. Hassel.** 1693. 4°. WV181.

1693 WALLIS, JOHN. De algebra tractatus. **Oxoniæ, e theatro Sheldoniano.** 1693. Fol. WW566.

1693 WALLIS, JOHN. A defense of the Christian Sabbath. Second edition. **Oxford, by L. Lichfield, to be sold by Thomas Bennet, London.** 1693. 4°. WW570.

1693 XENOPHON. Ξ ενοφωντυς λογος. **Oxford.** 1693. 8°. WX13.

1693 XENOPHON. Ξ ενοφωντυς λογος. **Oxford.** [1693]. 8°. WX14.

1694 [ALLESTREE, RICHARD]. The art of contentment. **At the theater in Oxford.** 1694. 8°. WA1093.

1694 BIBLE. ENGLISH. NEW TESTAMENT. **Oxford, by the university-printers.** 1694. 8°. WB2698.

1694 BULL, GEORGE, bp. Judicium ecclesiae Catholicæ **Oxonii, e theatro Sheldoniano, impensis Georg. West.** 1694. 8°. WB5418.

1694 CAESAR, C. JULIUS. Julii Cæseris portus iccius illustratus. **Oxonii, e theatro Sheldoniano.** 1694. 8°. WC202A.

1694 CAMPION, ABRAHAM. A sermon concerning national providence. **For Anthony Piesley in Oxford.** 1694. 4°. WC406.

1694 EDWARDS, JONATHAN. A preservative against Socinianism. Second part. **Oxon, at the theater for H. Clements.** 1694. 4°. WE219.

1694 [HALL, JOHN]. An answer to some queries propos'd by W.C. **Oxford, by Leon. Lichfield, for John Buckeridge in Marlebrough.** 1694. 4°. WH343.

1694 [HYDE, THOMAS]. Historia Nerdiludii. **Oxonii, e theatro Sheldoniano.** 1694. 4°. WH3875.

1694 [HYDE, THOMAS]. Mandragorias. **Oxonii, e theatro Sheldoniano.** 1694. 8°. WH3877.

1694 [HYDE, THOMAS]. Shahilvdium traditum. **Oxonii, e theatro Sheldoniano.** 1694. 8°. WH3878.

1694 JOSEPHUS, FLAVIUS. Josephi antiquitatem judaicarum specimen. [**Oxford.** 1694]. Brs. WJ1082.

1694 [JOYNER, EDWARD]. In obitum Mariae. [**Oxford.** 1694]. Brs. WJ1157.

1694 MALEBRANCHE, NICOLAS. Father Malebranche his treatise concerning the search after truth. **Oxford, by L. Lichfield, for Thomas Bennet, London.** 1694. Fol. WM317.

1694 MORGAN, MATTHEW. Eugenia: or, an elegy. **Oxford, by Leonard Lichfield.** 1694. 4°. WM2734.

1694 OXFORD, UNIVERSITY OF. Ordo baccalavreorum. **Oxonii, ex officina Leonardi Lichfield.** [1694]. Brs. WO926.

1694 PARDIES, IGNACE GASTON. Elementa geometriae. **Oxoniae.** 1694. 24°. WP347.

1694 PLUTARCH. The apothegmes of the ancients. βιβλιον ... quomodo. Εκ Θεατρου εη Oxovia. (1694). 8°. WP2632.

1694 [RAPIN, RENÉ]. Monsieur Rapin's comparison of Thucydides and Livy. **Oxford, by L. Lichfield, for Anthony Peisley.** 1694. 8°. WR261.

1694 WALLIS, JOHN. A defense of the Christian Sabbath. **Oxford, by L. Lichfield, for Thomas Bennet, London.** 1694. 4°. WW572.

1694 WALLIS, JOHN. A defense of the Christian Sabbath. Part the Second. **Oxford, by Leon. Lichfield.** 1694. 4°. WW571.

1694 [WHEELER, MAURICE]. The Oxford almanack for ... 1694. **Printed at the theater in Oxford.** [1694]. Brs. WA2697.

1694 WHITEHALL, ROBERT. A sermon concerning edification in faith. **Oxford, at the theater for Ant. Piesley.** 1694. 4°. WW1874.

1694 XENOPHON. Ξενοφωντυς λογος. **Oxford.** 1694. 8°. WX15.

1695 ABBADIE, JACQUES. The art of knowing oneself. **Oxford, by Leonard Lichfield, for Henry Clements and John Howell.** 1695. 12°. WA45.

1695 ABENDANO, ISAAC. An almanack for the year of Christ 1695. **Oxford, at the theater.** 1695. Sixes. WA1234.

1695 [ALLESTREE, RICHARD]. The works. Third edition. **Printed at the theater in Oxford, and in London, by Roger Norton for Edward Pawlett.** 1695. Fol. WA1084.

1695 BIBLE. ENGLISH. **Oxford, by the university-printers.** 1695. 12°. WB2366.

1695 CICERO. De officiis. Libri III. **Oxoniae, e theatro Sheldoniano.** 1695. 4°. WC4297.

1695 CONNOR, BERNARD. Dissertationes medico-physicae. **Oxonii, e theatro Sheldoniano, sumptibus H. Clement.** 1695. 8°. WC5885.

1695 EDWARDS, JONATHAN. Remarks upon a book lately published by Dr. Will. Sherlock. **Oxford, at the theater.** 1695. **To be sold by H. Clements.** 4°. WE221.

1695 FELL, JOHN, bp. Specimen. **Oxford, at the theater.** 1695. 8°. WF623.

1695 GREGORY, DAVID. Catoptricae et dioptricae. **Oxonii, e theatro Sheldoniano.** 1695. 8°. WG1883.

1695 HOMER. 'Ομηρου 'Ιλιας. Homeri Ilias. Εκ Θεατρου εν Οξονια. [1695]. 8°. WH2546.

1695 [HOWELL, WILLIAM]. The Common-prayer-book the best companion. **Oxford, at the theater, for John Howell.** 1695. 8°. WH3133.

1695 K[ENNETT], W[HITE], bp. Parochial antiquities. **Oxford, at the Theater.** 1695. 4°. WK302.

1695 K[ENNETT], W[HITE], bp. The righteous taken away from the evil to come. **Oxford, by Leonard Lichfield, for George West.** 1695. 4°. WK303.

1695 OXFORD, UNIVERSITY OF. At a meeting of the Vice-chancellor and the heads of colleges. [**Oxford.** 1695]. Brs. WO862.

1695 OXFORD, UNIVERSITY OF. In convento D. Vice Cancellarii & praefectorum. [**Oxford.** 1695]. Brs. WO889.

1695 OXFORD, UNIVERSITY OF. Ordo baccalavreorum. **Oxonii, ex officina Leonardi Lichfield.** [1695]. Brs. WO927.

1695 PHALARIS. Φαλαριδος ... Επιστολαι, **Oxonia, excudebat Johannes Crooke.** [1695]. 8°. WP1960.

1695 TANNER, THOMAS. Notitia monastica. **Oxford, at the Theater, to be sold by A. & J. Churchill, London.** 1695. 8°. WT144.

1695 THUCYDIDES. Proposals for subscription to. [**Oxford.** 1695]. Fol. WT1135.

1695 W., R. An essay on grief. **Oxford, by L. Lichfield, for Henry Clements, and John Howell.** 1695. 12°. WW91.

1695 WALLIS, JOHN. Opera mathematica. **Oxoniae, e theatro Sheldoniano.** 1695. Fol. WW596.

1695 [WHEELER, MAURICE]. The Oxford almanack for ... 1695. **Printed at the theater in Oxford.** [1695]. Brs. WA2698.

1696 ABENDANO, ISAAC. An almanack for the year of Christ, 1696. **Oxford, at the theater.** 1696. Sixes. WA1235.

1696 AESCHINES. Αισχινου ο κατα κτησιφωντος. Εκ Θεατρου 'εν Οξονια. **excudebat Johan Crooke.** [1696]. 4°. WA682.

1696 AESCHINES. Αισχινου ο κατα κτησιφωντος. Εκ Θεατρου 'εν Οξονια. **Oxon, e theatro Sheldoniano.** 1696. 4°. WA683.

1696 [ALDRICH, HENRY]. Artis logicae compendium. **Oxonii, e theatro Sheldoniano.** 1696. 8°. WA898.

1696 [ALLESTREE, RICHARD]. The lively oracles. **At the theater in Oxford.** 1696. 8°. WA1155.

1696 ASHWELL, GEORGE. Catalogus librorum. **Oxford.** 5 May 1696. 4°. WA3993.

1696 BIBLE. ENGLISH. **Oxford: by the university-printers.** 1696. 12°. WB2369.

1696 BIBLE. ENGLISH. NEW TESTAMENT. **Oxford, by the university-printers.** 1696. 12°. WB2702.

1696 BIBLE. ENGLISH. PSALMS. The whole book of psalms. **Oxford: by the university-printers.** 1696. 12°. WB2599.

1696 BRAY, THOMAS. A course of lectures. v. 1. **Oxford, by Leonard Lichfield.** 1696. Fol. WB4292.

1696 CICERO. M. Tullis Cicero de oratore. **Oxoniæ, e theatro Sheldoniano.** 1696. 8°. WC4298.

1696 COTTON, Sir ROBERT BRUCE. Catalogus librorum manuscriptorum. **Oxonii, e theatro Sheldoniano.** 1696. Fol. WC6483.

1696 DUPIN, LOUIS ELLIES. A new history. Third edition. **London and Oxford.** 1696-1725. 17 vols. Fol. WD2645.

1696 EUTROPIUS. Historiae Romanae breviarium. **Oxonii, e theatro Sheldoniano. Impensis Ab. Swall & Tim Child, Londini.** 1696. 8°. WE3436.

1696 IGNATIUS, saint. Epistolæ genuinæ. **Oxonii, e theatro Sheldoniano.** 1696. Fol. WI40.

1696 LITURGIES. BOOK OF COMMON PRAYER. Book of Common prayer. **Oxford.** 1696. 8°. WB3694.

1696 OVID. Metamorphoseos. **Oxonii, e theatro Sheldoniano, impensis A. Swall et T. Child.** 1696. 8°. WO682.

1696 OXFORD, UNIVERSITY OF. Comitia habita in universitate Oxoniensis ... Apr. 16. An. Dom. 1696. **[Oxford], e theatro Sheldoniano.** 1696. Brs. WO868.

1696 OXFORD, UNIVERSITY OF. Decreti Oxoniensis. **[Oxford].** 1696. 4°. WO872.

1696 OXFORD, UNIVERSITY OF. Decreti Oxoniensis. **[Oxford], excusa.** 1696. Brs. WO873.

1696 THUCYDIDES. Θουκνδιδου ... de bellos Pelopennesiaco. **Oxoniæ, e Theatro Sheldoniano. Impensis T. Bennet.** 1696. Fol. WT1133.

1696 [WHEELER, MAURICE]. The Oxford almanack for ... 1697. **Printed at the theater in Oxford.** [1696]. Brs. WA2700.

1696 XENOPHON. Κυρου 'αναβάσεως ιστοριων. 'Εν Οξονια. 1696. 8°. WX11.

1697 Animadversions on a late book entituled The reasonableness of Christianity. **Oxford, by Leon Lichfield for George West and Anthony Peisley.** 1697. 4°. WA3191.

1697 BECONSALL, THOMAS. The doctrine of a general resurrection. **Oxford, by Leon. Lichfield, for George West.** 1697. 4°. WB1656.

1697 BIBLE. ENGLISH. **Oxford: by the university-printers.** 1697. Fol. WB2372.

1697 BIBLE. ENGLISH. NEW TESTAMENT. **Oxford: by the university-printers.** 1697. 8°. WB2703.

1697 BRAY, THOMAS. A course of lectures. v. 1. **Oxford, by Leonard Lichfield.** 1697. Fol. WB4292A.

1697 Catalogi librorum manuscriptorum Angliæ et Hiberniæ in unum collecti. **Oxoniæ, e theatro Sheldoniano.** 1697. 2 vols. Fol. WC1253.

1697 DIONYSIUS Periegetes. Οιχουμηνης ... Orbis descriptio. **Oxoniæ, e theatro Sheldoniano, prostant apud S. Smith & B. Walford, Londinensis.** 1697. 8°. WD1523.

1697 EDWARDS, JONATHAN. A preservative against Socinianism. The third part. **Oxon., at the theater for H. Clements.** 1697. 4°. WE220.

1697 FELL, JOHN, bp. Grammatica rationis. **Oxonii, e theatro Sheldoniano.** 1697. 12°. WF611.

1697 HARDING, MICHAEL. Bibliotheca selectissima. **[Oxford. 1697].** Fol. WH700.

1697 HELLIER, HENRY. A treatise concerning schism. **By Richard Smith for Jo. Crosley in Oxford.** 1697. 4°. WH1381.

1697 LITURGIES. BOOK OF COMMON PRAYER. Book of common prayer. **Oxford.** 1697. 12°. WB3696.

1697 LYCOPHRON. Λυκοφρονος ... Lycophronis Alexandra. **Oxonii, e theatro Sheldoniano.** 1697. Fol. WL3523.

1697 [NEPOS, CORNELIUS]. Excellentiom imperatorum vitæ. **Oxoniæ, e theatro Sheldoniano.** 1697. **Excudebat, Johan Crooke.** 8°. WN426B.

1697 [NEPOS, CORNELIUS]. Cornelii Nepotis vitæ excellentium inperatorum. **Oxoniæ, e theatro Sheldoniano.** 1697. **Excudebat Johan Crooke.** 8°. WN434.

1697 OXFORD, UNIVERSITY OF. Comitia habita in universitate Oxoniensi ... Decemb. 2. **[Oxford], e theatro Sheldoniano.** 1697. Brs. WO869.

1697 PINDAR. Πινδαρου Ολνμπια... **Oxonii, e Theatro Sheldoniano.** 1697. Fol. WP2245.

1697 POTTER, JOHN. Archaeologiae Graecae; or, the antiquities of Greece ... volume the first. **Oxford, at the Theater, for Abel Swall, London.** 1697. 8°. WP3030.

1697 WALLIS, JOHN. A defense of infant-baptism. **Oxford: by Leon. Lichfield, for Henry Clements.** 1697. 4°. WW568.

1697 [WHEELER, MAURICE]. The Oxford almanack for ... 1698. **Printed at the theater in Oxford.** [1697]. Brs. WA2701.

1698 ABBADIE, JACQUES. The art of knowing one-self. **Oxford by L. Lichfield for Thomas Leigh, London.** 1698. 12°. WA48.

1698 ABENDANO, ISAAC. An almanack for the year of Christ, 1698. **Oxford, at the theater.** [1698]. Sixes. WA1236.

1698 ÆSOP. Fabularum. **Oxoniæ, e theatro Sheldoniano. Excudebat Johan Croke.** 1698. 8°. WA729.

1698 BARTHOLIN, CASPAR. Specimen philosophiæ naturalis. **Oxoniæ, typis Leon. Lichfield, impensis Henr. Clements.** 1698. 8°. WB974.

1698 BECONSALL, THOMAS. The grounds and foundation of natural religion, discover'd. **By W. O. for A. Roper, A. Bosvile, and G. West in Oxford.** 1698. 8°. WB1657.

1698 BIBLE. ANGLO-SAXON. OLD TESTAMENT. Heptateuchus, liber Job. **Oxoniæ, e theatro Sheldoniano, typis Jvnianis.** 1698. 4°. WB2198.

1698 BOETHIUS, ANICIUS MANLIUS TORQUATUS SEVERINUS. An. Manl. Sever. Boethii consolationis. **Oxonii, e theatro Sheldoniano.** 1698. WB3429.

1698 COWPER, WILLIAM. The anatomy of humane bodies. **Oxford, at the theater, for Sam. Smith and Benj. Walford, London.** 1698. Fol. WC6698.

1698   DODWELL, HENRY. Annales Velleiani. **Oxonii, e theatro Sheldoniano.** 1698. 8°. WD1802A.

1698   EDWARDS, JONATHAN. A preservative against Socinianism. The first part. Third edition. **Oxon. At the theater for Henry Clements.** 1698. 4°. WE218.

1698   GRABE, JOHANN ERNST. Spicilegium SS. patrum. **Oxoniae, e theatro Sheldoniano.** 1698-9. 2 vols. 8°. WG1464.

1698   [HUDSON, JOHN]. Geographiae veteris scriptores. Vol. 1. **Oxoniae, e theatro Sheldoniano.** 1698. 4°. WH3260.

1698   KEILL, JOHN. An examination of Dr. Burnet's theory of the earth. **Oxford, at the Theater.** 1698. 8°. WK132.

1698   LITURGIES. BOOK OF COMMON PRAYER. Book of common prayer. **Oxford, by the university-printers.** 1698. 8°. WB3698.

1698   [MARSHALL, THOMAS]. The catechism set forth. Tenth edition. **Oxford, at the theater, for T. Bennet, London.** 1698. 4°. WM806.

1698   OXFORD, UNIVERSITY OF. Ordo baccalavreorum. **Oxonii, ex officina Leonardi Lichfield.** [1698]. Brs. WO928.

1698   PATRICK, saint. Spicilegium. **Oxoniae, e theatro Sheldoneano.** 1698. 8°. WP727.

1698   PINDAR. Πινδαρου Ολυμπια. **Oxonii, e Theatro Sheldoniano.** 1698. **Prostant Londini apud Sam. Smith & Benj. Walford.** Fol. WP2246.

1698   VELLEIUS PATERCULUS. Annales Velleiani. **Oxonii.** 1698. 8°. WV182.

1698   [WELDON, JOHN]. Musica Oxoniensis, a collection. **Oxford, by Leon. Lichfield, to be sold by the widow Howell.** 1698. Fol. WW1279.

1698   [WELLS, EDWARD]. Elementa arithmeticae. **Oxoniae, e theatro Sheldoniano.** 1698. **Excudebat Johan. Croke.** 8°. WW1286.

1698   [WHEELER, MAURICE]. The Oxford almanack for ... 1698. **Printed at the theater in Oxford.** [1698]. Brs. WA2702.

1699   ABENDANO, ISAAC. An almanack for the year of Christ, 1699. **Oxford, at the theater.** [1699]. Sixes. WA1237.

1699   ANDERTON, WILLIAM. Bibliotheca Andertoniana. **[Oxford. 1699].** Fol. WA3111.

1699   BARLOW, THOMAS, bp. Αυτοσχεδιασματα, de studio theologiae. **Oxford, by Leon. Lichfield.** 1699. 4°. WB824.

1699   BARON, JOHN. A sermon preached, June 1. 1699. **Oxford, by Leon Lichfield.** 1699. 4°. WB879.

1699   BIBLE. ANGLO-SAXON. OLD TESTAMENT. Heptateuchus, liber Job. **Oxoniae.** 1699. 4°. WB2199.

1699   BIBLE. ENGLISH. **Oxford: by the university-printers.** 1699. 12°. WB2376.

1699   BIBLE. ENGLISH. NEW TESTAMENT. **Oxford: by the university-printers.** 1699. 8°. WB2704.

1699   BIBLE. ENGLISH. NEW TESTAMENT. **Oxford: by the university-printers.** 1699. 12°. WB2705.

1699   BOBART, JAKOB. Plantarum historiae. **Oxonii.** 1699. Fol. WB3377.

1699   Catalogus variorum librorum antiquorum & recentiorum ... (15) die Martii 1698/9. **Oxford.** 1699. Fol. WC1456.

1699   CRENIUS, THOMAS. Animadversiones philologicae et historicae. **Oxon., e theatro Sheldoniano.** 1699. 8°. WC6882.

1699   [DEFOE, DANIEL]. A letter to a member of Parliament, shewing. **Oxford, for George West, and Henry Clements.** 1699. 4°. WD837.

1699   HERODIAN. Ἡρωδιανοῦ ἱστοριῶν βιβλια ἠ. Herodiani historiarum. **Oxoniae e theatre Sheldoniano.** 1699. 8°. WH1580.

1699   HOLE, MATTHEW. Letters written to J.M. ... the second part. **For, and to be sold by J. Taylor, and T. Bever in London; H. Clements in Oxon, and J. Miller in Sherborn.** 1699. 8°. WH2410.

1699   HOLE, MATTHEW. The true reformation of manners. **Oxford, by L. Lichfield, for Henry Clements.** 1699. 4°. WH2414.

1699   KEILL, JOHN. An examination of the reflections. **Oxford, at the Theater for Henry Clemens.** 1699. 8°. WK133.

1699   LITURGIES. BOOK OF COMMON PRAYER. Book of common prayer. **Oxford, by the university-printers.** 1699. 12°. WB3701.

1699   MORISON, ROBERT. Plantarum historiae ... pars tertia. **Oxonii, e theatro Sheldoniano.** 1699. Fol. WM2772.

1699   MORSE, ROBERT. The clergyman's office. **London: for Tho. Bennet, and Henry Clement, in Oxford.** 1699. 4°. WM2815.

1699   Musarum Anglicanarum analecta: ... Vol. 1. Second edition. **Oxon e theatro Sheldoniano. Impensis Joh. Crosley & Sam. Smith.** 1699. 8°. WM3136.

1699   OXFORD, UNIVERSITY OF. Musarum Anglicanarum analecta. Vol. I. **Oxon. e theatro Sheldoniano, impensis Joh. Crosley.** 1699. WO899.

1699   OXFORD, UNIVERSITY OF. Musarum Anglicanarum analecta. Vol. I. **Oxon. e theatro Sheldoniano, impensis Joh. Crosley, & Sam. Smith, London.** 1699. WO900.

1699   OXFORD, UNIVERSITY OF. Musarum Anglicanarum analecta. Vol. II. **Oxon. e theatro Sheldoniano, impensis Joh. Crosley.** 1699. WO901.

1699   PATRICK, saint. Spicilegium. [Vol. 2]. **Oxoniae, e theatro Sheldoniano.** 1699. 8°. WP728.

1699   POTTER, JOHN. Archaeologiae Graecae: or, the antiquities of Greece ... volume the first. **Oxford, at the Theater, for Abel Swall, London.** 1699. 8°. WP3031.

1699   POTTER, JOHN. Archaeologiae Graecae: or the antiquities of Greece ... volume the second. **Oxford, at the Theater, for Timothy Child, and John Jones, London.** 1699. 8°. WP3032.

1699   THEOCRITUS. – Θεοκριτου τα ευρισκουενα. **Oxoniae, e Theatro Sheldoniano, impensis Sam. Smith, & Benj. Walford.** 1699. 8°. WT852.

1699   WALLIS, JOHN. Opera mathematica. **Oxoniae, e theatro Sheldoniano.** 1699. Fol. WW597.

1699   [WHEELER, MAURICE]. The Oxford almanack for ... 1699. **Printed at the theater in Oxford.** [1699]. Brs. WA2703.

1699   WHITBY, DANIEL. Ethices compendium. Second edition. **Oxonii, typis L. Lichfield; impensis Geo. West, Joh. Crosley, Joh. Wilmot, Hen. Clements, Mariae Howell, & Ant. Peisley.** 1699. 8°. WW1727.

1699   WHITEHALL, ROBERT. Catalogus librorum. **Oxon.** 1699/1700. 4°. WW1869.

1700 ABU BAKR IBN A TUFAIL. Philosophus auto-
didactus sive epistola. Second edition. **Oxonii, e**
theatro Sheldoniano, excudebat Johannes Owens.
1700. 4°. WA153.

1700 [ALLESTREE, RICHARD]. The art of contentment. **At the theater in Oxford.** 1700. 8° WA1094

1700 [ALLESTREE, RICHARD]. The ladies calling.
Seventh edition. **At the theater in Oxford.** 1700.
2 vols. 8°. WA1148.

1700 BARLOW, THOMAS, bp. Α'υτοσεχεδῑασματα, de
studio theologiae. Second edition. **Oxford.**
1700. 4°. WB825.

1700 BIBLE. ENGLISH. PSALMS. The whole book of
psalms. **Oxford: by the university-printers.**
1700. 12°. WB2626.

1700 Bibliotheca librorum rarissimorum. [**Oxford.**
1700]. 8°. WB2837.

1700 BUERDSELL, JAMES. Discourses and essays.
Oxford, by Leon:Lichfield. 1700. 8°. WB5363.

1700 Catalogus libris exquisitissimis. **Oxford.**
20 June, 1700. 4°. WC1429.

1700 CREECH, THOMAS. Catalogue of the library.
Oxford. 20 November, 1700. 4°. WC6872.

1700 CYPRIAN, saint. Opera. Third edition. **Oxonii,**
e theatro Sheldoniano. 1700. Fol. WC7712.

1700 DODWELL, HENRY. Dissertationes Cyprianicae.
Oxonii. [1700]. Fol. WD1811.

1700 DODWELL, HENRY. An essay concerning the
lawfulness. **For W. Hawes, [London] and Henry**
Clements in Oxford, and W. Burton, at Tiverton.
1700. 8°. WD1814.

1700 DODWELL, HENRY. A treatise concerning the
lawfulness of instrumental music. **For W. Hawes,**
London, and Henry Clements in Oxford, and
W. Burton, at Tiverton. 1700. 8°. WD1820.

1700 EUCLID. The elements of Euclid. Third edition.
Oxford, by L. L. for M. Gillyflower, and W. Freeman
1700. 8°. WE3402.

1700 GRABE, JOHANN ERNST. Spicilegium SS.
patrum. Second edition. **Oxoniae, e theatro**
Sheldoniano. 1700. **Impensis Joannis Oweni.**
2 vols. 8°. WG1465.

1700 GROTIUS, HUGO. Hugo Grotius de veritate religionis Christianae. **Oxoniae, e theatro Sheldoniano,**
impensis Ant. Peisley. 1700. 8°. WG2105.

1700 [HYDE, THOMAS]. Historia religionis. **Oxonii, e**
theatro Sheldoniano. 1700. 4°. WH3876.

1700 JOSEPHUS, FLAVIUS. Josephi antiquitatem
judaicarum libri quatuor priores. **Oxoniae, e**
Theatro Sheldoniano. 1700. Fol. WJ1081.

1700 LITURGIES. BOOK OF COMMON PRAYER.
Book of common prayer. **Oxford: by the**
university-printers. 1700. 8°. WB3703.

1700 [MARSHALL, THOMAS]. The catechism set
forth. Eleventh edition. **Oxford, at the theater.**
1700. 4°. WM807.

1700 OXFORD, UNIVERSITY OF. Exequiae desideratis-
simo principi Gulielmo. **Oxonii, e theatro**
Sheldoniano. 1700. Fol. WO885.

1700 OXFORD, UNIVERSITY OF. Parecbolae sive
excerpta è corpore statutorum. **Oxoniae, e**
theatro Sheldoniano. 1700. 12°. WO934.

1700 PINDAR. Serie chronologica Olympiadum.
Oxonii, e Theatro Sheldoniano. 1700. Fol.
WP2247.

1700 TATIAN, SYRUS. Tatiani Oratio ad Graecos.
Oxoniae, e theatro Sheldoniano. 1700. 8°. WT236.

1699 THEOCRITUS. Θεοκριτου ... Theocriti quae
extant. **Oxoniae, e theatro Sheldoniano.** 1699.
8°. WT851.

1700 TULLY, THOMAS. Praecipuorum theologiae.
Fifth edition. **Oxonii, typis L. Lichfield, impensis**
F. Oxlad. 1700. 12°. WT3250.

1700 [WHEELER, MAURICE]. The Oxford almanack
for ... 1700. **Printed at the theater in Oxford.**
[1700]. Brs. WA2704.

1700 WOODROFFE, BENJAMIN. Examinis, & examina-
ntis examen. **Oxoniae, e theatro Sheldoniano.**
1700. 4°. WW3466.

1700 WOODROFFE, BENJAMIN. A sermon preach'd
May 23, 1700. **Printed at the theater in Oxford.**
1700. 4°. WW3470.

1700 XENOPHON. – Ξενοφωυτυς λογος. Εκ Θεατρου
'εν Οξουια. **Oxford.** [1700]. 8°. WX16.

PETERBOROUGH

1691 The mischief of intemperance. **For J. Deacon**
and are to be sold by Geoffrey Bouchier ... in
Peterborough. 1691. 8°. WM2234.

PLYMOUTH

1641 JELINGER, CHRISTOPHER. The excellency of
Christ. **By I. L. for Fran. Eglesfield, and are to**
be sold by William Russell in Plimouth. 1641.
8°. WJ542.

1661 RICH, JOHN. Verses on the blessed and happy
coronation. **London, printed and are to be sold**
by John Ratkliffe in Plymouth. 1661. Fol.
WR1352.

PRESTON

1678 BUSHELL, SETH. The believer's groan for
heaven. **For Tho. Sawbridge and Philip Burton,**
at Preston, Lancs. 1678. 4°. WB6236.

READING

1661 CHEESMAN, CHRISTOPHER. An epistle to
Charles the second. [**Reading.** 1661.] 4°.
WC3773.

1693 [SANDILANDS, ROBERT]. An expedient for
peace. **Reading.** 1693. 4°. WS658.

ROCHESTER

1688 JAMES II, king of England. His Majesties reasons
for withdrawing himself from Rochester.
[**Rochester.** 1688]. Brs. WJ376.

1689 JAMES II, king of England. His Majesties reasons
for withdrawing himself from Rochester.
[**Rochester?**]. **Printed.** 1689. 4°. WJ377.

ST. ALBANS

1479 DATUS, AUGUSTINUS. Augustini Dacti scribe sup.
Tullianis eloganciis [sic] & uerbis. **St. Albans.**
[1479]. 4°. STC6289.

1480 ALBERTUS, MAGNUS. Liber modorum signifi-
candi. **Apd' villam sancti Albani.** 1480. 4°.
STC268.

1480 TRAVERSANUS, LAURENTIUS GULIELMUS.
Fratris laurencii guilelmi de saona prohemiū
in nouam rethoricam. **Ap. villā sancti Albani.**
1480. 4°. STC24190.

1481 LATIN. BIBLE. SELECTIONS. Incipiunt exēpla sacre sc'pture ex vtrooβ testamēto. **Ap. villā sancti Albani.** 1481. 4°. STC2993.

1481 JOANNES, canonicus. Expliciunt questioēs Johannis canonici super octo libros phisicorum aristotil. Quaestiones super Aristotelis physica. **Apud villam sancti Albani.** 1481. Fol. STC14621.

1483 ANDREAE, ANTONIUS. [Scriptum super logica]. **St. Alban's.** [1483]. 4°. STC582.

1485 [CHRONICLES OF ENGLAND. The Saint Albans chronicle]. Begin 2a. Here begynnys a schort ƶ breve tabull, etc. **Sanctus Albanus.** [1485]. Fol. STC9995.

1486 [The book of Hawking, hunting and blasing of arms.] [End]. Here in thys boke afore ar contenyt the bokys of haukyng and huntyng ... and here now endyth the boke of blasyng of armys translatyt and compylyt togedyr at Seynt albons ... mccccixxxvi. [**St. Alban's.** 1486]. Fol. STC3308.

1534 ALBAN, saint. Here begynneth the lyfe of Seint Albon prothomartyr of Englande. [**St. Albans, J. Herford**]. 1534. 4°. STC256.

1536 GWYNNETH, JOHN. The cōfutacyon of the fyrst parte of Frythes boke. [**St. Albans, J. Hertford for R. Stevenage**]. 1536. 8°. STC12557.

ST. ANDREWS

1622 LEECH, JOHN. Jani bifronti strena, sive cornua calendis januarii, 1622. **Andreopoli, E. Rabanus.** 1622. 4°. STC15370.

SALISBURY

1649 The resolutions of the private souldiery. [**Salisbury?** 1649]. Brs. WR1167.

1649 The unanimous declaration of Colonel Scroope's ... regiments. [**Salisbury?**], printed. 1649. 4°. WU28.

1650 DITTON, GEORGE. Symbolvm apostolicvm. **By Thomas Harper, to be sold by John Courtney, in Salisbury.** 1650. Brs. WD1706.

1658 PIERCE, THOMAS. Φιλαλληλια. Or, the grand characteristick. **London, by J. G. for R. Royston, to be sold by John Courtney in Salisbury.** 1658. 4°. WP2190.

1659 [MARTIN, T.] Mary Magdalen's tears wipt off. **By J. C. and are to be sold by J. Courtney, in Saulsbury.** 1659. 8°. WM850A.

1660 CREED, WILLIAM. Judah's purging. **For R. Royston, to be sold by John Courtney in Sarum.** [1660.] 4°. WC6873.

1662 PRIAULX, JOHN. Confirmation confirmed. **London, by I. R. for Iohn Courtney in Salisbury.** 1662. 4°. WP3330.

1664 [MARTIN, JOHN]. Lex pacifica: or Gods own law. **London, by J. G. for Richard Royston, to be sold by John Courtney in Salisbury.** 1664. 4°. WM843.

1675 ADDISON, LANCELOT. The present state of the Jews. **By J. C. for William Crook, and to be sold by John Courtney in Sarum.** 1675. 8°. WA526.

SHAFTESBURY

1673 E., W. A vindication of the ministers of Christ. **For John Pike of Shaftsbury.** 1673. 4°. WE44.

SHEFFIELD

1689 [BAXTER, RICHARD.] Now or never. **By B. Griffin for N. Simmons in Sheffeild.** 1689. 12°. WB1326.

1697 DRAKE, NATHANIEL. A sermon against false weights. **For W. Onley, for A. Bosvile; and N. Simmons, in Sheffield.** 1697. 4°. WD2127.

1697 MANLOVE, TIMOTHY. The immortality of the soul asserted. **London: by R. Roberts for Nevill Simmons, in Sheffield. And sold by George Coniers.** 1697. 8°. WM454.

1698 J[OLLIE], T[HOMAS]. A vindication of the Svrey demoniack. **For Nevill Simmons, in Sheffield, Yorkshire: and sold by A. Baldwin.** 1698. 4°. WJ890.

1698 MANLOVE, TIMOTHY. Præparatio evangelica: or, a plain and practical discourse. **London: for Nevill Simmons, in Sheffield: and sold by George Coniers, Yorkshire.** 1698. 8°. WM455.

SHERBORNE

1650 GOVE, RICHARD. A soveraigne salve. **By J. G. for R: Royston, to be sold by Thomas Miller in Sherburne.** 1650. 8°. WG1455.

1654 LYFORD, WILLIAM. The matching of the magistrates authority. **London, for R. Royston, to be sold by Tho: Miller in Sherborne.** 1654. 4°. WL3549.

1697 [ALLEN, WILLIAM.] A practical improvement of the articles. **For J. Taylor, and J. Miller in Sherborne, and in Yeovill.** 1697. 4°. WA1078.

1699 HOLE, MATTHEW. Letters written to J. M. ... the second part. **For, and to be sold by J. Taylor, and T. Bever in London; H. Clements in Oxon, and J. Miller in Sherborn.** 1699. 8°. WH2410.

1700 ENGLAND, JOHN. Man's sinfulness. **By J. Heptinstall, for John Sprint, and sold by John Miller in Sherborne, and Thomas Wall in Bristol.** 1700. 8°. WE739.

SHREWSBURY

1550 GRIBALDI, MATTEO. A notable and maruailous epistle. Tr. E. A[glionby]. **Worceter, J. Oswen; they be also to sell in Shrewesbury.** 1550. 8°. STC12365.

1550 VERON, JEAN. The godly saiyngs of the old auncient fathers vpon the sacrament of the bodye and bloude of Chryste. Newlye compyled and translated by J. Veron. **worceter, J. Oswen, also to sell at Shrewesburye.** 1550. 8°. STC24682.

1635 TERRY, JOHN. The defence of protestancie. Second edition. **For W. Millard, bookseller in Shrewsbury.** 1635. 4°. STC23911.

1642 BUSHELL, THOMAS. A just and true remonstrance of His majesties mines-royall. **Shrewsbury, by Robert Barker: and by the assignes of John Bill.** 1642. 4°. WB6247.

1642 CHARLES I, king of England. His Majesties speech and protestation ... 19th of September, 1642. **Shrewsbury, by R. Barker and the assigns of J. Bill.** 1642. Brs. WC2775.

1642 NEWCASTLE, WILLIAM CAVENDISH, earl of. An answer of ... to the six groundlesse aspersions. **Printed at Oxford, and reprinted at Shrewsbury.** 1642. 4°. WN875A.

1643 [CAPEL, ARTHUR CAPEL, baron.] Arthur lord Capell, lieutenant general ... to all commanders. **Imprinted at Shrewsbury, by Robert Barker; and by the assignes of John Bill.** 1643. Brs. WC470.

1643 CHARLES I, king of England. His Majesties declaration to all his loving subjects, after his victories. **Shrewsbury, by Robert Barker: and by the assignes of John Bill.** 1643. 4°. WC2227.

1643 CHARLES I, king of England. His Maiesties declaration to all his loving subjects, in answer to a declaration ... 3. Iune. 1643. **Shrewsbury, by Robert Barker: and by the assignes of John Bill.** 1643. 4°. WC2231.

1643 CHARLES I, king of England. The king's Majesties declaration to all his loving subjects of ... Scotland. With an act. **Shrewsbury, by Robert Barker: and by the assigns of John Bill.** 1643. 4°. WC2244.

1643 CHARLES I, king of England. Trusty and wel-beloved ... 23 January 1642 [3]. **Shrewsbury.** 1642 [3]. Brs. WC2841.

1643 The collection of all the particular papers that passed between His Majesty ... concerning the late treaty. **Shrewsbury, by Robert Barker: and by the assignes of John Bill.** 1643. 4°. WC5113.

1643 ENGLAND. PARLIAMENT. The articles of cessation of the Lords and Commons, March 22, 1642 [3]. **Printed at Oxford, and reprinted at Shrewsbury.** 1643. 4°. WE1233.

1685 BAYLY, LEWIS, bp. Yr Ymarter o dduwioldeb. **Mwythig, & en Thomas Jones** [1685?] 8°. WB1505A.

1690 [CROUCH, NATHANIEL.] Dwy daith: Gaersalem. **Yn y Mwythig, John Rhydderch** [Shrewsbury. 1690?] 12°. WC7313.

1695 DAWES, THOMAS. A sermon preach'd ... March 5. 1694/5. **By F.C. for Gabriel Rogers in Shrewsbury; to be sold by John Whitlock.** 1695. 4°. WD451.

1696 PRICHARD, RHYS. Canwyllyeymru: sef gwaith. **Atgraphwydyny Mwythig gan Thomas Durston.** [1696]. 8°. WP3404.

1699 BUNYAN, JOHN. Taith y peverin. **Mwythig, Thomas Jones.** 1699. 12°. WB5602.

1700 BAYLY, LEWIS, bp. Yr Ymarter o dduwioldeb. Fifth edition. **Mwythig, gan Thomas Durston.** [1700]. 8°. WB1505A.

1700 W., J. Cydymaith yr eglwyswr. **Mwythig, gar Tho. Durston.** [1700?]. 8°. WW50.

STAFFORD

1658 LINEALL, JOHN. Itur [sic] Mediteranium. **For the author, and to be sold by John Felton in Stafford.** 1658. 4°. WL2331.

1662 POWELL, EDWARD. The danger of the errors. **For W. Gilbertson, and are to be sold by John Felton in Stafford.** 1662. 4°. WP3046A.

1674 A short account of Blurton-Spaw-Water. **London for William Bateman, in Stafford-shire.** [1694]. Fol. WS3533.

STIRLING

1567 SEMPILL, ROBERT. The exhortatioun, etc. **Striuiling, R. Lekprevik.** 1567. Brs. STC22198.

1571 BUCHANAN, GEORGE. Ane admonition direct to the trew lordis mantenaris of the kingis graces authoritie. **Striuiling, R. Lepriuik.** 1571. 8°. STC3968.

1571 KNOX, JOHN. To his louing brethren. **Striuiling, R. Lekpreuik.** 1571. 8°. STC15076.

1571 SEMPILL, ROBERT. The bischoppis lyfe and testament. **Striuiling, R. Lekpreuik.** 1571. Brs. STC22188.

STOURBRIDGE

1661 M[ALPAS], T[HOMAS]. Monarchiæ encomium ... or a congratulation. **London, by T. Leach, to be sold by William Palmer, and by Joan Malpas, in Sturbridg.** 1661. 8°. WM341.

1686 CHAMBERLAINE, JAMES. Catalogus variorum librorum. [n.p.] **to be sold at Sturbridge.** 1686. 4°. WC1816.

STAMFORD, LINCOLNSHIRE

1690 TOPHAM, GEORGE. Pharisaism display'd. **London for Thomas Fox; to be sold by Mr. Caldecot in Stamford.** 1690. 4°. WT1907.

1690 The voyages & travels of that renowned Captain, Sir Francis Drake. **Printed at Stamford, Lincolnshire.** [1690?] 4°. WV748.

STRATFORD

1669 YOUNGE, RICHARD. Carnal reason. **By I.R. for the author, at Stratford.** 1669. 8°. WY142.

TAUNTON

1646 NEWTON, GEORGE. Men's wrath and God's praise. **London, by W. Wilson, for Francis Eglesfield, and are to be sold by George Treagle in Taunton.** 1646. 4°. WN1045.

1648 BATT, TIMOTHY. The waters of Marah sweetned. **For Francis Eglesfield, to be sold by George Treagle in Taunton.** 1648. 4°. WB1148.

1652. [FULLWOOD, FRANCIS]. The churches and the ministery of England. **By A.M. for George Treagle at Taunton, to be sold at London by William Roybould.** 1652. 4°. WF2498.

1652 NEWTON, GEORGE. A sermon preached the 11. of May 1652. **London, for William Roybould, to be sold by Georgle Treagle in Taunton.** 1652. 4°. WN1046.

1653 SCLATER, WILLIAM. Civil magistracy. **By T.M. for George Treagle, at Taunton: to be sold by William Roybould.** 1653. 4°. WS914.

1658 NORMAN, JOHN. Christ's commission-officer. **London, for Edward Brewster, to be sold by Edward Rosseter in Taunton.** 1658. 8°. WN1240.

1698 HOLE, MATTHEW. A correct copy of some letters written to J.M. **For H. Chanklin, in Taunton, and are sold by R. Knaplock.** 1698. 8°. WH2408.

TAVISTOCK

1525 BOETHIUS, ANICIUS M.T.S. The boke of comfort called in laten Boetius de consolatione philosophiæ. [Tr. J. Walton]. **in the exempt monastery of Tauestok by me dan Thomas Rychard.** 1525. 4°. STC3200.

TIVERTON

1696 NEWTE, JOHN. The lawfulness and use of organs. **London: by Freeman Collins, to be sold by William Rogers: and by Humphry Burton in Tiverton.** 1696. 4°. WN1040.

1700 DODWELL, HENRY. An essay concerning the lawfulness. **For W. Hawes, [London] and Henry Clements in Oxford, and W. Burton, at Tiverton.** 1700. 8°. WD1814.

TOTNES

1675 BURTHOGGE, RICHARD. Cavsa Dei, or an apology for God. **For Lewis Punchard in Totnes in Devon, and are to be sold by F. Tyton** [London]. 1675. 8°. WB6149.

TUNBRIDGE WELLS

1694 SELDEN, JOSEPH. The trades-man's help. **London, for the author, and sold by him at Tunbridge-Wells, and by Richard Wilkin,** [London]. 1694. 12°. WS2445.

UPPINGHAM

1692 DAVIS, RICHARD. Truth and innocency vindicated. **For Nath. and Robert Ponder, to be sold by Randal Taylor, by Mr. Coolidge at Cambridge, Mr. Prior at Colchester, Mr. Noble at St. Edmund's Bury, Mr. Haworth at Ipswich, Northampton, Wellingborow, Kettering, Oundle, Harborow, Litterworth, Upingham, Bedford, Kimbolton and Canterbury.** [1692?] 4°. WD435.

UTTOXETER

1687 SHAW, SAMUEL. Grammatica Anglo-Romana: or. **London, for Michael Johnson to be sold at his shops in Litchfield and Uttoxeter: and Ashby-de-la-Zouch.** 1687. 12°. WS3035.

WARMINSTER

1693 EXELL, JOSHUA. Plain and exquisite Scripture-proof. **For the author, to be sold by Thomas Parkhurst; and by William Langford, in Warmister.** 1693. 4°. WE3857.

WARRINGTON

1690 C[RANE], T[HOMAS]. Job's assurance of the resurrection. **For Philip Burton in Warrington.** 1690. 4°. WC6819.

WARWICK

1683 JEMMAT, SAMUEL. A sermon preached ... March the nineteenth, 1682/3. **Oxford, by Leonard Lichfield, for George Teonge, in Warwick.** 1683. 4°. WJ550.

WATERFORD

1643 Admonition by the supreame councell of the Confederat Catholicks of Ireand [sic]. **Waterford by Thomas Bourke.** 1643. 4°. WA593A.

1643 Admonitions by the Supreame Councell. **Waterford, by Thomas Bourke.** 1643. 4°. WA598.

1643 By the supreame Councell of the confederate Catholicks. **Waterford.** 1643. Brs. WI354.

1643 CASTLEHAVEN, JAMES TOUCHET, earl of. A remonstrance of the right honovrable Iames Earle of Castlehaven. **Printed at VVaterford by Thomas Bourke.** 1643. 4°. WC1236.

1643 DARCY, PATRICK. An argvment delivered ... 9 Iunii, 1641. **Printed at Waterford, by Thomas Bourke.** 1643. 4°. WD246.

1643 A declaration of the supreme council of the Confederate Catholicks. **Waterford, by Thomas Bourke.** 1643. Brs. WD769A.

1643 IRELAND. Forasmuch as after a long and serious debate ... 21 September 1643. **Waterford, Thomas Bourke.** 1643. Brs. WI394.

1643 Lawes and ordinances of warre. **Waterford, by Thomas Rourke.** 1643. 4°. WL696.

1644 By the supreme councell of the Confederat Catholicks. **Waterford, by Thomas Bourke.** 1644. Brs. WB6371A.

1644 C., P. The inquisition of a sermon ... by Robert Daborne. **Waterford, by Thomas Bourke.** 1644. 4°. WC94.

1644 ENOS, WALTER. Alexipharmacon, or a soveraigne antidote. **Waterford, by Thomas Bourke.** 1644. 4°. WE3129.

1644 Propositions of the Roman Catholicks of Ireland. **Printed at Waterford by Thomas Bourke.** 1644. 4°. WP3800.

1643 A remonstrance of grievances. **Waterford, by Thomas Bourke.** 1643. 4°. WR989.

1644 Titus, or the palme of Christian courage. **Waterford, by Thomas Rourke.** [sic]. 1644. 4°. WT1314.

1646 RINUCCINI, JOHN BAPTIST. The degree of excommunication ... 1 September 1646. [Waterford? 1646]. Brs. WR1521.

1645 A persuasive letter exhorting the natives of Ireland. **Printed at Wareford** [sic]. 1645. 4°. WP1670.

1651 COOK, JOHN. Monarchy no creature of Gods making. **Printed at Waterford in Ireland, by Peter de Pienne.** 1651. 8°. WC6019.

1652 COOK, JOHN. Monarchy no creature of Gods making. **Printed at Waterford in Ireland, by Peter de Pienne.** 1652. 8°. WC6020.

1652 COOK, JOHN. Monarchy no creature of Gods making. **Printed at Waterford in Ireland, by Peter de Pienne, and are to be sold in London, by Thomas Brewster.** 1652. 8°. WC6021.

1652 ENGLAND. PARLIAMENT. Ordered ... that this act be forthwith printed. **Waterford, by Peter de Pienne.** 1652. 4°. WE1749A.

WELLINGBOROUGH

1692 DAVIS, RICHARD. Truth and innocency vindicated. **For Nath. and Robert Ponder, to be sold by Randal Taylor, by Mr. Coolidge at Cambridge, Mr. Prior at Colchester, Mr. Noble at St. Edmund's Bury, Mr. Haworth at Ipswich, Northampton, Wellingborow, Kettering, Oundle, Harborow, Litterworth, Upingham, Bedford, Kimbolton and Canterbury.** [1692?] 4°. WD435.

WINCHESTER

1682 [KEN, THOMAS], bp. A sermon preached ... 30th of June, 1682. **London, by M. Flesher, for Joanna Brome; and William Clarke in Winchester.** 1682. 4°. WK279.

1684 [ANDERSON, HENRY.] Religion and loyalty maintained. **By J. M. for Will. Abington; and Will Clark in Winchester.** 1684. 8°. WA3092.

1684 [KEN, THOMAS], bp. A manual of prayers for ... Winchester College. Sixth edition. **For W. Abington, and W. Clarke in Winchester.** 1684. 12°. WK271A.

1686 [KEN, THOMAS], bp. An exposition on the church catechism. **London, for Charles Brome; and William Clarke in Winchester.** 1686. 8°. WK262.

1687 [KEN, THOMAS], bp. A manual of prayers for ...
Winchester College. "Sixth edition". **London,
for Charles Brome, and Will. Clark in Winchester.**
1687. 12°. WK273.

1688 [KEN, THOMAS], bp. A pastoral letter from.
**London, for Charles Brome, and W. Clark in
Winchester.** 1688. 4°. WK276.

1688 [KEN, THOMAS], bp. A sermon preached ...
30th June, 1682. Third edition. **London, for
Charles Brome; and William Clarke in Winchester.**
1688. 4°. WK280.

WOLSTON

1589 MARPRELATE, MARTIN, pseud. Theses
Martinianæ: that is, certaine demonstratiue conclusions. **Published by Martin iunior.** [Wolston,
J. Hodgkins, the assignes of Martin Junior, 22 jy
1589]. 8°. STC17457.

1589 MARPRELATE, MARTIN, pseud. The iust censure and reproofe of Martin iunior. By Martin
senior. [**Wolston?** J. Hodgkins, 29 jy. 1589].
8°. STC17458.

1589 MARPRELATE, MARTIN, pseud. The protesta-
tyon of Martin Marprelat. [**Wolston? 1589?**]
8°. STC17459.

WOLVERHAMPTON

1685 PLAXTONE, GEORGE. The loyal speech of
**London, by J. Leake, for Richard Grosvenor, in
Wolverhampton, to be sold by A. Jones** [London].
16[85]. Brs. WP2416.

WORCESTER

1549 BIBLE. ENGLISH. PSALMS. The psalter or
psalmes of Dauid after the translation of the
great bible, perfectly pointed. **Worceter, J.
Oswen.** 1549. 4°. STC2378.

1549 Certayne sermons or homilies. Newlye imprinted
in partes. **Worceter, J. Oswen.** 1549. 4°.
STC13645.

1549 H., H. A consultorie for all christians. **Worceter, J. Oswen.** 1549. 8°. STC12564.

1549 HEGENDORFF, CHRISTOPHER. The seconde
parte of the domesticall sermons. Tr. H.
Reiginalde. **Worceter, J. Oswen.** 1549. 8°.
STC13022.

1550 GRIBALDI, MATTEO. A notable and maruailous
epistle. Tr. E. A[glionby[. 8°. **Worceter, J.
Oswen; they be also to sell in Shrewesbury.** 1550.
8°. STC12365.

1550 VERON, JEAN. The godly saiyngs of the old
auncient fathers vpon the sacrament of the bodye
and bloude of Chryste. Newly compiled and tr.
by J. Veron. **worceter, J. Oswen, also to sell at
Shrewesburye.** 1550. 8°. STC24682.

1550 ZWINGLI, ULRICH. A short pathwaye to the
ryghte and true vnderstanding of the holye
Scriptures. Tr. J. Veron. **worceter, J. Oswen.**
1550. 8°. STC26141.

1551 BULLINGER, HEINRICH. A most necessary a.
frutefull dialogue betw. ye seditious libertin a.
the true christiā. Tr. J. Veron. **Worcester,
J. Oswen.** 1551. 8°. STC4068.

1551 BULLINGER, HEINRICH. A most sure a. strong
defence of the baptisme of children. Tr. J.
Veron. **Worcester, J. Oswen.** 1551. STC4069.

1551 HOOPER, JOHN, bp. Godly and most necessary
annotations in ye xiii chapyter to the Romaynes.
Worceter, J. Oswen. 1551. 8°. STC13756.

1552 LITURGIES. BOOK OF COMMON PRAYER.
Book of Common Prayer. **Worcester, J. Oswen.**
1552. Fol. STC16287.

1553 HOOPER, JOHN, bp. An homelye to be read in
the tyme of pestylence. **Worceter, J. Oswen.**
1553. 4°. STC13759.

1650 TAYLOR, JEREMY, bp. The rvle and exercises
of holy living. **For Francis Ash in Worcester.**
1650. 12°. WT371A.

1651 BARKSDALE, CLEMENT. Nympha libethris:
or the Cotswold muse. **For F. A. at Worcester.**
1651. 8°. WB804.

1654 TAYLOR, JEREMY, bp. The rvle and exercises
of holy living. Fourth edition. **For Francis Ash
in Worcester.** 1654. WT373.

1656 TAYLOR, JEREMY, bp. The rvle and exercises
of holy living. Fifth edition. **For Francis Ash
in Worcester.** 1656. 12°. WT374.

1657 [TAYLOR, JEREMY], bp. The rvle and exercises
of holy living. Second edition. **For Francis Ash
in Worcester.** 1657. 12°. WT372.

1658 DARLING, JOHN. The carpenters rule made
easie. **By R. & W. Leybourn, for John Jones in
Worcester.** 1658. 8°. WD260.

1660 NANFAN, JOHN. An answer to a passage in Mr.
Baxter's book. **London for John Jones in
Worcester.** [1660?] 4°. WN148.

1662 BAXTER, BENJAMIN. A posing question. **For
John Jones, in Worcester.** 1662. 8°. WB1173.

1662 H[OLDEN], S[AMUEL]. D. E. defeated. **For R.
Royston, to be sold by John Jones in Worcester.**
1662. 4°. WH2381.

1663 TAYLOR, JEREMY, bp. The rvle and exercises
of holy living. Seventh edition. **For Francis Ash
in Worcester.** 1663. 8°. WT375.

1663 Y[ARRANTON, ANDREW]. The improvement
improved. **London, by J. C. for Francis Tea, in
Worcester.** 1663. 8°. WY16.

1674 [FOX, GEORGE], elder. For all the bishops and
priests. [**Worcester. 1674**]. 4°. WF1819.

1675 The art of thriving. **Worcester, S. Gamidge.**
[?1675]. Brs. WA3796.

1676 BADLAND, THOMAS. Eternity: or the weighti-
ness. **For Sampson Evans in Worcester, to be
sold by N. Simmons.** 1676. 8°. WB390.

1676 DARLING, JOHN. The carpenters rule made
easie. Third edition. **For Tho. Sawbridge and
John Jones in Worcester.** 1676. 12°. WD261.

1676 Γραφαυταρκεια, or, the Scriptures. **For Sampson Evans, in Worcester.** 1676. 4°. WG1563.

1681 NANFAN, BRIDGIS. Essays divine and moral.
London, for Sampson Evans, in Worcester. 1681.
WN146.

1681 WALLS, GEORGE. A sermon preached ...
June 28, 1681. **By J. M. for Samson Evans in
Worcester; and Robert Kettlewell.** 1681. 4°.
WW623.

1682 NANFAN, BRIDGIS. Essays divine and moral.
Second edition. **London, for William Leach and
Sampson Evans in Worcester.** 1682. 8°. WM147.

1684 Γραφαυταρκεια, or, the Scriptures. **For Sampson Evans in Worcester, and sold by H. Sawbridge.**
[**London**]. 1684. 4°. WG1564.

1689 C[LARIDGE], R[ICHARD]. A second defence of
the present government. **For John Mountforth
in Worcester, and sold by Richard Baldwin.** 1689.
4°. WC4435.

1689   THOMAS, WILLIAM, bp. The Bishop of Worcester his letter to the clergy. **London, for Sampson Evans in Worcester.** 1689. 4°. WT977.

1691   STILLINGFLEET, EDWARD, bp. The Bishop of Worcester's charge to the clergy. **London, for Henry Mortlock, to be sold by Sampson Evans in Worcester.** 1691. 4°. WS5565.

1700   An earnest exhortation from a minister. **Worcester.** [1700?] 8°. WE97.

1700   The new art of thriving. **Worcester, S. Gamidge.** [1700?] Brs. WN553.

WREXHAM

1671   [EDWARDS, CHARLES]. Y Ffydd ddiffuant. Second edition. **Rhydychen [Oxford] by H. Hall, sold in Wrexham, Llanfyllin, &c.** 1671. 8°. WE193.

YEOVIL

1697   [ALLEN, WILLIAM.] A practical improvement of the articles. **For J. Taylor, and J. Miller in Sherborne and in Yeovill.** 1697. 4°. WA1078.

YORK

1507   LITURGIES. HYMNS AND SEQUENCES. SALISBURY. Expositio hymnorum. (Expositio sequentiarum). [Sarum use]. **Rothom per P. Violete, imp. G. Wansfort [of York].** 1507. 4°. STC16119.

1513   LITURGIES. BREVIARIES. YORK. [officia noua]. **Ebor., U. Mylner.** [1513?] 8°. STC15861.

1516   WHITTINTON, ROBERT. [Syntaxis]. Editio secunda de concinnitate grammatices. **Eboracum per Urysn̄ Mylner.** 1516. 4°. STC25542.

1530   LITURGIES. PROCESSIONALS. YORK. Processionale cōpletum. [**Rouen?**] imp. I. Gachet, **Eboraci.** 1530. 8°. STC16251.

1532   STANBRIDGE, JOHN. Accidentia ex stanbrigiana editione nuper recognita. **Yorke, Iohan warwycke.** 1532. 4°. STC23151.

1579   CATULLUS, CAIUS VALERIUS. Phaselus et ad eam, quotquot exstant parodiæ. **Eboraci, apud J. Marcantium.** 1579. 8°. STC4866.

1626   DEANE, EDMUND. Spadacrene anglica; or the Englishe spaw-fountaine of Knaresborow. [**M. Flesher**] for J. Grismand. Sold by R. Foster in **Yorke.** 1626. 4°. STC6441.

1642   [BOOTH, WILLIAM.] The humble petition of. **York: by Robert Barker, and by the assigns of John Bill.** 1642. 4°. WB3740.

1642   CASELEY, SAMUEL. The holy rebell. **Printed at York by Stephen Bulkley.** 1642. Brs. WC1209.

1642   CHARLES I, king of England. His Majestie's answer to a book, entituled, The declaration, or remonstrance. **York: by Robert Barker, and by the assignes of John Bill.** 1642. 4°. WC2093.

1642   CHARLES I, king of England. His Majesties answer to a printed paper intituled, A new declaration. **York: by Robert Barker, and by the assignes of John Bill.** 1642. 4°. WC2109.

1642   CHARLES I, king of England. His Maiesties answer to the declaration of both Houses ... concerning the commission of array. of the first of July, 1642. **York, by Robert Barker and by the assignes of John Bill.** 1642. 4°. WC2113.

1642   CHARLES I, king of England. His Majesties answer to the petition of the Lords and Commons. **York: by Robert Barker, and by the assignes of John Bill.** 1642. 4°. WC2136.

1642   CHARLES I, king of England. At the court at York. 28 Martii 1642. **York, Barker & assigns of Bill.** 1642. Brs. WC2150.

1642   CHARLES I, king of England. His Majesties declaration for the relief of ... Derby. **York, Robert Barker and the assigns of John Bill.** 1642. WC2203.

1642   CHARLES I, king of England. His Majesties declaration in answer to a declaration. **York, Robert Barker, and the assignes of John Bill.** 1642. 4°. WC2206.

1642   CHARLES I, king of England. His Majesties declaration to all his loving subjects, occasioned by a false and scandalous imputation. **York, by Robert Barker and the assignes of John Bill.** 1642. 4°. WC2238.

1642   CHARLES I, king of England. His Majesties declaration to all his loving subjects, of the 12 of August, 1642. **York: by Robert Barker and the assigns of John Bill.** 1642. 4°. WC2248.

1642   CHARLES I, king of England. His Majesties declaration to both Houses ... Martii 21, 1641 [2]. **York, by Robert Barker, and by the assignes of John Bill.** 1642. 4°. WC2266.

1642   CHARLES I, king of England. His Majesties declaration to both Houses of Parliament (which he likewise recommends). **Yorke: by Robert Barker, and by the assignes of John Bill.** 1642. 4°. WC2267.

1642   CHARLES I, king of England. His Majesties gracious message to both Houses ... from Nottingham the 25. of August 1642. **Imprinted at York by Robert Barker: and by the assignes of John Bill.** 1642. Brs. WC2332.

1642   CHARLES I, king of England. His Majesties instructions to his commissioners of array. **York: by Robert Barker: and by the assignes of John Bill.** 1642. 4°. WC2349.

1642   CHARLES I, king of England. His Majesties message sent from Beverley. **York: by Robert Barker; and by the assignes of John Bill.** 1642. 4°. WC2436.

1642   CHARLES I, king of England. His Majesties message sent to both Houses of Parliament, January 20, 1641. **Imprinted at York by Robert Barker, and by the assignes of John Bill.** 1642. Brs. WC2439.

1642   CHARLES I, king of England. His Majesties message sent to the high court of Parliament 8 April, 1642. **York, by Robert Barker and the assignes of John Bill.** 1642. 4°. WC2444.

1642   CHARLES I, king of England. His Majesties message to both Houses ... 28 April, 1642 declaring. **York: by Robert Barker, and by the assignes of John Bill.** 1642. 4°. WC2454.

1642   CHARLES I, king of England. His Majesties message to the House of Commons ... 13 August 1642. **Imprinted at York, by Robert Barker: and by the assignes of John Bill.** 1642. Brs. WC2476.

1642   CHARLES I, king of England. A proclamation by the King, dated at the court at York the 14th day of May, 1642. **Imprinted at York by Robert Barker, and by the assignes of John Bill.** 1642. Brs. WC2572.

1642   CHARLES I, king of England. A proclamation declaring our purpose. **Imprinted at York by Robert Barker: and by the assignes of John Bill.** 1642. Fol. WC2579.

1642 CHARLES I, king of England. A proclamation for the suppressing of the present rebellion. **Imprinted at York by Robert Barker: and by the assignes of John Bill.** 1642. Fol. WC2636.

1642 CHARLES I, king of England. A proclamation forbidding all His Majesties subjects belonging. **York, by Robert Barker and by the assigns of John Bill.** 1642. Brs. WC2646.

1642 CHARLES I, king of England. A proclamation forbidding all levies of forces. **York: by Robert Barker, and by the assigns of John Bill.** 1642. 4°. WC2650A.

1642 CHARLES I, king of England. His Maiesties second message sent. **York, by Robert Barker, and the assigns of John Bill.** 1642. Brs. WC2768.

1642 CHARLES I, king of England. His Majesties speech to the gentlemen of Yorkshire. **York: by Robert Barker: and by the assignes of John Bill.** 1642. 4°. WC2802.

1642 CHARLES I, king of England. His Maiesties speech to the knights, gentlemen and freeholders of . . . Lincoln. **Imprinted at York by Robert Barker; and by the assignes of John Bill.** 1642. Brs. WC2811.

1642 CHARLES I, king of England. Two speeches delivered by the Kings most excellent Majestie at Oxford. **Printed at York by Stephen Bulkley.** 1642. 4°. WC2864.

1642 CHARLES I, king of England. Whereas upon summons from vs, divers. **Imprinted at York, by Robert Barker and the assigns of John Bill.** 1642. Brs. WC2880.

1642 [CHILLINGWORTH,   ]. The petition of the most svbstantiall inhabitants of the citie of London. **Printed at York by Stephen Bulkley.** 1642. 4°. WC3882.

1642 The copie of a letter sent from divers knights and gentlemen . . . Nottingham. **York: by Robert Barker, and by the assignes of John Bill.** 1642. 4°. WC6142.

1642 A copie of a letter sent from the Lords Justices. **Imprinted at York, by Robert Barker and by the assigns of John Bill.** 1642. Brs. WC6151.

1642 CUMBERLAND, HENRY CLIFFORD, earl of. The declaration of. **York: by Robert Barker, and by the assigns of John Bill.** 1642. 4°. WC7576.

1642 CUMBERLAND, HENRY CLIFFORD, earl of. The declaration of. **Printed at York, by Stephen Bulkley.** 1642. 4°. WC7577.

1642 The declaration and protestation agreed on by the Grand Iurie. **Imprinted at York, by Robert Barker and the assigns of John Bill.** 1642. Brs. WD540.

1642 ENGLAND. PARLIAMENT. The answer of both Houses of Parliament, presented to His Majestie at York, the ninth of May, 1642. **York, by Robert Barker, and by the assignes of John Bill.** 1642. 4°. WE1219A.

1642 ENGLAND. PARLIAMENT. A declaration of the Lords and Commons . . . for the raising of all power. **York, R. Barker and by the assignes of J. Bill.** 1642. 4°. WE1427.

1642 ENGLAND. PARLIAMENT. The declaration of the Lords and Commons . . . to the subjects of Scotland. **Printed at York by Stephen Bulkley.** 1642. 4°. WE1472.

1642 ENGLAND. PARLIAMENT. The humble petition of the Lords and Commons . . . seventeenth of June, 1642. **York, by Robert Barker, and by the assignes of John Bill.** 1642. 4°. WE1573A.

1642 ENGLAND. PARLIAMENT. The humble petition of the Lords and Commons assembled in Parliament, presented to His Majestie at York, 26 of March, 1642. **York: by Robert Barker, and by the assignes of John Bill.** 1642. 4°. WE1576.

1642 ENGLAND. PARLIAMENT. The humble petition of the Lords and Commons assembled in Parliament, presented to His Majestie at York, 18 April. **York: by Robert Barker, and by the assignes of John Bill.** 1642. 4°. WE1577.

1642 ENGLAND. PARLIAMENT. The humble petition of the Lords and Commons assembled in Parliament, sent to His Majestie at York . . . 14 April, 1642. **York: by Robert Barker, and by the assigns of John Bill.** 1642. 4°. WE1582.

1642 ENGLAND. PARLIAMENT. XIX propositions made by both Houses. **York, by Robert Barker, and by the assignes of J. Bill.** 1642. 4°. WE1674.

1642 ENGLAND. PARLIAMENT. The petition of both Houses of Parliament presented . . . 23 of May 1642. **York: by Robert Barker: and by the assigns of John Bill.** 1642. 4°. WE2165.

1642 ENGLAND. PARLIAMENT. The petition of the Lords and Commons . . . 16 day of July. **York, by Robert Barker, and by the assignes of John Bill.** 1642. 4°. WE2174A.

1642 ENGLAND. PARLIAMENT. House of Commons. A complaint of the House of Commons and resolution. **Printed at York, by Stephen Bulkley.** 1642. 4°. WE2540.

1642 F[ERNE], H[ENRY]. The resolving of conscience. **Printed at York by Stephen Bulkley.** 1642. 4°. WF802.

1642 H., S. This last ages looking-glasse. **Printed at York by Stephen Bulkley.** 1642. 4°. WH125.

1642 The humble gratulation and petition. **York, by Robert Barker, and by the assignes of John Bill.** 1642. 4°. WH3416.

1642 The humble petition and representation of the gentry . . . of Cumberland. **York: by Robert Barker, and by the assignes of John Bill.** 1642. 4°. WH3442.

1642 The humble petition of divers barronets, knights, esquires . . . of Lincoln. **York, by S. Bulkley for M. Foster.** 28 July 1642. Brs. WH3452.

1642 The humble petition of divers noblemen and gentlemen. **York, by Robert Barker, and by the assignes of John Bill.** 1642. 4°. WH3458.

1642 The humble petition of 85 gentlemen . . . of Chester. **York, by Robert Barker.** 1642. 4°. WH3463A.

1642 The humble petition of His Majesties loyall subjects in . . . Lincoln. **York, Barker & assigns of Bill.** 1642. Brs. WH3465.

1642 The humble petition of the Commons of Kent. **York, by R. Barker, and by the assignes of J. Bill.** 1642. 4°. WH3495.

1642 The humble petition of the Countie of Cornwall . . . 26 June 1642. **York: by Robert Barker & by the assigns of John Bill.** 1642. 4°. WH3501A.

1642 The humble petition of the gentry, ministers, and freeholders of the County of York. **York: by Robert Barker and by the assignes of John Bill.** 1642. 4°. WH3508.

1642 A letter sent to Master Speaker, from the knights, esqvires ... of Lincoln. **Printed at York, by Stephen Bulkley for Marke Foster.** 28 July 1642. Brs. WL1620.

1642 M[OSSOM], R[OBERT], bp. Anti-Parœus. **Printed at York by Stephen Bulkley.** 1642. 4°. WM2859.

1642 NEWCASTLE, WILLIAM CAVENDISH, earl of. A declaration made by. **Printed at York, by Stephen Bulkley.** 1642. 4°. WN879.

1642 [PUTTOCK, ROGER]. An abstract of certain depositions. **York, by Robert Barker and by the assignes of John Bill.** 1642. 4°. WP4252.

1642 R., T. An honest letetr [sic] to a doubtfull friend. **Printed at York by Stephen Bulkley.** 1642. 4°. WR83.

1642 ROE, Sir THOMAS. The coppy of two letters from. **York, by Stephen Bulkley.** 1642. WR1777.

1642 RUDYERD, Sir BENJAMIN. A most worthy speech spoken ... Iuly 9th 1642. **York.** Brs. WR2188.

1642 A true relation of His Majesties successe at Brainford. **Printed at York by Stephen Bulkley.** 1642. 4°. WT2911.

1642 Two petitions to the Kings Majesty at Yorke. **Yorke.** 1642. 4°. WT3525.

1642 WORTLEY, Sir FRANCIS. Lines dedicated to fame and truth. **York, by Stephen Bulkley.** 1642. 4°. WW3638.

1642 WORTLEY, Sir Francis. To the Kings most sacred Majestie. The humble petition of. **Printed at York, by Stephen Bulkley, for Mark Foster.** July 23, 1642. Brs. WW3642.

1643 An answer to the late declaration of Scotland. **Printed at York by Stephen Bulkley.** 1643. 4°. WA3413.

1643 ARGYLE, ARCHIBALD CAMPBELL, marquis of. A letter from. **Printed at York by Stephen Bulkley.** 1643. 4°. WA3659.

1643 BRAMHALL, JOHN, abp. A sermon preached ... June 30, 1643. **Printed at York by Stephen Bulkley.** 1643. 4°. WB4233.

1643 BYRON, JOHN, baron. Sir John Byron's relation to the secretary. **York, Stephen Bulkley.** 1643. 4°. WB6409A.

1643 CHARLES I, king of England. His Majesties declaration to all his loving subjects, after his victories. **Printed at Oxford, July 30. And reprinted at York by Stephen Bulkley.** 1643. 4°. WC2226.

1643 CHURCH OF ENGLAND. A forme of common prayer. **York, Stephen Bulkeley.** 1643. 4°. WC4109.

1643 A copy of a letter written to his Excellencie the Marquesse of Newcastle. **Printed at York by Stephen Bulkley.** 1643. 4°. WC6174.

1643 [DIGGES, DUDLEY, younger.] A review of the observations upon some of His Majesties late answers. **Printed at York by Stephen Bulkley.** 1643. 4°. WD1460.

1643 A letter from a grave gentleman. **York, Stephen Bulkeley.** [1643]. 4°. WL1404.

1643 London's warning-peece, being, the common-prayers complaint. **York, by Stephen Buckley** [sic] 1643. Brs. WL2955.

1643 M[OSSOM], R[OBERT], bp. The King on his throne. **Printed at York, by Stephen Bulkley.** 1643. 4°. WM2862.

1643 M[OSSOM], R[OBERT], bp. The King on his throne. **Printed at York, by Stephen Bulkley.** 1643. 4°. WM2862A.

1643 M[OSSOM], R[OBERT], bp. The King on his throne. **Printed at York.** 1643. 4°. WM2863.

1643 NEWCASTLE, WILLIAM CAVENDISH, earl of. A declaration of the right honourable the. **Printed at York by Stephen Bulkley.** 1642 [3]. 4°. WN882.

1643 NEWCASTLE, WILLIAM CAVENDISH, earl of. A proclamation by. **York, S. Bulkley.** 1642 [3]. Brs. WN889.

1643 A short history of the Anabaptists of high and low Germany. **York, S. Bulkley.** 1643. 4°. WS3599.

1643 Tis a plaine case, gentlemen. **Yorke, by Stephen Bulkley.** 1643. Brs. WT1307.

1643 A true relation of the passages of the armie. **Printed at Yorke by Stephen Bulkley.** 1643. 4°. WT3014.

1643 A true relation of the Queen's Majesties return. **Printed at Yorke by Stephen Bulkley.** 1643. 4°. WT3031.

1643 Via tuta, the safe way. **Printed at York by Stephen Bulkley.** 1643. WV290.

1643 A vulgar or popular discourse. **York, by Stephen Bulkeley.** 1643. 4°. WV750.

1644 BIRCHALL, JOHN. The non-pareil. **York: by Tho: Broad.** 1644. 4°. WB2940.

1644 BRAMHALL, JOHN, abp. A sermon, preached ... January, 28, 1643. **Printed at York by Stephen Bulkley.** 1643 [4]. 4°. WB4234.

1644 CHURCH OF ENGLAND. A collection of prayers and thanksgivings. **Printed at York by Stephen Bulkley.** 1644. 4°. WC4094D.

1644 ENGLAND. PARLIAMENT. An ordinance of the Lords and Commons ... with an exhortation. **Yorke: by Th. Broad.** Septem. 26, 1644. 4°. WE2108.

1644 RANSON, WILLIAM. A sermon preached ... 19. day of May. **Printed at York by Stephen Bulkley.** 1644. 4°. WR249.

1644 SHAW, JOHN. Brittains remembrancer. Third edition. **York, by Tho. Broad.** 1644. 4°. WS3024.

1644 SHAW, JOHN. Brittains remembrancer. "Third" edition. **Printed at Yorke by Tho. Broad.** 1644. 4°. WS3025.

1644 SHAW, JOHN. Two clean birds. **Printed at Yorke by Tho. Broad.** 1644. 4°. WS3031.

1645 A declaration by direction of the committee at Yorke. **Printed at Yorke by Tho. Broad.** 1645. 4°. WD562.

1645 KAYE, WILLIAM. Satisfaction for such as oppose reformation. **Printed at Yorke by Tho. Broad.** 1645. 4°. WK41.

1646 MEEKE, WILLIAM. The faithfull scout. **Printed at Yorke by Tho. Broad, to be sold by Nathanniel** [sic] **Brookes in London.** 1646. 4°. WM1615.

1646 NEWMAN. An hundred and six lessons, or Christian directions. **Printed at York by Tho: Broad.** 1646. Brs. WN923.

1647 ALMANACS. WHARTON, Sir GEORGE. No Merline, nor mercurie; but a new almanack ... for ... 1647. **[York?], printed.** 1647. 8°. WA2674.

1647 BLAND, FRANCIS. The souldier's march to salvation. **Printed at York.** 1647. 4°. WB3156.

1647 CALVERT, THOMAS. Heart-salve. **Printed at York, by Tho:Broad, to be sold by Nathaniel Brookes.** 1647. 8°. WC323.

1647 H., R. From the rendezvous of the whole army. **Printed at York by Tho. Broad,** 7 August 1647. 4°. WH106.

1647 KAYE, WILLIAM. Satisfaction for all such as oppose reformation. **Yorke. by Tho. Broad, and are to be sold by Nathanniel Brookes in London.** 1647. 4°. WK40A.

1647 MEEKE, WILLIAM. The faithfull scout. **Printed at Yorke by Tho. Broad, to be sold by Nathanniel [sic] Brookes in London.** 1647. 4°. WM1616.

1647 P[ARKER], H[ENRY]. An ansvver to the poysonovs sediciovs paper. [n.p.] **Are to be sold by Ralph Brocklebank, at York.** 1647. 4°. WP396.

1648 CALVERT, THOMAS. The blessed Jew. **Printed at York by Tho:Broad.** 1648. 4°. WC321.

1648 I., I. Reasons why this kingdome, as all others. **Printed at York, by Stephen Bulkley.** 1648. 4°. WI7.

1648 SAMUEL. The blessed Jew of Marocco. **Printed at York, by T. Broad, to be sold by Nath:Brookes, London.** 1648. 8°. WS545.

1649 CARTWRIGHT, CHRISTOPHER. A brief and plain exposition of the creed. **Printed at York by T. Broad.** 1649. 8°. WC683.

1649 CALVERT, THOMAS. The blessed Jew. **Printed at York by Tho:Broad.** 1649. 8°. WC322.

1649 DEAN, EDMUND. Spadacrene Anglica: the English spaw. **York.** 1649. 4°. WD491.

1649 THORPE, FRANCIS. Sergeant Thorpe judge of assize for the Northern circvit, his charge. **Printed at York by Tho:Broad.** 1649. Fol. WT1071.

1650 CROMWELL, OLIVER. Several letters and passages. **Printed and sold in York by T. Broad.** Sept. 27, 1650. 4°. WC7167.

1650 L[LEWELLIN], E[DWARD]. Divine meditations grounded. **York: by Tho. Broad.** 1650. 4°. WL2621.

1650 L[LEWELLIN], E[DWARD]. Divine meditations grounded. **York, by Tho:Broad, to be sold in London by Nath. Brooks.** 1650. 4°. WL2622.

1650 Several letters and passages between His Excellency, the Lord General Cromwel. **Printed and sold in York by T. Broad.** Septem. 27, 1650. 4°. WS2769A.

1653 [FOX, GEORGE], elder. Truth's defence [n.p.], **for Tho. Wayt, in York.** 1653. 4°. WF1970.

1653 TOMLINSON, WILLIAM. A word of reproof. **London, for Tho. Wayte, to be sold in York.** 1653. 4°. WT1855.

1654 N[AYLER], J[AMES]. A lamentacion (by one ...) **For Tho. Wayt, in York.** 1653 [4]. 4°. WN292.

1655 BOWLES, EDWARD. The dutie and danger of swearing. **Printed and sold in York by Tho. Broad.** 1655. 4°. WB3871.

1655 EMMOT, GEORGE. A northern blast. **For R. Lambert, in York.** 1655. 4°. WE714.

1656 DU MOULIN, PIERRE. The love of God. **Printed at York by Tho: Broad for the author.** 1656. 4°. WD2588.

1656 HUNTER, JOSEPH. The character of a Christian. **York, printed and sold by Tho:Broad.** 1656. 4°. WH3765A.

1659 The rendezvous of General Monck. **York: for Richard Foster.** [1659]. 4°. WR1035.

1661 BRADLEY, THOMAS. Appello Caesarem, or, an appeal. **York, by Alice Broad.** 1661. 8°. WB4127.

1661 BRADLEY, THOMAS. A sermon preach't ... 23 of Aprill last. **Yorke, by Alice Broade.** 1661. 4°. WB4137A.

1661 [CROWSHEY, JOHN]. The good husbands jewel. Fifth edition. **Yorke, by Alice Broad, to be sold by Leonard Campleshon.** 1661. 8°. WC7408B.

1661 HUNTER, JOSEPH. Judah's restitution. **York: by Alice Broade.** 1661. 4°. WH3767.

1661 LOVELL, WILLIAM. The duke's desk broken up. **Yorke: by Alice Broade, to be sold by Francis Mawburne.** 1661. 24°. WL3247.

1662 FREWEN, ACCEPTED, bp. Articles of visitation. **Yorke: by Alice Broad.** 1662. 4°. WF2201.

1663 BRADLEY, THOMAS. At the metropoliticall visitation. A sermon. **Yorke: by Alice Broade.** 1663. 4°. WB4128.

1663 BRADLEY, THOMAS. Cesar's due. **Yorke: by Alice Broade.** 1663. 4°. WB4129.

1663 BRADLEY, THOMAS. A sermon ad clerum. **Yorke: by Stephen Bulkley, to be sold by Francis Mawbarne.** 1663. 4°. WB4137.

1663 BRADLEY, THOMAS. A sermon preached ... thirtieth day of March, 1663. **Yorke: by Alice Broade.** 1663. 4°. WB4138.

1664 [CROWSHEY, JOHN]. The good husbands jewel. "Fifth" edition. **York, by Alice Broad.** 1664. 8°. WC7408C.

1664 [HILDYARD, CHRISTOPHER]. A list or catalogue of all the mayors ... of Yorke. **York, by Stephen Bulkley.** 1664. 4°. WH1981.

1665 CHARLES II, king of England. His Majesties gracious speech to both Houses ... 10th of October 1665. **Reprinted at York, by Stephen Bulkley.** 1665. Fol. WC3053A.

1665 SMALLWOOD, ALLAN. A sermon preached ... Aug. 17, 1664. **York: by Stephen Bulkley.** 1665. 8°. WS4005.

1666 ADRICHOMIUS, CHRISTOPHER. A briefe desription [sic] of Jerusalem. **York, by Stephen Bulkley.** 1666. 8°. WA600.

1666 BRADLEY, CHRISTOPHER. The eye of faith. **York, by Stephen Bulkley, to be sold by Francis Mawbarne.** 1666. 4°. WB4124.

1666 CHARLES II, king of England. Charles R. His Majesty in his princely compassion ... fifth day of September 1666. **York, Stephen Bulkley.** [1666]. Brs. WC3089.

1666 HUNTER, JOSEPH. The dreadfulness of the plague. **York: by Stephen Bulkley, to be sold by Francis Mawbarne.** 1666. 4°. WH3766.

1667 A poem on the burning of London. **York, by S. B. for F. M.** 1667. Brs. WP2687.

1667 SMALLWOOD, ALLAN. A reply to a pamphlet called, Oaths no gospel - ordinance. **York, by Stephen Bulkley, and are to be sold by Francis Mawburne.** 1667. 8°. WS4004.

1667   WITTY, ROBERT. Scarborough spaw or a description of the nature and vertues of the spaw. Second edition. **York: by A. Broad for Tho. Passenger, to be sold by Richard Lambert. 1667. 8°. WW3232.**

1668   BRADLEY, THOMAS. Nosce te ipsum. **York: by Stephen Bulkley, to be sold by Richard Lambert. 1668. 4°. WB4134.**

1668   BRADLEY, THOMAS. The second Adam. **York: by Stephen Bulkley, to be sold by Francis Mawbarne. 1668. 8°. WB4136.**

1668   BRAMHALL, WILLIAM. The loyal prophet. **York, John Garthwait. 1668. 8°. WB4238.**

1668   S., P. A vindication of conformity. **York, by Stephen Bulkley, to be sold by Richard Lambert. 1668. 8°. WS124.**

1669   BADILEY, RICHARD. The life of Dr. Thomas Morton. **York: by Stephen Bulkley, to be sould by Francis Mawbarne. 1669. 8° WB387.**

1669   BRADLEY, THOMAS. Elijah's nunc dimittis. **York, by Stephen Bulkley. 1669. 4°. WB4132.**

1670   BRADLEY, THOMAS, Elijah's epitaph. **York, by Stephen Bulkley, to be sold by Francis Mawbarne. 1670. 4°. WB4131.**

1670   BRADLEY, THOMAS. Elijah's nunc dimittis. **York: by Stephen Bulkley, to be sold by Francis Mawbarne. 1670. 8°. WB4133.**

1672   CALVERT, JAMES. Naphtali: seu colluctationes. **Typis Andraeae Clark, impensis Ric. Lambert, Eboraci, et apud Jo. Martyn, Londini. 1672. 4°. WC319.**

1672   S[TOPFORD], J[OSHUA]. The wayes and methods of Romes advancement. **[York], printed. 1672. 8°. WS5745.**

1676   STAINFORTH, WILLIAM. A sermon preached March 6. 1675. **London, for R. Royston, and R. Lambert in York. 1676. 4°. WS5172.**

1672   WITTY, ROBERT. Scarbroughs spagyrical anatomizer dissected. **By B. G. for Nath. Brooke and R. Lambert in York. 1672. 8°. WW3233.**

1677   [BANCKES, MATTHEW.] The several ways of resolving faith. **York, by Stephen Bulkley, to be sold by Richard Lambert. 1677. 8°. WB632.**

1680   F., C. A letter to His Grace the D. of Monmouth, the 15th of July, 1680. **York. 1680. Brs. WF4.**

1680   GRAHAM, RICHARD. Poems. Upon the death of the most honorable, the Lady Marchioness of Winchester. **York, by Alice Broad, and John White. 1680. Fol. WG1476.**

1682   GOEDAERT, JOHANNES. Johannes Godartius of insects. **York, by John White for M. L. 1682. 4°. WG1003.**

1682   HICKSON, JAMES. A sermon preached July 26, 1682. **For Richard Lambert in York. 1682. 4°. WH1930.**

1682   LISTER, MARTIN. De fontibus medicatis Angliæ. **Eboraci [York], sumpitubus authoris. 1682. 8°. WL2518.**

1683   LISTER, MARTIN. Letters and divers other mixt discourses. **York, by John White for the author. 1683. 4°. WL2528.**

1683   MERITON, GEORGE. A York-shire dialogue. **York, by John White, and are to be sold by Richard Lambert. 1683. 4°. WM1814.**

1683   A York-shire dialogue. **York, by John White. 1683. 4°. WY49.**

1684   CHURCH OF ENGLAND. Articles of visitation ... Durham. **York, by John Bulkley. 1684. 4°. WC4033A.**

1685   [ALLEN, CHARLES.] The operator for the teeth. **York: by John White for the author. 1685. 4°. WA1020.**

1685   JACKSON, CHRISTOPHER. The magistrate's duty. **York: be [sic] Jo. White for Francis Hildyard. 1685. 4°. WJ68.**

1685   MERITON, GEORGE. Nomenclatura clericalis: or, the young clerk's vocabulary. **London, for Richard Lambert in York, are to sold [sic] by the booksellers of London. 1685. 8°. WM1807.**

1685   MERITON, GEORGE. The praise of Yorkshire ale. **York: by J. White for Francis Hildyard. 1685. 8°. WM1809.**

1685   STAINFORTH, WILLIAM. An assize sermon, preached August 3, 1685. **York, by John White, for Richard Lambert. 1685. 4°. WS5170.**

1686   KAYE, STEPHEN. Ειϲοπρον του χριϲτιανιϲμου, or a discourse. **York: by Jo. White, for Robert Clarke. 1686. 8°. WK31.**

1686   STAINFORTH, WILLIAM. A sermon preach'd ... 6th of February 1685/6. **York: by Jo. White, for Francis Hildyard. 1686. 4°. WS5171.**

1686   WYVILL, CHRISTOPHER. The duty of honouring the king. **York: by Jo. White, for Richard Lambert. 1686. 4°. WW3786.**

1688   DAVISON, THOMAS. A sermon preached on the 8 of January. **York: by J. White, for Joseph Hall, in New-Castle upon Tine. 1688. 4°. WD441.**

1688   A declaration by the nobility and gentry of this county of York. **[York. 1688.] Brs. WD565.**

1685   WHITTON, KATHARINE. A testimony for the Lord; and His truth. **[York? 1688]. Fol. WW2051.**

1689   HALLEY, GEORGE. A sermon preached ... fifth fourteenth February, 1688/9. **For R. C. to be sold by Rich. Lambert and Francis Hildyard in York. 1689. 4°. WH454.**

1689   PERSE, WILLIAM. A sermon preached ... fifth day of Novemb. 1689. **York: by John Bulkley for Francis Hildyard. 1689. 4°. WP1654.**

1689   STAINFORTH, WILLIAM. A sermon preached ... January 30th 1688/9. **London, for Walter Kettilby, and Francis Hildyard, in York. 1689. 4°. WS5173.**

1691   HALLEY, GEORGE. A sermon preach'd ... 30th of March, 1691. **For Robert Clavel, to be sold by Christopher Welburn, in York. 1691. 4°. WH455.**

1691   TULLY, GEORGE. A sermon, preached October, the 19, 1690. **York: by J. White: to be sold by Joseph Hall, New-Castle upon Tyne. 1691. 4°. WT3242.**

1692   CHURCH OF ENGLAND. Articles to be enquired of in the visitation. **York: by John White. 1692. 4°. WC4014.**

1693   LEIGHTON, ROBERT, abp. A practical commentary or the first two chapters ... of St. Peter. **York: by J. White. 1693. 4°. WL1028.**

1694   A testimony from the people of God, call'd Quakers. **[York? 1694]. Fol. WT814.**

1695   BOETHIUS, ANICIUS MANLIUS TORQUATUS SEVERINUS. Anticius Manlius Severinus Boetius of the consolation of philosophy. **By J. D. for Awnsham and John Churchill and Francis Hildyard, and in York. 1695. 8°. WB3433.**

1695   DRAKE, NATHANIEL. A sermon against bribery. **For Walter Kettilby, and Francis Hildyard in York.** 1695. 4°. WD2126.

1695   PERSE, WILLIAM. A sermon, preach'd ... 3rd of March 1694/5. **York: by J. White for Robert Clarke.** 1695. 4°. WP1655.

1695   R., J. L. An elegy on the death of her late sacred Majesty Mary. **York, by John White for Francis Hildyard.** 1695. Fol. WR39.

1696   [MERITON, L.] Pecuniæ obediunt omnia. **York: by John White for the author, and sold by Tho: Baxter.** 1696. 8°. WM1821A.

1697   MERITON, GEORGE. The praise of Yorkshire ale. Third edition. **York: by J. White, for Francis Hildyard.** 1697. 8°. WM1810.

1697   MERITON, GEORGE. A York-shire dialogue. **York, by John White.** 1697. 4°. WM1814A.

1698   CHURCH OF ENGLAND. Articles to be enquired of ... York. **York, by John White.** 1698. 4°. WC4091A.

1698   HALLEY, GEORGE. A sermon preach'd ... fifth of November, 1697. **Printed for, and sold by Tho. Baxter, York.** 1698. 4°. WH456.

1699   LOWDE, JAMES. Moral essays. **York, by J. White for Fra. Hildyard,** to be sold by Brad. Aylmer, and Tho. Bennet, London. 12°. 1699. WL3301.